# The Aalborg PBL model
– Progress, Diversity and Challenges

Anette Kolmos, Flemming K. Fink and Lone Krogh (eds.)

# The Aalborg PBL model
# – Progress, Diversity and Challenges

Anette Kolmos, Flemming K. Fink and Lone Krogh (eds.)


ISBN 978-87-7307-700-9

1. edition, 3. impression.

Copyright 2004 The Authors and Aalborg University Press

All rights reserved. No part of this book may be reproduced in any form by any electronic or mechanical means (including photocopying) without permission from the publisher.


Printed by J. Tengstedt offset & digitaltryk, Aalborg

Cover photos: Carsten Hansen
Cover: Mette Dyhr

Published by
Aalborg University Press
Phone + 45 96357140
Fax + 45 96350076
E-mail: aauf@forlag.aau.dk
http://www.forlag.aau.dk


This book was made in co-operation with:

Centre for University Teaching and Learning, Aalborg University, Langagervej 8, DK-9220 Aalborg Ø, Denmark.
Phone + 45 96358008
Fax + 45 98156542
http://www.puc.aau.dk/

UNESCO International Centre for Engineering Education, Centre for Problem Based Learning (UCPBL), Aalborg University, Frederik Bajers Vej 7 A1, DK-9220 Aalborg Ø, Denmark.
Phone + 45 96359836
http://ucpbl.org
Email: ucpbl@kom.aau.dk

# CONTENTS

**Preface**
Sven Caspersen ................................................................................................. 7

**Introduction**
THE AALBORG MODEL -
PROBLEM-BASED AND PROJECT-ORGANIZED LEARNING
Anette Kolmos, Flemming K. Fink and Lone Krogh .................................. 9

**Setting the scene** ........................................................................................ 19
THE STUDENTS' VOICE
Frances Jørgensen ......................................................................................... 21

EMPLOYABILITY AND PROBLEM-BASED LEARNING
IN PROJECT-ORGANIZED SETTINGS AT UNIVERSITIES
Lone Krogh and Jørgen Gulddahl Rasmussen .......................................... 37

PROBLEM-BASED LEARNING AS A WAY OF ORGANIZING
LEARNING AND TEACHING AT THE UNIVERSITY
Erik Laursen .................................................................................................. 57

**The Aalborg PBL Model**
**- Diversity and Challenges** ..................................................................... 73
DEFINING THE PROBLEM IN PROBLEM-BASED LEARNING
Palle Qvist ..................................................................................................... 77

REFLECTIONS ON PROBLEM-BASED LEARNING
Jens Christensen ........................................................................................... 93

NEW REALITIES AND THE IMPLICATIONS FOR PROBLEM-BASED
LEARNING. THE CASE OF BUSINESS ADMINISTRATION
Olav Juul Sørensen ..................................................................................... 109

A PROBLEM-BASED CANON - A Draft For An Alternative
Way To Enhance Progression In University Studies
Erik Laursen and Jørgen Gulddahl Rasmussen ....................................... 129

PEDAGOGICAL AND TECHNOLOGICAL CHALLENGES
IN ON/OFF CAMPUS EDUCATION
Ole Borch, Morten Knudsen, Ole Rokkjær ............................................. 149

PROBLEM-BASED LEARNING
IN THE FOREIGN LANGUAGE STUDY PROGRAMMES
Rita Cancino .................................................................................. 165

DOING ALMOST THE SAME THINGS
FOR SOMEWHAT DIFFERENT REASONS
Thomas Borchmann and Søren Lindhardt ................................... 183

PpBL® IN ARCHITECTURE AND DESIGN
Hans Kiib ........................................................................................ 195

EVALUATION OF LEARNING IN ARCHITECTURAL EDUCATION:
PROCESS AND PRODUCT
Michael Mullins .............................................................................. 209

INTEGRATED DESIGN PROCESS IN PROBLEM-BASED LEARNING
Mary-Ann Knudstrup ..................................................................... 219

THE CONCEPTS OF LEARNING BASED ON THE AAU TEACHING
MODEL IN CHEMICAL ENGINEERING EDUCATION
Erik G. Søgaard .............................................................................. 223

SEMESTER PLANNING IN A PROBLEM-BASED
LEARNING ENVIRONMENT
Bent Rønsholdt ............................................................................... 247

**PBL in Distance Education
and Work Based Learning** ........................................................... 257
QUALITY IN MASTER PROGRAMMESS IN CONTINUING EDUCATION
THROUGH PROBLEM-BASED PROJECT WORK
Annette Lorentsen .......................................................................... 261

BACK TO THE FUTURE - THEORY AND PRACTICE IN ADULT
PRACTITIONERS' PROBLEM ORIENTED PROJECT WORK
Annie Aarup Jensen and Helle Bækkelund ................................... 283

PROJECT-BASED COLLABORATIVE LEARNING
IN DISTANCE EDUCATION
Morten Knudsen, Christine Bajard, Jan Helbo,
Lars Peter Jensen and Ole Rokkjær ............................................... 301

EMPLOYABILITY AND WORK BASED LEARNING
Flemming K. Fink ........................................................................... 317

**Skills Development and Supervision** ......... 329

TEACHING PROCESS COMPETENCIES IN A PBL CURRICULUM
Lise Kofoed, Søren Hansen and Anette Kolmos ......... 331

SUPERVISION AND THE GROUP DYNAMICS
Søren Hansen and Lars Peter Jensen ......... 349

**Intercultural Perspectives** ......... 363

PROBLEM-BASED LEARNING AND THE AGENCY OF MAPPING THE CONTEMPORARY CITY
Gitte Marling ......... 365

THE AAU MODEL SEEN FROM A FOREIGN PROFESSOR'S POINT OF VIEW
Joachim Höhle ......... 381

**Notes on Contributors** ......... 391

# PREFACE

**By Sven Caspersen**

When Aalborg University was inaugurated in 1974, the problem-based and project-organized teaching model (PBL) was part of the university's innovative profile, along with close interaction and dialogue with the surrounding society.

From the beginning we were met with considerable scepticism concerning our educational philosophy. This scepticism came from colleagues at other universities, from future employers of our graduates, from the Danish educational system specifically, and from the public in general.

Thus, the first years were hard work but gradually our surroundings, our partners in the society, accepted that problem-based learning was adding new value and qualifications to our students, our graduates.

Time has shown that it was the right decision. The graduates of Aalborg University are well-received on the labour market and many educational institutions - primarily universities abroad - have followed in our wake and have implemented the PBL model to a small or a large extent. Throughout the years we have had many visitors from abroad who have experienced a concrete, alternative educational practice and brought ideas back home in order to implement some of these ideas in their own educational practices.

Aalborg University has always endeavoured to further develop the educational practice, which was founded in 1974, when the demands and the conditions were different from today. Some of the educational researchers and practitioners at the university have improved elements of the PBL, such as supervision, development of the students' PBL-competencies, variations in teaching methods, development of the analytic approach to PBL etc. Another group of educational researchers have further developed the model on the basis of new target groups, internationalization, and new technology used in education. These are important elements in the development of the educational principles and models used for distance teaching and international study programmes.

During the years a number of initiatives have been launched in which Centre for University Teaching and Learning and the IT-Innovation Centre at Aalborg University have been the central actors. Later, a more externally-focused centre has been established, UCPBL, University Centre for Problem-Based Learning, which adds to the profiling of Aalborg University's PBL-competencies.

This publication is special, as it primarily focuses on the teachers and how they reflect on their own teaching. It shows a large degree of internalization of the educational thinking in the system and it also shows that the development of the educational model takes place in close co-operation with the various university programmes. The coupling is necessary to ensure the survival and further development of the model.

I am sure that this publication will contribute to the understanding of the learning ideas behind and in problem-based learning, and I expect that it will inspire and motivate the readers to include PBL-thinking in their own development of new learning models.

# THE AALBORG MODEL
# - PROBLEM-BASED AND
# PROJECT-ORGANIZED LEARNING

Anette Kolmos, Flemming K. Fink and Lone Krogh

## 1. INTRODUCTION

This book is the result of an internal conference at Aalborg University focusing on development and variation of the Aalborg Model. Twenty-five teachers and researchers gave a presentation on the Aalborg University Model (AAU Model). There were 100 participants at the conference, and afterwards 30 teachers and researchers reflected on their practice, which resulted in 23 articles for this book.
This is a quite unique book, as the problem-based and project-organized models are not primarily reflected upon on the basis of educational theories, but rather upon the basis of the theories and methods of the various university programmes. Thus this book contains a profession-based approach to the further development of the problem-based and project-organized educational practice at the university. This profession-based approach, which has gradually developed at Aalborg University, shows that the educational ideas are alive and well at the decentralised departments, and that the educational model is integrated in relation to the various professions. This is a development which takes time - it takes time to integrate the educational ideas and philosophies and to develop models - but it also demands reflection and experience to discuss and develop the project-based educational approach on the basis of both professional and educational argumentation.

The contributions of the book will inspire further development of PBL at universities all over the world. Throughout the years, Aalborg University has been the object of large international attention due to the special educational model. There have been many visitors who have seen and experienced a different university system, and in the light of that experience they have been convinced that it is actually possible to practice the student-centred ways of teaching. To visit a university where the teachers are not only talking about new educational principles, but where they turn the educational principles into practise, has inspired many of our visitors. For the last 10 years there has been a strong interest in redesigning the engineering study programmes in particular, to achieve more up-to-date educational methods.

Although the educational model works at Aalborg University, it is still important to make continuous improvements to increase the students' learning output and to adapt the educational theories to new types of young and adult students. The continuous improvements are a part of the teaching and learning culture at the university. It proves that there is a constant wish to reflect on and develop the learning principles upon which the Aalborg Model is based.

## 2. THE CONCEPT OF PROBLEM-BASED LEARNING AND PROJECT-ORGANIZED LEARNING

The Danish PBL tradition dates back to the 1970'ies. At that time two new universities were inaugurated in Denmark: Roskilde University in 1972 and Aalborg University in 1974. Common to the two universities was that they were founded on new educational models.

The Danish problem-based and project-organized model was developed on the basis of ideas from, among others Illeris, who formulated principles as problem-orientation, project work, interdisciplinarity, participant directed learning, and the exemplary principle and team work (Illeris, 1976). The Danish concept of problem-orientation was more or less the same as the definition of problem-based learning: a learning method based on the principle of using problems as a starting point for learning (Barrows, 1984).

It is important for the Danish approach to PBL that it is a combination of a problem-based and a project-organized approach. The students analyse and define problems within a defined interdisciplinary or subject frame. The students work together in groups on their project and submit a common project report. Furthermore, the project group has a joint examination, but the students are given individual marks.

During the years, there have been many discussions about the Danish models: many questions have been raised, such as What is a problem? When is a problem a problem? What are the criteria? What is the role of the supervisor and how can the role be conceptualized and develop? How can the students' PBL skills be improved, so that they become more skilled in co-operation and project management.

At the international arena, PBL is not an unambiguous concept. In today's international literature it means both problem-based and project-based learning. If you search on the internet for problem-based learning, you will find more than 100,000 search results. If you search for project-based learning, you will get about 50,000 search results. Thus both problem-based learning and project-based learning seem to be well established concepts. The confusion increases still more when you compare how the PBL concept is used internationally, as the concept is also used at Maastricht University, the Netherlands, Linköping University, Sweden, and in the medical programmes of McMaster University, Canada. They are all new universities - established in the 1970'ies - and founded on a problem-based learning model (Graaff and Bouhuijs, 1993; Wilkerson and Gijselaers, 1996).

This book is about the Aalborg PBL model, and most contributors to the book use the concept problem-based learning as a meta-concept, covering the central learning principles of the educational model used at Aalborg University. However in the book a number of other concepts will also be used to describe the model, such as project-organized learning (POL) and problem-orientation.

## 3. LEARNING PRINCIPLES FOR PBL

Even though there are differences in how problem-based models are practised internationally as well at the university, they are founded on the same theoretical basis and thus the same principles of learning. Reference is often made to the theories of Piaget, Dewey and Lewin, who were some of the first learning theorists within this field, together with Vygotsky (Piaget, 1974; Dewey, 1933; Lewin, 1948; Vygotsky, 1978). Among the new theorists reference is often made to Kolb (1984), Lave and Wenger (1991) and Gardner (1993) (Bygholm and Dirckinck-Holmfeld, 1997; Hansen, 2000). Common to all these theorists is that they view the gaining of experience as an important approach to the further process of motivation and learning.

Still, it is not possible to explain practice only by forming a theory. There are so many elements involved in the problem-based and project-based models, as they represent the establishment of a quite new learning environment and have far-reaching consequences for the universities' culture and organization as well as for the students' development of competencies. The comprehensive understanding necessary to be able to analyse PBL models does not exist within the theory alone and can only be understood once the cognitive approach, the social learning, and the motivation and social psychologies are coupled. The PBL models have thus not developed on the basis of a consistent comprehensive theoretical understanding. Instead they have developed on the basis of a number of - often isolated - theoretical principles, which have found their way to a pragmatic development.

The central theoretical learning principles in both problem-based and project-organized learning concern three dimensions: the problem, the content and the team (Graaff and Kolmos, 2003). The problem approach means that *learning is organized around problems*. It is a central principle for development of motivation. A problem is the starting point for the learning processes. It can be all types of problems from a concrete, realistic problem to a theoretical problem. The problem serves as the basis for the learning processes, because it determines the direction of the learning process, and places weight on the formulation of a question rather than an answer. Integrated in the problem approach is learning in context. The formulation of problems allows the learning content to be related to the context, which promotes the students' motivation and comprehension. *Experience learning* is also an implicit part of the formulation of problems, and especially important in relation to which problems the students are attracted, and to which problems are formulated by the student on the basis on his/her own experiences and interests.

The content approach is especially concerned with interdisciplinarity and exemplary practice. *Inter-disciplinary learning* relates to the dimension of knowledge as the solution to the problem formulation and may span across traditional subject-related boundaries and methods. This principle is critical for the organization of the teaching, in that teachers often consider objectives within the known subject-oriented framework, and do not consider problems or situations. *Exemplary practice* is concerned with ensuring that the student's learning output is exemplary in terms of the framework of the objectives. This is an extremely central principle in that the student must engage in a deeper understanding of the selected complex problem formulation. On the other hand, it is an inherent risk in PBL that it does not provide a sufficiently broad subject-area overview. The students must therefore have the ability to transfer knowledge, theory, and methods from the learned areas to new material areas.

*Social learning* - or team-based learning - is the last core principle, and specifies that the majority of the learning processes take place in groups and teams. Also *student centred, self directed*, or the very Danish concept of participant directed learning, indicates ownership of the learning process and especially the formulation of the problem. Personal competencies are therefore implicitly developed in order to handle the group co-operation processes.

The above described principles are drawn from various learning theories and form an abstract theoretical level, a »point of reference«, for designing and modelling the concrete education. The principles cover the problem-based learning models, as they are practised for instance at the universities in Maastricht and Linköping; but they also cover the project-based models as they are practised in Aalborg and Roskilde.

## 4. THE TRADITIONAL AALBORG PBL MODEL

The project work model is used in all study programmes at Aalborg University within the Faculty of Humanities, the Faculty of Social Science, and the Faculty of Engineering and Science

The traditional Aalborg model is founded on problem-based project work, in which approximately one half of the students' time is spent on project work in teams, whereas the other half is spent on more or less traditional lectures. All project work is made in groups, and the same model is followed from the 1st semester until the completion of a masters' degree (10th semester). During the span of the university degree programme, the groups normally become smaller, starting with typically 6-7 students in the 1st year, and reduced to maximum 2-3 students in the final semester.

Project-organized, problem-based learning as it is implemented at Aalborg University is described in the booklet »The Aalborg Experiment - project innovation in university education« (Kjærsdam and Enemark, 1994; Fink, 1999). The main principles can be described as in figure 1.

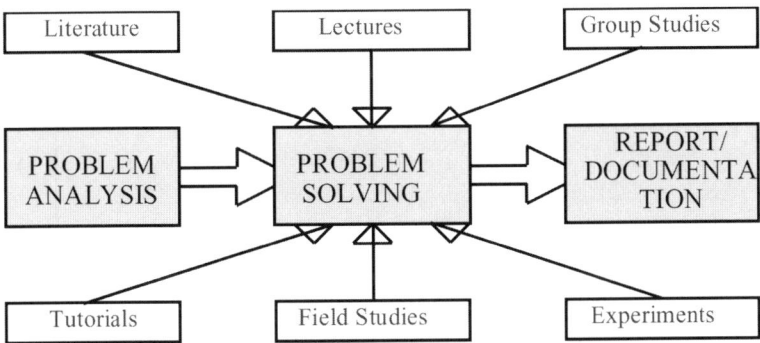

Figure 1: Principles of project-organized problem-solving
(Kjærsdam and Enemark, 1994)

The curriculum is organized into semesters - 10 semesters leading to a Master's degree, organized in a very deterministic structure with a very well-prescribed output. The project work is formulated within the framework of the given theme, related to the overall educational objectives, which can be a broad, open theme or a subject-related limited theme. The students are allowed to formulate their project proposal themselves, but there is always a supervisor who approves the proposal.

In each semester the project and the majority of the courses must relate to the theme of the actual semester. The students are supposed to attend the courses and apply them in their project work, and the output of the courses is assessed along with the project report at the end of the semester. The examination is a joint group examination with individual marks and takes up to six hours. The work with the project report and the courses - the theme - covers approximately 80 % of the semester, equivalent to 24 ECTS (European Credit Transfer System). A full semester is 30 ECTS points. The rest of the semester includes fundamental courses or other compulsory courses (study courses) assessed by more traditional examinations (see figure 2).

The structure of the curriculum is fundamentally progressive, and in addition each step in this progression implies a large degree of flexibility. Within a specific theme projects can and do change from year to year. A theme covers a great variation of problems - and as the projects selected will be a combination of 1) proposals from industry, public administration etc 2) interests among students, and 3) interests among staff etc., and new problems will always be in focus. Therefore, even though the purpose and the content of the theme is well prescribed using Bloom's taxonomy of learning depth (Bloom, 1956), the curriculum is very flexible and can follow the scientific development and integrate application of new research results.

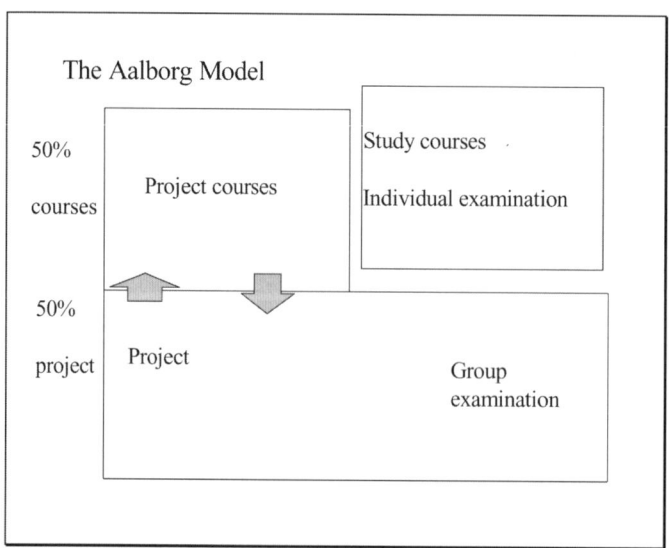

Figure 2: The traditional Aalborg PBL model

Each group has one or several supervisors (faculty member). The role of the supervisor is to respond to the students' project process along the way and to take the group through to the examination. The examination is a group examination, where both the supervisor and an external or an internal examiner are present.

## 5. VARIATIONS IN THE PBL MODEL AT AALBORG UNIVERSITY

The project-based model varies considerably in practice and these variations, which will be dealt with in this book. The subject, educational objectives, extent, placing in the study programme, group size, variations in the students' liberty of choice, the relation between courses and project, the form of examinations, and use of resources are just some of the differences that are often mentioned when project work at different institutions is compared.

In nearly all programmes the project work corresponds to half of the students' time. Although the typical project lasts five months, there are exceptions. In some programmes, for instance at the Department of Architecture and Design, the students work with a series of shorter projects of less extent, because that approach suits the educational objectives better.

The understanding of the educational principles will vary from department to department, and these variations will affect aspects of the program, including the implementation and the curriculum formulation:

- The **themes** can be defined in different ways as themes describing various types of problems, or as themes directed towards certain subjects
- The choice of **projects** can be based on open or more controlled problem formulations depending on the educational objectives and the understanding of »problem-based«. In the open situation the students are supposed to prepare and word the problems and the projects themselves, and in the more controlled situation the teachers make the preparation and wording.
- The definition of a **problem** can vary between professional areas. In some programmes the problem must be a dilemma or a social discrepancy, in other programmes the problem will be an issue calling for an engineering solution, or in other cases it is a question of turning the learning process in a certain direction.
- The definition of the **various phases** of the project, which may vary depending on the subject in question.
- The relation between **courses and project** will depend on the understanding of knowledge, traditions and culture of the various departments. For example there are large differences in the relation between courses and project

at the Faculty of Engineering and Science, and the language study programmes at The Faculty of Humanities. At the Faculty of Engineering and Science the students attend project courses, which supports the objectives of the project and the project itself. At some of the languages studies the students are offered a number of courses and they are free to choose 2-3 courses and write their project within in the framework of these courses.
- The extent of project **supervision** varies a lot - and is carried out in different ways
- The **group sizes** vary from 1st semester and up to 10th semester with more students in the groups at the beginning of the study. But the group sizes also vary from department to department.

More variations can be mentioned, and the above are just presented to illustrate that there are variations in the concrete execution of the model. Therefore, the formulation of learning principles and learning philosophies is an essential part in the development of models. There must be some core principles, with variations being allowed within a given framework.

## 6. THE CONTENTS OF THIS BOOK

In this book the authors refer to a number of themes, which are and have been on the agenda for many years. The many articles are grouped according to the following themes: Setting the Scene, The Aalborg PBL model, PBL in Distance Education and Work based Learning, Skills Development and Supervision, and finally Intercultural Perspectives.

All these themes are central in the development of PBL at Aalborg University. For each theme, there is a short introduction, included in order to explain the intention and the relevance of the theme as well as to render the inner logic of the book visible.

## REFERENCES

Barrows, H.S. (1984). *A specific problem-based, self-directed learning method designed to teach medical problem-solving skills, and enhance knowledge retention and recall*. In H.G. Schmidt & M.L. de Volder (Eds.), *Tutorials in problem-based learning* (pp 16-32) Assen (the Netherlands): Van Gorcum & Comp. B.V.

Barrows, H. S. (1996). *Problem-based learning in medicine and beyond: A brief overview*, in: L. Wilkerson and W. H. Gijselaers (Eds.), *Bringing Problem-*

*Based Learning to Higher Education: Theory and Practice.* Jossey-Bass Publishers, San Francisco.

Bloom, Benjamin S. (1956). *Taxonomi of Educational Objectives. The Classification of Educational Goals. Handbook 1: Cognitive Domain.* David Mckay Company, Inc., New York.

Bygholm, A. and Dirckinck-Holmfeld, L. (1997). *Pædagogik i det virtuelle læremiljø: metodiske overvejelser (Pedagogy in the virtual classroom - Methodological reflections)*, in O. Danielsen (Ed.), *Læring og multimedier (Learning and Multimedia)*, Aalborg University Press: Aalborg.

Dewey, J. (1933). *How We think: a restatement of the relation of reflective thinking to the educative process.* Heath, Boston.

Fink, F.K. (1999). *Integration of Engineering Practice into Curriculum - 25 years of experience with Problem Based Learning*, FIE'99: Frontiers in Education Conference - Engineers Designing the Future, Puerto Rico, November 1999.

Gardner, H. (1993). *Multiple Intelligences. The Theory in Practice.* New York. Basic.

Graaff, E. de and Bouhuijs, P. A. J. (Eds.) (1993). *Implementation of Problem-Based Learning in Higher Education*, Thesis publishers, Amsterdam.

Graaff, E. and Kolmos, A. (2003). *Characteristics of problem-based learning*, International Journal of Engineering Education, Vol. 19, no. 5. http://www.ijee.dit.ie/contents/c190503.html

Hansen, S. (2000). Vejledning og evaluering af den refleksive praktiker *(Advising and evaluation of the reflective practioner)*, Ph.D. Dissertation, Department for Development an Planning, Aalborg University.

Illeris, K.(1976). Problemorientering og deltagerstyring: oplæg til en alternative didaktik *(Problem orientation and participation: draft for an alternative didactic)*. Munksgaard, Copenhagen

Kjersdam, F. and Enemark, S (1994). *The Aalborg Experiment - project innovation in university education*, Aalborg University Press. Aalborg, Denmark.

Kolb, D.A. (1984). *Experiential Learning.* Englewood Cliffs. Prentice Hall.

Lave, J. & Wenger, E. (1991). *Situated learning - Legitimate peripheral participation.* Cambridge University Press, New York.

Lewin, K. (1948). *Resolving social conflicts; selected papers on group dynamics.* Gertrude W. Lewin (red.). Harper & Row, New York.

Piaget, J. (1974). Forord. In: Bärbel Inhelder; Hermine Sinclair & Magali Bover: *Learning and the development of cognition.* Harvard University Press, Cambridge.

Vygotsky, L.S. (1978). *Mind in Society. The Development of Higher Psychological Process.* Harvard University Press, Cambridge, Mass.

Wilkerson, L. and Gijselaers, W. H. (Eds.), (1996). *Bringing Problem-Based Learning to Higher Education: Theory and Practice,* Jossey-Bass Publishers, San Francisco.

# SETTING THE SCENE

In the first theme »Setting the PBL Scene« the purpose of the introduction is partly to relate the Aalborg Model to a large international PBL-pattern and partly to give initial bearings to the contents of the Aalborg PBL model.

In addition, three articles have been chosen, which set the framework of this book in various ways. The first article is about the students' voice. What do the students think of the Aalborg PBL model? Frances Jørgensen replies to this question and addresses various issues, all related to the students' experiences with PBL. . In her article, »The Students' Voice, the author summarizes and analyses data collected through both individual and group interviews conducted with students from the three faculties, primarily at the completion of their fifth semester, at Aalborg University. Through these informal, semi-structured interviews, the students share their thoughts on what PBL »in practice« means to them, their learning, and their expectations for the future.

The next article, »Employability and Problem-based Learning in Project-Organized Settings at Universities«, concerns the voice of the graduates, which is analysed by Lone Krogh and Jørgen Gulddahl Rasmussen. They report on a new study conducted with graduates from the two PBL-universities in Denmark, Aalborg University and Roskilde University Centre. In total, 6,758 candidates and 175 employers have answered questions concerning work, employability, and the match between competencies developed through the studies and competencies needed from the academic labour market and other related subjects. The analyses of the data focus on the question of the future role of the universities and the development of transferable skills by using PBL principles.

The third article sets up a framework for diversity and challenges. The Aalborg Model varies from department to department, depending on the teachers involved and their practice. In his article, »Problem-based Learning as a Way of Organizing Learning and Teaching at the University«, Erik Laursen describes PBL as a very flexible method that is adjusted to demands formulated at different times. The PBL methods are seen as a flexible educational frame for a broad variety of educational elements and methods. These elements and methods can be combined in different ways, as it has been the case during the 1990's. . Crucial contemporary challenges are outlined, and proposals for the future development are presented.

# THE STUDENTS VOICE

Frances Jørgensen

Abstract: The data presented in this paper were collected from interviews conducted with students who had been enrolled for five or more semesters in the Faculties of Engineering and Science, Humanities, and Social Science at Aalborg University. Through these informal interviews, the students shared their experiences with the problem-based and project-organized (PBL) approach to learning practiced at the university. For instance, the students explained what PBL has meant to them in terms of both theory and practice, how they have viewed the relationship between theory and practice in their project and course work, and what the role of supervision and IT has been in their studies. In addition, the students described some of the benefits and challenges of working in project groups as well as their learning and skill development while at the university.

## 1. INTRODUCTION

A quick show of hands in a class of students at the basis year at Aalborg University suggests that the vast majority chose to attend the university because they were attracted to the prospect of the »problem-based and project-organized (PBL)« approach to learning. Further probing reveals that these students were in fact motivated primarily by the idea of working on projects in groups: few could articulate a definition of problem-based learning at this early stage of their academic careers.

Again through casual questioning, it becomes apparent that many of the students share the perception that working in project groups at the university level will eventually provide them with an »edge« over graduates of the more traditionally structured universities in Denmark. Some had reached this conclusion based on surveys and newspaper articles they had read, others had been encouraged by high school teachers and advisors, and there are a few that reasoned that, because team work and project work has become such a part of the every-day work life, such an education would be beneficial to them in their future careers.

Even though the AAU model is clearly described in the information provided upon enrolment, most of the students at this point have only a vague understanding of how the courses and project work are structured and organized in order to support problem-based learning. As would be expected, a deeper understanding of what PBL and the AAU model are all about requires gaining experience with the group project work over time. For this reason, it was considered especially relevant to talk with students who had studied at the university for several semesters about their experiences with problem-based learning and project and group work.

The remainder of this paper is used to describe a series of interviews conducted with students and student project groups from the three disciplines of study at Aalborg University and to present the students' responses are summarized in this paper.

As only a handful of interviews were conducted for this paper, the summary provided here should not be considered comprehensive or representative.

## 2. METHODS

Data for this paper were collected through seven interviews with students and student project groups in the Faculty of Humanities, the Faculty of Social Science, and the Faculty of Engineering and Science. In all cases, attempts were made to interview assembled project groups; however, due to scheduling conflicts, this was only possible in 3 cases. Individual interviews with four students were therefore conducted to collect additional data for the paper. The groups interviewed included between 3-4 students, all at the end of their fifth semester at Aalborg University. Two of the individual interviews were also conducted with fifth semester students, the third with a seventh semester student, and the final interview with a recent master's level graduate.

The interviews were semi-structured, with open-ended questions derived from the main themes represented at an internal conference of teachers and researchers in the field of PBL at Aalborg University. Specifically, the interview questions were designed to gain an understanding of the students' experiences in terms of the following: their own understanding of PBL; the structure and organization of the courses and project work; the relationship between theory and practice in the courses and project work; the nature of cooperation (e.g. with group members, advisors, external contacts); use of resources; the role of IT; forms of evaluation and examination; and the perceived learning and competence development achieved thus far in the education.

Each interview lasted approximately one hour and all of the students participated in providing responses to the questions. In the case of the project groups, the responses were in the form of informal discussions between the group members and the author. In the next section, the students' responses to the interview questions are summarized according to the described themes. Although some similarities and differences between the three disciplines are highlighted in the next section, the small number of interviews conducted prevents any type of systematic comparisons. Further, there were no efforts to validate or verify any of the statements made by the students, as the focus here is on sharing the students' own perceptions rather than on reporting objective facts.

Over the years, a series of educational research-related studies and evaluations of PBL have been conducted among students at the university, though none in the last three years. Therefore, the editors chose to include the students' views and experiences in each of the above-mentioned themes; this paper has thus taken the form of a type of qualitative pilot study.

## 3. MAIN THEMES

### 3.1. What Does PBL Mean in Practice?

How PBL is understood from both a theoretical viewpoint and a practical viewpoint was one of the central themes among the teachers and researchers attending the conference held at Aalborg University. Likewise, it is interesting to hear how the students define PBL in their own words, on the basis of their experiences over the past five or more semesters. When asked, »What does PBL mean in practice?« the majority of the students readily admitted to a certain »naiveté« concerning PBL when they first became students at the university. Several students told that, even though they were given a definition of PBL in their first semester, it did not make sense to them until they had completed one or more projects. In particular, they claim that the concept of the problem defining the project-rather than the problem being developed from a project idea-first became real to them after having gained some experience with PBL. One student from the Faculty of Social Science explained that projects often change dramatically from how they are described in the project catalogue, once the research begins. For instance, in one project the initial idea involved building an understanding of foreign aid provided to underdeveloped companies, but the group soon discovered there was a great deal of controversy among various parties. The project therefore shifted course to explore the basis for this controversy, including the very different attitudes and objectives of those involved in economic decision-making. One student stated that »the project just develops a life of its own«, according to the problem formulation that emerges in the beginning weeks of the project work.

## 3.2. Structure and Organization of Project and Course Work

According to the original Aalborg model, approximately one half of the students' time is spent on group project work and the other half is spent on more traditional lectures. In the interviews, the students were asked to first to explain their own understanding of the relationship between course and project work at the university and thereafter, to describe their experiences with way in which the courses and project work have been structured and organized.

Students within all of the disciplines seemed aware of the »theoretical« (i.e. stated) relationship between study-related coursework and project work, although none of the students believed there was a »50-50« balance between the two in any given semester. Rather, it was generally reported that when viewed as a whole (i.e. the study over the 5-7 semesters), this balance might in fact be achieved. Only the students in the Faculty of Engineering and Science had been required to complete a project every semester (although exceptions are common due to apprenticeships and foreign study programs); in the Faculty of Humanities and Social Science, projects had been completed projects in three out of the five semesters at the university. In those semesters without project work, smaller tasks such as essays or reports, completed either individually or in groups, were assigned.

Generally, the smaller assignments were closely related to the content of one of the study-related courses. The students did not feel that completing assignments that were not directly tied to project work was in any way a disadvantage in terms of their learning, because these assignments were viewed as supplements to the project work in the other semesters. In addition, most of the assignments were completed by groups, just as in the case of the projects. The shift between full-scale project work and less extensive assignments each semester also provided students in these study programs with the opportunity to complete an apprenticeship or study abroad.

Students in each of the disciplines reported that lectures often seemed very broad and that it was difficult to make a connection between the content and the project work. One student in the Faculty for Social Studies estimated that approximately 10 minutes of each lecture attended could be directly or indirectly related to the content of the project work. She further explained that the opportunity to attend seminars on specific topics did not fully address this issue, as the groups worked with such diverse problem formulations. Still, this student believed that having too broadly focused lectures was a decided advantage over lectures that were solely focused on the project themes, as the latter would prove to be too limited. On the other hand, she expressed concern as to whether some of the courses would be relevant to her field of study.

The relationship between the project work and the course work is one of the most complicated aspects of the Aalborg model and this relationship can be quite difficult for the students to recognize, especially in the first semesters at the university. From the interviews, it appears that the students at the fifth semester (and upward) also had difficulty in this area. The students from the Faculty of Humanities also reported a very loose relationship between the study-related course work and the project work. In fact, the students claimed that the course work and the project work were basically viewed as »two separate entities«. The students in the Faculty of Engineering and Science agreed with those in the other disciplines and felt that there were definite advantages and disadvantages to study-related coursework that was not directly linked to the project work. For instance, they felt that such a structure forced them to learn theories and methods on their own in order to complete the projects, rather than being »allowed to draw only from what came out of the lectures«. At times being required to learn independently while digesting the lecture material served as a challenge, but one they felt was worthwhile. On the other hand, they mentioned that the study-related courses sometimes seemed planned somewhat haphazardly, without enough attention being given to overall coherence of the program (e.g. some subjects repeated in two courses or noticeable gaps in the course material over the first five semesters). Still, they and the students from the other disciplines claimed that they recognized a clear progression from the basis year to the point they had now reached. In other words, even though there may have been some problems with the organizing and structuring of certain courses in relationship to another, the students felt that the courses built on each other in some way so that they were not starting at the beginning each semester.

Most of the students in the three study programs stated that the balance between the number of lecture hours and hours to work on the projects and or conduct fieldwork had improved farther into their education. During the first two semesters, they felt that there were too many scheduled lectures, which left inadequate time to work on projects. One of the students explained that the time taken to actually form a relatively cohesive group did not seem to be taken into account during the basis year, and thus allocation of time was perhaps done according to the number of hours the actual project required. Most of the students agreed that the first semesters are characterized by many »wasted« hours-i.e. hours with the group that were not directly related to the project work. In retrospect, they perceive this time necessary for group development and learning group skills.

## 3.3. The Relationship between Theory and Practice

Several of the students remarked that the project work was invaluable in so far as helping them understand the theory presented in their lectures and in their own reading. One of the project groups from the Faculty of Humanities explained that, for example, models describing the role of politics in certain types of communication patterns first became understandable once manuscripts from a city council meeting were reviewed as part of a group project. They explained that when models or theory were read about in their course books and presented in lectures, they focused primarily on learning details that might be relevant in an examination. However, the overall meaning behind the theory and methods only first became apparent when they read through the manuscripts for themselves and related these back to the models.

Other students told that some courses and semesters seemed to be more tied to practice and others were more theoretical in nature. They felt that overall there was a reasonable balance between the two, but that it would be preferable if the teachers could make a more visible connection between theory and practice in each of the courses.

## 3.4. The Group Work

For many of the students interviewed, the choice to attend Aalborg University was based on the desire to participate in group project work. Although none of the students claimed that group work is easy, they all strongly believed that the benefits far outweigh the drawbacks. Some of the advantages they mentioned having experienced with working in groups included learning cooperation and collaborations skills, developing a sense of tolerance and understanding of differing viewpoints and ideas, patience and tolerance with working with others in general, synergy or creative flow of ideas in group processes, a greater sense of commitment to the education, and the social value of having others to encourage and motivate attendance and participation in the courses and assignments.

There was general consensus among the students that successful group project work requires the use of tools and methods taught during the first semesters. For instance, many of the group members related how it was now customary for the project groups to begin a new project with a discussion of the members' expectations and ambitions for the project, creation of verbal and/or written guidelines for the group, and both short and long term activity plans. A few of the students even commented that they had begun to use these methods in their personal lives, for making sure chores and other responsibilities were accomplished on time.

## 3.5. Group Formation

At the beginning of each semester (with the exception of the first semesters) a project catalogue for each study program is made available to the students; shortly thereafter a »group formation« day is held within each study program. On this day, the students are expected to select the members of their project group for that the semester. Although a teacher meets with the students to outline the group formation procedure, the students are left alone to decide on the group composition. One of the fundamental rules for the students is that the group formation is not complete until all students have found a project group. It is certainly no secret at the university that the process of group formation can be extremely difficult for the students.

Students from the Faculty of Engineering and Science appear to be more likely to remain in somewhat intact groups over several semesters than students from the other two disciplines and therefore tend not to be so involved in the group formation process. Normally, more than half of a particular group chooses to continue together to the next semester and one or two move to/from another group. The engineering students believe their desire to remain with the same group members stems from the progressive nature of the project work. In other words, many of the projects from the later semesters may include external contacts the groups established in prior semesters or they may involve more in-depth analyses using methods learned in a previous project.

For all of the groups, decisions related to group composition in the first few semesters were generally based on interests (i.e. project ideas). In later semesters, the students admitted that personal qualities played an ever-increasing role in group selection. Within each of the study programs, certain students had developed a reputation for being hard workers and others gained reputations as »free riders«. Those students who had demonstrated their commitment to the study program often formed their own groups, sometimes long before the actual group formation activities took place. Some of the students remarked that such a group selection process was problematic, in that good students with an interest in joining one of these groups might be excluded and there was a strong likelihood that feelings would be hurt.

### 3.6. Equal Work Effort and Commitment?

One of the issues that inevitably arises when talking with student about their experiences with group work concerns whether there appears to be equal commitment and work contribution on the part of all of the group members. In reality, situations in which a student contributes very little to a project yet nonetheless passes the semester due to the efforts of his/her fellow group members are quite rare at the university. Still, it appears that even one isolated experience may have a significant impact on the remaining group members and the feelings of »injustice« are discussed frequently among the students. This was also found to be the case with the students interviewed.

Although the students fully agreed that actual number of »free riders« was quite low in their respective study program and especially in the later semesters, all those interviewed had experienced project work with at least one such individual. Interestingly, many of the students shared some responsibility for the problem, stating that the group should have been better about defining norms at the beginning of the project, confronting students that did not fulfil their responsibilities, or involving the project supervisor when problems could not be solved at the group level. One student described a situation in which a student contributed only minimally to the project, causing the others to do much more than their designated tasks. The other students never confronted this student and never discussed the situation with the advisor. At the examination, the entire group was given the same marks, which caused all but the one student to be very dissatisfied. By the time the groups were to be formed in the next semester, this student had developed a reputation that made it difficult for him to be welcomed in any of the groups.

Several of the students interviewed suggested one way of dealing with some of the problems incurred while working in project groups would be to hold regular courses on group psychology, team work, group roles, etc. Although there are courses focused on these themes early in the study program, there are none offered during the later semesters. The students reported that they were unlikely to discuss these types of group problems with their advisors, as they preferred to use that time on the study-related aspects of the project.

### 3.7. Examinations

For all of the students interviewed, project examinations in which the entire group was evaluated, based on the written project, the presentation of the project, and the discussion of the project, were the most common type of evaluation. Although most of the students had also completed individual assignments and smaller group tasks, these did not generally receive marks. Variations as to how students were evaluated in the group examinations appeared to be related more to the particular advisor than the study discipline in which the students were enrolled. Students in all three study programs reported that some advisors were more likely to give the same marks to all of the students, while others generally give individual marks, based on each student's ability to participate in the discussion and present.

The students seemed to agree that a group examination was the most appropriate form of evaluation for the project work but as was mentioned previously, there have been cases in which students who had not contributed to the project were given the same marks as those who had. Several of the students said that a more fair system might include peer evaluations combined with project and presentation grades, but others were unsure as to whether the students would evaluate each other fairly. Other students believed individual marks were the best solution to the problem, but that this would only be possible if the advisor had some basis on which to make the evaluation.

The students all appeared to be aware of the recourses available to them if they felt the need to dispute the results of their examination. In fact, two of the students said that there were far too many opportunities for students to complain and/or have their efforts re-evaluated and that marks should be perceived as »final« unless there is clear cause for a reversal.

## 3.8 Learning and Skill Development

The students were asked to describe their learning and skill development thus far in their education, especially with respect what they believed would be most valuable to them in the future. In all of the interviews, skills related to group/teamwork were mentioned first. The students all believed that they had learned a great deal about themselves and how to work more effectively with others, as a result of their studies at the university. In particular, the students mentioned having gained a greater respect for others' opinions and ideas, how to express their own ideas in ways that could be understood by others, and how to support and encourage a group process (i.e. to support other members of the group in working towards a goal). Many of the students also mentioned learning about how their own strengths and weaknesses could both be used as assets in group work, the types of roles they could and should fulfil in a group setting, and how they learn and work best (e.g. under pressure, alone or in small or larger groups, on one or several tasks at one time). None of the students had difficulty imagining that these skills would be useful once they enter the job market.

On practical level, the students also mentioned having learned (and learned the value of) a great deal about project management, including establishing an agenda, time lines, milestones, short-term and long-term goals, and delegating tasks to individuals and sub-groups. One student said that even though he had listened to teachers explaining why these methods and techniques were important during the earlier semesters, he needed to experience all that can go wrong with a project under poor management before he could really believe it. Many of the other students interviewed agreed that the experimentation with many types of project management had helped them learn skills that could be used after graduation.

One of the students in the Faculty of Social Science said that while she has learned an enormous amount, both in terms of her study-area and group project work, she often wonders whether she would have learned more in a more traditional setting. Other students agreed that they had given this matter some thought, as they were just beginning to consider their options for working towards the master's degree. The majority of the students felt that the decision to attend this university-in other words, to study according to a PBL approach-had been the »right« one, but some were still worried that knowledge in their chosen professional field (i.e. discipline of study) might be weaker than students graduating from other universities. One of the students admitted that she often worried what she would do if she realized one day that she had chosen the »wrong« education (i.e. engineering), but rationalized that if that were to happen, she would at least have her group and project skills to fall back on.

## 3.9. Supervision

All of the students reported being satisfied with the number of hours of supervision they receive each semester and none could remember having an advisor that actually »counted his/her hours« when meeting with the groups or individual students. Generally, the students felt that the advisors were available to them when they were needed. Students in the Faculty of Social Science explained that advisors were assigned to the student groups, whereas students from the other two disciplines were more or less able to choose their advisors, as the advisors were linked to certain projects within their academic field. Thus, when students selected a study area in which to focus their projects, they were in essence also selecting their group advisor. Although the assignment of advisors in the Faculty of Social Science sometimes resulted in a mismatch between advisor and project study area (i.e. not the advisors area of expertise), the students did not feel this had been especially problematic as their advisors seemed very good at helping the students establish other contacts and at developing their own knowledge.

The students in the Faculty of Humanities feel that they are given lowest priority at the university in terms of budgeting and the availability of resources and one said she feared continuous budget cuts were leading to a »discount education«. The lack of (available and quality) resources were most apparent for these students in relationship to the quantity and quality of computers, copy machines and printing facilities, and reimbursement for travel expenses related to the project work. In all of these categories, the students rated the availability of useable resources far below satisfactory. Students in both the Faculty of Engineering and Science and Social Science expressed general satisfaction with the available resources, stating that reimbursement of travel funds and adequate allotment for copies and printing had not been an issue for them.

## 3.10. The Role of IT

The students were asked to describe the role that IT-for example, computers and networks, played in their course and project work as well as their study program in general. As mentioned previously, each of the group rooms are equipped with one university-owned computer. The students were all in agreement that the equipment tends to be older and somewhat outdated and that technical problems were common. Further, they stated that one computer per group, especially for those groups that share a group room, is inadequate. However, because many of the students have acquired their own laptops, this has not been a serious problem for the majority of the students interviewed.

One of the students suggested that the university should consider offering a type of cooperative financial loan program so that all students could afford to purchase a laptop computer. In his opinion, providing the students with an affordable way to purchase their own equipment would relieve the university of the financial burden of purchasing and updating computers and offering technical support for so many computers. Moreover, since the students would be most likely to purchase newer machines, recurrent problems with internal networks that might be caused by using the university's outdated software might be alleviated.

One a few of the students regularly use networks established by the university for communicating with their group members and file sharing, although all reported using some type of file sharing an email programs. Frequent technical problems with the university networks appeared to be the reason more students do not make use of this resource. Emailing between group members and advisors was reported as the most common means of communication and most considered this an efficient and effective way to stay in contact with each other, even though there were many stories of attached files being lost. Apparently, all of the students interviewed had experienced problems with inactive group email addresses assigned by the secretaries; therefore, the majority created their own via such programs as hotmail.

Many of the students also use various chat programs to stay in touch with group members when not working together at the university. They explain that being able to ask the other students questions while working at home allows them to get much more work done, as they do not have to wait until a group meeting is scheduled. All of the students reported using the class calendars posted online to make their own work schedules and most visited their teacher's homepages or course sites to retrieve copies of lecture overheads. Students were also accustomed to visiting Internet sites for those classes in which the teachers posted additional reading materials, but stated that updating of these sites could be better.

Those interviewed and especially the students in the Faculty of Social Science and Humanities said that they would like to see more courses offered in the use of IT and networks. They explained that while there was always at least one group member experienced with IT that could manage whatever the group needed, it would have been preferable that all could learn these skills and have the opportunity to practice them in their project work.

### 3.11. Availability and Use of Resources

The students were asked to give their own evaluations of the availability and use of resources such as group rooms, time with advisors, funds for project related travel, copies and printing, etc. Since the university's strong expansion through the 1980's-1990's, obtaining adequate physical facilities have been a recognized problem and the source of repeated complaints from the students.

There is a general understanding that group rooms are made available for each of the project groups during each semester. However, there seems to be considerable variation into the administration of the group rooms and whether the time allotted each group is sufficient. Students in the Faculty of Engineering and Science reported that they had been assigned their own group room each semester; there had occasionally been minor delays with room assignment, but once this was accomplished, the groups were free to use the room whenever they wished. The students reported that having free access to their own group room was a definite advantage to the project work, especially considering the diverse work patterns of the group members. For example, some students preferred to work in smaller groups late in the evening while others often met before and after lectures to compare notes or plan tasks. The students also mentioned that having such access to the group room allowed those without home computers and/or Internet connections to contribute to the project.

Students in both the Faculty of Social Science and Humanities reported that due to a shortage of group rooms, most of the groups were required to share rooms with other project groups. The secretary took responsibility for scheduling time for each group on a weekly basis. For those in the Faculty of Social Science, approximately two-and-one-half eight-hour days per week per group was considered standard. Students in the Faculty of Humanities reported that the number of hours per group varied considerably per semester, but that rooms were often shared between groups. In both cases, the students felt that not having a group room to themselves whenever it was needed resulted in additional pressure on the group members, especially in the beginning and ending phases of the project.

A few of the students explained that they had learned to tailor their own work patterns according to the limited availability of the group rooms, so that most of the work was accomplished individually at home and time in the group room was reserved for discussions and planning with the entire group. Still, sharing group rooms presented problems for all of these students, as time plans or notes written on the blackboard were often erased, files were occasionally damaged or deleted on the group room computers, and there were frequent scheduling problems so that two groups waited on one room. Students from both of these study programs remarked that they would set the attainment of additional group rooms as a high priority for their respective departments.

## 3.12. Development of PBL

The students were asked whether they were aware of development of PBL during their time at the university and if so, whether they felt that they had participated in this development in any way. For the most part, the students believe the model was constantly being fine-tuned and improved to meet the needs of the students and their chosen fields. The one possible exception to this perception was the student from the Faculty of Humanities who felt that budget constraints had jeopardized the positive development of PBL and the study program in general. The students had difficulty specifying the ways in which PBL had developed and stated that much of what they believed was based on changes they had heard about in the basis year or read about regarding continuing education at the university. Further, those interviewed believed that the projects themselves were developing each year, in order to better prepare them for the students for their future careers as well as to make the education more attractive to students with work experience.

Many of the students interviewed in each of the three disciplines had participated in student committees that sought to make improvements to the study programs. These committees focused primarily on the structuring and organization of the project and course work and the students' suggestions for improvement were channelled through a representative to the department heads. Although none of the students had followed any give improvement suggestion through to determine whether changes were made, they had the perception that their feedback was used and useful in the development of PBL. Two of the students who had not participated in this type of committee remembered completing a feedback questionnaire at some point in which they were asked to rate various aspects of the program, but they did not remember what was done with the results.

Some of the students claimed that they believed that PBL was developing in a positive direction, based on the many articles that had been written about the university during the past few years and the increased enrolment.

## 4. CONCLUSION

The purpose of this paper was to share students' experiences with PBL at Aalborg University. Although the students interviewed for the paper are from very different programs of study and the learning achieved relative to their professional field would be expected to vary greatly, there were many common experiences described by the students from the Faculties of Engineering and Science, Humanities, and Social Science. In particular, the students all agreed that through the PBL approach created a link between theory and practice that had enriched their learning. Furthermore, all of the students felt that they had developed project management and group skills that will prove valuable in their future careers. Many of the students also attributed much of their own personal development to the group project work, explaining that they had become easier to talk to, better at listening, more respectful of others, and more tolerant of individual differences.

The topics the students responded to and discussed in the interviews conducted in order to write this paper correspond roughly to the major themes in this book-themes that represent the main areas of focus of the teachers and researchers within the field of PBL that participated in the PBL workshop at Aalborg University. By including the students' own experiences with PBL in the book, a non-professional perspective is added.

**REFERENCES**

Easterby-Smith, M., Thorpe, R., & Lowe, A. (1991). Management research: An introduction. Sage Publications, London.

Graaff, E. and Kolmos, A. (2003). Characteristics of problem-based learning, International Journal of Engineering Education, Vol. 19, no. 5. http://www.ijee.dit.ie/contents/c190503.html

Kjersdam, F. and Enemark, S (1994). The Aalborg Experiment - project innovation in university education, Aalborg University Press. Aalborg, Denmark.

# EMPLOYABILITY AND PROBLEM-BASED LEARNING IN PROJECT-ORGANIZED SETTINGS AT UNIVERSITIES

**Lone Krogh and Jørgen Gulddahl Rasmussen**

**Abstract**: The discussions in this paper are based on data from a survey collected from nearly 6.758 masters who have graduated during the last ten years from Roskilde University and Aalborg University and from 175 employers. The data concerns a substantial number of questions concerning work, employability, and the match between competences developed through the studies and competences needed by the academic labour market and other related subjects. The data is discussed in the light of societal change, changes on labour markets, and the future role of universities in enhancing the employability of graduates. The data looks into changes in the demands and conditions for the academic workforce. These changes will be used to discuss consequences in the role of the university as the education institution and especially how other skills than specific subject knowledge can be developed in university education. The principles of problem-oriented project-work which have been used by the two universities since 1972 and 1974 will be presented - and the possibilities in using such a method will be discussed as a method to integrate subject-related as well as more general academic abilities in the qualification processes at the universities.

## 1. INTRODUCTION

In many ways we have seen societies and their labour markets go through dramatic changes during the last couple of decades. Such changes have had an impact on jobs, work functions, company structures as well as industry dynamics. However, it has also an important impact on the daily societal life and the dynamics of the economy and society. We have considered this as a change from the industrial society to the information society, the knowledge society, and even to the learning economy. Such changes in society and the economy are supposed to have not only an impact on society in general or on firms and institutions as such. The changes also affect the relationships between people in all their mutual activities and the ways in which people experience these relationships.

This in itself demands changes in the functions of educational institutions that support the development of the youth to become suitable as citizens, as work force, and as adapters of new techniques, culture, and ethics. In our opinion, the educational institutions are still believed to have an important significance in the diffusion of general and specific knowledge to society. Therefore the starting point for this discussion is the overall function of universities, but specifically we want to narrow it down to the educational function and especially focus on in its dissemination of knowledge to students other than the specific disciplinary (or subject) knowledge. This focus is interesting to discuss because changes here can be important, but at the same time not undisputed as an obligation for universities.

This subject is addressed from data about the daily practice of seven thousand masters and 175 employers in Danish (and a number of foreign) firms and institutions. At the same time parts of the same subject are for instance addressed for instance by the EU and their newest report on the European universities (EU Commission, 2003). This subject is also discussed in a large number of more theoretically oriented writings within themes as the new relationships between university and society, its part in the triple helix, (Dunne, 1999; Barnett, 1994.), the change from Modus One to Modus Two (Gibbons, et al. 1994; Nowothy, 2001) in the production, and diffusion of new knowledge.

The importance of these efforts to understand the relationship between universities and society is connected to that societal dynamics which can be described in the concept of the knowledge or the learning society. In this model of society all kind of jobs and other societal functions have to be dealt with more dynamically by individuals in those groups and the societal context to which he or she is attached. Therefore, substantial weight is put on all those buzzwords that are echoed within the daily debate such as flexibility, dynamics, human resources, skills for co-operation and individual and organisational learning. An important question is: What does this mean to university education? Is the university in fact not only the provider of such knowledge in an abstract manner and driven by a critical and autonomous pursuit for value free knowledge?

In an ideal world continuously driven or steered by such a noble pursuit, this could perhaps be the case. However, this is different in a world increasingly marked by discontinuity, by politics and many different interests, and by universities that are not fully able to meet the noble deeds of value-free knowledge production. While due to the introduction of these factors universities are also forced to behave as normal societal institutions. This is because of not only the way they have to operate to get funds for their research activities, but also to be able to function as institutions that are able to diffuse knowledge which as much as possible supports the Masters and Bachelors in developing relevant academic competences. Competences or abilities, which make it possible for these candidates to participate in producing and using the knowledge of tomorrow.

In this respect, it is also important to be aware that in our opinion this does not mean that university education should be totally market driven. This would not only harm the universities in one of their main functions, which is to act as an important corrective to society. To depend solely on the market would also risk creating a short-sighted academic work force that mostly was concentrating on how to use the skills well known to the firms and institutions of today, and not on how to use genuine methodological skills for producing the knowledge of tomorrow. Therefore, there are some skills and views on the production of knowledge coming from the production of disciplinary knowledge - and some more general university skills, which could be stored under the concept of »Bildung« (Bowden and Marton, 1998) counterbalancing the market orientation.

In the following we discuss the perspective of this difficult balance which of course affects the role of universities, and its main empirical basis and inspiration are the messages given in the above mentioned surveys with Masters and their employers. Masters that are working within a Danish industry and public sector context based on the degrees they have earned from the two universities.

## 2. DATA FROM THE SURVEY

A completely new set of data material from the two surveys (Kandidat- og Aftagerundersøgelsen, October 2002 and April 2003) on how the masters graduated from the two Universities and their employers looking at these aspects is the empirical background for this paper. The surveys contain responses from about 7000 Masters as employed in their present positions and from 175 of their employers in public as well as in private institutions. The survey covers the masters graduated from all programmes at Aalborg University and Roskilde University during the last 10 years.

---

[1] **A Note on the two Surveys**
The two universities in collaboration carried out the two surveys. The surveys are defined through a number of questions gathered in two different questionnaires, one for the Masters and one for the employers. Theses questionnaires were sent out by post to the masters and the employers. The masters were those who had graduated from the beginning of the nineteen nineties to 2001 and the employers were chosen among those who employ these kind of Masters. Nearly seventy percent of the Masters and nearly ninety percent of the employers responded on the questionnaires. This resulted in 6758 responses from Masters and 170 answers from employers 43% of the employers were also interviewed).

In this paper, we only present data, which we find important, related to our subject, and we will shortly describe the most general information from these surveysi. The first of these themes will be addressed in this paper and the second in a short appendix attached to this paper.

The data focussed in this paper contains information about how the Masters value the study they have gone through and how the knowledge and skills gained through the studies have helped them to get a job. But the survey also gives us some information about how useful this knowledge has been in their endeavour to understand the non-disciplinary requirements at the work place, and how this have helped them to become real professionals within their field. The second theme, which is about what the Masters also would have preferred to gain from their university studies, but which they think they did not gain, is also an important element in the survey. In order to have some information for discussion the second theme is highlighted more than the first theme.

This is done to make the following analysis that uses some of the data from the two surveys to focus especially on three themes. The first is called job qualifications and is related to information on what is seen necessary to manage a job as a Master. The second is called preparing for a job and relates to information on what is needed to get the first job. The third is called the general academic qualifications and relates to information on non-disciplinary knowledge for future development of competence.

## 2.1. At the job qualifications

The most impressive way to see the needs for qualifications expressed by these Masters is to focus on the gab between what they have learned at the university and what they have been asked to use at the work place. This can be divided into skills, which are in balance between learned and demanded, skills which they find they have gained too little of, and skills which they find they have gained too much of. This information is of course on the average of the entire sample, and is covering a broad number of job functions in a large number of different firms and institutions and a substantial number of Master programmes with quite different scopes.

The skills which obviously balance between what the Masters actually value they have learned during their studies and what they found was needed on the job is for instance the ability to acquire new knowledge. In general among the Masters in all areas they find themselves well prepared to work project- and problem-oriented, to acquire new knowledge and general theoretical subject related knowledge and to work interdisciplinary. This may be seen in the perspective that some of the most important intentions of these two universities are to ensure that the Masters have the opportunity to develop this competence. In the survey, which contains data from the employers it is expressed that the expectations they have to the Masters to work innovatively and project-oriented were also met. Also the general theoretical subject related knowledge seems according to the data from the employers to be well matched between what was needed and what the masters actually is able to handle.

Small differences were seen between acquired knowledge and needs within the specific subject related knowledge, but these differences were really small and may be seen as a result of the dynamics in the development and change within such kinds of knowledge areas. More substantial is the gab between the need for practical knowledge within the field and the actual practical knowledge and experiences the Master had before beginning their working life. From the survey it is also seen that many students during the studies actually try to compensate for this by having practical training as part of their education, part-time jobs beside their studies, and write study projects in co-operation with firms and institutions. Still half of the Masters confirmed that such gabs do exist.

Most in deficit seems to be the skills to handle communication and presentation techniques. The large majority stressed the need for such competences, but only a few found that they had gained such skills during their university study. Here we discuss areas that deal with rather personal competence. Obviously, it is the matter when we discuss competence or skills related to the ability to work autonomously and the ability to work under pressure which were also mentioned to be present on the deficit list. Concerning competence related more to the specific non-disciplinary skills area was the ability to handle information technology where only the civil engineers expressed a balance while all other Masters expressed a clear deficit.

On the opposite, we also see a gab between qualifications gained at the university where the competence seems to be larger than the competence actually needed for the work. This is the case when we talk about general theoretical knowledge within the specific field or discipline and also on a number of methodological qualifications on problem-based project-work. To the surplus of general theoretical knowledge, one might mention that this is perhaps self-evident because of the specific character of a job. The surplus on some methodological qualifications is probably to be explained through the broad array of different firms and job types. This might be a way to understand this because a more detailed look into these aspects shows an uneven distribution of this gab between different job functions.

## 2.2. Qualifications to prepare for an academic job

The survey shows that these master programmes lead to jobs in the ordinary labour market, and the survey shows an unemployment rate of 2.5 percent, which was lower then the national average at the time when the data was collected. The data, however, also shows that the time-period between finishing the Master studies and getting the first job differs between the Master programs. Within some educational areas it seems to be much more difficult to get the first job than within other areas.

The qualifications to prepare for a job-career have to be discussed within a framework of practical activities that might be effective raising these qualifications. One is the possibility to prepare for a job by writing the master thesis in co-operation with a specific firm or institution. In fact approx. twelve percent get the first job this way. The long-term consequences for those masters on the job market are not studied, but it could be expected to be neutral compared to other types of first job. Another way of preparing for job is to have a part-time job while studying. This is a way to gain experiences. The main problem is the difficulties of defining the relevance of a pre-master job for preparing for the academic job market.

What can be seen statistically from the survey is that only if pre-master jobs are combined with some elements of practical training and co-operation with firms as part of the study process the entrance to an academic job happens more quickly. The differences in the number of masters who got a job within three month having had such a job versus not having had one, however, was less than ten percent measured on the entire population. On the other hand the qualifications which is supposed to be gained through such activities seem to be valued positively not only by Masters, but also by the students. Therefore, it might have to be taken into consideration in the discussion on non-disciplinary qualifications.

## 2.3. What about the general academic qualifications?

It is interesting what we can see specifically from the employer survey about their explanation for an increasing demand for Masters in firms and institutions. To the employers this increase will happen mainly because it is related to an expected increase in the complexity of tasks and jobs. This seems to be the dominating explanation of the employers for hiring additional Masters. At the same time the survey shows that the large majority (3/4) of employers responds that while the demands for disciplinary qualifications will remain unchanged in quantity then on the other hand the demands for non-disciplinary qualifications will rise in the future. This rising demand contains qualifications as the ability to network, to work across disciplinary boarders, to change and to work in teams, but also the ability to understand the increasing political, social, economic and cultural inter-relatedness within society. Conclusively the employers point out that the need for a future academic workforce will be a complex combination of general academic (non-disciplinary) qualifications and specific disciplinary and professional knowledge. This raises the important question to which extent and how the universities have to meet with those expectations from the labour markets. In the following three sections, we will discuss some societal, economic, technological, cultural and pedagogical factors in a general setting.

## 3. DEMANDS IN GENERAL FOR NON-DISCIPLINARY KNOWLEDGE ON THE JOB

As mentioned above the employability of Masters is related, as it is shown on the employers' survey, to societal change, and the data can be seen as part of a general discourse on the future of the academic workforce. This future contains, at least according to the EU commission (the Commission, 2003), a number of characteristics on how the demands for university-educated workforce develop. This seems for the Commission to be connected to the knowledge-based economy, to the need for interdisciplinary competence, for an ability to work globally in the local community, and to be able to manage a strategy of progression in the adaptation of new knowledge. These means are in an EU terminology elements in forming a strategy to increase the European competitiveness and according to the Commission also ways to solve more specific problems for European universities. This is, however, without greater importance in our context. Instead, it is important to try to unfold some of these elements, which in several respects are rather similar to some of the data from the employers' survey. This is done to se how they define the present and perhaps future society and economy and in this way perhaps make a perspective on the empirical data, and make a basis for changes needed at the universities.

One of these elements behind such changes can be defined as the technology factor. To some extent, the universities have always been an important factor in the development of technology and its Masters have always been agents of technological and cultural change. This has been connected closely to the discipline and the discipline has defined not only the useful technologies, but also the way they should be used in an abstract form. This situation ended of course many years ago in its more specific form, for example the knowledge on how to build instruments for astronomy. What we see now, and what we have been able to se within many professions for a long time is the complete change in technology within a few decades. What is also to be seen is a crossover of technologies between different professions. An example can be health care technology, another the technologies for avoiding pollution.

These changes are both illuminating the need for being able to cross-disciplinary borders and they point at the need for being able to re-configurate ones own knowledge. This is connected not only to the demand for being able to adapt new knowledge after the Master education, it also point in the direction of building a capacity to do this both within a formal and informal educational setting. This also connects to the expressed need to participate in horizontal learning processes within the workplace and to some extent to have an ability to work or at least have some understanding on how to work within neighbouring fields. Seen in a learning perspective this stresses the need of being able to participate in production of new knowledge in the fields surrounding the new techniques. This means to be able to participate in many forms of learning processes, not only continuing education, but also in learning opportunities, suddenly appearing in the network of customers, consultants, and experts in neighbouring fields. In addition to this, the survey shows that for many of the recently educated Masters the direct participation in such processes is not enough, but that they after a short number of years are supposed to be able also to lead such operations.

Connected to these changes in technology are a number of changes in the expectations from the workplace, colleagues, clients, customers and management, which have been expressed by the employers on how a Master should be able to behave. Seen in an old traditional concept of an academic workplace the young Master started the career by working in a lower rank, and abilities to understand the hierarchy were preconditions for reaching higher ranks. As the data from the survey shows, today the great majority of the private firms and public institutions form a rather non-bureaucratic organisational setting both for the newly hired and for the more experienced Masters. This kind of organisational setting demands a more proactive style of work for many occupied in the private as well as in the public sector.

This means that settling into the workplace in many ways is much more complicated. As the survey shows the Master from the first day generally feels a pressure of being able to show the employer and perhaps colleagues that they are able to practice the profession. At the same time, the context for this praxis is increasingly unclear because the rate of changes is rising and the organisational structure is more unsettled.

The Masters in the survey point at the efforts during the education to be able to work on developing their personal qualifications. This is of course closely connected to handling the methods of the discipline, but it also points at the needs for competence to work innovatively, to act actively, to take responsibility for pushing the firm ahead, and even to be able to work as an entrepreneur. These areas represent the changing relationships between the individual Master and the workplace. It points out that employees with a Master degree no longer can expect to be placed in a work position where the unfolding of the disciplinary theoretical skills is governed by a fixed job description in a stable organisational structure. This is not only tied to a relationship between the individual Master and his workplace. It is also a result of increased expectations from the employer, colleagues and the firm or institution on the ability to co-operate.

Because Masters are supposed to participate in the development and diffusion of knowledge from the discipline also in cross-disciplinary settings then they have to take a function where they actively, directly or indirectly, work for changing the work methods. This, however, also happens together with the work force with a vocational, non-academic background. At the same time these changes have to obey the new rules, norms and culture within the organisation where the individual and personal competence concerning face-to-face communication, ability to work in groups, and to form groups around important change projects are key elements. When the survey is talking about the ability to take responsibility and to co-operate actively this represents a perspective on the new organisational reality.

This is not only a matter of working together and to take responsibility toward the interior. The present organisational structure and its values and culture are increasingly exposing Masters toward the environment of their firm. The old functions of many firms and institutions are under deconstruction (Normann, 2002). The result of this is that Masters increasingly become front-line-workers where they in earlier times mainly were placed in staff functions. The result of this can be seen in the survey for both the employers as the Masters as the need to work across traditional boarders, to be able to structure project, to work problem-based, and to be able to communicate and to present ideas. Perhaps also the clearly defined need for being able to work under pressure can be seen as connected to this context. The skills for the Master represented here can be summed up into the dynamic creative group worker, willing and being able to take individual responsibility.

The survey focuses on skills and competences at the workplace and connected to the job of Masters, and how they got into the first and following jobs. This is of course an important part of the interaction between disciplinary and non-disciplinary competence and does form some kind of focus on the employability of graduates from universities. But seen in the perspective of the total human life: as citizens, as workers, as social beings some ideas on how such functions are interwoven could also shed some light over the long-term employability in society at large. To some extent, the demands from the survey point in two opposing directions. One is to be ready for immediate workplace challenges. The second can be seen behind this, and it summarises some of that competence which is not only usable for work life, but also as general skills as citizen and as social being.

Nevertheless, even when this kind of competence can be interpreted into the words of the Masters it is important not to see this as uncomplicated to keep as an aim. Even when the data from the survey through the weight in the questions on job-related competence is biased away from the general knowledge then the general trend in prioritising the aims for university education are to a large extent also directed toward the workplace and individual, firm related and national / European competitiveness in a rather narrow sense.

## 4. HOW CAN UNIVERSITIES MEET SUCH DEMANDS?

It is clear that one way of looking at these questions is from the perspective of the traditional academic position. Expressed very shortly this perspective will say: It is not for the university to speculate on profane changes in society as long as the university education is based on the most advanced knowledge within the discipline. If firms, institutions and society in general do not understand this knowledge and how to make a benefit of it, then they have a problem - not the university! This traditional way of defining the problem does not only tell us that the demands expressed through the survey, but also the worries expressed by the EU Commission are irrelevant to the universities. In this perspective, the universities should concentrate solely on producing new knowledge within the disciplinary paradigm and go for valid knowledge, perhaps even the truth.

Not only as citizens and employees, but also as teachers and researchers, this ideal position, which can be heard, presented in situations of political turmoil around universities, seems irrelevant to us in today's integrated funding, aim defining and co-operative inter-relatedness between the universities and the environment. On the other hand, it is clear that there has to be some kind of line, which cannot and should not be crossed by the universities in the tasks they embark on and the methods they use. If not, after some period, they will have placed themselves in an untrustworthy position both concerning what they are doing and how they are doing it.

It is important to recognise that a firm and steady position between the total autonomous and the total submerging position never will be established in a society with strong technological, social and cultural dynamics. This means that what can be said about the task of the university, diffusions of non-disciplinary knowledge, and the development of employability can only become a kind of trajectory. To discuss the direction of this trajectory some of the elements from the survey can be used as markers.

The first marker can be the role of the university to engage in producing and disseminating knowledge about specific technologies. This is not a question which has a simple answer, because both the newly educated Masters and the employers would find it very practical if the Masters were »ready to use« from the first day at work. In addition to this many of the activities around the primary study activities, such as trainee periods and part time jobs parallel to studies aim to make the Master ready for use. But to make this as a primary educational task for the university, it risks to become so much vocationally oriented that the diffusion of general and abstract knowledge drowns in a large amount of disseminating activities on knowledge about specific technologies and how they should be used in specific firms. Therefore, this might be a dangerous strategy.

The second marker is how much responsibility the university has to create employability through training the students in understanding the workplace and entire firms or institutions and how they function. As long as the university was the only supplier of workforce to a limited number of functions within specific types of institutions and firms, this monopolistic position gave the university not only the knowledge on how things were shaped in those institutions. It also had some kind of upper hand in conducting those slow changes that happened due to the production of new knowledge within the trade or profession, because this knowledge was produced in the university. During a substantial number of years the universities have lost this position not at least because the workforce educated at the universities themselves have managed to become an important part in a production of new knowledge outside university. Many research divisions in big companies are several times as large as most university departments within the same field. In addition to this, many more development-oriented functions in large companies have taken methods developed in university research and re-shaped such methods to be used in the companies.

In those disciplines where the universities educate Masters to work in such kinds of systems and where the majority of Masters gets a job within such firms or institutions the workplace, practice and knowledge about company culture seem informally to become part of the common knowledge within the education. An important question is here to what extent the knowledge among teachers from their research co-operation with such firms is diffused systematically into the education as part of research-based teaching. One of the consequences of the increased number of students and the increased economic efficiency has in many departments and environments resulted in a more clear separation between studies and research, which to us seems to be a problematic strategy.

The third marker can be how far the university education can be stretched in the direction of training the students to become co-operative partners to colleagues in their future work life. In general, this is not a common subject in university education except for those educations where a professional involvement with other people is a main part of the professions and where practice is seen as a necessary part of the education. This trajectory does not have to be followed very far before it becomes easy to imagine that such skills are needed in many jobs and occupations. It relates to participating in informal learning in the workplace, to group-wise transformation of theory into action, to all kinds of entrepreneurship, to work with tasks and technologies that cross disciplinary boarders, and in general to be able to fit into a workplace and a firm. However, this also tells something about the complexity of such a task and how much it relates to social competences of the individual Master. This raises another problem on how these aims should be possible to reach for all students in disciplines where neither the motivation of the students nor the skills of the teachers always are turned that way.

The fourth marker can be seen as a kind of summary of the three previous because it relates to the general education or Bildung perspective. The motivation for general academic knowledge has to be connected to the discipline, but it cannot be governed from this perspective alone because this will make it too narrow and too much governed from the paradigm(s) of the discipline. This makes it very difficult to deal with not at least in a situation where the battle at the universities to some extent is between Modus One and Modus Two knowledge production (Gibbons et al., 1994). Where the traditional Modus One will try to define general knowledge as belonging directly to the discipline and the more recent Modus Two will define general knowledge as working with the applicability of the discipline in a cross-disciplinary context. To defend our case on improving the general academic knowledge we might gain some power from the idea of »universalis« which is an important part of the obligation of the universities.

## 5. PROBLEM-BASED LEARNING IN PROJECT-ORGANISED SETTINGS

Problem Based Learning and project-organisation will be discussed in the perspective of developing general and social competences integrated in developing disciplinary knowledge. This will touch upon some of the ways in which the universities can be inspired and learn from its environments on such subjects, and how such subjects can lead to an actual learning process for students.

It is important here to stress both the character of the learning institution the Masters in the survey have gone through and the working environment as it relates to the two specific universities with their distinct didactical principles. The two universities in Roskilde and Aalborg are both based on the ideas of experience-based learning as it was originally developed in Germany (Negt, 1975) and to some extent inspired by older Danish educational principles (Korsgaard, 1999). At the same time these ideas have parallels to South American education of peasants (Freire, 1970) as well as to North American training of medical doctors (Pettersen, 1999). The implementation of these principles happened at the same period as similar principles were introduced at for instance Maastricht University and Linköping University.

The didactic of Roskilde and Aalborg University has been developed from the original principles formulated around principles as: problem orientation and inter-disciplinarily, exemplarity, open curriculum and experience-based learning, peer learning, and cooperative learning in groups. (Kjærsdam and Enemark, 1994; Kolmos, 1996; Laursen, 1994; Olsen, 1993) This means that all the students in the survey have been through Bachelor and Master programmes which in different combinations are built on these principles. They work in projects on defining, analysing and solving theoretical as well as methodological problems. Some projects are empirically based on and are carried through in co-operation with firms, institutions and different types of organisations. The selection of a problem and the nature of the project are closely connected to for instance the type of Master programme, whether it is graduate or post-graduate programme, and under which theme it is defined. Such a project is also closely combined with a number of lectures and seminars, which both illuminate and govern the direction of the learning processes.

This work process has some similarities to some types of research work, but it is also related to types of work processes as they are seen in business not at least in project management and in combination with organisational learning. This kind of educational work makes it possible for the students to participate in defining the assignments they have to work on. In this context, there are similarities to the principles of Modus Two research. Especially in the last terms of the master programme, it gives students possibilities to transcend barriers of cognitive and affective aspects. This is done by having the students work in investigating learning processes that can be seen as types of pre-forms to research-processes. The intention is not to turn all students into researchers but to develop skills that are useful within their future professional work.

Seen from the survey some of these aims seem to be met according to the Masters and their employers. This can be said about the theoretical knowledge, the methodological knowledge and some ability to cross the traditional disciplinary boarders. In this respect, these pedagogical principles seem to meet some of the demands also outside and across the strict disciplinary knowledge, without loosing the learning of disciplinary knowledge - still in the perception of the employers and their employees. So these demands are fulfilled at least in the problem-based didactic as it is performed in these two specific universities.

This turns the perspective to those non-disciplinary elements that are not met sufficiently in the pedagogical form these masters have been going through. What are they and how could they be met by the university educational system? Important elements here are the deficits in building a capacity to communicate professionally and in using presentation techniques. Of course, these are also important competences to be acquired as Masters starting a new career within a public or private organisation. However, it raises the question: »What are the main obligations of the universities and what can be expected within the educational areas?« Is it possible to guarantee the development of narrow discipline related competences as well as all kind of non-discipline related competence? Aalborg and Roskilde University may to a certain extent benefit from the fact that the organisational structure, the culture and the educational traditions for many years have been based on principles which actually make it possible to establish a dialogue with the environments.

This is used to inspire students to participate in the discovery of new knowledge and problems in relation to future work situations and within society and permanently to use the inspirations from masters, employers and other interesting mediators of knowledge. However, maybe these two universities also have to discuss whether there are other PBL-compatible didactical methods, which might be useful in the creation of relevant academic disciplinary and non-disciplinary competences, not at least to participate more strongly in the creation of »lifelong« learning processes. This could gradually meet some of the non-disciplinary demands necessary for supporting the more long-term employability.

In relation to this, the main question has been addressed: How is it possible to secure the employability of students to an ever-changing labour market and society? How do we develop a complex combination of competence as to structure as well as to method? However, knowledge and understanding are and will always be essential elements in such processes, - and so it has always been within higher educational institutions. Teachers in higher education want students to develop abilities such as to understand important concepts and their associated facts and procedures within the different subjects (Ramsden, 1999). At the same time, they want the students to be able to think critically and to analyse different aspects of particular areas. Ramsden refers in his book to different surveys, which document this. No doubt the teaching methods and the ways in which the institutions and the teachers understand the learning processes are important to be aware of, when the university have to decide how to support the development of the relevant disciplinary and non-disciplinary competence.

## 6. STRATEGIES FOR THE UNIVERSITY ON CREATING EMPLOYABILITY

In general, the surveys point at some areas where employability might be improved if elements outside subject or disciplinary knowledge play an increasing role in the curriculum of the universities. At the same time the two universities, Roskilde and Aalborg who define the focus for these surveys are both institutions that have built themselves a reputation for not looking too narrowly, at what could be the educational role of the contemporary university. Therefore, a number of these areas are at present covered by the educational policies of these universities. On the other hand, many researchers and teachers at these two universities will stress the limitations to such policies of enlargement.

Seen in a several hundred years old and traditional perspective one of the main tasks of the university concerning the teaching part is to function as a kind of quality controller through exams. This control is primarily on the disciplinary qualifications of the graduating Masters. The rest - which means the rest of the learning activities, for instance the development of non-specific disciplinary qualifications - were to a large extent the responsibility of the individual student, perhaps more or less supported by professors as instructors, sometimes even paid for by the students directly. Seen in such narrow perspective employability was closely related to the ability to set the right criteria for the examinations so that those who passed also were directly employable. When this theme is raised here it is due to the fact that most universities already have taken responsibility for a much broader array of tasks at the same time as the direct link between exams and employability has become much more uncertain. This has to do with a more dynamic society and labour market where the functional relatively stable institutions such as the Church, the Courts and maybe even the State administration today in general play a much smaller role as employers than earlier. These institutions mentioned are today also increasingly parts of the same societal dynamics as opposed to private firms and other types of public institutions. Therefore, competences as abilities to develop and change products, services and production processes play a much more important role than traditions created and kept alive by the traditional institutional structures.

The examples of Aalborg and Roskilde show together with all other modern universities that to a certain extent it is possible to meet with the criteria of employability. However, we do not think that all demands from students and employers should be met, because trying to fulfil one aim will often harm the fulfilment of another important aim, which has to do with other obligations for the university. Consequently, it is important to avoid harming the obvious relevant disciplinary or subject-related aims in order to fulfil non-disciplinary aims needed by the individual firms or students.

An abstracting process will take some non-disciplinary elements into its own context and work on the similarities between several disciplines. This may result in the characteristics presented through the survey by the Masters on their education with its strong potential for at the same time to contain sufficient general academic knowledge, disciplinary knowledge and methodological skills at an abstract level. What seems to be in deficit are a number of more practical skills, perhaps also practical disciplinary skills. Such skills might with less difficulty be taught and learned in a more specialised education, but they can be more difficult to take into a broad and methodological oriented education especially in relation to the still growing variety within the student population. So there seems to be the well-known trade-off between abstraction and specialisation in these institutions.

At the same time and according to these educational principles abstraction is not to be reached as a kind of pure theory. What is presented for these Masters is a kind of practical abstraction defined as the ability to handle a complexity of problems by relating or even integrating theory into practice. The basic part of the problem-based learning is its ability to train students to work deeply in pointing out and analysing complicated problems, to find solutions and even to propose solutions and action. Because of the complexity of many theoretical problems, this offers no easy solutions. This means that the Masters, as they express, to some extent lack the abilities in finding the »quick and dirty« solution. Such competence has definitely to be learned in the »real world« after the studies at the university, something that in the perspective of employability can create some short-term difficulties.

The recommendations from the Masters from the two universities and their employers should be used to create the basis for a discourse for a general disciplinary interaction. A discourse between Masters, students and teachers on how the growing number of disciplinary and non-disciplinary elements can be assessed and used by the students during their studies at the university with the aim of improving their employability and their contributions to a dynamic society.

## REFERENCES

Barnett, Ronald (1994). *The Idea of Higher Education*. Buckingham: The Society for Research into Higher Education.

Bowden, John and Marton, Ference (1998). *The University of Learning*. London: Kogan Page.

Commission of the European communities (2003). *The role of the universities in the Europe of knowledge*, Bruxelles: Communication from the Commission

Dunne, Elisabeth (1999). *The Learning Society*. London: Kogan Page.

Freire, Paulo (1970). *Cultural Action for Freedom*. Boston

Gibbons, M. et.al. (1994). *The New Production of Knowledge. The Dynamics of Science and Research in Contemporary Societies* London: Sage

Kandidat og Aftagerundersøgelsen (2002/3) Roskilde Universitetscenter og Aalborg Universitet

Kjærsdam, Finn and Enemark, Stig (1994). *The Aalborg Experiment. Project Innovation in University Education*. Aalborg: Aalborg University Press.

Kolmos, Anette (1996). Reflections on Project Work and Problem-Based Learning. *European Journal of Engineering Education* Vol. 21 no. 2, p. 141-148.

Korsgaard, Ove (1999). »Undervisning af voksne versus voksenundervisning« in Conelius, Hans *Voksenunderviserens veje og udfordringer*. København. Undervisningsministeriet 1999.

Laursen, Erik (1994). *Evaluering af den samfundsvidenskabelige basisuddannelses på Aalborg Universitet*, 3. rapport. Problembaseret projektarbejde, Aalborg: Aalborg Universitet.

Negt, Oskar (1975). *Sociologisk fantasi og eksemplarisk indlæring*. Roskilde University Press.

Normann, Richard (2002). *Reframing Business. When the Map Changes the Landscape* New York: John Wiley.

Nowothy, Helga et al. (2001). *Rethinking Science*. London: Policy Press.

Olsen, Jan Brødslev (1993). *Kreativ voksenindlæring*. Aalborg Universitetsforlag.

Pettersen, Roar C. (1997). *Problemet først: Problembasert læring som pedagogisk idé og strategi*. Oslo: Tano Ascheoug.

Ramsden, Paul (1999). *Learning to Teach in Higher Education*. London: Routhledge.

## Some main results from the master survey

43% of the Masters are female, 57% male. 39% have graduated within the technical science and science, 35% within the social sciences and 26% within the humanities

- Half of the Masters have changed the type of job they would prefer several times during their study
- Half of the Master has got some kind of labour market supervision during their period of study
- Many Masters have got experiences from practice during their study and use these experiences in their study and in their first job
- Those with such experiences get the first job (a little) quicker than the rest
- 1/3 get their first job before they end their study, the additional 1/3 after less than three month
- Those who start their search for a job during the study period get a job most quickly
- The unemployment rate was very low

- Increasingly the Masters get their first job through informal channels, and the internet is also increasingly used
- 90% of the Masters respond that the important criteria for getting the first job was the right job qualifications and personal qualifications
- 97% are employees, half in the private and half in the public sector. The share in the private sector is growing
- Only 3% have their own firm (with an average of ten employees)
- An increasing share starts in non permanent jobs or as freelancers
- More than 90% have a full time job
- 1/3 has or has had managerial responsibilities and half of the Masters want such responsibilities in close future. As they see it, the chance for a managerial job depend entirely on their personal qualifications
- The job content is the most important factor in a job. Challenging tasks, responsibility, a stimulating environment and the possibility to influence the content of the tasks are very important
- The Masters in general assesses the master education positively. (Some of the reasons for this assessment are analysed in our paper)
- Nearly all participates in shorter further educational activities, 15% have participated in further education resulting in formally recognised competence. The masters themselves take the initiative for participating in such activities
- The most wanted areas within this field are management and organisation
- 1/3 uses the general competence gained at the study, but works outside the traditional area of their master education. At the same time a relatively large flexibility are demanded from the Masters

**Some main results from the employer survey**
- The employers expect an increased demand for employees with higher education, also compared with other types of employees
- The employers are utmost satisfied with university Masters as employees
- The large majority knows that the Masters from Roskilde and Aalborg have special problem based qualifications and they generally find that such Masters and Masters from more traditional types of university education supplement each other
- They see masters from Roskilde and Aalborg as particularly competent in project management, co-operation and innovation
- They also see the traditional ties between certain types of job and certain disciplines loosen up. This is related to the increase in complexity and the obsolescence of disciplinary skills. This demands flexibility, adaptability, and general academic competences
- The personal qualifications of an applicant is the most important factor in getting a job
- The master should according to the employers be competent during the

study time to enter the labour market and have a realistic view on his / her own competence

# PROBLEM-BASED LEARNING AS A WAY OF ORGANIZING LEARNING AND TEACHING AT THE UNIVERSITY

## Some contemporary problems and future possibilities

Erik Laursen

**Abstract**: After almost thirty years problem based and project organized methods have established themselves as a successful, quiet normal and at some places, like Aalborg and Roskilde, even obligatory way of teaching and learning at university level in Denmark. In this article the methods are seen as a flexible educational frame for a broad variety of pedagogical elements and methods. The intention of using the frame is to integrate the elements in a functional way in the nineties the success of the model was largely due to its power to organize a supportive frame for the development of competencies of application and Meta cognitive reflections. Four crucial contemporary problems related to the use of the methods are outlined, and finally some proposals for the future development of the problem-based and project-organized methods of teaching are presented.

## 1. INTRODUCTION

Almost thirty years have past since teachers and students at the new university centers in Roskilde and Aalborg established and started the development of Problem-based and Project-organized Studies at university level in Denmark.

Looking back at the thirty years it is interesting to notice, how different this method of teaching and learning has been perceived and evaluated through the years. I think it is possible to make a distinction between three periods:

- *First period* was the seventies, characterized by strong emotions. Enthusiasm and the spirit of pioneers from the supporters, while the adversaries showed skepticism and even offered harsh criticism.

- *Second period* was the eighties, with a strong sense of doubt and defeatism from the supporters and by certain sense neglect from everybody else. The fact is, that *Problem based Project organized Studies (PBL[1])* was in deep troubles at the end of the decennium, and even at Aalborg University there were heated arguments and discussions pro and contra the idea, that problem based, project organized ways of teaching and learning also in the future should be an important element in the advertisements of the University.

Anyway, this story holds a happy end: The nineties, the *third period* of development, has indeed been a triumphant one for PBL. A period of regained confidence shared by the Institution on behalf of its pedagogical base. At the same time PBL has enjoyed a remarkable growth of popularity in the rest of the educational field of the society. Today PBL is used in numerous variants on almost all educational levels and fields. And what's more: PBL has even become normal *and obligatory*.

## 2. A WORLD TAKEN FOR GRANTED VS. THE EXOTIC PRACTICE OF THE NEIGHBOURS

What are the consequences of having success, and being considered normal and obligatory as well? In short it means that this way of teaching has become a part of normal teachers »normal way« of teaching. If this way of teaching is used at Aalborg University or the University Center of Roskilde, you don't have to explain anything. By having won the status of being obligatory this method of teaching has been a part of the taken for granted reality of the Institutions. Of course it is still accepted as normal and necessary to discuss the quality of the projects of the students and even of the supervision of the teachers, but normally you don't question whether the educational goals of a certain semester really should be reached by this method or by some specified alternative.

Normally this way of perceiving a given practice does not add much to the innovative development of the practices of an organization. On the other hand it is characteristically for the development of the PBL-method at the University of Aalborg, that it is a differentiated and de-centered development, which has been heavy influenced by the various studies. Of course it is possible, as I will try to demonstrate later, to outline some characteristics, which could be found everywhere at the institution, but strictly speaking

---

[1] The point of reference for this article is the Problem Based studies at Aalborg University, characterized by Problem-*based, Project-organized* student activities, mainly done in *groups* with fellow students. Consequently the most precise abbreviation, referring to these activities might be »PPS« which stands for Problem-based, Project-organized Studies (including as teaching as well as learning). Anyway, as I don't want to add further to an already confusing field of different abbreviations, I shall use the more common abbreviation »PBL« (Problem-Based Learning) instead throughout this article.

there exists a plurality of variations, which makes it hard to speak of the Aalborg Model.

This is quite interesting. At one hand the institution has developed a way of seeing the existing way of teaching as an integrated part of a taken-for-granted institutional reality. On the other hand there are in fact substantial differences in the ways the PBL-method has been developed different places in the organization, all depending on the study at hand. As a consequence of this paradoxical situation, it should be possible to stimulate some innovative fantasy and critical thinking merely by establishing a more comparative frame of reference for the didactical reflections going on at the studies at the university.

The first thesis of this article is then: *The PBL-method ought to be seen as a flexible organizational frame for a broad variety of pedagogical elements and methods. The most important objective for using the frame is to integrate the elements in a functional way, letting each element supporting the other.*

## 3. THE »NEW« CONCEPT OF LEARNING

Now, what were the real reasons behind the successful revival of the PBL method in the nineties? Why this change of the conjunctures?

The second thesis of this article might be a possible answer to this question. *There is a connection between the success of the PBL-method in the nineties and what could be called a shift of focus in the didactical and pedagogical discourses, which went on at the same time inside the educational sector. A shift, which could be described as a shift of interest between »teaching« and »learning«.*

But this »answer« immediately triggers a new question: why this increased interest in how the students are to acquire the contents of the studies, and why this relative neglect of how the teachers support the learning processes of the students?

Now to answer this rather complex question it is necessary to point out, that we are talking about a change of »interest« and a shift in *»the focus of discourse«*, -opposed to a change in actual behavior. We are talking about a change in the way many teachers and other professionals think about education, and not necessarily including a change in the way educational activities are organized and carried out.

In the last 15 years our ways of understanding and reflecting on educational activities have been heavily influenced by *constructivist understanding of the learning process*. The core elements of this understanding go back to the important theoretical and empirical works of *Jean Piaget* on the cognitive development of the children (Piaget, 1971). Most important Piaget described cognition and learning as active processes. In order to accomplish learning, the student must act, and reflect on the actions. Another important element is the idea of seeing learning as a *constructive process*, where the student must build her own picture of how the world is structured and how things are done. As human beings we imitate, copy and repeat what we are experiencing, but it is all installed in our special ways of constructing our own reality and own projects of living. *John Dewey* pointed out, that everything we learn, must be perceived as meaningful in relation to those projects of action we try to carry out in the world. A third element in the constructivist understanding is that the learning process must be seen as a reaction on the »disturbance«. What are disturbed are the expectations of the student in relations to how the context will react on the actions of the student (Piaget, 1971; Bateson, 1973; von Glasersfeld, 1995). We must change our understanding and knowledge on a given phenomenon when it is not behaving as we expected it to.

This conception of learning is important and non-trivial. It asks us to move our focus on educational activities from the actions of the teacher to actions of the student, while asking the question: what are the possible and necessary actions of the student inside this educational frame? and what does the student learn from doing them? To complete the picture of the »new concept of learning« I should like to add two further elements:

- The importance it puts on competencies *of application*, as a consequence of seeing learning as a context-*related process* (Bateson, 1973). From this perspective the question of, how to transfer what is learned inside an institutionalized context of formal education to other frames of action in the work sphere of society, becomes an important one. *Learning competencies* forms a special but important category of competencies of application. Learning competencies refer to knowing how to develop competencies as a consequence of ones actions. In the nineties the acquisition of learning-competencies, often referred to as »learning-to-learn« (Bateson, 1973), became one of the most popular mantras of the period.

- Secondly the new concept of learning stresses the ability to reflect on knowledge and competencies, also referred to as *Meta cognition or self reflection* (Flavell, 1976) Meta cognition is a reflection on the cognitive processes, the competencies or the learning processes one holds or carries out. One example could be the competencies to work out a diagnosis of missing competencies in relation to the demands put by the solving of a certain problem. Meta cognition typically have the critical evaluation of the results of own actions as its starting point and tries to make a relation between the results of ones actions and the competencies which are related to these actions.

Learning competencies and Meta cognitive competencies can be put together under the concept of self *directed learning*, which is an important condition for the ideas of *lifelong learning*. (Smith, 1983)

The competencies of self directed learning could be described by putting a sequence of questions, which the competent person should be capable of answering:

a. What must I know to accomplish this task?
b. What must I learn? (What competencies do I miss?)
c. How can I develop these competencies?
d. How do I want to acquire them?
e. What did I learn, and what do I still miss?
f. How did I accomplish the task?

The diffusion of the competencies to ask and answer these simple questions is an important precondition for the realization of the political high priority goals of lifelong learning and education for most of the population. This helps explaining the extensive and positive interest towards educational methods, facilitating the development of this kind of competencies.

## 4. THE MODEL AND SOME POSSIBLE REASONS OF POPULARITY

We have seen how a certain way of reflecting on the educational activities, inspired by the constructivist understanding of learning, have acquired a widespread popularity during this period.
If this set of ideas, concepts and theories are to be transformed to practical educational activities the PBL method have been by far the most popular way of organizing this transformation.

I have already claimed, that the PBL method at Aalborg University exists as a plurality of variations, which makes it hard to speak of the Aalborg Model. Parallel to this internal differentiation, I think it is also correct to notice that there exist some important and interesting differences between Roskilde University Center and Aalborg University in their development of the model (Ulriksen, 1997). Still it is possible to point out some common basic principles for the ways the model is developed at Aalborg University. I will try to outline the most important of these principles, and later I shall make a comparison between these principles and »new concept of learning«.

As we are referring to« Problem-based Project-organized Studies« it might come as a surprise, that by following this method, the students are to accomplish a project, including producing a rapport. Furthermore this project in principle makes up the overall frame for all the other educational activities.

In fact there are important differences in just how big a part of the educational activities are framing. At certain studies a substantial part of the courses are parallel activities placed outside the context of the project-related activities, while other studies work hard at getting all-important activities integrated under the umbrella of the project.

Furthermore the PBL-model is problem based and most often organized in groups.

If we are to express these main elements: *Projects, Problems* and *Groups* in limited sets of principles for the education, it could f.ex. be done by these four propositions:

1. *The project is a frame around a set of different teaching and learning systems* (Laursen, 1994 & 2002). The group organized, project- and problem based study typically includes the individual and solitary learning processes of the student, alone in her room, trying to understand the complex argument of a text. Or following quite traditional courses and seminars. The important thing is whether the project creates a frame, which integrates the various elements in a way, which makes each element of study meaningful and useful for the student.

2. *The educational frame demands an offensive orientation towards action from the student.* The educational use of problem-based projects presupposes that a subject and a problematic motivate the students that she really wants to make it the object of a rather demanding working process. Curiosity and the ability to design and follow a plan, reflecting own interests and ideas are also an important precondition for a successful realization of this method.

3. *The project is directed by a problem, formulated by the student.* At one hand the problem must be subjective interesting to the student. On the other hand it must be relevant in relation to the curriculum and the educational objectives of study. A problem is a »disturbance«, that is a perceived difference between what is expected and what actually happens.

Furthermore we have a difference between practical and theoretical problems as well (Kjærsdam & Enemark, 1994; Adolphsen, 1985). The common sense reflection is normally focused on the practical problems of everyday life, while the theoretical problems quite often only exist as problems inside the theoretical discourse of a certain discipline. Consequently it is not always an easy task to combine theoretical- and practical reflections, re-formulating the practical problem as a theoretical one.

4. *The individual learning processes are supported by » theory-enriched« and problem orientated dialogues integrated in the project work. These dialogues are partly taking place in the relation between the supervisor and the student, and partly between the students. These dialogues play a crucial role for the development of met cognitive competencies.* A theoretically enriched dialogue presupposes the ability of both parts to master the relevant codes of theoretical discourse as well as the rules of academic discussions. Meta cognitive competencies are partly learned by internalization of this critical dialogue.

Together these four propositions make it possible to develop a context of teaching and learning, where all the five major elements in the constructionist concept of learning are used:

(1) Acting as the precondition of learning: Proposition no. 2:
    The offensive action orientation.
(2) Learning as a process of construction: Proposition no 3:
    The principle of problem orientation.
(3) Learning as a reaction on disturbance: Proposition no 3:
    The principle of problem orientation.
(4) The importance of competencies of application: Proposition no 1 and 3:
    The project as a frame of application steered by a defined problem.
(5) The importance of Meta cognitive abilities: Proposition no 4 and 1: The handling of a problem in an academic way, in the dialogical context of a group work and supervision.

This strong connection between the PBL model and the constructionist concept of learning leads us to formulate a third thesis: *During the nineties the success of the PBL model became depended on its ability to organize a supportive frame for the competency development of application and - Meta cognitive reflections.*

## 5. HAVE THE CRITERIA OF SUCCESS CHANGED?

One possible critical comment on this thesis might be, that the development of competencies of self directed learning right from the start has been one of the most important criteria of success for the use of the PBL-model, and consequently one should not expect it to be addressed as a specific aspect of PBL in the nineties.

It is perfectly true that the development of personal- and application competencies has been used as an argument in favor of the PBL already in the seventies, but with one very important reservation: The groups of teachers and students who developed project organized studies at the universities mainly saw this argument as a much needed legitimation of a rather controversial way of organizing the university studies. The driving forces behind the development of project-organized studies at the universities in the seventies were a strong critical movement against the traditional disciplines and the traditional and hierarchical ways of organizing life at the university. This movement was inspired by a set of high profiled, normative conceptions concerning what a decent content of the studies and a decent way of organizing the institution should be.

I should like to stretch this argument a little further. In doing this I will introduce the Didaktik triangle (e.g. Künzli, 1998; Laursen, 2002; Bering Keiding, 2003) as a useful tool. The didaktik triangle gives a simple schematic representation of the core elements in the educational processes of teaching. In all teaching we have a *Subject* or *Content* to be taught. We have a Learner or *Student*, the person who shall learn the content, and finally we have the *Teacher* the person who tries to mediate between the learner and the content. We also have three important relations involved. First the relation between the student and the content, we call this Acquisition *axis* (A). Secondly we have the relation between the teacher and the content, which we call the Representation *axis* (R), and thirdly we have the relation between the teacher and the student, the Interaction *axis* (I).

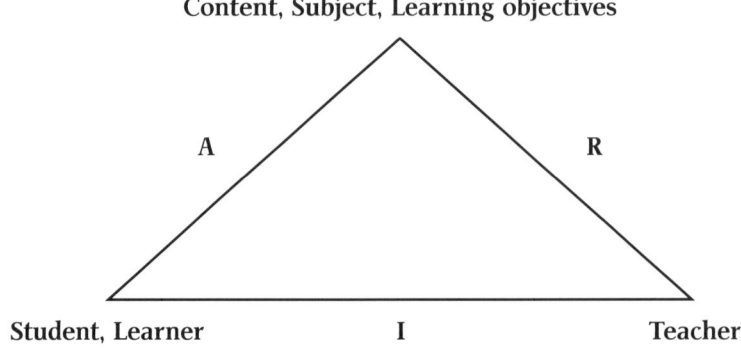

As mentioned above, the motivating forces behind the development of project-organized studies in the seventies was an interest to change the content and the relation between students and teachers. These interests were based on a set of well-defined alternatives. In *Knud Illeris'* important book on problem based and project organized studies (Illeris, 1974), Piaget's theoretical understanding of the learning process plays an important role in the argument in favor of the problem based project work, but in everyday practice of teaching and learning at the universities, the constructionist theories of learning never had any important influence in the seventies. Most of the »formulated problems« of the projects at that time could hardly be seen as »disturbances« in the constructionist meaning of the word, and even today the formulated problems of the projects are better seen as broad frames for the project work, with its integrated set of concrete problems and disturbances (Laursen, 1994; Keiding & Laursen, 2003).

I shall conclude, that the »*learning aspect*« of the acquisition axis *didn't* mean much for the development of PBL-methods at that time. The important aspect for Illeris and his contemporaries in relation to the student was not »learning« but »influence!, that is: who are to decide, what the student should learn? Illeris' book was quite appropriately titled: *»Problem orientation and self governance of the participators«*. The important point of the book was, that the students should have influence on the content of their projects, and the problems which forms the context of the project work should be »subjective meaningful« to the student. In fact this apparently very student centered approach only accepted student influence on the question of the content of the problems of the project work, [MN1][MN2][MN3]while influence on the decisions concerning which theories and models to be used in the project work was definitely not allowed. Consequently, the essential part of, what the student should learn, was in fact not an issue for negotiation and influence. This part was only up to the teachers to decide.

I think it is possible to conclude, that the PBL-model as it developed in the seventies had a strong - and teacher defined content as its precondition.

In the *nineties* the educational context changed quite a lot. The content lost most of its well-defined character: The limits between the various disciplines have grown increasingly weak. Many disciplines had been »de-centred« to a situation, where several competing paradigms, theoretical directions and sub disciplines were fighting to accomplish the hegemonic dominance over the discipline, but never getting it. There have been a radical growth in production of knowledge and information, and in most disciplines the sheer mass of new theories, concepts and research results are simply grueling. Furthermore, the outline of the field of practice of most studies and professions have also been developing in a more complex way. Consequently, it can be difficult today to decide in many professions, what the important »core-competences« are or will be in the next ten years.

The relation between the teachers and the students has changed from the symmetrical ideal of the seventies to the asymmetrical or even complementary one, where the teacher are expected to know and teach in relation to a certain, well defined element of content, while the student is expected to learn, - not to produce new knowledge, with a learning potential for the teacher!

In opposition to this very traditional way of organizing the interaction axis, the acquisition axis, relating the student with the content have changed in a way, that reflect several widespread tendencies in the late-modernity (Beck, 1992; Giddens, 1991). Today the students in fact have substantial control in relation to which contents they want to learn. Not only which problems, but also which theories, methods and paradigms. Paradoxical enough, many students today don't want this influence.

Of course they want to have influence on what elements of content they sho-uld learn, but they want to make these decisions in a context of well-defined disciplines or core competencies of the relevant professions. To make those priorities and decisions they turn to the teachers and ask them to tell, what pieces of content (knowledge, skills) there are important and consequently must have high priority, when they decide on, which problems and which modules of study they are going to choose.

One of the really hot pedagogical mantras of the nineties was »AFEL« (e.g. Responsibility For Own Learning; Bjørgen, 1995). As it turned out, the teaching practice of this model tended to leave the student with the responsibility, - not only of *how* the content should be learned, but also of *what* should be learned as well.

I will conclude, that the context of PBL has changed radically from the seventies to the nineties: In the seventies we had a strong teacher-influence on the question of what theories, methods and paradigms should be studied. At the same time we saw a rather symmetrical relation between teacher and student, which made an open and free discussion on specific ways of »reading« or interpreting theories and ways of analyzing sets of data.

In the nineties and even today students in general have a strong influence on what should be studied and learned. But at the same time the teacher- student relations are rather asymmetrical and hierarchical organized. The teachers are having traditional symbolic authority (Bourdieu & Passeron, 1977) over various »packages« of knowledge. But still they can be considered as »salesmen« for these packages. It is up to the customers, the students to decide, what to buy.

I will conclude, that the criteria of success for the problem-based, project-organized methods of teaching and learning have indeed changed. The character of the change of criteria (thesis number four) is:

*Today success of the PBL-method depends on whether it succeeds in handling a situation, where the definition of content is very weak, combined with a demand on the studies to qualify the students at the highest level of knowledge, plus a considerable influence of the students on the selection of contents. This situation is generally handled by focusing on the development of general competencies like application competencies, meta cognitive competencies and personal competencies* (Rasmussen & Laursen, 2003).

## 6. SOME CONTEMPORARY PROBLEMS

Is it possible, on this background, to conclude that the use of PBL-methods on a university level in the present situation can be considered as a complete success? Hardly.
I should like to point out four different kinds of problems:

a. *The various forms of teaching and learning, framed by the project, are not functional integrated. Instead they make up a fragmentary, often rather confusing and overwhelming totality.*
   Often we see that the project work and the courses are stealing time and energy from each other, and sometimes there are even made separate examinations. I see this tendency as a result of the »de-centering of the disciplines«, where the weak definition of the content are handled by an extension of the curricula and the courses. This de-centered situation also makes it hard to formulate criteria of quality, used by the students to critical self-reflection and self-evaluation in relation to the project work.

b. *The progression of the competencies and the knowledge of the students, thorough the line of study is generally too weak, characterized by a tendency to avoid the dull and difficult elements of content. Combined with a tendency to repeat what already have been learned.*
   As we have seen above, the flexibility- and the weakly defined contents of the studies is an important precondition for the contemporary use of the

PBL-method, combined with very few indicators of relevance, to be used by the students as points of navigation.

c. *Exciting individualities - dull communities*
The individual learning processes are to be supported by » theory-enriched« and problem orientated dialogues integrated in the project work. These dialogues are partly taking place between the students. Unfortunately these dialogues often are time-consuming, difficult to establish and maintain, and although these dialogues play a crucial role for the development of meta cognitive competencies, the students' motivation to take part in them are generally weak.

d. *Too arbitrary examinations*
Weak definitions of content combined with diffuse objectives of study often produce problems in relation to the examinations. Often the question of what exactly should be tested and what are left to some kind of intuitive understanding between the censor and examiner. The examinations are at risk of developing into one of the really sore spots of the Universities in the near future, where the confrontation between personal selected routes of individual competencies and the teachers, are carrying the responsibilities as the keepers of the disciplines, can be rather sharp.

## 7. FUTURE POSSIBILITIES -PROJECT WORK FOREVER!

Regarding project-organized problem- based method of teaching and learning, it is important to stress, that this method must be considered as one among other methods for students organising learning processes. Just how this frame are to be structured depends on three aspects of the context where the method is to be used: The qualifications of the students, the learning objectives and the content (Keiding & Laursen, 2003).

PBL is a robust and flexible method, where most of the elements can be considered as variables.

One example of this could be the *formulated problem*, which can be outlined in accordance with how much structure or freedom the students should have in the process of selecting and formulating a problem. This depends on the learning objectives and the qualifications of the student. Another variable is that *field of resources*, that is: theories, models, methods and data together making up for the »raw material« of the project work. How open or closed is the field of possibilities outlined for the students to use?

As mentioned above confronting the problems it is important to stress, that the general trend is, that learning objectives ought to be formulated as *competencies of self directed learning and problem solving* with references to special fields of knowledge and professional work. Furthermore I should like to make three proposals for the future development of the PBL method:

*The studies must produce a set of learning objectives and criteria of quality, to be understood and used by the students, and useable as a tool for the examination and in the self-evaluation of the student.* These objectives should be articulated in a form that makes it possible to use them to evaluate the projects and to decide on the relevance of projects. The pedagogical reflections can not solve the problems produced by the de-centring of the disciplines, but problem-based project work cannot be used as a frame for the development of competencies of self directed learning unless the task is solved.

*The problem of how to establish a clear progression through the line of study, in relation to the most important competencies and educational objectives, -must is solved.* This progression should be described in terms of using methods, solving problems and handle different kinds of complexities.

*A differentiated concept of problems- and projects must be developed.* The idea is to establish a better-informed and more precise connection between the learning objectives and the qualifications of the student on one hand, and the selection of the educational frame (Laursen, 1994; Keiding & Laursen, 2003).

## REFERENCES

Adolphsen, J. (1985). *Problemer i videnskab: En erkendelsesteoretisk begrundelse for problemorientering.* Aalborg Universitetsforlag, Aalborg.

Bateson, G. (1973). *Steps to ecology of mind.* Paladin, London.

Beck, U. (1992). *Risk society: Towards a new modernity.* Polity Press, Cambridge.

Bjørgen, I.A. (1995). Læringsprocesser i gymnasiet. In : K.S.Iversen & K.Svejgaard(ed): *Læreprocesser i 90'erne.-Ansvar for egen læring?* Statens Erhvervspædagogiske læreuddannelse, Århus.

Bourdieu, P. & Passeron,J-C (1977). *Reproduction.In Educagtion,* Society and Culture, Sage Publ..London.

Flavell, J.H. (1976). *Cognitive development.* Prentice Hall, New York.

Giddens, A. (1991). *Modernity and Self-Identity.* Polity Press, Cambridge.

Glasersfeld, E. von (1995). *Radical constructivism : a way of knowing and learning.* Falmer Press, London.

Illeris, K. (1974). *Problemorientering og deltagerstyring: Oplæg til en alternativ didaktik.* (Problemorientation and Selfdirected Learning: Towards an alternative didactic.) Munksgaard, Copenhagen.

Keiding, T.B. (2003). *Hvorfra min verden går.* Institut for Læring. Aalborg Universitet, Aalborg.

Kjersdam, F & Enemark, S. (1994). *The Aalborg Experiment. Project innovation in university education.* Aalborg University Press, Aalborg.

Künzli, R. (1998). The common frame and the Places of Didaktik. In: *Didaktik and/or curriculum.* Ed: Gunden,B.B. & Hopman,S. Peter Lang Publ., New York.

Laursen, E. (1994). *Evaluering af den samfundsvidenskabelige basisuddannelse på Aalborg Universitet.* Aalborg Universitet, Aalborg.

Laursen, E. (2002). Projektpædagogik, konstruktivisme og individualisering. In: *Projektpædagogik i udvikling.* Ed: Kolmos,A. & Krogh,L. Aalborg Universitetsforlag, Aalborg.

Laursen, E & Keiding, T.B. (2003). The relation between types of problems and learning outcome. in: *Teaching and learning in higher education: New trends and innovations.* University of Aveiro, Aveiro.

Laursen, E. & Rasmussen, J.G. (2003). A problem based Canon - A draft for an alternative way to enhance progression in university studies. In: Kolmos, A. et al.(eds): The Aalborg PBL-model - *Progress, Diversity and Challenges,* Aalborg University Press, Aalborg.

Piaget, J. (1971): *The construction of reality in the child.* Ballantine Books, New York.

Smith, R.M. (1983): *Learning how to learn.* Open University Press.London.

Ulriksen, L (1997): *Projektpædagogik - hvorfor det?* Erhvervs- og uddannelsesgruppen. Unipæd-projektet nr 7. Roskilde Universitetscenter, Roskilde.

# THE AALBORG PBL MODEL
# - DIVERSITY AND CHALLENGES

This part of the book contains concrete descriptions, reflections, challenges and comparative analyses of the Aalborg model. The articles show how the Aalborg model is adjusted in many different ways to be adapted to the various study programmes - in terms of practice, development and idea development - and the authors touch upon various central elements. The articles also show that there are number of interdisciplinary challenges in adapting the model to the study programmes.

What is a problem? How do you define a problem? That has been a general discussion throughout the years at Aalborg University - and it is one of the central questions within PBL. In the article, »*Defining the Problem in Problem-Based Learning*«, Palle Qvist analyses definitions of the understanding of the problem in project-based learning in order to set up a broader definition of the problem. The new definition must be well defined, easy to understand and easy to practice. The definitions that have been analysed in this article does not necessarily cover all definitions or traditions developed or in use at the university, but rather the most well-known ones. .

However, the most crucial issue related to PBL is to ensure an open approach to its practice , Jens Christensen argues in, »*Reflections on Problem-Based Learning*«. Perceptions of learning and knowledge and PBL are interpreted differently, depending on the time and situation. The article develops a framework for discussing the complexity of PBL, which should be manageable at a university in the year 2003. This framework gives a survey of the starting points of exemplary learning in relation to general and transferable competencies. It is argued that exemplary learning may be initiated either by problems, potentialities, or values, or by an interaction between those. Furthermore, the personal and affective involvement of the student is a precondition for promoting a learning process.

Olav Juul Sørensen points out several more challenges with PBL in the article, »*New Realities and the Implications for Problem-Based Learning*«, which concerns the case of Business Administration at the Faculty of Social Science. The article focuses on the history of the university and the new realities. The hypothesis is that the changes (global, business related, and in terms of individualism) that have taken place during the last 30 years necessarily create new challenges for the educational model. Close co-operation with reality, focus on creation and action, more possibilities for individual performance, lifelong learning, and the integrative use of ICT and the internet are all elements demanding adjustments to be made within these study programmes.

Erik Laursen and Jørgen Gulddahl Rasmussen formulate the challenge of constructing a new kind of methodical canon in their article, »*A Problem-Based Canon - A Draft for an Alternative Way to Enhance Progression in University Studies*«. Central trends of crisis for contemporary university studies are presented, reasons and possible remedies are discussed, and a new kind of canon is defined by using principles taken from general knowledge production combined with core educational elements. The main subjects to be addressed in this perspective are: the goals for university education, the contemporary university student, and the suitable means for changing the didactics. Finally, an example of this strategy for transforming the didactics is presented.

However, lifelong learning, ICT, etc. and their impact on learning are different in on-campus and off- campus learning, Ole Borch, Morten Knudsen, and Ole Rokkjær emphasise in the article, »*Pedagogical and Technological Challenges in on/off Campus Education*«. A new educational format - i.e. educational resources, scenarios, composing, activities and technological support - has been developed to strengthen the individual learning process. Experiences with individual learning in distance education are fine, since individual learning responsibilities are naturally leaving out alternative learning options. Still, on-campus students do not benefit from the new format. Changing the on-campus learning process to be more reflective and using the new format for courses may improve the learning behaviour and merge material maintenance and development.

Rita Cancino presents an overview of the language studies at The Faculty of Humanities in the article, »*Problem-Based Learning in the Foreign Language*

*Study Programmes«*. Most of the projects in these study programmes deal with issues and topics from the different foreign-language countries in order to integrate the context. Both the literature used in the project and the project reports are written in the foreign language and the oral exam is held in the foreign language as well. The students studying foreign languages are really challenged as they not only have to study various subjects such as economy, law, etc., but they have to do it in the language they are studying. Content and educational methods merge.

Thomas Borchmann & Søren Lindhardt, who are also from the Faculty of Humanities, reflect on the communication studies in the article, *»Doing almost the Same Things for Somewhat Different Reasons«*. In this article they focus on the different understandings of the rationale(s) for using problem-based project work as a vehicle for student learning. These understandings are present in the daily conversations as a fragmented manifold of arguments, perspectives and vocabularies, which influence perceptions of problems and perceptions of possible action strategies for problem-solving. These various local understandings and practices are defended in this article.

Hans Kiib, in *»PpBL® In Architecture and Design«*, describes the challenge of creating a new understanding of PBL. The article describes the educational experiences and reflections leading to the development of a new Master's in Engineering programme within the field of Architecture and Design, which was established at Aalborg University in 1997. Adjustments to the traditional PBL model at Aalborg University were necessary in order to use PBL in Architecture and Design. The PpBL concept (»Problem- and Play-Based Learning«) was developed on the basis of the relationship between the intuitive and the goal-oriented aspects in university education. The article's concluding sections offer preliminary experiences with this interplay between reflection and play in PpBL on one hand, and spatiality as another educational dimension on the other.

Michael Mullins points out the importance of assessment in the article, *»Evaluation of Learning in Architectural Education«*. The integration of civil engineering and architecture within the Institute of Architecture and Design embraces paradoxes and contradictions. There is a difference between engineering and architecture in their evolutionary backgrounds and their varying degree of emphasis on natural science. In addition, the pervasive influence of assessment on the learning process must be recognized. 'Successful' learning is essentially defined by the criteria on which it is assessed. Information and computer tools now pervade most expressions of modern society and not least, the way in which the built environment is designed and built. These tools have direct influence on education by impelling change in prevalent educational models.

Mary-Ann Knudstrup reflects on the educational experience during the first years of the curriculum in Architecture & Design in her article, »*Integrated Design Process in Problem-Based Learning*«. Activities and methods are outlined which have been developed during the semester when working with an Integrated Design Process combining architecture, design, functional aspects, energy consumption, indoor environment, technology, and construction. Also the dilemma between courses and project work is addressed, as the number of courses in the learning model often clashes with the demand for time and scope for reflection, which the students need in order to concentrate, mobilize creativity and find the personal design language, which is a precondition for making good architecture.

In the article, »*The Concepts of Learning Based on the AAU model of Teaching in Chemical Engineering Educations*«, Erik G. Søgaard describes a version of the AAU model used to educate chemical engineers in a long series of projects performed in corporation with industries, companies and other universities departments of natural science. The necessary ingredients in a project are presented and a model of learning that creates the basis for the arrangement of the project is described. In this model of learning a model of memorising is integrated. Also the storytelling concept is integrated in both the model of learning and the model of memorising.

The last article in this section is also from chemistry department and deals with the planning of a semester, described by Bent Rønsholdt in his article, »*Semester Planning in a Problem-Based Learning Environment*«. As the title indicates, the case involves the first year programme, which had the overall theme 'Reality of the Models' and the sub-theme 'Equilibriums', under which themes project proposals for student projects were generated. These projects were supported by a project course 'Chemical Equilibrium and Reaction Kinetics'. The objective of this course was to provide a broad theoretical basis for the projects as well as being the first common basic chemistry course in the associated undergraduate programme in biotechnology, chemistry, and environmental engineering. Both sub-theme and course contents were subject to constraints due to the problem-based learning, which are discussed.

# DEFINING THE PROBLEM IN PROBLEM-BASED LEARNING

**Palle Qvist**

Abstract: The vision of this paper is to formulate a new and broadly based definition of the problem in PBL. The objective is by drawing on former definitions published in books (perhaps in the beginning published as booklets or stencils) by teachers at Aalborg University, to build a new definition containing the important elements of the older attempts to define a problem. The new definition must be well defined, easy to understand and easy to practice. After going through the older definitions published a new exact definition is drawn. The definitions mentioned in the article does not necessarily cover all definitions or traditions developed or in use at the university. The article does not draw eg. on definitions or practice formulated in drafts or stencils at department levels, articles in periodicals, anthologies or booklets not later published by a publishing firm.

## 1. INTRODUCTION

Problem-based learning (PBL) starts with a problem. The goal of the knowledge process is to find one or more answers, which can explain or solve the problem. (Kjersdam and Enemark, 1994, Qvist, 2002).

The selection of the problem is essential in PBL. Early it was pointed out that it was important in relation to the effect of learning and very important for the feeling of success or failure and motivation of the students in relation to the project and the teamwork (Berthelsen *et al.*, 1977).

The selection of the problem ought to be the student's responsibility. This was also very early a crucial element in PBL. The students should be active and creative. They should decide themselves and be responsible.

The specific chooses and a formulation of the problem is as an ideal the student's responsibility. The teachers - called their advisers - are responsible for the criteria of a reasonable problem selection and for criticism and suggestions in relation to structure and improvements (Berthelsen *et al.*, 1977).

There has been many attempts to facilitate the students choose of the problem by formulating different criteria's (Berthelsen et. al., 1977). Today it is often the study boards or groups of teachers, which formulate such criteria's. The choosing of the problem must be within certain areas or subjects, , which the study boards or the teachers find important for the students to study at the specific level of their education. At some studies the teachers formulate very specific suggestions to projects within their own interest or research areas instead of more broad areas where they have competence's.

In other studies they maintain the principle that it is the students themselves, which choose the problem within areas where there are teaching resources available.

In some other studies the practice is more flexible. It is not a violation of the principles that the students in the first and perhaps also in the second year are introduced to very specific suggestions to problems, they are allowed to choose. In addition it is said to be the goal that the students themselves later on choose and formulate the problem they want to settle.

The final goal is that the students themselves take responsibility for all aspects of the learning, also the formulation of the problem.

To know the definitions of a problem is therefore an important implication for the possibility to identify and formulate a problem. With a theoretical definition of a problem is it possible for the students themselves to decide if the problem they want to settle might be called a problem, or if it is something else - e.g. a subject or a simple question.

## 2. IN THE BEGINNING

Already in the early days of the University it was obvious that the question of what might be called a problem could start heavy discussions between the teachers and between the teachers and the students. Particularly the question, what a good problem, was caused discussions.

To answer the question the literature was studied. Teachers from outside the University wrote two of the books. One of the first attempts to define a problem in the Danish literature is found in a book of Jenny Winter called »Research Methods and Report Writing« (Winter, 1973). She defines a problem in this way:

»*A problem is a wondering, which takes the concrete form of a question*«. (Winter, 1973 p. 14)

But not all questions are a problem. The wondering Winter talks about often originate from an observed phenomenon which is different from what is expected.

She did not define what should be understood by a phenomenon. Studying her literature might give the answer. Johan Asplunds book »Wondering Towards Society« is mentioned in the references. Asplund mentions Stephen Toulmins understanding of a phenomenon. A phenomenon is here defined as an event or occurrence which must be explained, something which is deeply problematic in one way or another (Asplund, 1972).

Winter says that there arises a tension between the understanding in advance and the facts as they are seen. It is the difference, which creates the wondering. And you want to know why there is a difference. You ask »Why ....?«

The understanding in advance was by Winter called the normal condition of the phenomenon. Because the understanding in advance is limited it is sensitive towards new facts. It is the new facts, which make you wonder. Winter reaches the following point:

»*A problem can be characterised as a discrepancy between a hypothetical normal condition and a fact which diverge from it*« (Winter 1973, p. 15).

In the chapter where the problem is formulated the wonder must be described. The precise problem to be solved is then defined. You want to find knowledge of the defined problem.

Four years later Berthelsen, Illeris and Poulsen published their definition of a problem. They wrote:

»*Problems are forms of appearance for contrasts, conflicts and contradictions*«
(Berthelsen et al., 1977 p. 291).

They deal with how the individual meet, experience or register something as a problem. It can be met emotionally, intellectual or as preventing actions. They write:

»*The individual register emotionally that something is a problem if »it« is connected with frustration, something unpleasant, sorrow, indignation - if reality contradicts the ideals, if the individual feels within one self or outside one self a need to act contrary to ones own values. Intellectually a problem can appear as an unsolved question in relation to causes, about how and why the conditions have developed to the level of today. In relation to knowledge the problem appears as lack of information, uncertainty among validity of facts or as a lack of a coherent structure in segments of knowledge. And in relation to taking action a problem can pop up as hindrance for action, uncertainty between alternative strategies or lacking understanding of existing or future possibilities of action«* (Berthelsen, et. al. 1977, p. 291).

Approximately at the same time as Winter and Berthelsen et. al. formulated their definitions of a problem, teachers and researchers at Aalborg University started to publish their definitions. There was a small difference at the three faculties - the faculty of human science, natural science and social science.

## 3. HUMAN SCIENCE

Problem-based teaching and learning can be understood as the students learning of theories, methods and techniques when analysis of the problem or the complex of problems in question demands it, Eva Hultengren wrote in 1976 (Hultengren, 1976). It was a question of »choosing concrete problems from reality of society«. She defines it the following way:

*»Choosing concrete problems from the reality of society means to have starting point in something which is nor abstract or (lost in) thought. It means to choose something which has happened, happens or will/might happen«* (Hultengren, 1976, p. 14)

Concrete problems have some forms of appearance. She reaches the point in stead of saying that it is a question of choosing concrete problems from the reality of society, one might say that it is a question of having starting point in some concrete observable forms of appearance, for something, which will show up to be a problem of practical or educational interest. Later on she describes a problem as a historical or actual observable phenomenon. But in addition to that it should be possible to perspectivate the phenomenon into an insight in relation to society and furthermore it should be possible to test hypothesises to a degree not defined. Hultengren does not define what should be understood by a phenomenon except it has something to do with reality. Nor does she define what should be understood by reality of society.

She formulates the following description of a problem:

»A problem  *- is something which you wonder about*
*- is something you would like to know more about*
*- is something you have heard or have seen with your eyes*

*- is something which you find a scandal«* (Hultengren, 1976 p. 85; Hultengren, 1981 p. 85)

Almost 15 years later Jan Brødslev Olsen and Lisbeth W. Sørensen write their introduction called »Problem-based learning« (Olsen and Sørensen, 1995). Their objective is not directly to define a problem. They try to explain what PBL is in another way. They say that PBL has something to do with answering the questions of »What ...?« and »Why ... ?«

They introduce a difference between descriptive or empirical projects and projects seeking motive or causes. Later on they call the latter for the literary project.

In the descriptive or empirical project you are looking for an answer to the question about »What ... ?« while in a cause seeking project you are looking for answers on the question of »Why ... ?«. In the first case it is a question of knowing something. In the second it is a question of understanding something.

They write:
*The difference between the two types of projects is that we first and foremost will be interested in »The What ...« ... and in the second we want an explanation. Either of the two questions we choose will influence the design of the project in a decisive way...*
*A special variety of the motive or cause seeking project is the question of »Why ... ?« which contains an anomaly* (Olsen and Sørensen, 1995 p. 13).

In other words Olsen and Sørensen differs between a question of »Why ... ?« and a question of »Why ... ?« containing an anomaly. To explain this difference they distinguish between a curiosity and a qualified curiosity or a wondering. By curiosity they mean an interest in investigating a phenomenon. According to the two writer's curiosity is perhaps one of the most driving forces in development of the human being. The qualified curiosity or the wondering is a curiosity connected to assumptions on beforehand of the phenomenon in question. They write, that the concept is connected to the concept of anomaly. About the anomaly they say:

*»A phenomenon is an anomaly if it appears in a way which differs from what we had expected it would. The phenomenon make us wonder. One example could be that you find shells many kilometres away from the sea. »The solution« of the anomaly is that the sea once upon the time was more spread«* (Olsen and Sørensen, 1995 p. 58)

Olsen and Sørensen do not define what should be understood by a phenomenon.

In the light of the above-mentioned it should be possible to conclude that they understand a problem as a phenomenon which creates a curiosity or a qualified curiosity (wonder). The phenomenon can be an anomaly, which means that it differs from the expected.

## 4. ENGENEERING AND NATURAL SCIENCE

Helle Algreen-Ussing has together with different co-writers - latest Niels O. Fruensgaard (Algreen-Ussing, et al., 1974, 1975; Algreen-Ussing et al., 1986; Algreen-Ussing et. al., 1990) dominated the understanding of the problem at the Faculty of engineering and science.

Back in 1975 Algreen-Ussing published the second issue of »Writing a Report and Problem-Based Education« together with Skov-Petersen and Fruensgaard. The word »problem« is not mentioned as a word to be defined. But it is possible to see a kind of definition when it is said:

»*The project must start with a situation where something is needed, you are lacking knowledge or a »mechanic thing« carry out a function of one kind or the other*« (Algreen-Ussing *et al.*, 1975 s. 5).

Later on it is set up in items. In connection with the description of project's starting point, the starting point will be a confrontation with a situation of lack and needs, meaning lack of knowledge or function (Algreen-Ussing et. al. 1975).

In the book from 1986 a problem is defined as:

»*a defined, existing conflict/contrast or a defined, uncovered need/wish*« (Algreen-Ussing *et. al.*, 1986 p. 55)

It is stressed that working with a problem is qualitatively different from working with subjects and tasks. An important precondition is that the problem is known and experienced as a conflict, a contrast, a need or a wish of those who are working with it.

Conflicts, contrasts, wishes and needs are experienced different from individual to individual. For Algreen-Ussing et. al. it has something to do with fantasy, feelings and impressions and it is assumed that it is possible to imagine something different even though straight away it is not possible to see how it could be possible to reach it.

About the problem Algreen-Ussing *et al.* write:

*»The first formulation of the problem must be starting, seeking, open, e.g. something like*
*- I wonder why ...*
*- Could there be a relationship between...*
*- I would like this to be possible in stead ... »*(Algreen-Ussing et. al., 1986 p. 56)

Algreen-Ussing et al. differ between the real problem and the initiated problem. The first formulation of the problem is called the initiated problem. It has always form of appearance in practice, which is defined as the reality of society. It is an impression of something experienced, something, which has happened or is happening or something, which one might fear, will happen or wish to happen. Because the initiated problem always has forms of appearance in real life and can be perverted so that the problem looks like a technical problem, it must be uncovered and analysed. This is done in the problem analysis.

The problem analysis is defined as the first step in the project. The problem analysis leads to formulating the problem. About this Algreen-Ussing *et al.* say:

*»In the formulation of the problem the initiating problem is a short general or overall question - at best formulated as a direct question. And all partial problems are hereafter described as series of questions, of which the group will seek an answer. ... Partial problems in the problem-based project can be descriptions of subjects or settling tasks but this work will be part of a bigger project connection and will be defined from the problem«* (Algreen-Ussing et al., 1986 p. 59-60).

Experience show that the concept »a problem« is difficult to handle Algreen-Ussing and Fruensgaard write in 1990 (Algreen-Ussing and Fruensgaard, 1990). They find it necessary to mention that a problem in daily speech is not the same as a problem suitable for a study project. Now they define a problem as:

*»Problems in study projects are forms of appearance for contrasts or conflicts in society«* (Algreen-Ussing and Fruensgaard, 1990 p. 43)

The initiated problem is also introduced in 1990. It is identical to the first formulation of the project problem. And it is defined in the same way as the problem:

*»The initiate problem is a form of appearance for a contrast or a conflict in society«* (Algreen-Ussing and Fruensgaard, 1990 p. 55)

The idea of Algreen-Ussing and Fruensgaard is that after the formulation of the initiated problem there should be a well documented and formulated chapter in the project leading up to a narrowed and clear formulated problem. This could be done in many ways. But something is common. The initiated problem must be analysed to show its existence. It must be placed in its social context. It happens during the problem analysis, which is a chapter as well. The conclusion is the formulation of the problem. When the problem analysis is finished and has been done properly, well documented and well structured, there can be narrowing to the partial problems selected. What should be understood by partial problems are not defined, but it is the impression of the authors that partial problems can be a description of subjects or a matter of settling tasks. But it shall be part of the project and limited by the problem.

## 5. SOCIAL SCIENCE

In »Problems in science« Jes Adolphsen (Adolphsen, 1985) says that problems can be anomalies. He differs between practical and scientific problems. A practical problem is a problem in relation to human practice. Something around you behaves in another way than expected or wanted. A practical problem can be settled by chance or disappear as problem without you know why it happened. With theoretical problems it is not like that. It is the theoretical problems which are interesting and which are made object for knowledge or comprehension at universities. Adolphsen also calls the theoretical problem for a scientific problem. It is defined this way:

*»A theoretical problem or a scientific problem can be said to be an anomaly in relation to our knowledge or our theories about the world. A theoretical problem in an anomaly in relation to our former experience or understanding of the world a problem in relation to our former comprehension, understanding or explanations of the world regardless of our comprehension is from dealing with the world or from conscious activities of comprehension«* (Adolphsen, 1985 p. 31)

Theoretical problems often stem from the contrasts you are confronted with as practical problems. To every practical problem there is a theoretical problem. The practical problem changes to a theoretical problem in the same moment you ask: Why is the practical problem there?

It is not all theoretical problems which stem directly from practical problems or contrasts confronting one. There are theoretical problems to which there is no practical problem. Adolphsen writes:

*»Theoretical problems can be formulated from practical problems, from normal, imaginative wondering or from known theories.*

*It is common for all theoretical problems that their starting point is our daily life world. Their starting point is our nature background and our socio-economic, cultural and material conditions of life. It is because our conditions of life restrict us and because our conditions of life often result in unintentional, negative consequences of our acts. Dealing with theoretical problem makes sense because of contrasts in our life world.*

*Also theoretical problems have starting point in our daily life world because our background in nature and our life conditions determine which theoretical problems we see and confront ourselves with«* (Adolphsen, 1985 p. 33).

In »Formulating The Problem - an a,b,c« (Qvist, 1988) Palle Qvist defines a problem in the following way:

*»A problem is an anomaly. An anomaly is something, which is deviate from the rule or the usual, something irregular. Something which is not understood«* (Qvist, 1988 p. 2)

Qvist sees problems as relative. Some anomalies are only anomalies for some, not for others.

*»Problems are anomalies in relation to the knowledge you have on beforehand in relation to former experiences or understandings of the world. In relation to ones former comprehension's, understanding and explanations of the world«* (Qvist, 1988 p. 4)

Then he asks without giving a full answer, that when do you have a problem, is when you e.g. have two sets of facts meeting in a contrast. It means having e.g. a paradox. When you acknowledge, you try to answer the question of why »something« is as it is or you try to answer the question of how do I change »something« to »something« else. PBL is not as some think the same as explorative, investigating or descriptive research.

In 1991 in »ABC in Problem Formulation, Problem Settling and Project Writing« (Adolphsen and Qvist, 1991) Adolphsen and Qvist write - perhaps a little polemic -that all orderly comprehension starts with a problem. They define problems in the following way:

*»Problems are anomalies in relation to the knowledge you have on beforehand. In relation to ones former comprehension's, understandings and explanations of the world* (Adolphsen and Qvist, 1991, quoted after 1995 p. 26)

Adolphsen and Qvist distinguish between problems in daily life and other problems but also between forms of understanding in daily life and understanding and comprehension of society. A lot of problems start, as a problem in the common and everyday consciousness of the human being and comprehension's suitable in ordinary life. Such problems might turn out to be not real problems. The comprehensions of everyday life and the forms of understandings in everyday life are stamped by twisted and ideological conceptions.

When you comprehend you seek - according to Adolphsen and Qvist - to find the answer of »Why ...?« or »How ...?«. The answers are sought with help from theories or theoretical insight. In this way you are free of the knowledge and comprehension of daily life - free of understandings and limits by the consciousness of daily life.

In »Production of Knowledge« (Nielsen, 1994) Peter Nielsen indirectly defines what he understands by a problem. He says:

*»A problem is basically impression of a tension or a contrast between two conditions:*

*Condition of desires} ——————— {actual condition«*
(Nielsen, 1994 p. 28)

According to Nielsen the contrast often is abstract and weak formulated at the staring point. Therefore the problem must be exactly and explicit formulated. The problem must also be argued.

In »Creative Chaos in Project Working« (Kupferberg, 1996) Feiwel Kupferberg differs between problems of daily life and scientific problems. Because the same word is used in common language and in science many believe that it is the same. According to Kupferberg the problems of daily life are dilemmas.

He does not define how dilemma should be understood. It is a manifestation of which you cannot decide what you want. But problems in daily life are not the same as in science. What is manifested from the single individual, as a dilemma is for the scientist a problem, which can be formulated in terms of a contradiction, according to Kupferberg. He does not define what he understands by a contradiction. But he writes that what happens when you formulate a scientific problem, is that a dilemma in the real world is transformed into a possible contradiction in the world of thoughts.

But scientific problems are not just that. When there is a clear contradiction between ideal and reality, between how things ought to be and how they really are, there exists a scientific problem as well. Kupferberg concludes:

*»A scientific problem will normally contain a contradiction of some sort«* (Kupferberg, 1996 p. 60)

## 6. SUMMING UP AND PRESENTING A DEFINITION

Teachers and expert in PBL at Aalborg University have through the years formulated different definitions of a problem although elements and ideas are equal. Some of the definitions are quite broad and not very precise, others contain words defined or possible to define. Below they are classified.

*Figure 1:* Definitions of a problem

| Unspecific or soft | | Specific or hard |
|---|---|---|
| ← | | → |
| Wonder | Conflict | Anomaly |
| Something which has happened | | Paradox |
| Something which happens | | Contrast |
| Something which will happen | | Contradiction |
| Something which you would like to know more about | | |
| Something heard or seen | | |
| Something you find a scandal | | |
| A phenomenon creating curiosity | | |
| A phenomenon creating qualified curiosity | | |
| A lack of knowledge | | |
| A lack of function | | |
| Uncovered need | | |
| Uncovered wish | | |
| A practical problem | | |
| A contrast between a wish and reality | | |

As Figure 1. shows all or almost all the most of the unspecific or soft definitions are covered by the specific definitions. A wonder implies an anomaly. A wish is related to a contrast between what you have and what you would like to have. A conflict might be an anomaly, paradox, contrast or contradiction. And so on.

The ambition is now to formulate a precise and broad definition drawing on all the definitions, mentioned above. The idea is to establish continuity to what has been. A definition must be precise and as exact as possible. Therefore the definitions to the right in Figure 1. are the most interesting. But the idea is also to formulate a definition broad enough to contain the differences and traditions for comprehension, learning and the use of knowledge. A broader definition must be expressed in well-defined concepts and must be formulated so it is possible to understand and use it. It must also contribute to new comprehension, knowledge and solutions.

It seems to be possible to define a problem as:

*A documented or argumented anomaly, paradox, contrast or contradiction.*
*An anomaly is in scientific language an abnormal condition, something diverging from the norm or the rule, the expected, the lawful or the usual (Lübcke, 1983; Hanneborg, 1994).*
*A paradox is a claim about e.g. a relation, which is well-founded eventually correct but in contrast or discrepant with the prevailing opinion or what can be found empirical (Lubcke, 1983; Hanneborg, 1994)*
*A contrast is a relation between something, which is quite different from something else, which belongs to the same category, types or art (Dahlerup, 1932, second edition 1968).*
*A contradiction is simultaneous statements or relations in reality which mutual excludes each other (Lübcke, 1983; Hanneborg, 1994)*
*That the anomaly, paradox, contrast or contradiction are documented means that they are empirical grounded, established, supported or proved by a collection of claims where one - the conclusion - is formulated as grounded by the others.*
*That the anomaly, paradox, contrast or contradiction are argued means that they are supported by a collection of allegations where one - the conclusion is formulated as grounded by the others - the premises.*

The *purpose* with the answering or solutions of the problem - the work with the project - can be:

(1) *Understanding or comprehension.* During the working with the project you seek answer of »Why ... ?«

(2) *Change* (e.g. construction or solution - theoretical or in practice). During the working with the project you seek answer of »How ...«? (How is e.g. a new situation, a relationship, a new construction obtained.

(3) *Understanding and change.* During the working with the project you seek answer of »Why ... and how ... ?«

## 7. EXAMPLES

Multinational corporations often use a common tongue - e.g. English - in internal and external communication. Often the employees misunderstand each other. Such misunderstandings cost money for the corporation. The corporation uses a common language because they want to avoid misunderstandings. It happens anyway. It is a problem. The group wants to know why. Perhaps another group wants to find out how it can me minimised or even avoided. A third group wants to know why it happens and how to settle the problem.

A group of electronic engineering students will try to find out if it is possible to construct a ghetto blaster using fewer batteries, but having same volume as the ordinary ghetto blasters at the marked.

Their starting point has been - perhaps without realising it themselves - a contrast between what exists and what they would like to have. A contrast between a situation of status quo and a possible other situation - a vision. They can document the status quo. And they can argue for their vision. It might even be possible for them to document that it is a good idea to seek the vision realised.

A group of chemistry engineering students experience as an anomaly that the drinking water is polluted with coli bacillus. They can document the anomaly. They would like to know why the water is polluted. But they would also like to find out how it is possible to secure non-polluted water to the households.

A group studying social science registers that more and more unemployed are older than 50 years. They also register that in public and between politicians and members of organisations on the labour marked it is normal to talk about the importance of the seniors for effectiveness and benefits of organisations, corporations and public institutions. Even seniors are called Grey Gold. It is a paradox. The group wants to find out why there are more and more people above 50, whom are unemployed, when people belonging to the same group are Grey Gold for employers.

## 8. CONCLUSION

The starting point of a PBL-project is a *problem*. During the year's different definitions of the problem have been published in books by teachers at Aalborg University. Some are soft and some are harder or specific. The aim of a definition is normally to be precise and exact. All or almost all the most of the unspecific or soft definitions published during the years are covered by the specific definitions. A wonder implies an anomaly. A wish is related to a contrast between what you have and what you would like to have. A conflict might be an anomaly, paradox, contrast or contradiction. And so on.

The aim of this article has been to formulate a new and broad definition containing all the previous published definitions. Is it suggested that a problem is something, which is *documented* or *argumented* as an *anomaly, a paradox, a contrast or a contradiction*. The purpose with the answering or solutions of the problem - the work with the project - can be *understanding* or *comprehension, change* or *understanding and change*.

## REFERENCES

A free copy of this article is available in Danish at http://go.to/abznet

Adolphsen, J. (1985). *Problemer i videnskab*, Aalborg Universitetsforlag, Aalborg.

Adolphsen, J. and Qvist, P (1991 & 1995). *ABC i problemformulering, problemløsning og projektskrivning*, Forlaget edupax, Gistrup og Gyldendal, København.

Algreen-Ussing, H., Skov-Petersen, B. and Fruensgaard, N. O. (1974 & 1975). *Rapportskrivning i projektorienteret undervisning, Den teknisk-naturvidenskabelige basisuddannelse*, Aalborg Universitetscenter, Aalborg.

Algreen-Ussing, H., Fruensgaard, N. O., Nørgaard Nielsen, J. and Stubkjær E. (1986). *Metode i projektarbejdet ved teknisk-naturvidenskabelige uddannelser*, Aalborg Universitetsforlag, Aalborg.

Algreen-Ussing, H. and Fruensgaard, N. O. (1990). *Metode i Projektarbejdet. Problemorientering og gruppearbejde,* Aalborg Universitetsforlag, Aalborg.

Asplund, J. (1972). *Om undren overfor samfundet,* Hans Reitzel, København.

Berthelsen, J., Illeris, K. and Clod Poulsen, S. (1977 & 3rd edition 1979). *Projektarbejde - erfaringer og praktisk vejledning,* Borgen, Holstebro.

Dahlerup, V. (2$^{nd}$ edition 1968). *Ordbog over det danske sprog,* Gyldendal, København.

Hanneborg, B. and K. (1971 & 2$^{nd}$ edition 1994). *Filosofisk ordbog,* Høst, København.

Hultengren, E. (1976 & 1981). Problemorientering, projektarbejde og rapportskrivning, Institut for uddannelse og socialisering, Aalborg Universitetscenter & Aalborg Universitetsforlag, Aalborg.

Kjersdam, F. and Enemark, S. (1994 reprinted 1997). *The Aalborg Experiment. Project Innovation in University Education,* Aalborg Universitetsforlag, Aalborg.

Kupferberg, F. (1996). *Kreativt kaos i projektarbejdet,* Aalborg Universitetsforlag, Aalborg.

Lübcke, P. (red.) (1983). *Politikens filosofi leksikon,* Politikens Forlag, København.

Nielsen, P. (1994). *Produktion af viden - en praktisk metodebog,* Teknisk Forlag, København.

Olsen, J. B. and Sørensen, L. W. (1995). *Problembaseret indlæring,* Aalborg Universitetsforlag, Aalborg.

Qvist, P. (2002-). *abznet,* http://go.to/abznet

Qvist, P. (1988 & 1989). *Problemformulering - en a,b,c. Den samfundsvidenskabelige basisuddannelse,* Aalborg Universitet, Aalborg & Forlaget edupax, Gistrup.

Winter, J. (1973). *Undersøgelsesmetodik og rapportskrivning,* Munksgaard, København.

# REFLECTIONS ON PROBLEM-BASED LEARNING

**Jens Christensen**

**Abstract**: Perceptions of learning and knowledge are subject to historical changes, and they appear as complex phenomena. This is true also for the concept of problem-based learning (PBL). The article develops a framework for discussing the complexity of PBL, which should be managed at a university of year 2003. The framework gives a view on the starting points of exemplary learning in relation to general and transferable qualifications to be learned. It is argued that exemplary learning may be initiated either by problems, potentialities, or values, or by an interaction between those. However, the most crucial is an open approach. General and transferable qualifications include not only specific skills of the profession, but also existential enlightenment, social responsibility, and a reflective approach to learning and knowledge. Furthermore, the personal and affective involvement of the student is a precondition for promoting a learning process. The main aim of the article is not the specific framework as such, but to contribute to the explicit discussion of the underlying intentions of PBL, and by means of the argumentation that leads to the framework.

## 1. INTRODUCTION

Like all kinds of ideals, also the ideal of problem-based learning (PBL) is in the risk of going into one of two opposites.

The first risk is that the ideal stagnates to a rigid ideology. This may happen, if PBL is interpreted literally and hence equal to learning based on problems. A rigid interpretation is that learning should always start with a problem, then an analysis of the problem, and finally a search for a solution to the problem, this being independent of any other kinds of aims for the learning process. If an interpretation like this is insisted, then PBL looses its function as a corrective to practise, because practise will develop its own inertia and a high degree of variety. The ideal will not be taken serious among open-minded practitioners, and PBL becomes only a catchword.

The second risk is that the ideal is regarded so widely that it is likely to become interpreted at one's own convenience. All kinds of educational practises may be named PBL, only in order to legitimate that the actual development of the practise is within the frame of PBL. Also in this case, the concept of PBL looses its meaning as an ideal that can function as a corrective to the self-inertia of practise and as a leitmotif for the development of educational programmes and didactics.

This article reflects learning in respect of the very ideal of PBL, and in a way that expresses a movement in between the poles of a very rigid and a too open interpretation. Thereby, the article aims at contributing to an explicit discussion of the underlying intentions of the ideal. A main view is that a perception of learning and knowledge, such as PBL, is complex and historically changeable; and study boards as well as teachers should be able to deal with a complexity. A framework for further discussion is developed, showing the complexity in a way, which is open to many practical variations, but also decisive on a normative basis.

The first part of the article discusses different approaches to exemplary and project-organised learning, which can initiate a reflective process of cognition. The second part discusses general and transferable qualifications to be learned, in order to develop the students into reflective and responsible members of the society. The third part develops the framework, by combining views from the first and second part. Finally, a few comments are given about the relevance of didactics, which are different from PBL.

The article may be perceived as essayistic or tentative. The statement of the article being tentative is not the same as to say that the reflections are not really genuine. Only, it should be emphasised that the article is not based on comprehensive studies in theories of learning and education. Primarily, the article is initiated by my own teaching experiences and by reflections on these experiences. This is mainly referred to my function as a supervisor on study projects at The Faculty of Science and Technology, and especially first year projects (the basic year). Some of the reflections, however, are based on my research, which is within the field of theory and philosophy of science and knowledge, but with focus on issues different from those dealt with in this article.

## 2. EXEMPLARY AND PROJECT-ORGANISED LEARNING: FROM WHAT STARTING POINTS?

### 2.1. Problems, potentialities and values

Should a 'good' learning process always start with a problem? This question is important, when we think in terms of *problem*-based learning. The predicate of 'good' is used to express an undefined value-orientation, and in order not to limit the normative perception already from the beginning.

Before going any further with an attempt to answer the question, we must specify the concept of a problem. With reference to Karl Popper we can distinguish between two types of problems, practical and theoretical (Popper, 1979: 263). A practical problem can be said to exist, when a phenomenon which influences our living conditions, either socially or technically, is experienced as being 'wrong', 'bad' or 'unsatisfying'. A practical problem may also appear as a dilemma. A theoretical problem can be said to exist, when we just wonder at the character or the background of a phenomenon.

Practical problems prompt us to search for solutions, which are characterised as changes in the real world. Theoretical problems prompt us to search for solutions by a better understanding, interpretation, or explanation, and thus changes in our consciousness. Practical problems lead to the questions of 'how?', while theoretical problems lead to the questions of 'why?'. However, the two kinds of problems are also interconnected. In order to solve a practical problem we will need to achieve an understanding of the problem, including the reasons for the problem. We must search an answer for 'why?' before we can give a qualified answer to 'how?'. (Adolphsen, 1985: 30-36).

If we take the concept of problem-based learning literally, then learning should always take its starting point either in a practical or a theoretical problem. My experience from supervising study projects is that a 'good' learning process can have different starting points than problems only. This is not the same as to say that all approaches to projects rank equally.

The question is: How can we keep an open-minded approach to the starting points of exemplary learning in project-organised studies, in respect of underlying intentions of PBL[1], but also without interpreting PBL so overtly that the concept looses its meaning?

An example of a project's starting point, which I would consider good, will lead to a fundamental postulation. The example concerns the development of harbours. Many harbours of today are subject to changes, as the commercial use of the harbours tends to cease, and the water-front areas become available for other uses. Also the harbour of Aalborg is subject to this kind of change. Similar to many other groups in the society, as well as decision-makers, a group of students has become interested in the development of

---

[1] This sentence might lead to an analysis of the background of the ideal of PBL, and in order to analyse underlying intentions historically. As already mentioned, my approach is mainly based on practical experience with PBL, and the perception of 'underlying intentions' (which is a normative perception, not only subject of description) will appear as implicit in the following discussion.

such areas for new purposes, and the project-group has chosen the waterfront of Aalborg as a case. The students may have a vision of creating an aesthetic attractive environment, visually related to the firth, with a kind of connection between the water-front and the town centre. The vision may also include an imagination of an environment with lots of life of people.

It is not a practical problem, which has initiated this project, as there is nothing 'wrong'. Neither is the project initiated by a theoretical problem. At least the concept of 'problem' should be stretched to an extreme, in order to give the starting point the predicate of a problem. It would be more honest to say that the project starts with a possibility for something else to happen, it means a potentiality. If the students already from the beginning have a vision about the future development of the waterfront, even how diffuse this vision may be formulated, then another starting point may also exist, namely a value-oriented approach. However, when the students analyse the potentialities and reflect the values, problems will appear, and thus the project will lead to the analysis and the solving of different problems.

My postulation is that there are three equal kinds of starting points to exemplary learning: *Problems, potentialities, and values*. Three brief statements will throw light to this postulation.

1) A phenomenon appears as a problem only by virtue of a human consideration of the phenomenon as problematic. Consideration of a phenomenon as problematic is equal to an assessment, and an assessment is rooted in values. The incentive to try to solve the problem is based on an imagination of the existence of potentialities for change. This is true, even if beforehand we have no ideas about the potentialities. My suggestion is that problems, values, and potentialities are three closely interconnected categories.

2) If a project, as a first step, starts with a problem, then a second step will be to search for possible solutions. A search for possible solutions equals entering into a process of discovering potentialities for such changes which can contribute to the removing of the problem. A third step will be to choose one solution among the different potentialities. This choice is based on values. My suggestion is that project work does not need to develop as a linear process, but often the working process will include simultaneity between the three categories or a circulation between them.

3) The third statement is more fundamental, and based on the view of man. As humans, by nature we are not only problem-solving beings, but we are also potentiality-searching and value-creating beings. Basically, as a charac-

teristic of human existence, we do not only react to problems, but we also search for and create potentialities, and we search for and create meanings or values, for instance perceptions of 'the good life'.

In general it is my point of view that every project, if not explicit, then at least implicit, includes aspects of problems, potentialities and values in all its phases. This view does not imply that the problem-oriented approach to a project is degraded, but it is extended. The extension consists in the addition of two kinds of approaches, namely potentialities and values.

A second example will contribute to the emphasis of this viewpoint. Imagine a factory who has become known as a 'successful project', for instance as frontrunner in regards to an environmentally protective production. A study project is initiated by *values*, which is expressed through an assessment of the project in the real world as successful. The study project is also initiated by the assumption that this successful project may express transferable *potentialities*, which means potentialities that could be transferred to other factories. The attention on transferable potentialities is based on an interest in contributing to the solving of practical problems. In this case the *practical problems* are environmental problems. The project will search an answer to a *theoretical problem*, namely by asking the question: Why has the factory developed into a good example? What factors influenced the development of the factory, and by which technical means did the factory arrange its production? In such a study project, it is obvious that the focuses on values, potentialities, and practical as well as theoretical problems, are closely interrelated.

## 2.2. An open approach

Now, an example of a starting point will be presented which in my opinion does not respect the underlying intentions of PBL. A proposal for a study project might be »Make a one man helicopter!«, or in general »Make X!«, where X stands for a technical apparatus. Such proposals pre-decide a solution, without any problem to solve. They are not open to the discussion of human life values, neither to a search of potentialities. Such proposals may very easily lead to a subject-centred learning process only, within specific technical disciplines, and with no challenges for the students to discover problems, potentialities, or values.

On a meta-level we can distinguish between *open* and *closed* starting points. The proposal of 'Make a one man helicopter!« (or any apparatus named 'X') is closed. An alternative starting point might be the search for new means of transport, for instance with a specific purpose such as rescue, or more generally based on the perception that human mobility is a value. Such a starting point would have an open character.

When as a starting point a project is closed, either by a set problem, a set potentiality, or a set value, then the students will not really become challenged to do their own reflections. My suggestion is that an open character of the starting point of a project is crucial and more important than the specific category of the starting point. The reason for this suggestion is that an open approach is a precondition for the students to enter into a reflective process of cognition, and that this is a decisive aspect of 'good learning'.

It is a field for further discussion, whether the three mentioned approaches to exemplary learning are exclusive, or whether other good approaches exist. Two brief examples, only for promoting the discussion. A project may start with a wish to examine a hypothesis, as a potential explanation of a theoretical problem. A project may start with a wish to evaluate a theory, a method, or a model, which involves an examination of the potentiality of the theory, method, or model in relation to solving the problems in respect of values. Two questions arise: In which ways can such starting points be characterised as open and thereby challenging to a reflective process of cognition? How can their relation to problems, potentialities, and values become further developed?

## 3. GENERAL QUALIFICATIONS: FOR WHAT AIMS?

### 3.1. What is meant by professional qualifications?

Exemplary learning is not for the purpose of developing the students' ability only to handle the example in question. Exemplary learning is a way to develop qualifications of a general and transferable character. By working with the above mentioned case, the water-front of Aalborg, the students will not be able to deal only with this specific waterfront. To a certain degree they will get knowledge of, how to deal with water-fronts in general, but first and foremost the students will achieve professional qualifications of a still more general character. They will acquire qualifications within the field of physical planning, transferable to other cases than just water-fronts.

Exemplary learning is a way to achieve professional qualifications. The question is: What is meant by the concept of 'professional qualification'? Is it only skills within the field of theories and methods, as well as active knowledge within the subject area of the profession in question? Or do the concept of professional qualification include something more? If so, what should the general qualifications of a profession then include?

For throwing light to this question, and in order not to answer from the most immediate position, we should take a step backwards. We should ask about perceptions of learning and knowledge, including perceptions of the aims of general qualifications. Such perceptions are historically changeable and culturally multiple. When we stand before changeable and multiple perceptions, a way to bring perspective to an immediate perception is to ask for the historical changes as well as the cultural differences.

Instead of asking for perceptions of learning and knowledge in the most general sense, we can take the starting point in an undoubted supposition, namely that learning centres such as universities have a positive purpose, or that such learning centres are meaningful. Reflective practitioners will pose the question: »Why are we doing what we in fact are doing?«. As teachers and supervisors at a university we might ask: »Why has a society universities?«. More generalised the question might sound: »Why has a society specific learning centres?«.

Asking this kind of questions urge us to rethink the meaningfulness of universities, for instance Aalborg University in the year of 2003. Whenever we organise and arrange education, at least if we want to develop the education on a reflective basis, we should ask, on which perception of learning and knowledge we would develop a university, were we in the situation of developing a new university.

## 3.2. Examples on perceptions of learning and knowledge

During Western history different kinds of learning centres have existed, and with different and still changing perceptions of learning and knowledge. Main examples are the Platonic Academia, the Roman rhetor schools, the monasteries from the Middle Ages, the universities from the 12th century and until today, the technical high-schools during the latest couple of centuries. Other cultures may have other traditions for learning centres, or rather we can think of non-centres as for instance kinds of 'craft's apprenticeship'. In shaman cultures, for instance, where the shaman is considered as the most learned or wise man or woman, the single novice may learn from the single master.

Table 1 illustrates some different perceptions of learning and knowledge, tentatively, and not based on any deep historical analysis.

|  | Platonic Academia | Monastery, Early Middle Ages | University in year 2003 (normative) |
|---|---|---|---|
| The ideal of the cultural formation of individuals | Virtue ethics | Piety, inward search for devotion to God in Heaven | Existential enlightenment (freedom and interdependency, reflection of values) |
| The social tasks and duties of individuals | Participate in the public affairs of the Greek city-state (polis) | Represent a religious and moral ideal | Social responsibility (problem-solving and creative development) |
| The condition for fulfilling the social tasks and duties of individuals | The position as a free and male citizen | Admission to a monastery, exclude influence from the secular world | Position within the economic sphere of the society |
| The superior ideal of learning and knowledge | Philosophy | Bible reading as a prayer | Reflective approach to (scientific) knowledge |
| The idea about promoting a learning process | Socratic dialogue | Discipline / self-discipline | Personal and affective involvement |

Table 1. Examples on perceptions of learning and knowledge

Horizontally are three examples: The Platonic Academia, a monastery from the Early Middle Ages, and a university such as Aalborg University in year 2003.

The vertical dimension needs further comments. Asking for perceptions of learning and knowledge during history (as well as in different cultures), then the first question may be, how we can analyse perceptions of learning and knowledge. Clearly, a framework of historical analysis, such as the factors in table 1, is influenced by the actualised position, from which we carry out the analysis of what have happened in history. We ask for history or culture, but we ask from our own historical and cultural position. This dilemma is well known from hermeneutics, and here it is not the place to go any deeper into a discussion of the dilemma; just to indicate it.

Following, five factors of analysis are pointed out. The first two factors are based on the assumption that in every historical epoch there is a dominating perception of both the individuality and the sociality, and a perception of the relationship between the individuality and the sociality. The first factor is the ideal of the cultural formation of individuals (the ideal of personality)[2]. The second factor is the perception of the role of individuals in society, the social tasks and duties of the individuals. The third factor is the social conditions, especially the preconditions that makes it possible for the individuals to fulfil their social tasks or duties. The fourth factor is the superior ideal of learning and knowledge, meaning a doctrine that should be achieved, in order to be acknowledged as a learned person. The fifth factor is the idea of the basis, on which the intended learning is promoted and the intended knowledge is acquired.

---

[2] German: Bildungsideal.

*The Platonic Academia:* The free male citizens in the ancient Greece had the tasks and the duties of participating in the public affairs of the city-state (polis), and a precondition for taking part in the public affairs was the position as a free male citizen. Virtue based ethics played an important role, among others in the Platonic philosophy. As moral individuals, the free male citizens should let their decisions be ruled by reason, and not by desire or temperament. The ruling class should consist of wise men, specifically philosophers. Philosophical reflection was promoted by Socratic dialogue. By use of a modern concept we could say that Socrates posed 'facilitating questions', in order to develop a reflective way of reasoning.

*A monastery of the Early Middle Ages:* The learned men in the Early Middle Age were monks, living in a monastery. According to the ideas of Saint Augustine, the individuals should draw their attention to an inward search for devotion to the transcendent God in Heaven. With reference also to Saint Benedict's code of practice (Regula) the monks should avoid all kinds of influences from the secular world. If the monks had any tasks or duties of relevance for the outer and secular society, then their duty was to represent a moral or religious ideal. The precondition for fulfilling the religious duty was admission to the religious community of a monastery. The superior ideals were not learning and knowledge in our sense of these words, but rather to read the Bible as a prayer, and to take part in the prayers of the canonical hours. By means of discipline and self-discipline, not at least by developing the ability to direct ones own will, the inward devotion to God was promoted.

Although these historical remarks are extremely brief and simplified, they serve to show that perceptions of learning and knowledge are normative, and therefore also subject to a normative discussion, related to the historical circumstances and the dominating historical values. The same is true, when we pose the question; why do universities exist in society? Universities are not just 'universities' in only one conception of the term 'university'. During one thousand years the aim and the role of universities have changed. The concept of PBL in itself is a normative concept, originated in Western culture, and influenced by historically developed circumstances and values. When asking about the perception of learning and knowledge at a university of today, answers will become normative, depending on the values of the answering person. As the answering person himself is a historical and cultural being, the answer will have the impression of the actual circumstances and the actual zeitgeist, as well as an interpretation of the circumstances and the zeitgeist.

What should be the perception of learning and knowledge characterizing the education at a *university in year 2003?* A general statement is that the education should not only initiate a reflective process of cognition as stated in part 1, but also develop the students into reflective and responsible members of the society. Referring to the above table, more specific statements may be as follows.

*The cultural formation of the individual* should respect the tendency of our age to search for individual freedom and personal development, not in an ego-centred way, but as a socially and culturally interdependent person. 'Existential enlightenment' might be a key concept for the reflection of one's own identity in a perspective of freedom as well as interdependency, including the ability to reflect social and cultural values. Existential enlightenment may be perceived as a counterpart to 'scientific enlightenment' within the field of theoretical and factual knowledge.[3]

*The social tasks and duties of individuals:* Social responsibility may be a keyword. Social responsibility includes responsibility in relation to socially weak groups and to natural environment. The concept also includes a responsible way of interacting with different cultures, based on a respectful attitude towards people from other cultures and on an understanding of cultural traditions different from ones own. In order to carry out the duty as social responsible beings, individuals should develop qualifications to understand and solve problems, but they should also develop abilities in the field of creativity. Creativity includes the ability to search for unnoticed potentialities with an open-minded attitude, as well as the ability to contribute to the development of social values. From this viewpoint, attention to the three above mentioned categories, problems, potentialities, and values, is important, in order to behave socially responsible.

*The condition for fulfilling the social tasks and duties of individuals:* A precondition for fulfilling a social role is the ability to sell ones resources of knowledge for money within the economic sphere of the society, whether as a wage earner or as a self-employed person. The way, in which our society is established, a position within the economic system is a precondition for most professionals, in order to contribute in a responsible way to the technical and social development. To be in such a position, qualifications within the field of professional leadership are also important. Without further discussion of this point, it just ought to be mentioned that in many cases such a position may also be a way, in which to contribute in a non-responsible way, namely when money becomes more important than morality. The crucial point is that a person, who cannot sell his or her labour force at the labour market, is

---

[3] The distinction between the concepts of existential enlightenment and scientific enlightenment is inspired by Jesper Garsdal (a Danish philosopher, ph.d. from Aalborg University).

in danger of becoming excluded from positions with social influence. Determined by the historically developed social structures of our age, it is necessary that the learning of professionals is directed towards acquiring skills within the field of exactly the subjects appreciated within the economic life.

*The superior ideal of learning and knowledge:* A superior ideal of knowledge of our age is the specific category which is named scientific knowledge. This category is based on historically developed ideas about knowledge within Western cultures. Scientific knowledge, however, cannot be learned only by imitating the scientific knowledge of other people (as for instance teachers), or by imitating their way of acting based on scientific knowledge. An important aspect of learning scientific knowledge is the development of an ability to reflect knowledge as such. A reflective approach to knowledge should be based on theories of knowledge, not only as specific skills, but more precisely as a precondition for a reflective approach to knowledge. This approach is important for developing at least three different abilities: the ability to continuously learn; the ability to interact in an interdisciplinary group; the ability to interact with people from cultures based on ideas of knowledge which are different from one's own ideas.

*The idea about promoting a learning process:* A teacher may urge a student to cognition, which includes existential enlightenment, social responsibility, skills within specific subjects, a reflective approach to learning and knowledge. After all, the process of learning depends on the interest of the student. An affective involvement of the student is a precondition for the intended learning process to proceed. The model of learning must respect that a learning process cannot be controlled from outside. The learning process may be initiated by teaching, but the way of initiating must go together with the personal involvement of the student. It is important that each student has the feeling of 'owning' his or her own learning process. Thus also a schism may occur between the intended learning process and the actual learning process. The learning model should acknowledge and respect the existence of this schism.

A question was posed: What is meant by the concept of 'professional qualification'? The answer is that professionalism includes the entire complex of indicated general qualifications. These qualifications should not be regarded separately, as they are all closely interrelated with each other. For instance, in order to get an understanding of social responsibilities and the implications of this concept, existential enlightenment is a precondition. Furthermore, subject-oriented skills, as well as a reflective approach towards knowledge, are important, in order to be able to act in a social responsible way, when candidates achieve a position within the economic sphere of the society.

Learning centres may differ from universities. The Danish folk high schools, for instance, aim not directly towards the vocational orientation. They aim among others at the promotion of young people's ability to participate in democratic processes, including the ability to reflect and discuss social and cultural values, which is precisely existential enlightenment. Even when admitting the job-orientated focus at the universities, in some respects the universities could learn from the folk high schools.

## 4. THE CHALLENGE OF HANDLING A COMPLEX APPROACH

It appears that there is an intricate interplay between exemplary learning and general qualifications, between the starting points of learning and the resulting knowledge, between intended learning and the basis on which a learning process is initiated. Figure 1 outlines a framework for discussing the complexity of approaches to learning and knowledge. The intricate interplay between approaches is shown with a focus on three components:
- The starting point of exemplary learning in project-organised studies.
- The intended qualifications of a general character, transferable from one example to another.
- The precondition of promoting a learning process.

In exemplary learning, for instance within a project-organised model, the interplay between many approaches should be taken seriously. It follows from this statement that the aims and the contents of a project should not be decided only based on problems, which a literal interpretation of PBL might suggest, but based on a complex of influencing components. First, a project may be initiated by a problem, a potentiality, a value, or a mutual interaction in between, but first and foremost by an open approach. Second, the aims and the contents of a project should be influenced by intended qualifications of a general and transferable character, with a reference to such intended qualifications which are outlined in figure 1 (compare the discussion of table 1). Third, the personal and affective involvement of the students is a precondition for the learning process to take place. My suggestion is that altogether the three components, including the contents shown in the figure, form the constituents of 'good learning'.

The challenge of the study board who decides the framework of a project-organised study, as well as the challenge of each supervisor, who proposes projects and assists the students to carry through the project, is to handle the interplay between the many components. The study board as well as the supervisors should be able to manage the art of 'juggling' with this interplay.

In fact, the actual study curriculum of the first year of technological and scientific studies at Aalborg University expresses the importance to manage complex approaches to the learning process.[4] Many of the supervisors are aware of the complexity involved, both in the formulation of proposals for projects, and in the practical supervising situation. The contribution in this article, in general, is an explication of a framework for further discussions of, how to develop the project-organised and problem-oriented studies. More specifically, this framework challenges any narrow understanding of problem-based learning as being only 'learning based on problems'. The question may be posed, whether we ought to find another concept than PBL, which is more expressive of the complexity of the learning-model?

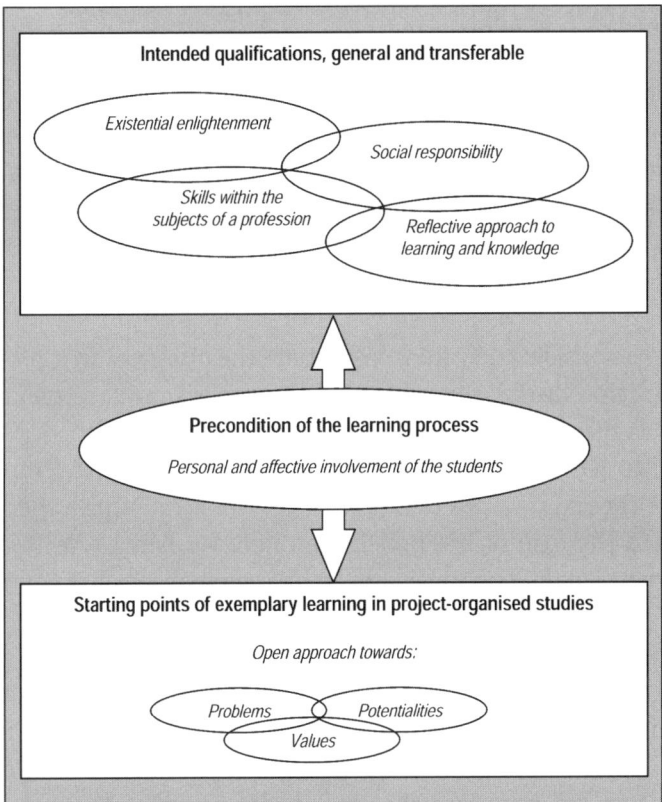

Figure 1. A framework for discussing the complexity of approaches to learning and knowledge

Although a framework for further discussion is explicated, the framework as such is not the most important message of the article. The framework, which is outlined, is not the only possible one, but is an example and thereby also

---

[4] A brief description of the study programme of these first year studies, also showing a complexity, is given by the head of the study board, Egon Moesby, in Moesby, 2002.

subject to continuous discussion. For the aim of contributing to the explicit discussion of the underlying intentions of PBL, the argumentation that has lead to the framework is more important than the resulting image in figure 1. The crucial point of this argumentation is that a perception of learning and knowledge is a complex phenomenon, subject to historical changes and to cultural differences. Discussions of ideals of learning and knowledge should pay attention to the complexity, the historical changeability, and the cultural variety. In an actual situation, when discussing the perception of learning and knowledge at a university in year 2003 for instance, explication of frameworks for the complexity may be fruitful for promoting the discussion.

## 5. CALL A SPADE A SPADE!

One question still ought to be given. Is the case that only one proper kind of didactics exists, for instance a variety of the concept of PBL, or may other didactics, which are different to PBL, be relevant or 'good'? Should we open our mind to the relevance of different didactics, in relation to different aims of learning and knowledge, actualised in different study-elements during the progress of an education?

The following consideration will substantiate the question. In a project-organised model, and during the process of the project work, relevant theories and methods should be applied. In order to apply relevant theories, the students need to have a profound knowledge of these theories. Proper knowledge of the theories is a precondition, firstly when choosing a theory, which is relevant to the case of the project, secondly for being able to apply the theory. However, a dilemma may appear. In a project, which is centred about a case, the students should apply relevant theories, but they cannot do this, if they have not learned about the theories.

Theories may be learnt by means of participating in courses and by reading theoretical textbooks. In order to acquire a deeper understanding of specific theories, it may be important that the students work with cases, in which these specific theories will have to be used. Then, in some study elements, it may be relevant that cases have their starting points in the theories that should be learned, not in 'problems, potentialities, and values'. For the specific purpose of such study elements, it may therefore also be relevant to formulate a case as a specific task, such as 'Make the apparatus X!'. Particularly, with reference to a specific purpose, a case like this may be 'good'. However, as it is emphasised above, the project has a rather closed character. If fundamentally PBL is defined by an open approach, then the project is outside the framework of PBL.

My suggestion is that we call a spade a spade, and that we search for suitable concepts for different didactics. Should this not be the case, we may loose the ability to distinguish. If we use the concept of PBL so widely that it covers all kinds of 'good learning', then the consequences are that the concept will loose its function as an ideal. Hence it will not be considered a leitmotif for the development and the assessment of practise.

## REFERENCES

Adolphsen, Jes (1985). *Problemer i videnskab. En erkendelsesteoretisk begrundelse for problemorientering.* Aalborg Universitetsforlag, Denmark.

Moesby, Egon (2002). *From Pupil to Student - a Challenge for Universities: an Example of a PBL Study Programme.* In: UICEE, UNESCO International Centre for Engineering Education. Global Journal of Engineering Education. *Vol. 6, N° 2, page 145-152.* Melbourne, Australia - Aalborg, Denmark.

Popper, Karl (1979). *Objective Knowledge. An Evolutionary Approach.* Clarendon Press, Oxford.

# NEW REALITIES AND THE IMPLICATIONS FOR PROBLEM-BASED LEARNING

## The Case of Business Administration

Olav Jull Sørensen

**Abstract**: The background for this article is the big changes we have experienced since the idea of the problem-based learning model at Aalborg University was conceived in the beginning of the 1970'ies. Assuming that no teaching model is context free, the challenge is to confront the basics of the problem-based learning model with the new realities of today. Three new realities are discussed, the new global realities, the new business realities, and the new realities at individual level.

The new realities challenge the problem-based learning model. Adjustments are needed in terms of closer co-operation with reality and thus integration between formal and experiential knowledge; more focus on creation and action (not just reflection); more possibilities for individual performance and the orchestrating of individual study programmes, and more focus on seeing the problem-based learning model in terms of long-life learning and, finally, the integrative use of ICT and the Internet. If these modifications are made, the problem-based learning model will be able to cope with the new realities to a larger extent than more conventional university models.

## 1. INTRODUCTION

The problem-based learning model - the Aalborg University version - can celebrate its 30th anniversary. The idea was conceived and the experiments started in Aalborg in 1972 as part of the establishment of the 3-years B.Sc.-Degree Programme in Business Administration under the auspices of the Copenhagen Business School. At that time, we barely could put words on what we were doing, but the experiences from the experiments in these first two years before the Aalborg University Centre (now Aalborg University) were used and very influential in the decision to adopt the model for the whole of the university. The author was together with a small group of colleagues [1] responsible for the experiments and for assuring that the 60 students on the programme would be able to graduate and be able to get jobs based on this new pedagogy, embedded in the concept of problem-based learning.

30 years have elapsed and the problem-based learning model has established itself as a reputable way of developing young people at university level. The basics of the model are still the same, but it has been refined and different versions have been introduced. The model has also been debated continuously and vigorously and the model itself has »graduated« to become subject for scientific investigation alongside other modes of learning. This has recently culminated in the establishment of a separate Department for Learning at Aalborg University.

The aim of this article is to confront the problem-based learning model with the new realities of today. Many changes, from the global to the local and individual level, have taken place since the problem-based learning model was conceived and developed 30 years ago. The question is if the model is able to adjust to and absorb the changes that we can observe at the global level as well as at the individual level. The challenges are multiple: Concurrent with the internationalisation of Aalborg University, will, for example, the problem-based learning model be able to accommodate different cultures; Concurrent with increasing environmental turbulence and uncertainty, will the reflection oriented problem-based learning model be able to deal with this turbulence, and concurrent with the tendency to see learning as a life-long process, can the problem-based learning model be enhanced to view students as partners beyond the graduate level. These and other major changes - the new realities - will de discussed in relation to the problem-based learning model.

The article comprises six sections. Section two briefly describes the pedagogical experiments from 1972-74 within the framework of the mentioned B.Sc.-programme in Business Administration. Section three presents and discusses the new realities, that any university pedagogy must be able to handle, and section four, under the heading of »the next generation of the problem-based learning model«, discusses the further development needed for the model to be a cutting edge learning and knowledge development instrument. Finally, section six summarises the discussions.

## 2. THE EXPERIMENT IN THE EARLY 1970'IES

In 1972, it was decided to start a Bachelor's Degree-Programme in business administration in Aalborg under the auspices of the Copenhagen Business

---

[1] Among them are the present Rector for Aalborg University, Sven Caspersen, Preben Sander Kristensen, and Svend Petersen. This group was later joined by Bengt Åke Lundwall, Jørgen G. Rasmussen, Ruth Emerek, Lennart Nørreklit, Poul Israelsen, and Flemming Larsen.

School. I.e., two years before the new Aalborg University would be established but alongside the planning of the new university. New staff members were recruited, the author of this article being one of them. The new faculty consisted of very young people (around 30 years of age most of them), coming from the two existing business schools in Denmark and a few from Sweden. They represented the various academic disciplines of which a general business administration degree is composed. More important, perhaps, is the fact that the new staff-members had more or less actively supported and taken part in the student revolts and experiments in the 1960'ies. Politically, the picture was somewhat mixed, but most were leftist oriented.

The debates among this new staff were often long and heated both over content and over the pedagogy to be applied. However, time was short. [2] The authorities of the Copenhagen Business School had to agree to the proposals and, most important, the group of young staff-members wanted to take advantage of this opportunity to create a new educational model. This made the group agree in the end and the new studies took of September 1972 with around 60 students.

Looking back in the personal archives of the author, it appears that some of the key words of the planning documents were: Inter-disciplinary and multi-disciplinary research, critical research, problem orientation and definition, group and project work, co-operation with business, alternative perspectives to the conventional ones in business, methodology related to problem-based projects, etc. The same words dominate today but at that time, we were uncertain as to what they meant.

The context in which the new pedagogy was to be implemented was not discussed to any large extend. It was clear that the class struggle of Capitalism was the overriding framework for understanding business and this made us focus on employees and workers, work organisation and the relations between workers/employees and management and the capital owners. Globally, the content reflected the virtues of the models of Communism, Socialism and Capitalism respectively and their empirical manifestations in the USA, the Soviet Union, China, Yugoslavia and the developing countries. The Centre-Periphery theory was the core theory for understanding the global reality. The content of the curriculum was not revolutionised. The key word was to put conventional business wisdom into perspective.

Students were assumed and believed to be were much like us, i.e. critical ori-

---

[2] The first official meeting of the new colleagues took place in May 1972, 31/2 months before the first batch of students would be in the classroom.

ented and eager to be more participative in the organisation and conducting of their studies.

The business community was not directly consulted, but some were sceptical as indicated by an article in the local newspaper with the title »What is it they give us«, criticising the pedagogical approach. In the very second year of the new programme, however, we made a very decisive move towards the business community by developing the concept of »The Holistic Firm« as a framework for co-operating with a number of local companies. The idea was that each group of students would work closely together with a company for a semester and identify crucial problems and their solutions in the course of the project period. Letters in my archives indicate that we prepared well for the project and that it was not easy in the first year to get the nine companies we needed. However, we succeeded and the business community gradually welcomed the initiative. The fact that the this very component of the business programme still exists, and pretty much unchanged, testifies to this break-through for the problem-based learning model's acceptance by our environment.

In general, the model developed through these early experiments had the following main features:

- Lectures and project work in a 50:50 split
- Project work in groups of student (5-8)
- Project work was directed by means of themes
- Focus on problem formulation and methodology for how to solve the problem
- Problems were real life ones; i.e. business or business related problems.
- Close supervision of students' project work
- Theory-practice integration.
- Few exams and exams based on the projects rather than on the courses

As the experiment ran alongside the planning of Aalborg University, obviously these fresh results from the field were eagerly received and used in the planning process, including used to convince the more sceptical parts of the coming university.[3]

---

[3] The author left Aalborg University for 21/2 years for Ghana from 1976 and summarised his experiences in a working paper: (Sørensen, O. J. 1977): On Theory and Practice in Education - with special emphasis on Education in Business Administratioon. Working Paper Series, vol. 77-1, School of Administration, University of Ghana. The paper did not pave the way for similar changes in the School of Administration. Similarly, the experiences are summarised in (Kristensen, 1975) and the Aalborg model for business education is also presented and discussed in a special issue of Civiløkonomen: Uddannelsen ved AUC (Educational Programmes at AUC): Civiløkonomen, vol 24, no. 10.

## 3. THE THREE NEW REALITIES

Moving from the early experiments to the new Millennium, the new realities, to which the problem-based learning philosophy must adjust as well as influence and shape, will be discussed under three headings:

- New Global Realities.
- New Business Realities
- New Individual Realities.

### 3.1 New Global Realities [4]

A new global context is emerging, driven by especially economic liberalisation and technological innovations and with political and cultural changes tailoring these two main drivers. The new global reality is best described as »complex« and »uncertain« as to its trajectory and destination, issues, which have severe consequences for both the content and the pedagogy of educational programmes. Before elaborating on the implications, the content of the new global reality will be discussed in some details.

The liberalisation trend and thus the globalisation of the economy started in the 1980'ies when more and more developing countries accepted the World Bank's national restructuring programmes. The trend got momentum in the 1990'ies, when the World Trade Organisation (WTO) replaced the GATT as the forum for discussions and agreements on liberalisation and especially when the Soviet Union and its East European satellites collapsed and opted for a market driven and open economy.

The liberalisation has made the flow of goods, services and money more free, while the free flow/movement of people has faced many obstacles and is a highly politicised issue. The free movement of labour is just one of the issues. Refugees is another, cross-border criminality a third, and »green-card«-programmes a fourth. The problems related to the free flow of people have also educational implications. First of all, it slows down the creation of a global educational market and secondly, it creates problems for establishing exchange programmes for students on a global scale.

The second major trend is the emergence and development of multiple new technologies. The technological drive is led by information and communica-

---

[4] See, for example, (Dicken, 2003) for a discussion of global trends.

tion technologies (ICT), but many other technologies, the potential of which we cannot even imagine, are on the agenda, including materials technology, nano-technology and biotechnology. Every day, the media report on one or more new technologies, which we never thought of.

The complexity and uncertainty related to the globalisation of the economy and the technological innovations imply that it is difficult, if not impossible, to find any pattern of development compared to more stable periods and situations. Forecasting and planning, based on past patterns, become increasingly difficult. We can take note of what happened, but it cannot be used for forecasting and planning. Every day must be created anew, so to speak.

This situation has implications for both research and teaching. When science finds fewer »universal laws«, the teaching must be altered towards a more participative pedagogy. Furthermore, the development of the IC-technologies implies access to more information and knowledge through the Internet, which comprises a large chunk of what we know today. The IC-technologies also provide opportunities to communicate and interact virtually in time and space and be instrumental in the innovation processes. How can the face-to-face and reflection oriented problem-based learning model adjust to this situation?

The multiple new technologies have given rise to what today is called the knowledge society and economy. This term indicates that technology is not just a technical matter. The new technologies have implications of how we organise our economic life and society. The new technologies cannot be developed unless we turn society in general and firms in particular into learning and knowledge generating institutions. Simple learning is not enough. We must also learn how to learn.

The new global reality has, as mentioned, also a political and a cultural dimension. The high speed with which liberalisation has occurred has not been paralleled by an equally high speed in the creation of political and cultural institutions, which can match and thus create a proper framework for the development of an ethical and sustainable global market economy. It is only natural that it takes time, because while global companies know of no borders, the border is the very essence of a nation state and thus of the power of the politicians managing the state. Certain non-governmental organisations, e.g. Green Peace and human rights organisations, may in fact match the economic liberalisation better than the political institutions and they are also in the lead concerning promoting a global orientations and mind among ordinary people across nation states.

The new global reality, across the dimensions elaborated above, makes it paramount that morals, ethics, aesthetics and values in general are put in the forefront. Many of the new technologies will challenge our conventional values related to human beings; the globalisation of the economy will confront different cultures and thus value system; the quest on natural resources will require that we develop a set of nature-human related values, and the speed of liberalisation makes it essential that managers and investors are provided with a set of values, which are in accordance with an ethical and sustainable business community.

Thus, overall, the new global reality implies complexity and uncertainty alongside the need for solid technological skills to take part in the innovation process and the knowledge economy at large. These qualities must be embedded, so to speak, in an ethics and moral codex. Is the problem-based learning model, with its focus on particular problems, able to develop such a complex graduate or human being?

## 3.2 The New Business Reality

How do the new global realities transform into new business realities? Broadly speaking, the agenda of business today consists of four items:

- Globalisation/internationalisation of mind and activities
- Innovation and development
- Legitimacy
- Environmental sustainability

Appropriate answers to these four points on the agenda transform into the conventional business virtues; Efficiency, effectiveness, competitiveness and profit.

***Globalisation/internationalisation of mind and activities.*** As the business community needs graduates with qualifications (skills, competence, and appropriate values and orientations) related to one or more of these agenda points, obviously it is essential to discuss the agenda in more details to formulate a platform for appropriate educational programmes and discuss the extent to which the problem-based learning model is able to deliver.

International positioning of products has been on the agenda in most companies for a number of years, but the internationalisation agenda is increasingly turning into a globalisation agenda. This means that all business functions and activities (not just sales) are globalised, including production abroad, outsourcing, finance, and innovative strategic alliances with partners abroad, employment, etc. Globalisation is thus a complex venture and a journey into uncertainty as each step in the process takes the firm into new land.

**Innovation and development** is crucial for survival and competitiveness of companies. To build an innovative company involves:

* Competence in core technologies
* The building of a learning and entrepreneurial organisation
* The creation of global network and positioning in dynamic clusters to get access to resources controlled by others.

Solid knowledge in a technological or managerial field and thus classical university virtues is crucial for companies, but it is not enough. Innovation at a high speed also involves an integration of formal and experiential learning and knowledge and it involves the virtues of the entrepreneur, embedded in an existing company. Furthermore, innovation is not today a question of concealed labs, but innovation at a high speed and at an advanced level often takes place within a network of partners with complementary resources.

**Legitimacy** is increasingly on the agenda of companies. Conventionally, a business is legitimate if the market accepts its products. Today, it is not that simple. Many stakeholders around the company keep an eye on how the company behave: The stockholders are interested in the bottom line; customers interested in quality and green customers also in the environmental friendliness of the products and the production process; Workers are concerned with work conditions, career possibilities, image, etc.; »green organisations« watch the environmental sustainability of firms, and human rights organisations watch for violations such as in case of child labour, poor work conditions, etc. Values come to the forefront and companies increasingly present their values in terms of »a positive story«, »branding«, and the preparations of various accounts, e.g. a green account, and various events and community supports. The moral and ethical standing, the loyalty, and the understanding of the corporate culture of the employees become crucial to the companies.

Finally, *environmental management* has become an essential part of a company's strategic planning both because of regulatory requirements and market pressures, but also because greening a company may mean cost savings, healthier employees, new products, etc. Ecology is not just a constraint on the company's activity. It is increasingly becoming a competitive parameter.

Looking across the four points on the business agenda, it appears that companies look for graduates and thus educational programmes which give the graduates solid skills, innovative and entrepreneurial competence, social capital and communicative skills, team-spirit, and a set of values which match the culture of the firm. Is the problem-based learning model ready for this mix of academic virtues and personality traits and values?

### 3.3 The New Individual Reality

The final of the three new realities concerns the changes in individuals, their personality traits and behaviour. Compared to the time, when the Problem-based Learning pedagogy and the underlying worldview was conceived, have the youth culture in general and the student culture in particular changed?

In a recent investigation of Aalborg University concerning students' inclinations to become entrepreneurs or intrapreneurs (Sørensen and Ivang, 2002 and 2003), it was, among others, found that students want to create something, make a difference so to speak, and that they want to use the knowledge they receive through their studies as a platform for their creations. They are also performance oriented and want to show their capabilities. Furthermore, they are, based on the philosophies of the 1960'iesgeneration, brought up with having to make decisions and take a stand on hundreds of issues and the number of issues have increased tremendously since the 1960'ies, far beyond the imagination of the creators of this philosophy of independence. [5] Today, students increasingly want to compose or orchestra their own life and their own studies both in terms of content, time and space.

Compared to the 1960'ies and the time when the problem-based learning model was conceived, it is commonly held that young people today are individualistic and even egoistic. It is, as observed above, true that young people want to perform and in general want to »stage themselves«, i.e. orchestrate their own life. However, this is not the same as labelling them individualistic as such. On the other hand, they are not group- or collective creatures as assumed in the early versions of the Problem-based Learning model. They are more like team players in the sense that they know the virtues of the group, but they also know its weaknesses. Perhaps, we can say that they try to combine the strengths of the group (diversity, synergy, capacity, etc) with the strength of the individual (action, entrepreneurship, etc.). The group is to the students a forum and they are members of many such fora. At the same time, the new global realities, as indicated above, both create many opportunities and threats, which the group cannot resolve for the individual students.

---

[5] This section draws on (Andersen's studies of youth culture 2001).

Two final characteristics of the students relate to the mode of studying. It was already mentioned that a tendency for each student to orchestrate his/her own studies in content, time and space could be observed. To this can be added, that today there is a tendency for students not to read a complete book and reflect over its content, including its understanding of reality. Today, students »search and make surveillance«, in particular on the Internet, which, with its millions of web pages, contains much of what is known today. The term, »to go and Google«, has become part of the vocabulary and learning mode of students.

Finally, already at the time when the problem-based learning model was developed, it was clear that the »filling station model« of a university was left behind and replaced by a »reflection model«. Instead of just providing theories to students, who then, after graduation, would apply them as part of their job, the problem-based learning model would teach students, how to integrate theory and practice when on the job. The importance of practice (read experiential learning) in the problem-based learning model, even made this author write an article on the time, when universities were not needed anymore. However, what was not foreseen at the time when the problem-based learning model emerged was the need for continuous or life-long learning. As indicated in the discussion of the new global realities, new knowledge is generated at a very high speed, and it is therefore important that students both get solid basic knowledge and learn how to learn. Already today, students do come back to the universities for a refill. However, this is only the simplest of life-long learning methodologies. We can envision much more integrative models between theory and practice, between university and former students based on ICT and the former students in much more intensive dialogues with each other, with present students and with the researchers from the university. In fact, the dialogue, it may be envisioned, will often result in the mutual generation of new knowledge.

In addition, there is a trend for students, after graduation, not just to accept various courses, seminars and training programmes as part of life-long learning, but that they see this learning as part of their career path and thus want certificates, diplomas and degrees, that can be used to get interesting jobs and thus a career to their liking.

## 4. THE NEXT GENERATION OF THE PROBLEM-BASED LEARNING MODEL

In the opening statement of this article, I mentioned that the problem-based learning model is not context free and the aim of the article is to find out, if the model will be able to cope with the three new realities presented and discussed above. In this final section, I will try to give an answer.

Basically the answer is YES and I will go as far as to say that a university cannot survive if it does not adopt the basics of the problem-based learning philosophy. They may develop different versions, but they cannot escape the basics of the model.

The three new realities have, however, implications both in the content of the educational programmes and in the pedagogy used. It has also implications in the relations between teaching and research.

## 4.1 Closer Contacts to and Interaction with Business

»The problem« is the starting point for the problem-based learning model. Different groups, even within Aalborg University, have interpreted this term differently. Within engineering studies and to some extent also business studies, the term has been interpreted as finding a solution to a real life problem in a real life business. Others have not seen problem-based learning as »the action research of business« [6], but used actual problems for purposes of reflections over and understanding of real life. In this case, the students may not even have direct contact to real life people, but use literature, studies, etc. Finally, some have interpreted the term as also encompassing »theoretical problems«, e.g. the combining and integration of two theories. An example is a student group, which attempted to combine psychology based consumer behaviour theories with cultural theories.

The new realities outlined earlier make it imperative that the interaction between real life firms, organisations and institutions becomes more direct and intensive. As reality is complex and uncertain with no universal patterns to rely on and as the firms, organisations and institutions are themselves part of the process of constructing the new realities; it is essential for students to be in close contact with reality.

To elaborate, by participating, students learn about the complexity and uncertainty at the same time as they participate in the very construction of the new realities. The close interaction is thus not to make the work of the

---

[6] In the 1960'ies and 70'ies, much research was critical of especially the operations of multinationals. The author wrote, for example, two critical papers: »Business Research: The Action Researh of the Firm« (together with Jørgen G. Rasmussen, 1980). The paper was presented at a Conference for Socialist Economists. In another paper, the author used his knowledge of business economics to create a platform for consumer movements:«Towards an Action Parameter Model for Consumers«. (Sørensen, O. J. 1977)

students instrumental to the firms and organisation with whom they co-operate. It is for the students to learn how to learn and thus reflect over and generate new knowledge based on real world problems.

The same tendency can be observed in research. When reality is turbulent (in the words of the journalist), uncertain (in the words of the manager), and complex (in the words of the scientist) and it is difficult to find any patterns, routines and other manifest expressions of what direction reality is moving in, the only way to deal with it, is to be more engaged and get hands-on insights which can be used for reflections and theorising. Thus, students and researchers have a common interest in a closer co-operation with real life firms, organisations and institutions and the problem-based learning models have the basic qualities for this move towards closer interaction and co-operation.

## 4.2 Students Wish to Create, Perform and Orchestrate own Studies

The problem-based learning is well known for curbing the dominance of the teacher and turning him/her into a supervisory or even mentor role. Students (in groups) are expected to become more active and work independent under guidance. It varies from one educational programme to another, but often students have direct influence on up to 50% of the educational activities.

At the same time, due to the close relations between the various educational activities during, for example, a semester, the problem-based learning model work with »packages«, which cannot easily be broken.

To be able to cope with the new individual realities, adjustments are needed in the following areas:

From group-work to teamwork enabling flexibility as to group size, exam forms, and project form. The group may be a network or a forum and the project can be a set of individual papers around a common theme. Some exams should be individual exams, even if the project is a group work, in order to give the students an opportunity to test their own performance capacity (and thus how much they are able to contribute to a group). In general, the project should be closer to reality as indicated above and often more action oriented as in case of creating a new company. In addition, different sizes of projects may be used.

As to how to cope with the tendency among students to orchestrate their individual educational programme, it is obvious that the mentor role of the teachers take on new dimensions. Basically, each student has to have a »global« mentor who discusses the educational programme as such with students. This augmented role would include issues such as:

• Studies versus job and career
• Studies abroad
• Internships and in general the integration of theory and practice
• The purpose of study leaves to develop other qualities
• Personality development and communicative abilities

## 4.3 The Multi-cultural Setting

Although the global educational market is not yet a reality, a number of educational programmes at many universities are already recruiting globally. From this trend towards a global market for education, it is clear that the problem-based learning is not context free.

In general, foreign students, coming from more conventionally structured universities, find the problem-based learning model attractive. They experience for the first time, that someone will listen to them, and what they say and think matters. However, this love at first sight also is a source of frustrations when the students realise that it involves more than reading a text and presenting it. The study culture around problem formulation, methodology discussions and theoretical reflections is complex and, at times, in contrast not just to their own study culture but in relation to their national culture. Bringing these students from universities based on »listening and reproducing« to be able to practice independent thinking under democratic forms and being reflective, critical and constructive at the same time, is a challenge. When such issues as language barriers, loosing face-issues, and away from a comforting network are added, the challenge is even bigger. Obviously, special attention to these students is required and the only reason that the problems may be overcome is that the students from such societies are highly motivated and able to work hard. Furthermore, each student is of course unique but even so, it is possible to define some main differences between students from Asia, Africa, the former Soviet Union and Latin America and, thus be able to pay special attention to each group of the students.

## 4.4 Life-Long Learning

As argued earlier, learning in the new knowledge economy is a life-long venture. A little reflection mayreveal, however, that life-long learning is not as new as we may think. Previously, implementing the received knowledge in actual jobs followed university studies. In learning terms, formal learning of science-based knowledge was followed by experiential learning from doing and acting in, for example, a business reality. If the experiences obtained are reflected, they become useful knowledge to the firm.

Life-long learning in the contemporary understanding of the concept does not have this clear distinction between formal and experiential learning and knowledge. In fact, the knowledge economy cannot become a reality unless we blend the two categories of learning.

The blend required of formal and experiential learning and knowledge, will vary over time. Teaching students with little experience is very different from teaching when the participants have an extensive practical experience. In short, in the first case, students need reality events to see that theoretical concepts have a real manifestation. In the second case, the participants need new words and concepts to be able to create some order in the multiple experiences in the form of actions, observations, discussions, etc.

In the simplest form, life-long learning can be viewed as a knowledge refilling process of the former students. They are updated with the latest scientific/formal knowledge, including ways of looking at reality, new theories and new tools. This extension of the problem-based learning model seems not very appropriate and productive given the three new realities. A more advanced model is one where professors, present students and former students form a network, which continuously interact within the framework of a problem-based learning model.

An example will illustrate the more advanced model. A company has signed a contract with a university, the contract stipulating that the university is charged with the task of developing the employees within a certain section, e.g. the sections related to international activities. A problem-based learning model is used, including the possibilities for the employees to »graduate« at various levels from the programme. Included is also that projects for regular students will be part of the contract in order to explore the issues, both more ample and profound than it would be possible if the employees did it alone. Students will thus work together with the employees. The teachers will supervise but may even have their own research agenda as part of the contract and thus, alone or in conjunction with company employees build new knowledge and theories.

## 5. INTERNATIONAL BUSINESS AS AN ILLUSTRATION

The establishment and development of the M.Sc.-degree in International Business in 1984 at Aalborg University may serve, as an example of how some of the changes in realities have been dealt with and what still needs to be done.

In 1981, what was to become the Centre for International Studies started operating. The first initiative was to develop a specialisation year within »development studies«. Later in 1984, a M.Sc.-programme in International Business was established. [7] Both programmes were based on the problem-based learning model as outlined in section 2 with one major exception related to the interaction with companies and organisations.

Closer contact to and integration with business: The experiences from the bachelor degree in business administration in relation to co-operation with local companies during an entire semester were used to take the integration between theories and practice one step further. Students of International Business were (and still are) expected to take an internship abroad in a Danish or foreign company. Thus, instead of being located at the university and work in groups, which includes time-to-time visits at a company to interview and compile data, the internship-model positions each individual student within a company abroad. As outlined in the Guidelines for internships[8], the purpose of the internship is four-fold:

1. Practical work experience
2. Cultural insights and understanding
3. Integration of theory and practice
4. Enhance language capabilities

These four objectives are tested through two reports, the Experience Report outlining the tasks which the student has carried out, the culture within which he/she has worked as well as a description of the company, and the Project Report, which deals with and solve an actual business problem of the company.

*A multi-cultural setting:* In the late 1980'ies, we started internationalising the M.Sc-programme in order to be able to participate in the exchange of students within the EU-programmes. At first, the 2nd semester was converted into English and offered to our EU-partners. Gradually, we converted all four semesters into English, making it possible not just to have exchange students but to recruit students for the programme globally, and thus preparing the programme for the participation in the global educational market.

The internship abroad was attractive to many students and a selling point of

---

[7] Some years later, a European Study Programme was established followed by an engineering programme on International Technology Transfer focusing on developed- countries in transition. All programmes were based on the same ideas: Recruiting international and including a traineeship abroad as part of the programme.
[8] WWW.business.auc.dk/ivo.

the education. Around 2000, it became, however, clear that the problem-based model needed to be revised.

The issues related to the integration of foreign students are not new, but with 50% of the students being foreigners, it seems essential to pay special attention to the students to avoid isolation and fragmentation. Instead of seeing culture as a barrier, the point is to build on the potential synergies of having different cultures in the class. For example, in a project on youth culture and buying behaviour, a multi-cultural group is able to build the project by comparing the cultures in the countries they come from.

*The wish to orchestrate own study programme.* Apart from the cross-cultural issues, it also became clear that students wanted more flexibility. Some want to study abroad already in the first or second semester of the programme; some want a more intensive programme and a possibility to show that they can perform; some want to create their own business and look for opportunities during their studies to prepare themselves. To deal with such individual issues, the semesters have been redesigned and organised around »theme blocks« where two-three fields (problem areas) are integrated and where the students under various forms (case, mini-project, and seminars) work on these themes alone, as teams with a mix of individual and group performance, or in groups with collective efforts. Exams are in some cases individual and in other cases it is a group exam. Within these blocks, it is easier to cater for the special needs of certain groups of students, including training them in delearning old study habits. The blocks with a blend of topics also provide us with flexibility, making it possible to adjust to frequent changes in business reality.

Life-long learning: Life-long educational programmes are on the agenda, but have not seriously been dealt with until now. In 1985, however, an experiment was conducted in collaboration with the Association of Exporters in North Jutland. The experiment was based on problem-based learning principles and the aim was to develop the international activities of companies. The 10 participants were export managers with strategic responsibility for the internationalisation of the companies. Apart from lectures and discussions, groups of companies were formed to discuss future strategies of each of the member companies in the group. Each group had one-two facilitators from the university to manage the collaboration and to put into perspectives the multiple experiences presented by the companies. Apart from having the strategies and activities of ones own company analysed and discussed, the participating managers had the opportunity to train themselves in analysing and providing recommendations to other companies. The results of this experiment are described in (Sørensen, O. J. 1985).

# 6. SUMMARIES AND CONCLUSIONS

What triggered this article were the big changes we experienced since the idea of the problem-based learning model was conceived in the early 1970'ies as part of building a new Bachelor's Degree in Business Administration and in conjunction with the establishing of Aalborg university in 1974. Assuming that no teaching model is context free, the challenge was to confront the basics of the problem-based learning with the new realities of today.
The new realities were described at three levels, the new global trends, business oriented new realities, and new realities pertaining to the individuals - the students.

The new global realities comprise the liberalisation of the economies, implying a freer move of goods and money and a freer move of people although this has become a very sensitive area politically, related both to employees, pensioners, refugees and students. Thus, the global educational market is yet to be seen. The new global reality also includes the new multiple technologies, which at the same time create an abundance of possibilities, complexity, and uncertainty as to what is to come. Over and above the concrete new technologies, the concept of the knowledge society/economy has been coined to indicate that technological development is accompanied by deep restructuring of our organisations and institutions to both take advantage of the possibilities and cope with the consequences. It is not enough to learn. Increasingly we must learn how to learn and thus build a learning company or society.

At company level, the second new reality, the agenda reflects the new global reality. Internationalisation and innovation are two major points on the agenda. In addition, the firms are concerned with their legitimacy and the handling of the many stakeholders around the company. Small events can travel fast through the Internet and have severe consequences for the company. The legitimacy question has become even more important due to the speed of liberalisation and the lack of political institutions to regulate and manage the liberalisation. This has put at risk an ethical and sustainable market economy.

The individuals, i.e. the students, have also changed. It is commonly held that young people today are very individualistic and even egoistic. It may be more correct to say that they are team players with a blend of individual performance and collective support and responsibilities. Clearly, young people want to create, perform and stage themselves in various ways. Teamwork is part of it.

Confronting these three new realities with the problem-based learning philosophy, it is found that the model is still valid. In fact, it may be the only model, which can cope with the challenges embedded in the three new realities. However, adjustments are needed and the model has to be used in a flexible way.

In summary, the problem-based learning model must be altered as follows:

- Closer co-operation with reality, i.e. moving towards a higher degree of participation
- More flexibility as to projects, groups, exams, etc. to accommodate the inclinations of students to create, perform, and orchestra their own studies
- Develop special means to cope with foreign students from more conventional study cultures and national cultures, which have less focus on independence, own decision-making, etc.
- Develop different blends of formal and experiential learning and co-operate more intensive with firms, organisations and institutions in order to be able to organise life-long learning.

One new reality has only briefly been touched upon, that of the global educational market both for students and life-long learning. Does the problem-based model have a change, when it comes? Does the model have any selling points? It has been claimed that the pure model has no unique selling points anymore as so many universities have adopted elements of the model. This is true, but it is also true that most of those, which blend the conventional model with the problem-based one, will not be able to get the same results under the new realities. The reason is that the problem-based learning model, in the version presented here, will be able to generate new knowledge alongside bringing students to the graduate level. However, it is essential that the problem-based learning model is being »branded« more clearly.

## REFERENCES

Andersen, J. (2001). *Mellem hoved og krop. Om ungdomskulturer.* (Between Mind and Body: On the cultures of the youth). Systime, Viborg.

Dicken, P. (2003). *Global Shift. Reshaping the Global Economic Map in the 21st Century.* 4th edition, Sage, London.

Kristensen, P. S. (1975). *Problemorienteret erhvervsøkonomi (Problem-based Teaching in Business Administration).* Erhvervsøkonomisk Tidsskrift, vol. 39, no. 1.

Rasmussen, J. G. and Sørensen O. J. (1980). *Erhvers økonomi - kapitalens aktionsforskning. En karakteristik, kritik og nogle muligheder* (Business Economics - the Action Research of Business). Paper presented at Workshop on »Business Administration, Sector Analysis and Business Accounting«. Association of Socialist Economists. Copenhagen, February 23-24.

Sørensen, O. J. (1985). *Erfaringsbaseret og handlingsorienteret undervisning. Ny formel for efter- og videreuddannelse* (Experience Based and Action Oriented Teaching. New Formula for Post-Educational Training). *Erhvervsøkonomisk Tidsskrift, no. 2, 1985*.

Sørensen, O. J. (1977). *On Theory and Practice in Education - with special emphasis on education in Business Administration.* Working Paper Series, vol. 77-1, School of Administration, University of Ghana.

Sørensen, O. J. (1977). Efterlyst: En forbrugernes forbrugeradfærdsteori (Towards an Action Parameter Model for Consumers). In: Forbrugerproblemer og forbrugerpolitik, ed. by H. R. Rask and F. Ölander. Det danske forlag: Albertslund.

Sørensen, O. J. and Ivang, R. (2002). *Mod en innovations- & iværksætterkultur på Aalborg Universitet. Jeg vil gerne.. Tør jeg...?.* (Towards an Innovation and Entrepreneurial Culture at Aalborg University. I want ...but do I have the Courage..?). Part I. International Business Research Group, Department for Business Studies, Aalborg University.

Sørensen, O. J. and Ivang, R. (2003). *Mod en innovations- & iværksætterkultur på Aalborg Universitet. Jeg vil gerne.. Tør jeg...?.* (Towards an Innovation and Entrepreneurial Culture at Aalborg University. I want...but do I have the Courage..?). Part II. International Business Research Group, Department for Business Studies, Aalborg University.

Uddannelsen ved AUC *(Educational Programmes at AUC)*. Civiløkonomen, vol. 24, no. 10.

In addition, materials from the author's archives 1972-75 and 1983- were used.

# A PROBLEM-BASED CANON[1]

## – A draft for an alternative way to enhance progression in university studies

Erik Laursen and Jørgen Gulddahl Rasmussen

Abstract: In the article central trends of crisis for contemporary university studies are presented and reasons and possible remedies are discussed. The construction of a new kind of »methodological canon« is considered as a central remedy. The main subjects to be addressed in this perspective are: the goals for university education, the contemporary university student, and the suitable means for changing the didactics. Finally an example of this strategy for transforming the didactics is presented.

## 1. INTRODUCTION

The aim of this article is to discuss the possibility of solving, what we call a »difficult situation for the students« in contemporary university studies. A situation which could shortly be described by referring to three modern trends of the development of the universities. The discussion raised in the article is about the possibility of solving this situation by defining a new kind of canon using principles taken from general knowledge-production combined with selected pedagogical elements.

The accomplishment of this task requires more than a new pedagogical method. In the article we will argue in favour of the construction of a methodological canon by defining what goals to aim at for the educational activities. In addition we will look upon methods that are available within the present university didactic.

---

[1] A canon could be either: a) a general rule, standard or principle by which something is judged. b) a list of sacred books accepted as genuine (Oxford Advanced Learner, 1997). In this article we refer to both sets of meaning. The question can be defined the following way: What interpretation of the concept forms the basis of the ways the curriculum of university studies is organised?

## 2. CONTEMPORARY SIGNS OF CRISIS

For some years the universities in the western world have shown some distinctive tendencies of crisis. One tendency has been the de-centering of the disciplines and the studies. This de-centering has two aspects, one being a radical extension of the volume of information and knowledge in most disciplines taught at the universities. The other has been a growing tendency of the coexistence of a plurality of competing paradigms and theoretical schools and directions within most of the disciplines.

A second tendency refers to the fact that a growing part of the university students seems to perceive the universities as kinds of secondary schools. Schools where the teachers are expected to tell the students straight out what it's all about, including what is good, and what is bad, and exactly what is high quality. But most importantly they expect the teachers to specify which elements of knowledge and what competence the students have to learn if they are to play it safe and secure themselves a career. As a consequence of this attitude such students do not develop sufficient competence to reflect on their own study activities, or develop sufficient competence to make realistic evaluations of their own efforts and resources. Instead they demand strong and well-defined structures, short well-defined periods of study, precisely defined job opportunities, and an increasing number of exams.

Thirdly the university studies to a growing extent have developed into a number of loosely coupled modules, where it is up to the students to make choices between various alternative modules. Through sequences of such choices the students in principle can develop an individual profile of competence. But for many students the choice of specific modules is more precisely described as a way to avoid »unpleasant modules« and by doing this they try to survive yet another semester of study. The consequence of this tendency to prefer the easy alternatives is that the difficult and dull, but important elements of knowledge, offered to the students, tends to be avoided and consequently not learned by this group of students. What should have made up a nice progression throughout the entire program risk in this respect to become a repetition of already mastered methods to understand modules of disciplinary knowledge not properly tied together.

Although the issue discussed in this article is the possible future developments of a specific pedagogical method which is the problem-based, project-organised (pp-pedagogy) way of teaching and learning it seems evidently clear that the substantial part of these problems has not been created by specific pedagogical methods and strategies. More possible the factors behind are to be found in the social context and in the knowledge base for higher education in the age of late modernity. On the other hand it is also evidently clear to the authors of this article, that the contemporary tendencies of crisis for the universities in the western world, mentioned above have produced some severe problems especially for this specific pedagogical method. Let us point out a few of the most acute:

- In the principles of a pp-pedagogic it is up to the students within a framework defined by the Bachelor or Master program, to make a decision on which projects and problems they want to work on within a specific semester/term of the program. Together with the module-structure of contemporary program, to which we referred above, this causes to many students problems in defining a goal for their studies.

- An important aspect of pp-pedagogic is that it makes it necessary for the students constantly to evaluate their academic performance and of their learning process as well along the entire process of doing a project. This very important process of self-evaluating which should develop the vital modern competence of meta-cognition and meta-learning is severely limited. This limitation is caused by the tendency to ask for strong frames strong structures and the tendency to let the teacher alone carry the responsibility of deciding what is »relevant knowledge« and when the quality of the academic performance is acceptable.

- When the disciplines are developed into a complex mass of competing paradigms and discourses most programs try to handle the situation by expanding the curriculum and especially the courses. The consequence of this development is that it to a growing extent is impossible to deal with substantial parts of the course subjects through the projects accomplished in the semester. The consequence of this development is that a growing part of the courses is seen as irrelevant to the projects of the students. This situation creates to sets of problems. Firstly: how to evaluate those parts of the curriculum and projects, which are not part of the projects? Secondly: How to motivate the students for the growing part of the courses which to them form no immediately use-value for the project?

## 3. A DISCIPLINARY PERSPECTIVE ON THE PRESENT CRISIS

As mentioned above, the problems of contemporary higher education might have more profound discipline related reasons behind what more superficially could be taken for pedagogical problems for not always functioning well. One of the problems discussed in this article comes from the present development within most disciplines. Following the rapid development of knowledge important processes of de-centering appears. Today, most disciplines are on their highest ontological level not any more able to define one clear and undisputed centre or one uniting paradigm, but instead several different concepts and paradigms are found to influence the discipline, from its most everyday application to its most abstract level. This is of course very interesting and motivating seen in a research perspective. But as this article addresses university teaching and the learning of students the situation is not always felt so exiting, instead it often results in a number of learning difficulties not seen before.

What is the discipline all about, and what is the »core-competence« of the profession, is an increasingly important question. De-centring of the disciplines, where each discipline develops a plurality of centres fighting each other to become the main yardstick of truth and relevance, produces this unclear situation. This is definitely not any new development, but to an increasingly extent a new paradigm that is gaining ground within the discipline does not conquer the scene entirely and destroys the previous one. Today old and new paradigms coexist inside the discipline together creating a kind of stalemate situation. A situation that supported with the growth in disciplinary knowledge becomes one of great complexity.

Today, a large part of the students are confronting difficult problems when trying to learn what can be described as the necessary »core-competence« for their later professional life. This is especially true, if we do not focus on the group of students who are most suited for university studies and who seems to be able to survive and to learn even in the most difficult situation, but on the rest of the students. An important part of these problems are produced by difficulties in selecting and grasping the core information from the broad multitude of elements within the discipline combined with difficulties in understanding the relationships between these different elements. At the same time we can hear teachers complaining about difficulties in getting enough time and space to present all the new developments within the discipline for the students.

In fact these problems can be seen as coming from the increasing number of new findings, theories and models that develop within all disciplines. The cure is often seen as making the communication through teaching more efficient with an aim to get more disciplinary elements presented within a shorter period of time. To increase efficiency is of course possible to a certain extent, but as we see it from a position of a problem-based didactic, we have also been able rather quickly to see the limits for addressing more disciplinary elements. So we have to find a solution to this problem, and to find this is not just to add new elements to the curricula. The solution could instead be to set priority between the different elements. This is the development seen in the ongoing specialisation, which also can be found within many disciplines. But to set priority which also means to throw some elements away is perhaps not so easy. The difficulties emerge from the unclear criteria of what is relevant, what is important, and what is valid.

As mentioned earlier, this dynamic and unstable situation within the disciplines has always been an inspiration for researchers. The unstable dynamics of disciplinary development and the different trails of specialisation to explore are challenging. It also makes some students interested in engaging in the research work, but for a large group of students this situation where different paradigms are presented in their real complexity makes for them the study process unclear, threatening and somewhat irrelevant. What they see are perhaps models and theories belonging to different paradigms where the origins of these models are not clearly understood by them as students. Students who try to get a clear overall picture are in this situation caught in this unclearness, and they are increasingly asking for clearness. A demand communicated in questions on specific guidelines, textbooks, curricula, tools and techniques. A clearness that often unfortunately cannot be found the way it was found decades ago without ruining the contemporary validity of the discipline, which today is based on a multi-paradigmatic dynamic. Where this situation, years ago, was steered by the one and only canon of the discipline, then the post-monopolistic period of paradigms does not allow one but several often competing non-holistic canons to exist side by side within a discipline.

The discussion raised in this article is about the possibility to solve this difficult situation for students in another, perhaps unorthodox, way where the non-solvable problem of uniting the different paradigms into one traditional disciplinary canon is acknowledged. In this perspective also the support for the progression in knowledge and the motivation of students are taken into account. The task here is to try to define a new canon made from a more solid material that does not corrode so easily than the traditional one. This material has to be taken from some of the very old academic deeds of university, but melted and shaped in a new way. To do this we try to use principles taken from general knowledge-production and to support such principles by some important pedagogical elements. In this way the learning process aims through the interplay between theory and practice made by the student to make him/her able to learn at a higher methodological level and thereby bypass some of the difficulties presented above.

To do so requires more than just a new pedagogical method. Non-reflected use of problem-based learning does not give better results on this field than the more traditional methods of university teaching. Instead we will argue in favour of the development of a methodological canon created by defining what goals to aim at in a master program, and an analysis of the present situation of those students who is supposed to benefit from this canon. In addition we will look upon methods that are available within the present university didactic. These analyses have to be done before the structure of the actual pedagogical canon is outlined.

## 4. DEFINING THE GOALS

The aim of this reformulation of the canon is to make it easier to tie together the goals of a university education, needs of contemporary students and the increasingly dynamic process of disciplinary development. In this context the goals of university education will be the first theme to discuss.

The objective that can be specified into goals of the university concerning education can be formulated in one sentence: to diffuse knowledge at the highest disciplinary level to students who have met the criteria for attending the university. In addition to this it is necessary to add that this knowledge has to be adapted of the students in ways so that they as Masters or Bachelors can make a living and fulfil a function in society and its firms and institutions. This might be further extended by stressing that in a dynamic economy and society this knowledge diffused to students have to be moulded by the same students in a way so it for them also in a longer time perspective keeps its value as constantly belonging to the highest level. This opens for a more detailed way of formulating the educational objective for the university into an academic, a professional and a practical goal. This way of seeing the goals also opens for ways to work on how they can be dealt with in practice to be fulfilled.

The academic goal of university education is formally the oldest and has to some extent been present throughout the entire history university education. From the beginning it was to understand and diffuse the Bible in the correct way. Later it was to understand the universe in different versions as this knowledge developed and changed during the following centuries. Today it is perhaps mostly to understand that final explanations for anything have not been discovered yet. But this only underlies that the primary goal is still of the same nature. It can be defined as an endeavour constantly to use critical methods to become a bit more knowable on what could be right and what definitely seems to be wrong. At the same time the word university in itself underlines that this knowledge has to be tested toward its context, previous understandings and its immediate consequences for existing knowledge. If the word, university, is going to have a meaning in the future, in our opinion these academic goals both have to contain the critical and constructive handling of the discipline, and some kind of general knowledge (the Bildung aspect of university). The reason for this is not the old traditions of university, but instead that it relates to the necessity of such elements for the contemporary Master as a partner in the continuing development of the discipline.

This weight on the academic goal is sometime seen as in opposition to the capability to act as professional within a work setting. The conflict that comes from this is understandable not at least because these two goals easily can be defined as fighting for the same limited amount of time, resources, and attention. Sometimes this discussion seems to build on a division between some Masters who are seen as professionals and some who are seen as academics. This division that might come from an older institutional division within the trade as well within the educational system - and problems in the not always successful integration of the binary system into one integrated - seems unproductive and should be forgotten.

To be able to forget, this demands instead that a dividing line between which types of work areas that in the future have to be handled by the combination of academic and professional competencies and what can be handled by a professional capability alone. This division is important because in earlier concept of university education it was possible to get the impression that work could be mastered by academic capability alone. What seems to be the reality today is that even theoretical research demands a lot of professional skills perhaps in the same amount as what is needed for a medical doctor, a barrister or a nurse. So when university education is on the agenda, the question should be how the academic skills that seems to be needed in a growing number of work areas and professions should be learned within the university, and which types of programs therefore should be taught at the university.

The interaction between the academic and the professional goals might roughly be described within the following elements:
- A broad general understanding, and acceptance, of the values and cultures of the profession and the work area.
- Competence to understand and taking part in the communication within the profession related to the various tasks of the profession.
- Knowledge of the most used models, concepts, methods and techniques used by the professionals within the field to understand, describe, analyse and solve typical work-related problems. And related to this general knowledge, having an understanding of the existence of different theoretical and methodological ways of interpreting and handling the complexities of the

field of practice, combined with a broad knowledge about the dynamic interaction between theory and applied theory.
- Competence to become a part of the day-to-day development of concepts models and techniques and so contribute to the continuous development of knowledge base of the profession.

These skills are related to how the third goal on practice is understood. To say that a university education also has a goal of diffusing practice and how methods and techniques are used in the practical work situation are met with very different reaction from the different disciplines and their agents within the university. These differences come from the practice and culture of the discipline, from the history of the discipline within university and from its techniques, models and paradigms. This will not be the subject here. Instead it will be seen as a fact that Masters and students increasingly asks for knowledge about practice, examples on how techniques are used at the work place, and for tools that can be used directly when they as fresh Masters are meeting their first assignment on the job.

These demands seem not only reasonable; they also today have great support among employers, union representatives, politicians, and civil servants within the educational sector. But such demands are not easy to cope with for the university. There are different reasons for this. One is that the university as an institution should not concentrate on techniques and tools already used today, but instead of those developing out of the theories and models of tomorrow. Another reason is that the increasing differentiation and speed of diffusion of new techniques makes it impossible for the university seriously to follow more than a few trends in the development of techniques. Thirdly to teach the students to operate the present techniques could have the effect that they stick to the well known, also when they operate as professionals.

On the other hand the university cannot in the zeitgeist of integrating the university into the society and into co-operation with knowledge-producing institutions in the form of private business and public institutions avoid this demand on knowledge about practice. So important is not only in research to avoid becoming too much involved in the development business. It is also to develop methods so important dimensions of practices become integrated in the educational tasks of the university in ways so that they support the attainment of the other two goals instead of becoming some kind of a hinder. The way this can be dealt with educationally is closely connected to what pedagogical and didactical concepts are developed.

In this perspective we could start by seeing the three educational goals connected to pedagogical perspectives at the different levels. To see such levels is not something new within the field of pedagogical theory, but can be followed back several decades. The four levels we want to refer to in this context are:

- The ability to learn techniques, methods, theories, models and concepts as they are under development within the discipline.

- The ability to reflect- and evaluate on these elements both in relation to a certain problem and in relation to a broader, general discourse.

- The ability to reflect on, and evaluate, how appropriate own skills and knowledge are in relation to the tasks and problems, which are to be confronted.

- The ability to participate in the development of the knowledge base of the discipline and of the profession

As we see it, this can be understood as a broad framework within which each study can define its own objectives in a more specified and concrete way. We also propose, based on our own experiences, that a concept of a methodological canon is based on problem-based learning. This includes the development of a concept of specific combinations of elements such as the selection of types of projects with specific qualities and learning potentialities. It also demands a selection of specific subjects or fields of study for the projects and of the types of problems which structure the specific set of academic or the student working on a project must accomplish professional problem solving that. The main question being: What types of projects- and problems, relating to which fields of study, must a student learn to master in order to become a competent professional in this very area?

This idea of a methodological »project-canon« is based on a constructivist concept, which defines that the disciplines are constructing their reality, epistemological- and methodologically speaking. This constructing process is carried out by producing a range of discipline-defined problems and the development of a specific set of practices to act, and reflects on the problems. To fulfil this in a problem-based methodological way the idea is that the sequence of projects the students have to work on through their of study should be structures in a way which leads them to develop the necessary competence to become a professional within their field of study. As a consequence of this specific criteria must be set in relation to each project of the students. This criteria is that the projects must be in accordance with - and as a whole cover the important elements of the canon of the discipline, defined as: ». A range of (the most important types of) discipline-defined problems and the range of a practices to act - and reflect on the problems« which constitute the discipline.

This position is in opposition to another understanding of the pedagogical use of project work. This is an understanding that considers project work a relatively open field of exploration and creativity where the students rather indiscriminately are free to follow their subjective interests within a broad context of discipline- and study-defined theories and methods. Our idea is, to develop the project-organised form of study into a more structured form, where it is the responsibility of the program to formulate a set of explicit, didactically-based demands on the form and content of the projects.

## 5. CONTEMPORARY STUDENTS

It has already been mentioned that the reason for addressing this subject is partly based on experiences we have done ourselves and problems pointed out by colleagues. It is that a substantial group of students reacts inadequately on the challenges they are presented for in their university studies. We want to underline that this is not reaction from all students, because the largest group of students works efficiently with the adaptation of new knowledge, and they seem to get substantial results out of their university studies, for some, nearly independently of the didactic used. So the students as input to university education discussed here are those who have formal qualifications to study, and to a large degree fulfil their studies, but with results not exploiting their full potentials. The more high-level students can be put in focus another time, but as we see it they will also be able to benefit from the principles presented here.

It should for many university teachers from their daily practice seem evident what type of students that is in focus here. They are those who in many ways behave in a manner they might have found appropriate in high school and in secondary school. They act, using a negative expression, as pupils. This can be heard in their requests for firm and solid answers, for knowing exactly and in detail what have to be read before the next lecture - although many teachers sometimes express a doubt about the actual reading of the defined texts before the next lecture. These students simply ask for more exams, and they express wishes for short well-defined study periods with clear goals attached to these activities. Demands which in many ways are logic if it was not for the nature of university studies - to build a competence to deal with the new and unknown within a conceptually and paradigmatic very complex area.

Of course some colleagues will say that such students are unable or unqualified to complete academic studies, and they should have become better instructed in primary and secondary school if they at all should have be allowed into the university. This is the easy answer for university teachers, but maybe this answer builds on two misconceptions. One is that these students substantially can learn better study practice during their basic schooling. The other is that the university can avoid this group of students. A group that meets normal standards to be allowed into the universities and at the same time looks as a growing share of the population of university students. At the same time these students are not to blame, what is to blame is a learning system not able to exploit their full potentials. So before raising the entrance level some background factors should be studied.

Several potential factors for the described behaviour can be examined. To narrow it down, it will here be defined as what the students have as input for university studies, including their biographical and contextual factors containing societal, institutional and personal elements that of course are interrelated, but here will be discussed preliminary in three separate paragraphs.

The societal element refers to the daily life in which the students are engaged outside university. Especially the immense input of information and the very influential channels of information play an increasingly strong role for all students. Hardly any students use newspapers and traditional periodicals as sources for information. On top of this the pleasure of reading seems to be left unnoticed by many students. Reading is for school or for specific useful information, but for information of other kinds the Internet and the mobile phone is increasingly important. This not only changes the informational landscape dramatically, it also challenges the school, the teacher, and the textbook on their expected validity and reliability seen from the perspective of the students.

The educational institutions are not only challenged by the competing channels of information, the system is also challenged by the so-called massification of higher education as it has been the reality for the last two decades. In many ways this increase in the number of students has not generally been met by new methods of instruction and training. Instead the increasing number of students and the diminishing amount of resources - at least per student - have been dealt with in the form of traditional cost cuts within the same basic educational structure. This has resulted in more students per group, per class and per lecture, which again has made it even more difficult for those students in focus here to get a profound understanding of what all these learning activities are useful for. Seen pessimistically the picture is that didactical experiments are symbolically supported, but not carried through, well-qualified teachers has fled into the work of research, and students have increasingly been asking for the confirmed result: »How do I have to perform to pass the exam?«

These problems are perhaps also a result of change in the »average« personality of students. Perhaps not in the form as it is often presented i.e. the new personality profile of the youth - such models seldom last for more than half a year, because then a new clever styling or advertising bureau has discovered the next profile. But behind this the overall change in society and its institution plays a role in the direction that the symbols of speed, of change and of discontinuity, which have an increasing impact on all of us, also mould the ways the youth senses their environment. Former norms of authority, hierarchy, tradition steered validity and continuity are not any longer part of symbolic world of the new students, not even to fight against.

To sum this up it is important to say that this does not result in a less qualified youth or in students, which are not able to study and to become competent Masters within their specific trade. On the contrary it represents the new generation of the knowledge-based society with its unclear trajectories, its contradictory goals and its broken and unfinished learning spirals. Therefore it is also important to recognise that these conditions not only defines a group of university students that most efficiently learns in a new way, it also defines an important need to transform major educational routes within the university. This article tries to give one perspective on this.

## 6. MEANS FOR TRANSFORMING THE DIDACTICS

As this article is published in an anthology on problem-based learning and due to the facts that both authors have worked with such learning methods for more than 25 years, such methods will form this presentation of means and relationships between means important for such a transformation. This does not mean that it is not possible to work on reforming the traditional canon by using other pedagogical means, but ideas for this is not within our field. At the same time it is important to say that for us problem-based learning has a potential to deal with these pedagogical tasks when it is used the right way though combination of the different learning elements [2].

Seen from the entrance position of the students and the goals to be reached in university education the combination of means have to have great importance as also the last thirty years' debate on increasing the quality in university teaching shows. These means are all those methods and techniques that

---

[2] The point of reference for this article is clearly the Problem Based Studies at Aalborg University and the example on how it might be solved, which is brought later in the text, is situated at the Business Administration Studies at the Social Faculty of this university. Anyway we see the theme raised in the article as much broader than the development of problem based studies in this field of study.

have been used to improve learning for more that 500 years will come into play, and they have to be scrutinised. The colloquium, the lecture, the assignment and the exam are important means, but also the group work, the project, the co-operation with external partners and the problem as means for increasing leaning are part of this.

Underlining the total sum of means is done to make it clear that the ability to reach the goals of university education is connected to all kinds of activities done by the students and not only the didactic of lecturing or the didactics of project supervision. At the same time the efficient organising of means is not only to reach the best possible technical cognition mechanism among the students, it is also a question of creating motivation, engagement and commitment among students as well as teachers. The most important mean to reach those goals is perhaps the most underestimated: The will and interest of the individual student to function as a moderator in these processes in the middle of her fellow students. To reach those goals together with the students means to support active students to act as learners for themselves individually, and as mentors for their fellow students as well, in a group and in the class.

What will be present here is an array of means we as teachers have used in our educational work or means we as developers of disciplinary or cross-disciplinary study programs have been assessing. Shortly these means can be outlined in the following conceptions: Problem, theme, group, class, exam, external collaboration, supervision, lecturing, guest lecturing, moderating, and semester/term. Within these conceptions it should be possible to outline the basic element of the problem-based learning process, i.e. the extended concept of a project. This basic concept contains different combinations of the elements mentioned above, and is as well a leaning tool for disciplinary knowledge, a method to look critically into strong and weak sides of this disciplinary knowledge, and a tool for engaging in development of new knowledge within the disciplinary field.

A project in this extended version could cover the entire study activities within a semester; it can be defined to cover half a semester or perhaps half of the student's time in a whole semester (the example could be 30, 15 or even 7.5 ECTS). Important is that this concept in an integrating form covers all forms of input; all forms of study activities, and all examination activities. At the same time a project in this concept is defined within a theme that can be disciplinary or cross-disciplinary. Therefore such a project will be able in content both to include theoretical, methodological and practical / empirical elements.

To call this a project refers to the organising principle, which structures the interplay between the elements. The overall idea is that the students are asked to write a project paper or -thesis, which describes the different ways the students have worked on a defined problem, using a selection of student-relevant methods, theories, concepts and models. Still the »project« is not only defined as the work the students put into writing the paper. As mentioned above the »project« is (re)- defined to cover the totality of student activities accomplished in a certain period organised under a certain theme.

Such a project unit starts with a presentation of the theme. Such a presentation can be done by a combination of persons practising within the field as operators, developers or producers of theory. From the start it should be clear that the students have to produce new knowledge within the theme and to present this in some way as part of the examination. Lectures should be given to students by scholars and from professionals. These lectures have to be followed by colloquiums or seminars where the students have a responsibility together with teachers to get to results including new knowledge about the theme. Here the teacher operates with a number of different functions: Facilitator, lecturer, moderator and evaluator. These activities together with textbooks, articles, visits outside the university - real or virtually - are all inputs to the work done by the students on the assignment which is an important part of the project, and the examination is also a part of the project with considerable weight on its feedback.

Two main principles are behind this didactical form. One is that all educational activities are integrated within the theme. The other is that the theme activities are a combination of inputs from academics and professionals, student activities and combined activities. These activities can take place in all kind of group sizes. Lecturing can be executed for all students within the theme, seminars can be executed in classes of 20 to 30 students, and activity on assignments can be worked upon students individually by students gathered in groups with size of four to seven and in large groups of perhaps 15 students. In fact entire classes can be divided into groups, which together share a common responsibility for exploring important aspects within the theme. The exams have to serve two purposes. One is to act in its normal control functions the other is to round off the theme and to define what should be learned.

There are two kinds didactical frames build up around the project. Firstly, there is the theme which outlines the possible contents of the projects, the students are allowed to choose to work on. Secondly, there is the selection of methods the students are obliged to work with doing this specific project. The didactical goals of each project-period is defined as competencies in relation to specified academic actions like comparing, describing, evaluating, criticising, explaining, constructing, etc. The progression the students are to accomplish during their line of study is mainly described through organising the order of methods the students have to learn through the study.

The combination of the defined theme and the selection of obligatory methods used in relation to the theme offers to the students a structure, a direction, and tells them what the relevant student activities are. At the same time this frame also leaves free space in relation to the selection and articulation of the concrete problem as the object of their project where the students can make their own independent decisions in accordance with their interests.

## 7. DIDACTICAL PBL STRUCTURES - AN EXAMPLE

The educational elements integrated within themes are the basic structures that should be gradually advanced throughout a bachelor and a master program. These different themes form together the specificity of the program of the discipline and form the progression necessary to reach the goals of university education. This integrated form is not only introduced to secure that one-way teaching activities are not left alone and their output quickly forgotten. It is also introduced, because experiences done by us, and by colleagues of us, have shown that this integrated form really motivates the great majority of students to participate and learn more actively.

The basic form contains the three kinds of goals to be reached at different learning levels in a number of learning activities. As the weight on the different goals can differ from discipline to discipline the learning levels can be attached differently by using different combinations of learning activities. But the integration within the single theme, the progression from theme to theme and the composition of learning levels has to be structured throughout the entire program. This is not a didactical form that is completely steered by students or by the students and teachers within a single theme. This is a didactic that demands an overall strategic steering which leads to reaching the educational goals for all students.

This specific structuring has to be decided by those in charge of the different disciplinary programs, in our case the study boards. Therefore this article will only give an example from disciplinary fields we are familiar with. We will here use examples from a program, which is under way and which is a Master program within business administration specialised in management of innovation. This program has not yet fulfilled all the educational goals we have presented above, because it is under construction, but these goals are constantly parts of an educational discourse within the planning group.

The way the didactical principles have to be used can be illustrated firstly by examples from the start of this program in business administration (the MIKE program). A program that is attended by students of different nationalities and with bachelor exams from different institution and that has to build a bridge between experiences of the students from different cultures. This demands from the start an overall presentation of the state of the art of the discipline with a balance between presentation of commonly accepted stepping-stones within the field and an opening toward the existence of contradictory paradigms. These elements have to be presented by academics, but stressing the relationship to the professional world can be done through inviting practitioners in as guest lecturers. For the students it is important that they start to learn the discipline by some individual or group work on rather fixed assignments resulting in an oral or written presentation that is assessed in an exam.

This will be followed by a number of lectures and seminars where the students are presented for and urged to discuss in seminars on important fields within the field they have chosen. In this program these fields are integrated into a theme containing: Theories of the firm, industrial dynamics and entrepreneurship. These seminars are followed by a very short project work of one week where the students work on a theme defined assignment, and the outcome that is a short written report is part of the input to the oral examination. These activities contain approximately half a semester. After this exam the students are allowed in groups to do project-work on a problem specified by the group, but defined by a theme determined by the subjects of the previous seminars. Integrated into this project activity the students participate in a seminar on methods in understanding problems, making analysis and presenting results on the disciplinary areas they. The project work and its methodological and disciplinary aspects are the material for a project exam at the end of the first semester.

Having passed this exam and having gained not only their marks, but also a more broad assessment by the supervisor the students are gradually within the same superstructure engaging into more demanding and autonomous assignments both defined within the following seminars and by a methodological specification of the following project. Important is here that the students slowly is gaining increasing responsibility for the activities at seminars. Such seminars could partly bee steered by the students, invited guests and the teachers in collaboration, but with a fixed theme. But the following project could at the same time be defined within the theme in a form that allows the students to co-operate with a firm or institution with strategic interest in the theories and methods of the curriculum. This co-operation should end in a project where the students includes important parts of the curriculum in this project by using it analysing and handling important practical and professional problems inspired from their collaborator outside the university.

During the following two semesters, which in this example define the last year of the master education, degrees of methodological freedom are gradually introduced at the same time as the students are confronted with demands that cover important elements within the discipline. Specifically these elements cover areas as applying theory on practice, communicating theoretically oriented solutions to practitioners, immediate problem solving and merging data from practice into new theoretically oriented frameworks. Generally expressed the study process during these two semesters puts new structural demands on the projects parallel with gradually increased degrees of freedom on the student's choice of theories and problems. This ends in the thesis semester with demands entirely connected to the content, level and structure of the master thesis, and where the students define how they within the resource framework together with the supervisors build a structure that supports the advanced learning process. The master thesis is, when it has been concluded, assessed in the normal way for such a university activity.

## 8. THE METHODOLOGICAL PRINCIPLES OF THE PBL CANON STRUCTURE

The example above was used, because it is a program only running over a two years period from start to finish, and because it is under construction right now. But what we are trying to say both through our more abstract discourse and through the concrete example is that a disciplinary or cross-disciplinary program can be structured in a way that not only reflects the main elements of the academic, professional and practical expectations toward an university education. It can also be done so by using the more active and inspired effort by all students that develops when the right combination of steering and autonomy is used. This demands not only some abstract principles on problem-based learning that many students are not able to grasp in a situation where disciplines are overcrowded with knowledge, where many kinds of specialisation are competing and where paradigms are fighting each other. It demands instead that the students will be met where they stand and gradually let toward an increased independence and responsibility on learning the trade.

The example above tries to illustrate some steps within this process, but it is also possible in a more abstract way to outline some organising principles on how this should be done. These principles are based on some of the general principles of learning where complex processes combining practice and theory have to be dealt with and where the end result is not only to understand these complex processes. It is also done to prepare for building a capacity for the individual Master in co-operation with others to further develop these processes and to become a member of work force that deliberately follows its academic obligations.

As we mentioned from the start of the article, we are not in a position where these conditions are already fulfilled in our daily teaching work and we just have to present the practical results of our efforts. Instead these pages are written, because we observe increasing problems for a part of the university students that the way traditional university pedagogy or traditional problem-based learning are used do not solve. Therefore we are interested in continuing a process of further developing the problem-based methods. This will be done in ways that some of our colleagues certainly will find problematic, either because they perhaps think it tries to steer the learning processes of the students too much or the method demands efforts from supervisors and lectures that they are not able to comply with.

Despite of this, or perhaps because of this, we will once more by summing up present the main principles of how we see out problem-based canon. This can be done be stressing the following elements:
- The students have to be met where they are - also with the internet and their mobile phone as their main sources for information
- The present situation for all disciplines and areas for university programs cannot be simplified into one paradigm and one traditional cannon
- University teachers do not have the monopoly for diffusing disciplinary knowledge
- Most students are not prepared from the start of their university studies to grasp the variety and incompatibility of disciplinary knowledge (and some of them never develop this ability with the present didactical methods).
- Problem-based learning is not in itself a sufficient way to solve this problem, but have to be integrated in a broader didactical framework.
- At the end of a master study the student have to be able not only to write a master thesis, but also to handle important intra and extra mural means of the discipline or program area
- A bachelor or master program has to start relatively steered and gradually in a progression to introduce degrees of freedom to the students.
- Didactical means have to be used to illustrate the discipline and at the same time to be introduced as varied as possible.
- The study activities have within the specific periods of study to be integrated within a theme or another kind of disciplinary framework.

## REFERENCES

Beck, U. (1992). *Risk Society*. Sage, London.

Foucault, M. (1972). *The Archeology of Knowledge*. Tavistock, London.

Foucault, M. (1979). *Disciplin and Punish*. Penguin, Harmondsworth.

Gibbons, M. et.al (1994). *The new production of knowledge*, Sage Publ., London.

Savin-Baden, M. (2000). *Problem-based Learning in higher education: untold stories*, Open University Press, Buckingham.

Seltzer,K & Bentley, T. (2000). *Kreativitetens tidsalder*. Dafolo, Frederikshavn.

Simonsen, B. (1997). *RUC-lærer - himmel og helvede*. 8.delrapport fra UNI-PÆD-projektet. Roskilde, RUC.

# PEDAGOGICAL AND TECHNOLOGICAL CHALLENGES IN ON/OFF CAMPUS EDUCATION

Ole E. M. Borch, Morten Knudsen and Ole Rokkjær

**Abstract**: Supporting the learning process for off-campus and on-line students is needed to establish a structured and motivated competence development. New pedagogical format - i.e. pedagogical resources, scenarios, composing, activities and technological support - has been developed to strengthen the individual learning process. Experiences from distance education in individual learning are fine since individual learning responsibilities are natural leaving out alternatives learning options. On-campus students did not benefit from the new method and especially the challenges expected to support preparation for the preceding attendance teaching, an understandable fact since the classroom teaching is a high quality of service alternative. Changing the on-campus learning process to be more reflective and using the new format for courses may improve the learning behavior and merge material maintenance and development. This requires new competences in the learning organization, and the problem is if the willingness for changes exists among staff and in the organization as long as competition from the educational market is small.

## 1. INTRODUCTION

At the end of the last century, extra attention was made on competences development of employees in industry. The reason was to attract and keep employees and at the same time to increase the potential knowledge inside the plant for competition purposes. The result was making plans for individual competence development also useful to the plant - education became a competition parameter. One more aspect became obvious; the wish to relate the employee's educational activity closely to the working situation, so relation and motivation became important factors. Adapting learning processes to the industry and problem-based learning (PBL) became trends in the competence development strategy, and thus focusing on learning methods and learning processes. Changes in competence development were then evident in industry and influenced the educational institutions too. In the didactic triangle as shown in figure 1, focus was moved from the teacher's corner to the learning part. The major flow of knowledge should now go from the knowledge producer in the top of the triangle to the learner and less via the teacher, who now should have a dominant moderator and facilitator role. Conditions for the learning process are more defined by the learning part (customer, employee, plant etc) then before when it comes to continuous education, but is not the case in the traditional educational schools.

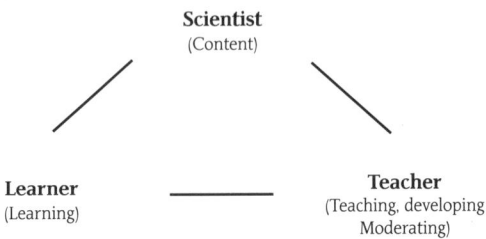

Figure 1: The didactic triangle (Erik Laursen, 2003)

The educational institutions customers are gradually changing to fulfill requests for re- education and continuous learning, based on flexibility in both on-campus and off-campus and on-line education. Off-campus on-line continuous education is setting strong demands for competition skills since the customers are able to choose among numerous operators where content, methods, flexibility and price are important for the selection. As long as the educational institutions still have their major income from on-campus customers, the competition between institutions is minimum and the teacher driven teaching may continue as usual. The demand from customers for off-campus activities is not yet strong enough to motivate a more learning oriented attitude, but a lot of analysis and design is going on. From a customers point of view it is also a problem to leave the relaxed social room where attendance teaching is performed. If the drop out of the education is to be low, the focus on the learning process must increase to bring didactic, pedagogic and technology together at such a high quality level which attracts the customer and improvements must be made by the educational developer. In distance learning it is important to get the learning process to work supporting the ability for individual learning thus increasing continues competence development and also, that the learner is aware of it.

More and more on-campus students are going on-line at home, and it would be reasonable to investigate if individual learning to a larger extend can be used intensively reducing the traditional attendance teaching with the same factor. This will help to merge development and maintenance recourses for both on-campus and off-campus learners. Increasing individual learning is not easy but can be supervised and planned by the developers by using appropriate pedagogic format and technology. This is what this article about.

A pedagogical format can be defined as (Borch et al., 2003.a):
• The information in itself (the pedagogical resources)

- The way the information can be read and navigated (the pedagogical scenarios)
- The graphical style of the published supports (the pedagogical composing)
- The pedagogical actions expected from the learner (the pedagogical activities)

## 2. ON-CAMPUS

The interpretation of PBL used at Aalborg University (AAU) for more than 25 years is problem oriented and project organized, and the results are very fine in terms of motivation and learning (Fink, 1999). The fixed theme for the project work and the supported courses are fundamental anchors in the personal learning process. The project organized group work is forming a professional and social room keeping the individual in a tight consuming and producing community. The group supervisor is guiding and helping the project to follow the track going through the most important topics and looking after an equally distributed workload between members concerning complexity. The supervisor also encourages the group members to setup reflection and reading processes to stimulate the learning process.

Traditionally and scheduled teacher driven courses are given to support the project work (PE-courses evaluated via the project) building up parallel competence for group members to be able to improve and work together on equal basis. The problem with those courses is the balance between theories, methods and direct instructions useful for the project work. Another problem is the course scheduling itself, which seldom is matching the progress in the project work and thus out of phase in terms of motivation.
Other courses are also given (SE-courses) which have a special exam and thus indirectly motivates. For all types of courses, students are not well prepared before the teaching session. This influence the teaching session to be more one way-process with few questions from the audience to be more clearing up than reflective. If the individual preparation could be stimulated, it will improve the learning process dramatically, witch has been observed where a course - due to a small audience - was turned into a study group. Subgroups of 3 to 4 participants on shift took the responsibility to prepare themselves and present topics for the rest of the study group. Another subgroup was selected to be the opponent group and the rest of the participants were encouraged to put up reflective questions.

In short, the on-campus project organized group work is forming a tight effective social forum for development, where communication and reflections takes place in a communicative high bandwidth environment. The way courses are developed, managed and scheduled gives problems in terms of lack of preparation and out of phase motivation.

## 3. OFF-CAMPUS

When AAU started developing off-campus on-line education, it was obvious to use the same PBL interpretation as on-campus. After 2 years of operation in the Master of Information Technology (MII) distance education a lot of results were collected and the experiences are used in the new design and implementation (Knudsen et al., 2003).

At the distance the virtual project room has large communication delays and the social environment is weak. Compensations were needed and all sorts of appropriate communicative applications were used like email, news-groups, chats, and audio-meetings. Reflective forums were established, but rarely used. An important feature of the MII was the regular physical meetings where project discussions, status and planning took place. The responsibility for the project among members of the group was strong, and the major (only) place for anchors in the learning process. This strong focus on the project work removed resources from courses and thus the method and theory providing activities (Knudsen et al., 2003). On the other hand, the students requested knowledge when they needed it, and therefore the motivation was dominant for searching and reading. It turned out, that traditional courses dumped on the Internet media was less attractive for the project work than courses developed to help and guide the students in the individual learning process. Alternative courses from other providers then from AAU were also used by students, fitting better into the individual wishes in terms of presentation and pedagogical methods.

At the course side, the students were also left alone in the virtual classroom and nobody to discus with and no group to reflect immediately in. On the other hand, taking the course freely in time and space and synchronized with the project work improves the learning and stimulates self-reflections. Still group reflections are typical missing on course topics.

To secure the parallel competence development among group members, a well formed time schedule for the project work must exist along with well defined learning goals. Only by using such milestones, it is possible to collaborate on equal basis. At MII it was observed, that dropping out of the study was also due to increased distance in specific competences.

Sub-conclusion
In short, the project work is also very attractive when it comes to on-line education, even in the virtual classroom missing proximity and immediate reflective environment. Courses are only attractive in the virtual classroom if they are developed to fulfill the individual expectations in terms of pedagogical methods, project supported contents and accessible free in time and place too. Reflective environments, such as news-groups, are seldom used.

## 3.1. Course development

Providing courses and other services for participants in an on-line environment requires an appropriate way of organizing recourses to be accessed at one single site related to the specific education. The user interface should be created to make interactions possible accessing resources stored at the educational site. Many different tools are used at the client side (consumer actor) so different converters and viewers are needed at the server side.

Some standards are available for presentation and storage of educational resources on a digital platform. LMS (Learning Management System) is a standard expected to manage activities during the training and LCMS (Learning Contents Management System) is expected to manage content production before the training. In figure 2 the deployment diagram is shown. The content actor is managing the content to be used in services to the consumer actor like students, printers and application programs. The database is the storage for the content leaving out any kind of presentation and XML (eXtensible Mark Up Language) is the appropriate logical storage format to use. The presentation style is chosen according to the consumer actor, e.g. the presentation format HTML, which is constructed by using a XSL (eXtensible Style sheet Language) script to interpret the XML.

Realizing the learning management helps to organize and develop digital platform services faster and at the same time optimizes reusability and collaboration between educational providers. The UniFlex (University Flexible learning tool) digital platform (Uniflex, 2002) is one simple example which stores information's in a simple SQL database, and when requested by a HTML client, the generator extracts data from the database in the XML format and associates an XSL scripting file.

The teacher is the moderator for the learner and must prepare materials to facilitate the learning process. This is the task for the teacher in the developer role. The ingredients are the content subjects, pedagogical format and technology. In the attendance classroom the teaching process is based on a subject and the pedagogical format used may be planned and changed dynamically during the teaching session. The technology used to support the teaching process is very teacher specific.

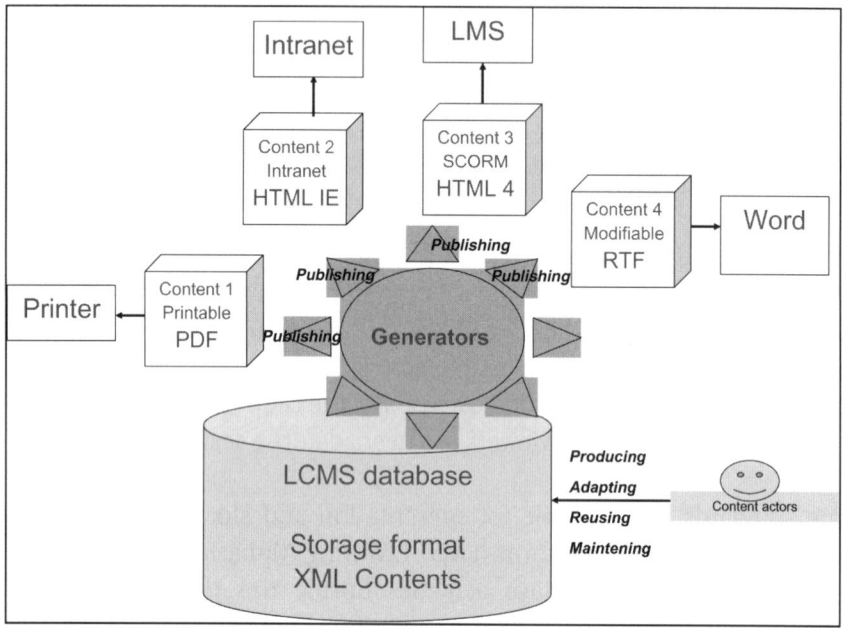

Figure 2: Deployment diagram for LCMS and LMS nodes. The architecture is typical used in a digital platform (a Borch O, et al., 2003). SCORM= Sharable Content Object Reference Model (http://www.adlnet.org/)

When it comes to distance teaching, the pedagogical format used must be selected carefully in the planning phase and supported by appropriate technology. How a course is delivered is a matter of the digital platform and the quality of service in the network infrastructure. A web-based interface is recommended bypassing firewalls, and at the same time meeting the most commonly used internet client tool - the Internet browser.

The developing path is shown in figure 3. Materials are collected and the operating environment is recognized such as communication facilities, developing tools offered, system constrains like minimum network requirements and user requirements.

The collected raw materials are structured according to the recommendation script offered via a template, which contains two major elements described in the next chapters:
• Course structure
• Learning path

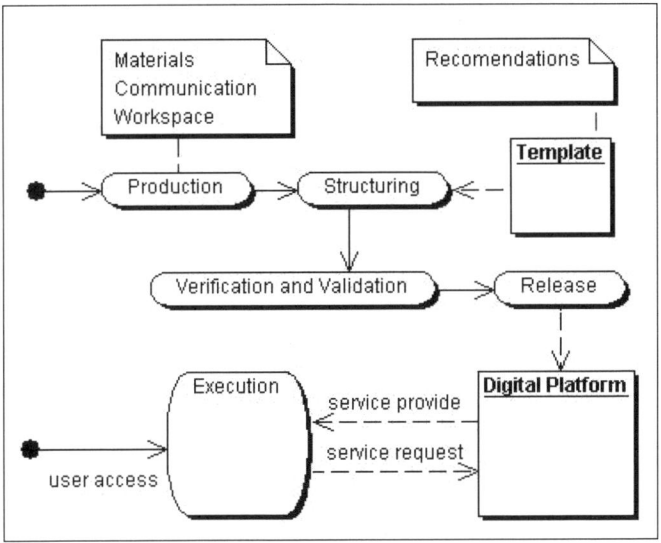

Figure 3: Course developing path to be used by the teacher in the developer's role.
(UNITE 2000;a Borch O., et al., 2003)

Next the structure is verified towards the study regulations and syllabus and validated towards the learning principles and the behavior of the learner target group.

When finished, the product is released by uploading to the digital platform inside the LCMS to provide services to the user. An upload is essential for more reasons:
• A fixed product release
• Stable document infrastructure such as stable anchors and hyperlinks
• Controlled authorized access to protect materials or at least a user registration
• Possibility to monitoring access activities
• Backup support

The digital platform is acting as a service provider for user requests, and the service access point at the client side is recommended to be organized in 4 major groups:
• Communication
• Information
• Courses
• Project work

One example of a digital platform is UniFlex (J. Helbo, 2001; Uniflex, 2002; Borch et al., 2003.b) developed at AAU offering the 4 groups of services and the services provided in each group are depending of the user profile (teacher, developer, student, supervisor and guest). The communication group is more than email, aliases and general discussion it also contains forums for each course and for each project work used in reflective sessions.

## 3.2. Course structure

The course structure used in the template in figure 3 is defined in figure 4 and can be constructed by using different type of authoring tool. One example of a powerful tool is FrontPage from Microsoft which has a graphical user interface for constructing and maintaining the structure - called a web. Validation checks of hyperlinks, internal navigation and maintenance of a structure file for later use in the digital platform are important features (course template example can be found in: Uniflex, 2002). Simple tools are a lot more time consuming for the same quality and stability.

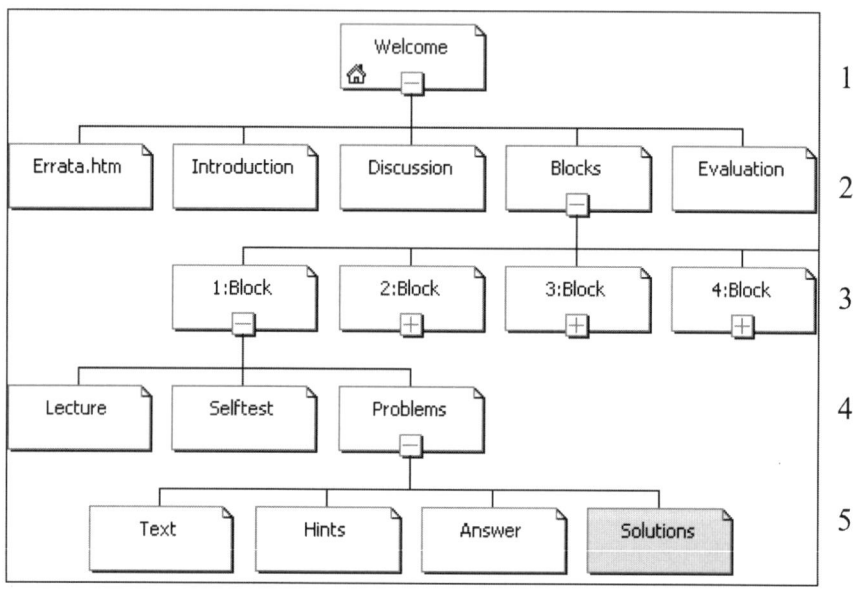

Figure 4: Recommended course structure as a set of interconnected elements.
(b: Borch O., et al.,2003)

The structure must be simple and well formed to separate different kind of activities. The internal navigating must be logical and easy to adapt, so the knowledge of the structure itself must be known by all users and fulfilled by the course developer.
For the course, the welcome layer (layer 1) is about the course and followed by a management layer (layer 2). Layer 3 - the session layer - is a set of topic specific learning blocks encapsulating the learning activities. Every block has the same structure in layer 4 and 5.

## 3.2.1 Layer 2 - The management layer

This management layer contains information's needed for taking the course such as defining the environment, context, conditions and constraints. By collecting and encapsulating information in a structured way, it helps the customer to navigate and find information's needed. There are 5 management elements.

Errata element
When a new version of the course is released by the developer, the changes (when, where and what) since last upload are registered in the 'Errata' table element. Thus the user is able to take action like downloading the new version of the course and to make corrections according to the modifications made. The developer must be aware only to release few new versions during the course taken and focus on increments rather then iterations. The table is cleared before the course is delivered once again.

Introduction element
This element is the container for aggregated resources such as course environment, conditions, and resources among others and specified in the following list.

* Study load as specified hours spend in average
* Course syllabus or a link to the study board maintained site. This includes prerequisite, objectives, results and list of content.
* Explanation of course structure
* Used communication channels advising how to communicate when taking the course
* How problem solving is organized in terms of help and submission of solutions
* How self test should be used and description of the value for the user and the teacher
* How the evaluation of the course is performed
* List of references such as books with online graded recommendations, online hyperlinks and link to local CD supporting the course
* Recommended and required tools and related links

Discussion element
The objectives for this element are to describe and set up the context and motivate the participant by using considerations as 'carrots' to inspire the participant. Also a course content overview description and especially why the course should be taken are described.
The course position in the continuous competence development process is

described. Facilities such as FAQ (Frequently Asked Question) and examples are very much used as motivated aggregations.

Blocks element
Distribution of subjects into learning blocks is described such as importance, load and complexity. Argued and recommended learning path and use of additional external learning activities are mentioned here.

Evaluation element
The course itself may be evaluated here by using an electronic form, but also conditions for examine and evaluation of the participants goes here. Link to the discussion forum is also inserted as well as the possibility to submit remarks to the course.

### 3.2.2. Layer 3, 4 and 5

The main learning activity takes place inside a block.
At level 3 the block itself is described with:
• Objectives for this learning activity
• Study load
• List of topics and brief introduction
• Reading information, recommendations and reading advisory
• Result of this learning activity

Layer 4 and 5 is a structure of elements supporting the recommended learning path inside a block as shown in figure 5.

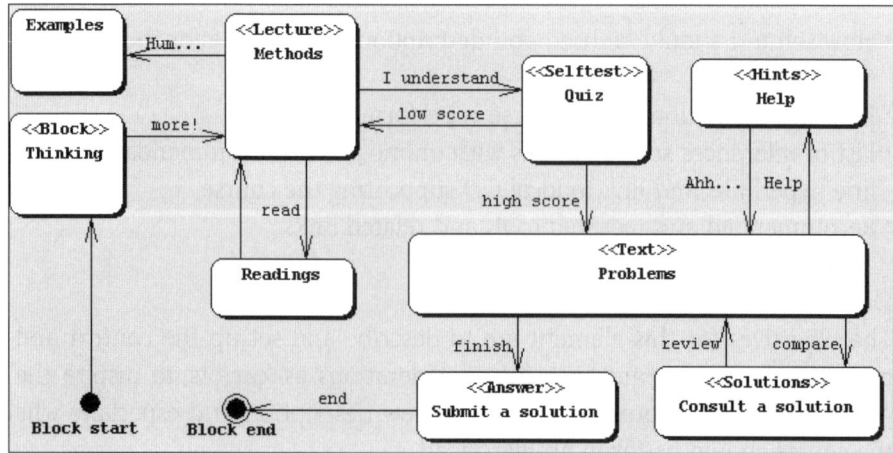

Figure 5: State diagram for the learning process in each block. (Borch et al.,2003,b)

The support of such a state diagram for learning process is a valuable guide for remote studies, since the supervision is not available like in on-campus sessions, where the teacher often is managing the process. The activities also contain a self-test facility for guiding the participant when to leave the lecture part and take the training exercises. The lecture element is replacing the classroom teaching activity. Like in the classroom the lecture quality is based on pedagogical methods chosen, teacher style and variations in use of effects. Examples, best praxis, discussions and reflections are important activities as well, strengthening the learning process.

The lecture element should motivate and guide the learner through the topics for the block. First the materials are presented, and then one of more topic blocks are filled in as a) context motivation presented as an overview pointing out important areas to prepare the learner for the readings for the following b) advised reading activity. The lecture element can be supported by examples, questions, audio and video clip.

The lecture element contains:
1. About materials used in this block such as slides, audio, video etc.
2. Topic block (one or more)
    - Topic motivation and FAQ (This is an important and valuable task)
    - Detailed list of readings

The *quiz element* contains information's about the area tested and the conditions such as repeated self-test possibilities, one try only and if the results are registered. The quiz itself may be located on a general purpose quiz server, where the teacher has uploaded questions and answers, and from where a specified URL is returned and may be stored in the quiz element.

The *problem element* contains the objectives and conditions for the problem solving activity. The problem to be solved is in the text element and links to the on-line helper *hint element* are embedded in the text. If the results are going to be submitted, the conditions and method is described in the *answer element*. If the teacher's solutions are offered to students for comparison, the *solution element* is part of the course element navigation.

Sub-conclusion
The course template developed has a structure supporting a learning path, which filled in as described may guide and help the learner to adapt the contents in a better way when it comes to individual learning.

## 4. MERGING EDUCATIONAL ENVIRONMENTS

Seen from the educational organization, it could be reasonable to consider first of all to improve the learning processes and then to optimize resource spending in development and maintenance of on-campus and off-campus environments.

Taking the best from the two activities, organizing the learning processes and using the same materials is an option to a large extend, but changes in behavior and styles among students, teachers and in the organization might be a difficult innovative process.

## 4.1. Courses - (off-campus influence on-campus)

Investing in course material containing high quality of pedagogical methods and using the appropriate technology has shown an improvement in self-training in the off-campus environment. At the same time preparation activities and reflections among on-campus students are not satisfactory, so it could be a good idea to adapt the course development from off-campus - as described in the previous chapter - to be used on-campus as well. This requires a change in the way courses are given on-campus so a 'teaching' session will be turned into a more reflective session, which was a success in the study group mentioned in chapter 2. One course session instruction scenario could be:

> »*Within the next 5 days, you prepare yourself from the course material (URL=xx) session 3 for the next course reflection session. You also must take the multiple choice test. Peter, Poul and Mary are going to put up questions in the forum[1] starting the reflective process. All other course participants - including the 'teacher' - will join the reflective process on session topics.*«
>
> »*After the reflection session the problem solving is performed in the project groups and compared with a suggested solution released dd/mm/yy on the course news forum.*«

For students, the change in the learning style is a major change in mentality, since they have been using the classroom for years in the education system and got used to traditional 'teacher controlled' teaching. The new style in the sense of preparation before the session is seen as waste of time if the usual attendance teaching style is offered for at the on-campus students too. This was observed in a course, where the new course style was offered the on-campus students. Asking the students in the classroom, they found the on-line material very good, but few took the opportunity to prepare themselves - as some students said: »Why do self study if the teaching is still performed« (It is easier just to listen!) The student's workload will increased by using the new style, since more reading in advance is required to participate qualified in the reflective session. From experiences in study groups, some students can

---

[1] Forum may be a classroom for on-campus students and a course reflection news forum for of-campus students. The start and length of the reflection session is defined in advance.

attend passively, which is of course not wanted. From the Virtual University in Monterrey in Mexico this is avoided by requesting the students to write down reflections in a personal reflection logbook, which is taken into account at the exam.

For teachers, the new style is also a challenge, both in the developer role and the teaching/moderator role. The major obstacle for the innovation process is the well acquired autonomy and right in using pedagogical methods and technology. Competence development in the organization is required to learn how to reduce teaching as instruction giving and increase teaching in theory, methods and to stimulate interactive reflection processes. Supporting the new style also means to follow recommended pedagogical methods and technology, witch also is a barrier for developers.

## 4.2. Project work - (on-campus influence off-campus)

Project work is working very well on-campus at AAU (Fink, 1999), but the reflective processes related to the supporting PE-courses and the support from those courses could be better. Off-campus project work also seems to be well organized by taking the courses before starting the project work (Knudsen M. et al., 2003). At on-campus this sequence is controlled by scheduling activities in class rooms and group rooms, and at off-campus an on-line calendar is used not as a control facility but as a recommendation.

Using the on-campus way on the off-campus doesn't mean that the on-campus method is good enough.
• Should PE-courses disappear and be replaced with activities in the project work to increase motivation as a kind of work based learning?
• Should the project work include formal reflection sessions and a personal learning logbook or portfolio?
Anyway, in both 'campuses' a well defined project work time schedule taking the learning goals into account is required to obey the demand for parallel competence development.

## 5. CONCLUSION

Higher educational institutions are able to collaborate on a free competitive educational market by focusing on the learning process. Reaching such a state needs new management competences and teacher competences at the LCMS level. Reusability, standards, new pedagogical format and advanced technology are keywords reaching high quality on an open market. Building in that quality in the on-campus educational environment will also improve the individual learning process in terms of preparations for reflection sessions.

Not underestimating the effort for changes, it is possible to merge on-campus and on-line activities gradually with an open mind and getting inspired and learn from institutions which already have been on its way for a long time. The changes need new competences and reorganizing resources rather than increasing costs.

A common set of activities and styles for on-campus and on-line educations in terms of development, maintenance, teaching and learning is possible, but the barrier is the mental change and the willingness for changes among students, staff and in the organization.

The used style for courses has been tested in the off-campus situation, but need to be tested on-campus along with the new teaching method turning classroom teaching into reflection sessions.

## REFERENCES

Borch O. et al. (2003.a). *»Digital Platforms«*, Working Group 1 (WG1), Part of EU project. To appear in an EU report published 2003.

Borch O. et al. (2003.b). *UniFlex: A WWW-environment for project-based collaborative learning 4th International Conference on Information Technology Based Higher Education and Training,* ITHET03, Marrakech, MOROCCO.

Laursen E., (2003). *Speech at Pedagogical Conference in Problem Based Learning,* March 4, 2003. Aalborg University.

Fink F. K., (1999). *Integration of Engineering Practice into Curriculum - 25 years of experience with Problem Based Learning.* FIE'99: Frontiers in Education Conference - Engineers Designing the Future, Puerto Rico, November 1999.

Helbo J., Knudsen M. , Jensen L.P. , Borch O. , and Rokkjær O. (2001). *Group Organized Project Work in Distance Education.* ITHET 2001 Conference, Kumamoto.

Knudsen M. et al. (2003). *Project-Based Collaborative in distance education*. In this anthology.

EUNITE Task force 1 (2000). *Digital Learning Platform & Digital Campus*. Final report version 1.2 December 1.

Uniflex prospect (2002).
http://www.mii.auc.dk/uniflex/common_info/uniflex_update_03.pdf and login example (visitor/guest) http://uniflex-proactt.itorg.auc.dk/.
Course template is to be found at
http://uniflex.itorg.auc.dk/downloads/FPcourseTemplate.zip

# PROBLEM-BASED LEARNING
# IN THE FOREIGN LANGUAGE STUDY PROGRAMMES

**Rita Cancino**

**Abstract**: This article presents an overview of how problem-based learning at The Faculty of Humanities, Aalborg University, is practised, particularly in the Foreign Language Study Programmes. Most of the projects in these study programmes use project themes and topics from the different foreign-language countries. The literature used in the preparation of the project should be in the foreign language; the project reports are written in the foreign language; and the oral exam is held in the foreign language. The students studying foreign languages are really challenged as they not only have to study various subjects such as economy, law, etc., but they have to do it in a language very different from their mother tongue.

## 1. AALBORG UNIVERSITY

The nature of study at Aalborg University is rather different from that of most universities in Denmark and in other countries. This is because of the emphasis which the university puts on group work and project writing e.g. problem-based learning (PBL) where students take the responsibility for their own learning.

As the students in a problem-based learning curriculum work with a problem, they should be able to identify what they need to learn and what resources they are going to use to accomplish that learning. In this way the students can design their learning to meet individual needs and career aspirations. By having the opportunity to assume this responsibility under faculty guidance, students are prepared to become effective and efficient life-long learners.

The three faculties at Aalborg University all use project work, Humanities, Social Sciences, and Engineering and Science, but in particular one faculty is more successful than the two others, due to its nature. At the Faculty of Engineering and Science problem-based learning prospers with many projects on concrete development tasks, very often in connection with projects raised by companies in the private sector. This means that the faculty benefits from external resources as these firms pay for many of the projects. It is the only faculty, which is capable of raising funds from outside the university.

## 2. THE FACULTY OF HUMANITIES

At the Faculty of Humanities the collaboration with business is very small. Due to the nature of Humanities the students will not be able to solve development problems or design new devices for trade and industry. This means that the possibilities of joint projects with the trade and industry in Northern Jutland and the rest of Denmark are almost non-existing. The private firms are not able to see what humanistic research can do for their financial results and for the competitiveness. They may not even recognise the necessity of employing persons with foreign language skills at a very high level such as the graduate students from the Faculty of Humanities' language studies.

The Faculty of Humanities embraces many different study programmes which no matter their nature all use the pedagogical model which characterises the university, i.e. the problem-based learning. The programmes are as different as foreign languages, philosophy, communication, information technology, music, music therapy, psychology and many more. The red thread linking together the many different studies is the problem-based and project-based learning where the students work in small learning teams. From every stage on their university studies students are asked to design and write academic projects with a high degree of autonomy and intellectual freedom. They are faced with a number of challenging problems, i.e. deciding on the direction of their research, collecting materials, information and data, working out a structure of their project report etc.

Among the many different study programmes at the Faculty of Humanities project work is used in different forms, but all the programmes use project work from the very first semester. For most of the new students at the Faculty of Humanities project work is a different and new way of working with a topic. In addition, it is a new way of acquiring knowledge. This can lead to frustrations and great anxiety, but also to a feeling of happiness and development. When working with the first projects most students will feel uncertain and fumbling as regards both the professional and the social aspects of the project work, but it turns out that most students later become very satisfied and competent in preparing project reports and working in groups.

In this article it would become quite impossible to describe the project work in all the study programmes. Consequently, I have chosen to focus on some particular programmes: the Foreign Language Study Programmes, describing their procedures and ways of practising problem-based learning. These programmes have an important and special component in common, the foreign language, which necessarily has to play an important role in the project together with the other specialised subjects. As all the more theoretical parts of the general project have already been described in all possible ways, this article will mainly deal with other dimensions of the project work, i.e. the linguistic dimension. Furthermore, emphasis will be on the project models chosen by the two different language study programmes to which attention will be paid in this article.

## 3. THE BUSINESS COMMUNICATION STUDY PROGRAMME

### 3.1 The Department for Languages and Intercultural Studies

As the Faculty of Humanities among other things is characterised by many language study programmes, the foreign-language dimension has to play a major role in the projects of these studies. If Aalborg University is unusual in its teaching structure, the Department for Languages and Intercultural Studies at the Faculty of Humanities is also somewhat unusual in the number of different academic disciplines which it covers. Unlike many other departments, this department is truly interdisciplinary, with teachers, researchers and students working in a variety of different fields and with different perspectives, aims and assumptions. At a certain level, different academic subjects - literary criticism, linguistics, social history, the social sciences, business communication, etc. have similar kinds of requirements. In each case, the student must be able to state a position, construct an argument, demonstrate an understanding of the relevant issues, discuss hypotheses, work critically, with others' research etc.

In the Business Language and International Business Communication Programme four different languages are taught and spoken: English, French, Spanish, and German. These languages are combined into many different study programmes, e.g. English and Spanish or one language together with Information Technology and Communication, e.g. French and IT-Tools/Communication (http://www.auc.dk/fak-hum/studordn.htm). These programmes focus on a particular dimension of the language viz LSP - Language for Specific Purpose -, which differentiates them from the other language study, programmes, the Foreign Language Study Programmes, where focus is partially on the classical language study, partially on a more international dimension in the language studies. The classical language studies are related to English and German, the international dimension to English and Spanish.

## 3.2 Project Preparation

Already in the very first semester of the Studies of Business Communication the new students meet the project model and the project evaluation. (http://www.sprog.auc.dk/ciek/uv.html). During the first weeks the new students have to attend lectures dealing with project work and project method. This is meant to prepare the students for the project awaiting them when the project-preparation teaching ends. Normally, the first semester has a length of 10 to 12 weeks during which the students follow different subjects, many of which are evaluated by group projects, whereas others are evaluated by individual exams.

In due time before the first semester ends the students can check the department's website in order to see how the groups are formed. As the students do not know each other yet, the group formation is made administratively this first time, normally with 4 to 6 students in each group and within the same language combinations in order to ensure that the students have received the same inputs during the preparing lessons. Later in the studies the students organise the groups themselves according to their interests.

In the lectures on project work the students will be presented to the formal requirements in connection with the project where the framework is particularly important. In this first group project the framework theme is: Language, culture and method. (http://www.sprog.auc.dk/ciek/uv.html) This theme makes it possible for the students both to choose some topics within Danish society, but equally to choose topics from the country whose language or languages they are studying,

In connection with the first project the students are allowed to turn in a project with a maximum number of pages of 20 per student (a normal page corresponds to 2800 keystrokes. Enclosed material is excluded from the designated maximum of pages that the student may write. During the lectures on project work they are informed of the deadlines for both the project report and opponents' paper. The oral evaluation normally takes place at the end of the semester.

At International Business Communication's website a handbook -the project handbook written by teachers and researchers at Aalborg University - is at the disposal of the students. This handbook deals with all practical issues in relation to the work process itself and the working out of the final product - the project report. In addition, information can be found on project work, the practical work in the group, the project report (for example, footnoting and quotations), the evaluation, etc. The most important issue in relation to the work is the main requirement: the project has to be problem-based and analytical. This handbook can be downloaded and used as a student's bible during the years at the university. (http://www.sprog.auc.dk/ciek/uv.html).

For many students it is the first time they meet with the project work, which means that they have to act in relation to many practical issues. For instance, they have to find out whom their supervisor is going to be. This information can also be found on the department's website. Here they find information on the administrative allocation of group rooms, etc.

Early in the project course the students have to make a provisional problem formulation. This problem formulation has to strictly follow the formal guidelines described in the project handbook. When the students are working with the process of choosing a topic, e.g. the different aspects of the topic and the formulation of the problem, they have access to a large number of sources of inspiration. Besides the inspiration from the media around them, they have received a lot of inspiration during their classes. The first semester they receive, besides the inputs from their language studies, inspiration from other disciplines such as business communication, social, political and cultural studies, etc. Furthermore, they attend courses and lecturers in communication theory; text, discourse and genre analysis; and media analysis, text types and discourse functions and finally rhetoric. They might as well have been inspired by attending guest lecturers on topics relevant to all the students, irrespective of the language, or attending more specific lectures in some of the foreign languages given by visiting teachers from the partner universities around the world.

## 3.3 Different forms of project evaluation

The project is evaluated at a group exam on the basis of the project report elaborated by the group. The evaluation is oral and is either in the foreign language or in Danish with the supervisor as the examiner and often with an internal or an external examiner. At the first semester all evaluations are in Danish regardless of the student's foreign language. At this early stage of the studies the students' foreign language competence is not sufficiently strong to allow them to take part in a discussion in a foreign language using professional terminology at the same time.

Some projects are evaluated internally, which means that the »external« examiner is a professor from Aalborg University who has not been the student's supervisor during the semester. (http://www.sprog.auc.dk/is/sup.thm, p. 28). Other projects are evaluated externally, which means that the external examiner is appointed by the Ministry of Education and does not teach at Aalborg University. An external examiner may come from another educational institution or from a company or an organisation.

The students at the programme of International Business Communication will during their studies be exposed to two different forms of evaluation.

1. Project exam with project group and opponent group
2. Project exam exclusively with project group.

### 3.4 Project exam with project group and opponent group

A project exam with a project group and an opponent group takes places as follows: The evaluation is initiated with the project group's supplementary comments on the project report and aspects in that connection.. Subsequently, each member of the group makes a short presentation of different aspects in the project. The individual presentation must be of no more than five minutes. As everybody, including the supervisor and the external examiner, knows the content of the report, this presentation should not be a summary or a repetition of the project, but it should take up some new points in relation to the topic. A presentation should never resemble a speech learned by heart before the exam. It is important that the students prepare the paper by means of keywords and then make the presentation using the keywords. This improves the presentation and the mark considerably. (http://www.sprog.auc.dk/is/sup.thm, p. 29).

The students themselves are responsible for the presentation. When they have handed in their report, the supervisor changes roles and becomes an examiner. Before the exam the group can consult the supervisor on important matters and general guidelines in connection with the exam, but the supervisor cannot and is not allowed to evaluate the project report beforehand or to approve possible presentations for the oral exam.

The presentation should form a whole and might, for example, summarise the main points of the project and point to problems, which the students would like to discuss in more detail. The students may also place the project in a larger context or put it into perspective by pointing to new problems that have arisen in continuation of the project. During the presentation the students are invited to use overheads, video, power point presentations, computer, etc. When all the students in the project group have made their part of the presentation or possibly several parts per student, the group now proceed to respond to the opponents' criticism. The project group has received the opponent group's report with the points of criticism some days before the exam in order to prepare themselves for the criticism that will be stated.

When giving their criticism the opponent group must already have distributed the different parts of the paper among themselves. They have to be aware that each student at least once has to have the possibility to state some criticism. Moreover, the students have to be prepared for some further remarks in connection with their criticism once the project group has defended themselves.

In their paper the opponents can for instance evaluate if the group's problem formulation corresponds to the real content of the project and the conclusions. Furthermore, they can evaluate if the exposition is well structured and logical, if the material is sufficient to subject the central aspects to a critical analysis: if the students have shown independence and used analysis instead of quotations. It is extremely important that the language is clear and comprehensible as the students are language students.

When stating their criticism the opponent group must be conscious of stating both positive and negative criticisms and doing so in a decent way. In addition, they have to be open and positive to the defence given by the project group. Correspondingly, it is expected that the project group is capable of receiving both positive and negative criticisms in a constructive way without getting offended. Under no circumstances is it acceptable that the defence develops into a vehement debate or discussion, it has to take place in a quiet and orderly way, with the participants showing mutual respect and listening to each other. (www.sprog.auc.dk/ciek/uv.html, p. 14).

During the whole process the supervisor and the external examiner follow the discussion from the sideline while they make notes about all the students in both groups for the evaluation. They only have to interfere if some aspects have to be treated further or if the discussion takes a wrong direction. It happens now and then that some students forget the distribution of the roles and keep on talking, without making it possible for other students to make any remarks. In that case the supervisor has to interfere in order to make it possible for the more quiet students to make their questions or answers.

For the students it is always necessary to be aware of the fact that in connection with this form of exam they both have to be evaluated at an exam where they participate as members of the project group and at the same time, in another exam, they play the role of the opponent group. Normally, the diploma will only state one aggregated mark for the exam. This mark reflects the total result for all the components of the project exam. In the evaluation of the project defence both the project report, i.e. the individual student's contribution, and the oral defence form part.

## 3.5 Assessment

In connection with the earlier described form of evaluation only the mark passed/failed is used. According to the Curriculum both parts of the exam have to be passed separately, i.e. both as a member of the project group and as a member of the opponent group in order to consider the exam as passed (http://www.sprog.auc.dk/is/sup.thm, p. 29).

The project exam both consists of the project report, i.e. the individual student's section and the oral defence. In this evaluation, the language proficiency, i.e. the ability to communicate in a precise, balanced, well-structured and idiomatic manner, will be included in the assessment of all written assignments, whether in Danish or in a foreign language. Furthermore, the following criteria form part, too.

* Linguistic competence
* Professional overview and comprehension throughout the report, not only in the individual's contribution.
* Clear and logic coherence in the project report
* Accordance between the problem formulation of the project report and the real content/conclusion
* Progression, i.e. is the project report well structured and logically advancing
* Independence in the elaboration of the project formulation, argumentation and exposition
* Terminology

In the evaluation of the opponents' presentation the following criteria should be emphasised:

* Critical position to the content of the project report (including the professional overview and understanding in the total report)
* Linguistic competence
* Terminology

The oral communication of the assessment takes place in separate rooms for the project group and the opponent group, respectively. The marks for the project group are communicated by the examiner, while the external examiner gives the marks for the opponent group. If the groups are very numerous two external examiners shall be present with one acting as an »observer« in order to ensure a fair evaluation.

## 3.6 Project exam exclusively with a project group

The groups at this exam are usually smaller, with three to five students in each group. This exam form differs from the former in the absence of the opponent group. Thus the project group does not receive any report before the exam, as was the case with the project exam with opponent group. The advantage of this report is that the project group will be prepared for the critical questions and the topics of discussion in advance (http://www.sprog.auc.dk/is/sup.htm, p.29).

In this case, too, the exam is initiated by the project group's presentation of their supplementary remarks on the project report and the different aspects concerned. When all the participants have made their presentation on different aspects of the project, the examiner and possibly the external examiner will ask some questions about the project report. The project group will not know in advance the questions to be put forward from the examiner or possibly the external examiner. It could e.g. be elaborations concerning illustrations or tables. Questions could be raised because of misunderstandings in the text or even contradictions or the examiner might need some further remarks on some unclear sections.

Normally, there will the questions directed to each student in the group, as the examiner through the table of content is able to identify each student's contribution to the project report. Nevertheless, all participants of group are responsible for the project and they all have to know every part of the report i.e. their fellow students' contribution in order to be able to answer questions about the entire project. The evaluation time is approx. 20 minutes per student, including the time for discussion about the individual students used by the examiner and the external examiner, including the time for communication of the result.

## 3.7 Language proficiency

As mentioned before the language proficiency, i.e. the ability to communicate in a precise, balanced, well-structured and idiomatic manner in Danish will be included in the assessment of all written assignments. The standards required increase as students are expected to progress through their programme. Furthermore, the language proficiency of the foreign language as well should be evaluated in the projects as the students are foreign language students. This concerns both the written foreign language and the oral language.

It is mostly in the exam with only a project group that the foreign language competence and proficiency is evaluated. The project report is written in a foreign language, the students make their presentation in the foreign language, the students defend their project in a foreign language and the discussion with the examiner and possibly the external examiner takes place in the foreign language. It is, of course, a double and severe trial for the students as they are expected to handle the project exam using the foreign language with a simultaneous command of the project's specific terminology, i.e. their wording abilities are put to the test.

In all language studies projects, the students' written proficiency in the foreign language is evaluated and strong emphasis is put on the same components as what regards the Danish language: grammatical correctness, use of correct idiomatic expressions, terminology, linguistic competence, etc. The student's linguistic level in the foreign language is evaluated together with the all the other elements of the project.

In some of the project exams the students oral proficiency in the foreign language is evaluated separately with a particular mark for the oral performance where emphasis is put on the correct pronunciation, fluency, grammatical correctness, idiomatic language and of course knowledge of the specialised terminology in the relevant field.

During oral examinations that are not oral proficiency exams, a high frequency of grammatical errors and mispronunciations will not affect the assessment of the student's command of the subject. The ability to speak in a clear and precise manner does, however, influence the assessment because it affects the student's ability to communicate views on the academic subject being discussed. (www.auc.dk/fak-hum/uk/eksklage.htm).

In the evaluation of the project defence both the project report (as well the foreign-language proficiency) and the individual student's contribution to the project form part. This evaluation form mostly makes use of the Danish 13-marking scale.

In the first semester there are several individual exams besides the project exam. During the following semesters the students will be altering between project work and individual exams. There is a project in the third semester; there are two in the fourth semester, one in each foreign language. Again in the sixth semester there will be a project, the so-called Diploma project which can be written individually or in groups. As the projects very often aggregate the teaching in more than one subject and thus represents many hours of work and teaching they are weighted quite strongly in terms of ECTS. The average number of ECTS is 12 to 15 ECTS per project.

## 4. THE FOREIGN LANGUAGE STUDY PROGRAMMES

### 4.1 Classical and modern studies

As mentioned the Foreign Language Study Programmes include the foreign languages English and German as classical studies, the so-called »general« studies. Simultaneously, the Foreign Language Programmes embrace the SIS-Programmes, the Language and International Studies, too. Here the students can dedicate themselves to Spanish and English studies from a more international point of view. At the Master's Programme: Culture, Communication and Globalisation, KKG, all three languages are represented together with French.

The Foreign Language programmes normally have semesters of a shorter duration than what is known from the International Business Communication. The semesters are of approx. 8 weeks with courses and lectures and afterwards the project work begins. Thus the project-preparatory courses have a duration of eight weeks with approx. two lesson per week per subject. These courses are often denominated area studies, which clearly indicates that here is an area where the students can find a topic for this or the next semester's project. The Foreign Language Study Programmes all include a project in the first semester. The framework of the first semester's project is: Culture and Social Conditions in Europe.

### 4.2 Project method

The project-based form of work at the Faculty of Humanities and Aalborg University is intended as a first step towards the acquisition of a scientific way of working. Therefore, to some extent, the project is subject to the same requirements as is other academic work such as a refereed article. This means that investigation into »the real world outside« (empirical investigation) must be conducted according to certain principles and the students must be aware of the consequences of choosing one method above another. Depending on the student's interests or the method they choose in order to conduct empirical investigation there will books describing this methodological dimension.

The new students at Foreign Language Study Programmes are offered a course in project work during the first semester. This course is meant to introduce new students to the structure of the project and to the requirements for the final product. The course deals also with the learning dimension - how to learn an academic work form - and how the project form is applied to the many different studies at Aalborg University

Groups are formed according to common interests, where the participants' prerequisites in the form of knowledge and interests are presented. The possible project topics are discussed, it could for instance be Political Points of View on the War in Iraq; Cultural Angles on the Indians' Life in Latin America, something about the Basque Country and ETA, etc. (http://www.sprog.auc.dk/is/Diverse/lanprof.htm).

### 4.3 The project work

The Foreign Language Study Programmes organise their group formation differently from International Business Communication. In connection with the intro groups, the students from the first semester are put together in random groups because this solution is the most simple and easy. When it comes to the very project during the first semester and all the following semesters, the students themselves choose with whom they wish to work in the groups. At that moment they may have found some fellow students with whom they share interests and attitudes.

At the first semester the groups can consist of up to eight students, while on the later semesters they can consist of 6 persons as a maximum. The most usual number of participants is four to six on the first semester and three to five later in the course of the studies. If the students want to form a bigger or a smaller group they have to apply for dispensation. Irrespective of in which semester the student is working on a project, the group work is hard work and the student is exposed to strong requirements in all fields (http://www.sprog.auc.dk/is/sup.htm., p. 11)

The department's website informs students about the date at which the project should be handed in.. Normally the students should hand in three copies of the project report at 12 noon on the designated date. Projects that are handed in too late without permission will no be evaluated until the next exam period.

## 4.4 The cooperation contract

In order to formalise the relation between the supervisor and the participants of the group, a cooperation contract has been worked out. (http://www.sprog.auc.dk/snf/coop_agr.html). The supervisor should bring this cooperation contract to the first meeting and fill it out together with the students. Afterwards both parties receive a copy. Every semester a certain number of hours per student are allocated to the supervision of the project groups. When the supervisors of the different groups have been designated, they are now able to calculate how many hours of supervision the different groups can get in total. From this cooperation contract appears the number of hours available for supervision of the group, of which a certain number of hours can be used for meetings. The hours for consultations with the supervisor also include the supervisor's time for reading the group's working papers.

The contract also indicates how many business days before a meeting the group has to turn in their work sheets including the meeting appointments that are mandatory on the first and second semester. On the following semesters they are only an offer to the students. Furthermore, the contract includes agreements concerning cancellations, absence, etc. Finally, the contract contains information on the supervisor's telephone number, e-mail address and office hours. Also the corresponding information on the students in the group is added so that the parties can be in touch and be kept informed.

## 4.5 Evaluation at the Foreign Language Study Programmes

The oral exams are usually group exams, which means that the entire project group is examined at the same time. It normally has the form of a discussion among the participants, including the external examiner. In the later semesters the external examiner will often play a minor role, though there are some external examiners who are active players. Also there are external examiners who practically do not interfere at all. The external examiner's primary role is to ensure that all the students receive equal and fair treatment and that the rules are obeyed. The external examiner is a person who guarantees that the student receives fair evaluations based solely on the project report and the oral exam. It could be agreed that the external examiner is the students' ombudsman, he ensures fair play during the exam. The students are very often quite afraid of the external examiner, but they ought to be very happy about this person as they are ensured the evaluation by two different persons, not only from the supervisor who may know them or the group too well at this stage.

The evaluation in connection with the project exam at the Foreign Language Studies does not defer considerably from the one described at the Business Communication Studies. Nevertheless, there is one important difference, as the Foreign Language Study Programmes never use the project group exam with opponent group, but exclusively the project group with the supervisor as an examiner and normally a external examiner, too. The exam is oral and is either in the foreign language or in Danish. On the first semester all evaluations are in Danish regardless, of the student's foreign language.

According to the exam regulations and the curriculum each student must be evaluated individually as well. In order to ensure that each student's contribution to the report is evaluated individually, the report must include a review of each student's written contribution. This means that it is unacceptable if several group members share responsibility for each central chapter. Individual sections can, of course, be written by several group members (for example short sections, introduction and conclusion) or have several responsible parties. The supervisor can demand a specification of each group member's contribution if a group report is handed in without a list of each students contributions to the report. The evaluation should include an assessment of each student's contribution to the report as well as the oral exam. (http://www.sprog.auc.dk/is/sup.htm, p. 29).

The result of the evaluation may be that all group members receive the same mark. This is often the case on the first couple of semesters, because the project is meant to be a shared learning process for all the members of the group and because writing the project and presenting it at the exam ought to be an equal co-operation between all members of the group. The mark is, however, always individual, and the group can easily receive different marks. On the later semesters this in fact often the case.
(http://www.sprog.auc.dk/is/sup.htm, p. 29).

Both the project report and the oral defence form part of the final assessment of the project. Both the group and its individual members are responsible for contributing to an equal and fair discussion in which everybody is allowed to participate. Academically, the student's ability to relate to the project's theoretical implications and possible empirical research and to consider the consequences of using one theoretical approach over another is emphasised. In addition, the student should demonstrate that he or she understands the basic theoretical concepts and is able to use them actively in the discussion.

# 5. PROJECTS IN THE FOREIGN LANGUAGE STUDY PROGRAMMES

## 5.1 The Diploma Programmes

The following description of the projects at the Spanish and English Studies (SIS) is given as an example of the project work in the Foreign Language Studies as it is not possible to give a complete description of all the projects in the different languages..

At the Spanish Studies (SIS) the students are introduced to the project work already on their first semester. At this stage they defend their project in Danish, but on the subsequent semesters, i.e. on the second, fourth and sixth semesters, they have to do other projects, but this time they have to write in Spanish and to defend the project in Spanish. This means that the students have to search for literature in Spanish in order to write the project report with the correct terminology.

According to the Curriculum the students should work with the following area studies (http://www.sprog.auc.dk/is/Diverse/lanprof.htm).:
* Language (Area Study 2)
* History and social analysis (Area Study 3)
* International social analysis (Area Study 4)
* Culture analysis and Intercultural Communication (Area Study 5)

The structure of the English Studies (SIS) follows the pattern of the Spanish Studies with four additional area studies between the second and the sixth semester:
* History and society (Area Study 2)
* Linguistics (Area Study 3)
* International social analysis (Area Study 4)
* Intercultural Communication (Area Study 5)

## 5.2 The Master's Programme

The problem-based learning and the project work continue on the Master's Programme - KKG, Culture, Communication and Globalisation, where the project framework on the seventh semester is either Intercultural Studies or International Social Conditions. The same framework is used and continued on the eight semester, meaning that the students during these two semesters have to write two projects using both themes.

At the end of the ninth semester the student has to prepare an internship project based on problems relating to an internship in an international organisation abroad during this semester.
(http://www.sprog.auc.dk/is/Praktik/infoguide1.htm, p. 3). The project report should be based on the internship in one of two ways. The student can either formulate a problem based on the tasks he has performed personally at the internship placement or he can base his report on a problem, which is relevant for the internship organisation in general. It could be analysis of market conditions, competition, cultural differences, political conditions, etc. The internship project report is part of a graduate studies programme and therefore not identical to a report written for the internship placement. The purpose of the project report is to combine theory and practice where the university is almost only interested in the applied method. Thus the internship report must include an account of the theoretical framework within which the problem has been treated.

The following titles of projects are examples of ongoing projects at this moment (October 2003) at the KKG Studies' seventh semester:

- Organizational Leadership
- US/UN Relations
- Consumer behaviour in a tourism context. Culture. Communication.
- Modernidad, Cultura
- España: Punto de vista. Migración, medios de comunicación y cultura
- Latinos en EEUU
- Germany's role in Europe
- La vie politique en France aujourd'hui

## 6. CONCLUSIONS

The students at the Foreign Language Study Programmes work with a wide range of projects covering social history, literary studies, intercultural communication and linguistics e.g. discourse, formal linguistics, sociolinguistics, psycholinguistics and applied linguistics. As the foreign-language students always have to work with theoretical problems in a foreign language, they have to write project reports and defend the project in a foreign language, these students have to defend themselves in many ways. The project-based learning is an instructional method that challenges the students to »learn to learn« and prepares our students to think critically and analytically. They learn how to find and use appropriate learning resources and the many long processes when working with the project, using their foreign language when discussing the different angles of the problems make them learn more as the project-based working process enlarges the time where they actively work with their foreign language. In fact, you could say that the problem-based learning make the students study more.

## REFERENCES:

Bennett, Andrew et al.(1994). *Languages and Cultural Studies - an introduction to study skills and methodology*. Publication of the Department of Languages and Intercultural Studies, Aalborg University.

## Curricula:

BA- Erhvervssprog og International Erhvervskommunikation
http://www.auc.dk/fak-hum/studordn.htm

BA - SIS-Spansk ved Aalborg Universitet
http://www.auc.dk/fak-hum/studordn.htm

BA SIS-Engelsk ved Aalborg Universitet
http://www.auc.dk/fak-hum/studordn.htm

Kandidatud i Kultur, Kommunikation og Globalisering ved Aalborg Universitet http://www.auc.dk/fak-hum/studordn.htm

Other web-addresses:
Guidelines for exam complaints and appeals - June 2003
http://www.auc.dk/fak-hum/uk/eksklage.htm

Internship guidelines: (Internship)
http://www.sprog.auc.dk/is/Praktik/infoguide1.htm

Oral examinations: (Oral)
http://www.sprog.auc.dk/is/Diverse/lanprof.htm

Pages on courses and projects (Courses)
http://www.sprog.auc.dk/is/Diverse/lanprof.htm

Project handbook for Foreign Language Studies - Study Board of Foreign Language
http://www.sprog.auc.dk/is/sup.htm

Project handbook for International Business Communication
http://www.sprog.auc.dk/ciek/uv.html

# DOING ALMOST THE SAME THINGS FOR SOMEWHAT DIFFERENT REASONS

## - A note on »variations« within the Aalborg model

**Thomas Borchmann and Søren Lindhardt**

Abstract: In this presentation we will focus on variations within the Aalborg model. The variations we have in mind are not the minor differences that one can find in the outward materializations of the semesters within the different departments, but rather the different understandings of the rationale(s) for using problem-based project work as a vehicle for student learning. These understandings can be said to be present in our daily conversations as a fragmented manifold of arguments, perspectives and vocabularies that influences our perceptions of problems as well as our perceptions of the scope of possible action strategies for problem-solving, as we will try to illustrate by drawing on examples from our own work within the Department of Communication. Finally, we turn our attention to the question of the merits and potential value of the praxis of »doing almost the same things for somewhat different reasons« and claim that this praxis can be defended.

## 1. INTRODUCTION

When asked about our pedagogical practices, we often start by mentioning problem-based project work and sometimes even the Aalborg model. But what are we really referring to when we use such headings? Are we pointing to a shared way of doing things and a shared set of beliefs or justifications for doing what we do - or are we rather referring to a diversity of practices and a number of different views on why we do what we do? Here we shall argue that we might reasonably be said to refer to a common way of doing things, that is a fairly common way of organizing the semesters, but also that there is a variety of different understandings of the rationale(s) for doing so. Understandings, that can be said to both manifest themselves in - and actively influence - the perceptions of problems within our daily work - as well as our perceptions of the scope of possible action strategies for problem-solving and curriculum development.

Stated as three separate claims we can say I) *that there is an overall model, although some variations exist,* II) *that this overall model can be grounded in a variety of different rationales, and thus be understood differently,* and III) *that the different understandings are present as a fragmented mix of arguments, perspectives and vocabularies that influences the perceptions of problems and scope of possible action strategies within our daily work.* Each statement will be accompanied by some supplementary comments and justifications in the following section 2, before we turn our attention towards an illustration of the third statement in section 3. Finally, in section 4 we will present some views on the merits and potential value of the praxis of doing almost the same thing for different reasons, and claim that this praxis can be defended.

## 2. SOME COMMENTS AND JUSTIFICATIONS

In this section we offer some justifications for the three claims: I) *that there is an overall model, although some variations exist,* II) *that this overall model can be grounded in a variety of different rationales, and thus be understood differently,* and III) *that the different understandings are present as a fragmented mix of arguments, perspectives and vocabularies that influences the perceptions of problems and scope of possible action strategies within our daily work.*

### 2.1. There is an overall model, although some variation exists

The first part of claim (I), *that there is an overall model*, is to some extent obvious, as we would (probably) not speak of an Aalborg model unless there were some kind of common denominators for our actions. Hence we might learn something from trying to list these features and also a little from noticing what would not be included on the list. In our attempt to list these features, we are not going to depart from the extensive literature on problem based project work or the history of the Aalborg model. Instead we will concentrate on the folder distributed to accompany the announce-ment of the conference. The main reason for doing so is that the folder can be viewed as containing a straight-forward answer of what the shared characteristics are (as well as what they are not), which can be said to capture our current situation better than an answer derived from a survey of literature or history could.

Quoting from the conference folder (UCPBL & PUC 2003) the shared features or characteristics are:

- Half of the students time is spent on project work, the other half on courses
- One project per semester
- Each group has it own room and an attached supervisor
- In the first semesters, the number of students in a group is 6 - 8 students. In the latter semesters 2 -3 students

At first glance, what could be viewed as odd by an outsider, is that these characteristics all consist of (at best) very generalised descriptions of how we organise the semesters and that there is no mentioning whatsoever of any ideas or principles which specify/justify why we are doing things this way. That is to say, there is no mentioning of learning principles or declarations of the overall educational goals, just as there are no specifications of the character of projects, the freedom or influence granted to students, or the restrictions enforced or recommended, etc. If someone wanted to claim that this is because there exist a fixed and commonly shared understanding of why we do what we do, which hardly needs explicating at a local conference setting - or to paraphrase; that »model« here just mean the overall guidelines for unfolding this shared understanding - we would argue that this is not - and cannot be - the case. Rather than just referring to our own experience, we will try to suggest some evidence for the claim, that this cannot be the case, by pointing your attention to the fact, that these guidelines in their vagueness allows for a multiplicity of interpretations and realizations, which had to be deemed problematic, if such an understanding really did exist. (As an example you might notice, that the first guideline allows for different placements of the project work within the semester plan.) Without any specifications or restrictions, the guideline really only states that there has to be project work. Here we might also add that the next guideline »one project per semester« cannot be viewed as a supplementary restriction, as in praxis it is understood as »minimum« one project. Secondly, one might also notice that a lot of diversities exist within issues that such an understanding probably would require uniform views on if it really did exist. A few examples follow; in some places the choice of project theme is left to the students and in other places a fixed stock of project suggestions exists. In some places, the students are required to reflect on the exemplary qualities of their work, whereas in other places emphasis is put on more personal reflections concerning »process-lessons« learned or on reflections concerning science philosophy. Taken together this evidence not only offers support for the claim that a more common understanding of what the Aalborg model means cannot be said to exist, beyond what the folder itself suggests, but it also trivially supports the second part of claim (I) that variations exist within this *overall model*.

## 2.2. The overall model can be grounded in a variety of different rationales, and thus be understood differently

Whether viewed from the privileged position of the contemplative theoretician or from the more modest perspective of a participant in our daily conversations and engagements, the second statement (II) *that this overall model can be grounded in a variety of different rationales, and thus be understood differently*, should not be controversial either. Both speaking from the second position we do not intend to do a thorough statement of these rationales - let alone a critical, historical study of the pro- or regressions in the dominant arguments for the model. Instead we will just do a short (and somewhat polemical) juxtaposing of different answers to the question »Why project work?« in order to show the variety of focuses and terminologies that these answers produce. A supplementary reason for doing so is that it is precisely in this fragmented form that the rationales and understandings manifest themselves in our daily conversations and actions.

If we define project work as a learning oriented activity where students in a group choose - and set out to explore or solve - one or more problems, which supposedly carries within it/them a potential for exemplary learning and where the problem/problems therefore is/are allowed to serve as a reference point for the students choice of theories to be used and methods to be applied, we seem to have five central characteristics; It is *problem-based*, it is *group-organized*, it is *democratic* or *participant directed*, it aims at *exemplary learning* and is (or can be) *interdisciplinary*. However, each of these characteristics can be understood and weighted differently; similarly, there is a wide variety of different arguments supporting these as indicated respectively in the following.

• The idea that project work would benefit from being centred around the exploration of - or attempt to solve - a problem can be supported by at least three different reasons; 1) A structure-oriented reason according to which the problem will serve as a basis for creating focus, direction and continuity in the learning process, 2) a motivational reason according to which, the departure from a problem would serve to stimulate the interest of the learner, and 3) a goal-oriented reason according to which the problem-crushing or problem solving activities would allow the students to acquire important real-life skills. These reasons do not necessarily conflict, but nor do they necessarily fit smoothly together. That they can conflict can be observed, when we address the question of what an appropriate problem would be. Here one could claim that a possible conflict existed between what the learner(s) would conceive of as an appropriate problem and the appropriateness of the problem qua its potential for exemplary learning.

- With regard to the concept of exemplary learning, this concept must be said to have different meanings based primarily upon the definitions given by Wagenschein (Wagenschein, 1968) and Negt (Negt, 1981) In the first definition the notion of exemplary learning means exemplary for a specific field or discipline, whilst the other states that the learner acquires critical consciousness, that is an understanding of how both your own and others ideas and understandings, etc. are shaped by the(ir) historical and socio-economical setting. Hence the arguments put forward for the necessity of exemplary learning can include anything from the simple claim that almost any field or discipline is too »large« to be studied completely, and therefore necessitates exemplary selections of »parts which reflects the whole«, to the claim that critical consciousness (or »true« consciousness) is something which any student should acquire as a future citizen, and professional administrator - or transformer - of the disciplines. Arguments which can be said to offer different views on the existing borders between the disciplines, different degrees of interest in the previous/primary socialization of students and the character of their experiences, as well as a difference in their view of the obligations and contributions of education to society.

- Considering the different meanings given to the word, »exemplary« different views on the necessity or possibility of interdisciplinary approaches also seem possible. Here we might separate a critical orientation according to which the existing parcelling up of knowledge domains (and knowledge constitutive interests) is considered to be problematic, and a non-critical orientation according to which the chosen problem - and not fixed disciplinary borders - should serve as the reference point for the students choice of theories and methods.

- With regard to the democratic or participant directed character of the project work, we can distinguish between reasons which focus on motivational gains, reasons which point to the gains of self-censorship, and reasons which point to either the outcome of the process or aspects of the process itself, in that it is claimed that the students will acquire important competencies by participating - or be objects of a problematic suppressive socialization if not granted democratic/participatory rights. As with the reasons put forward for the idea that project work would benefit from being centred round the exploration of a problem, these reasons do not necessarily conflict. Different emphases can however be given, just as too rigid interpretations might also carry along with them the seeds of conflict.

- Arguments for the group organization of students could also be said to differ. Some would point to the output - that is the positive experience of democratic values and principles - others to the »synergetic effects« seeding the process or the »team-player« competences acquired. Competences, which some would judge to be more (and some to be less) than the positive acknowledgement of democracy. Finally, it is also possible to point to the group organization as a forum for reduction of anxiety, sharing of experience and experience objectification, and means to safeguard the students against hidden learning plans.

### 2.3. The different understandings are present, as a fragmented mix of arguments, perspectives and vocabularies that influences the perceptions of problems and scope of possible action strategies within our daily work

Considering the mix of arguments and focuses put forward above, the first part of the third statement (III) *that the different understandings are present as a fragmented mix of arguments, perspectives and vocabularies*, should also be easily understood. The second part of the statement *that (this mix) influences the perceptions of problems and scope of possible action strategies within our daily work*, needs however some supplementary comments as well an »exemplary« illustration. If we depart from a view of human individuals (and teachers) as something less than disciplined conscious individuals with consistent world-views, we might find the statement plausible, but we might also find the fragmented character of our understandings problematic, because it permits unreflective practices as well as constantly shifting influences. If, however, we are willing to think of ourselves as something more than unconscious automatons (or lazy opportunists or unreflective dogmatists), we might, on the other hand, find no reason to despair by the outlook to this »grand reservoir« of divergent understandings. At least that is what we will try to argue in section 4. Before that, we will turn our attention towards an illustration of how a fragmented mix of arguments, perspectives and vocabularies can be said to influence the perceptions of problems and scope of possible action strategies. Here we will draw on examples from our own work with a semester in the Department of Communication.

## 3. AN ILLUSTRATION

The material, which we will use as an illustration of how a fragmented mix of arguments, perspectives and vocabularies can influence the perceptions of problems and scope of possible action strategies, is based on our own work with the fifth semester in Humanistic Informatics, a semester, for which we have been jointly responsible for a period of two years.

### 3.1. The semester and its project unit

The theme of the project unit on the semester is »*Communication in Organizations*«. In our interpretation this heading cannot be said to dub a specific *field* - although you can find a variety of textbooks or textbook chapters dealing with a fairly wide subject called communications in organisations - just as it cannot be said to point out a specific *approach* to the study of organisations or a specific *view* of organisations as communication or communicative systems. So, what is it about? It is about making analysis of communication and communication patterns in which the influence of the context(s) on the communicational exchanges is taken into consideration and made an object of reflection. In the fifth semester, the notion of context introduced is »organisation« and not context in terms of say époques or cultural settings (although you might view an organisation as a cultural setting amongst other things).

Analysis of communication in an organisational context can roughly be said to require explicit understandings of different conceptions of organisations, (for example as consensus- or conflict-driven systems, pluralistically determined systems or social systems where other specific internal dynamics are stipulated), explicit views of speakers as inhabitants of organisations (whether they are free, role-determined or over-determined individuals/actors) and a vocabulary for describing (and identifying) specific communicational moves, patterns, phenomena, etc. Part of this vocabulary is acquired in earlier semesters, but in the fifth semester the students are introduced to the vocabularies stemming from the family of discourse- and conversation-analysis approaches (Fairclough, 1995, 2001; Potter, 1996; Laclau & Mouffe, 1985) as well as the vocabularies stemming from the variety of approaches to the study of organisations as cultures. (Schultz, 1995; Alvesson & Deetz, 2000 among others). The students are free to investigate any theme of communication, but to further complicate things communications about organisation, work, leader-ship, technology, etc. are recommended as interesting objects of study, partly because these themes - or communications - are thought to contain a variety of visible displays of how communicational interactions are shaped by their context and partly because it is an area that the students will work with - or in - later in professional life. Hence, ideally the students are not just introduced to different conceptions of organisations and different approaches to the study of communication in organisations, but also to central concepts, themes and ideas within management theory.

Historically the semester has had different teaching staff attached and a changing emphasis with regard to the interpretation of theme of the project unit and the courses offered, leading some years to an emphasis on making cultural portraits of organisation and in others to an emphasis on the study of the quality of dialogue qua dialogue in organisations. However, these changing emphases had also resulted in a certain plurality in the projects engaged in by students; a plurality which could not just be described as positive, as patterns of problematic character could also be detected.

### 3.2. Perceived problems and action courses

One pattern, that could be detected, can best be described as an element of single-sidedness within the plurality. This single-sidedness showed itself in a low frequency of projects, which used discourse- and conversation-analysis approaches and a frequent use of previously learned analytical vocabularies as a substitute for the new ones introduced. Another aspect of single-sidedness had to do with the themes chosen, in that a majority of the projects were looking at popular or main stream themes and in a lot of cases incidents of »old wine in new bottles« without ever discovering them to be so. Thirdly, one could also track a tendency to perceive the problems that were discussed within the communications studied as instrumental problems, that is as problems where goals were taken as given or assumed to be something shared, and where anything but a submission to the quest of an effective realizing of these would be perceived or modelled as irrational. In other words, the students showed a certain blindness or ignorance of the political aspects of - and power relations in - the communications and contexts studied.

Different diagnoses of these problems as well their possible causes were offered by the group of teachers involved with the semester. We basically agreed that a lot of projects could not be said to be exemplary, taken in the first sense of exemplary stated earlier on in section 2, because they did not include an analysis of communication in which the influence of the context(s) on the communicational exchanges was considered, just as they did not display a satisfactory acquisition of supplementary theories and vocabularies for the analysis of communications or an ability to relate the modern themes studied to their historical roots. We also agreed that a large part of the projects could not be seen as exemplary in the second sense of exemplary. A lot of projects could be said to indicate a heightened critical insight in the sense of being conscious about the implications of choosing one or the other perspective/approach and to document a heightened ability to critically examine a theory or an approach in terms of the evidence presented for it, etc. but both the ability to critically reflect on your own belief and biases and their possible roots, and the ability to make externally oriented examinations of theories, their possible roots and ideological components, etc. were not documented to the same extent. Hence we ended up addressing the following four questions; 1) *Why is there such a low frequency of projects, which reflects the influence of the context(s) on the communicational exchanges and what can we do about it?* 2) *Why is there almost no use of discourse- and conversation-analysis approaches and what can we do about it?*, 3) *Why are modern organisational themes studied not related to their historical roots and what can we do about it?* and 4) *Why is there a tendency to perceive problems as instrumental problems and no self-interrogation of this tendency and what can we do about it?* Here we found ourselves able to offer many different perspectives, which each influenced our views of the scope of possible courses of action.

With regard to the first question we agreed that the low frequency of projects, which sought to reflect the influence of the context(s) on the communicational exchanges, could be seen as a consequence of at least three different factors: a) The way the semester had evolved its »plurality« under the influence of changing emphases and interpretations eventually leaving open the possibility of doing projects which did not reflect the influence of context on communicational exchanges, b) the many possible interpretations still open to students as well as teachers, when introduced both to organisational theory as prescriptions about organisation, the study of organisation and the study of communication in organisations and c), an established »stock« of previously done projects from which the students sought inspiration believing these to be exemplary projects. As for the second part of the question of what to do about it, we basically agreed on the necessity of making the theme of the project unit clearer, as well as clarifying the relations between it, the semester courses offered and previously offered courses. However, we did also discuss the possibility of formally placing further restrictions on the project unit with regard to theme as well as approach, but we decided against it in favour of attempts to present more exemplary projects during the courses. One consideration here, which was weighted against the attempt to control through the imposing of further restrictions, was that of the students' needs to be allowed room for their own translations of the project theme. Needs, which were not just formulated as »rights«, but needs which perhaps could be met and qualified by postponing the start of the project work until a more thorough introduction to the semester, its courses and its goals was given.

With regard to the second question several possible causes to the low frequency of discourse- and conversation analysis approaches were also pointed out. Some thought a major reason was to be found in the »economic« behaviour of students leading them to opt for previously tried and mastered approaches rather than trying out new and more work demanding dittos. Others thought of students as somewhat stifled by the introduction to the seemingly abstract vocabularies of discourse-analysis and conversation-analysis, although the perceived abstractness could also be thought to be generated by a certain unwillingness. Also the placement of the course giving an introduction to discourse and conversation analysis and its relation to other courses on the semester were considered, before we eventually decided to give the course a higher priority on the semester with regard to placement and scope, as well as deciding to incorporate examples of discourse analysis and a usage of the discourse vocabularies in other courses on the semester.

With regard to the third question, we all agreed that the lack of historical understanding was due to two factors. Namely a) a lack in the existing curriculum with regard to providing an overview and b) that a lot of the new concepts tended to present themselves as new and never seen before. Hence we decided to put in an historical overview of the developments within organisational theory and management theory, an overview which itself would allow for important exemplifications of the tensions embedded within a lot of organisational and managerial prescriptions as well as give ample opportunity for a de-masking of the emperor's newest clothes.

With regard to the students´ tendency to perceive the problems as instrumental ones, without an explicit understanding of - or critical reflection on - this tendency, the differences in our views on possible reasons primarily stemmed from our divergent perceptions of students as individuals with a lack of experience and students as »over-experienced«. Divided between the equally »square« perceptions of students as »clean slates« and individuals, each holding the conviction that the best chance of breaking with your own oppression was to become an oppressor yourself, we reached an agreement to try to link the introduction of every organisational and management theme with illustrations from the students own (and shared) experience as university students. However, we also decided to reintroduce or strengthen a public space between the lectures and the group forum in the form of plenary sessions and workshops, in which both confrontational discussion and shared investigations could take place. This decision was motivated by a view of the group as a forum, which could not automatically be thought of as a forum for fruitful experience-sharing, especially since this experience was thought to be absent or, alternatively, to be present but only in the form of experiences already dealt with individually.

To sum up the following changes were made: We examined and changed the course-curriculum in order to ensure that a) different conceptions of organisations were introduced and contrasts high-lighted, b) an overview of the emergence of themes and traditions within management and organisational theory was given, and contrasts as well as similarities were high-lighted, c) that different approaches to the study of communications in organisations were given and exemplified. We also d) postponed the starting point of the project work in order to let the student get a grasp of the semester, its content and goals, instead of prematurely starting off from the students´ expectations thereof, just as we e) introduced plenary sessions and workshops in connection with every lecture. Among other changes made, we also decided f) to participate in each other's courses, so that there would always be at least two teachers present, see also (Lindhardt & Borchmann, 2002).

## 3.3. Outcomes and some process reflections

In general, we were all pleased by the outcome of the semester that followed. Considering the many contemporary changes made - as well as our reformist eagerness, which probably also manifested itself in our interactions with the students - it would, however, be somewhat futile to try to point out any clear lessons on causes and effects. But nor was this an overall objective for the presentation. Rather we would like to point to the process, and especially to the fact that we all found it fruitful to be able to draw on different understandings of problems and their possible solutions while working. Here, we refer in particular to understandings which all stemmed from different emphases given in our answers to the question »Why project work?« Also today, our divergent emphases show their value in our ongoing evaluations and discussions of future efforts to improve the semester. For example, one issue here is a discussion of the potentials of a more radicalised democratic approach as a way to reach a shared interpretation of the project unit, another concerns the proper balancing of the gains of clear instructions and the gains of getting it yourself. It is also with these experiences in mind, that we will now turn to the question of the merits and potential value of doing almost the same thing for somewhat different reasons.

## 4. ON THE MERITS AND POTENTIAL VALUES OF DOING ALMOST THE SAME THINGS FOR SOMEWHAT DIFFERENT REASONS

Departing from our own experiences and the felt values of having divergent understanding of the rationales for using problem-based project work as a vehicle for student learning, we will of course defend the potential values of the praxis of doing almost the same things for somewhat different reasons. This defence must however not be confused with a defence for pluralism per se in that we both accept and sympathise with the need for shared guidelines within a university, which aims at producing its own educational profile. That these guidelines are needed does not mean, however, that one cannot envisage and fear the sterility that could follow from attempts to establish a final and uniformed answer to the question »why problem-based project work«. A uniformed answer, which in our view is not attainable, but probably remains as a quest that someone would find worthy of pursuit for reasons other than just an improvement of our educational practices. Finally, we would also like to add, that different understandings do, as a matter-of-course, require living dialogues and cooperative experiments in order to be able to enrich our shared praxis. Here we particularly welcome the conference, which we hope will be followed with more to come.

# REFERENCES

Alvesson, M. & Deetz, S. (2000). *Doing critical management research*. Sage, London.

Fairclough, N. (1995). »*Critical Discourse Analysis*«. Longman, London.

Fairclough, N. (2001). »*Language and Power*«. Longman, London.

Laclau, E. & Mouffe, C (1985). »*Hegemony and Socialist Strategy*«. Verso, London.

Lindhardt, S. & Borchmann T. (2002). »*Udviklingstiltag på 5. semester*«. Institut for Kommunikation. Aalborg Universitet

Negt, O. (1981). »*Sociologisk fantasi og eksemplarisk indlæring*«, Kurasje, Copenhagen.

Potter, J. (1996). »*Representing Reality: Discourse, Rhetoric and Social Constructivism*«. Sage, London.

Schultz, M. (1995). »*On studying Organizational Cultures: Diagnosis and Understanding*«. Walter de Gruyter, Berlin.

Wagenschein, M. (1968). »Zum begriff des Exemplarischen Lehrens« in »*Verstehen Lehren*«. Beltz Verlag, Basel.

UCPBL & PUC (2003). »*AAU-modellen; Variation og udvikling*« Conference-folder.

# PpBL® IN ARCHITECTURE AND DESIGN

## Hans Kiib

**Abstract**: This article recounts some of the pedagogical experiences and reflections that teachers and students have developed in the M.Sc. in Engineering programme of Architecture & Design at Aalborg University, since its start in 1997. A new model for problem-based learning has been developed. We call it PpBL, which is the acronym for »Problem and Play Based Learning«. It places the focus on the interplay between the intuitive and the goal-oriented aspects in university pedagogy. Future development work must strengthen the initiatives that have already been started in the area, by including intuitive and reflective tools, artistic progression and critical interpretation. This also embraces a changed vision of development in the learning environment - both the physical and the virtual. The article's concluding sections offers preliminary experiences with this interplay between reflection and play in PpBL on the one hand, and spatiality as a fourth pedagogical dimension on the other.

## 1. ARCHITECTURE AND DESIGN IS A NEW CREATION IN THE ENGINEERING FIELD

In the summer of 2002, the first graduates emerged from Architecture and Design (A&D) at Aalborg University. These young graduates will create careers within architecture and engineering firms, in the development fields of industry or within larger municipalities. We also believe that some graduates will find jobs in information and service concerns, and that others will have the courage to start their own practices and firms, as the educational programme also supports the insight of leadership, collaboration ability and precise communication.

### 1.1. Integrated design

The new graduates are spread across three specialisations: Architecture, Urban design and Industrial design. All have received a broad education with a focus on »technical and aesthetic design«. We have strived to educate professionals with strong abilities within their core specialisations; they can design and build and are, like other graduates of Aalborg University, well equipped for cross-disciplinary teamwork.
In this education, we work from a concept of 'integrated design'. Regardless of the scale of design, the programme's aim is to enable graduates to convert functional, aesthetic, and technical, production and environmental demands

into excellent design. Buildings should have high architectural qualities; cities should be exciting and stimulating. They should be functional and flexible enough to satisfy changing demands. Designs of products, information and virtual »space« have a central significance to our quality of life and identity. The design should last, be beautiful and functional, but it should also narrate meaningfully. This implies a combination of creativity, analytical and technical abilities, aesthetical confidence and technical competence.

## 1.2. The structure of the programme

Students in the first year have followed a particular programme with focus on design. In the $3^{rd}$ to $5^{th}$ semesters, projects have focussed on architecture, urban design and product design, with emphasis on form-making skills, graphic and digital presentation. The projects have been supported by a number of courses within architectural and design history, design methods, communication, CAD, GIS, 3D modelling, construction, materials and indoor climate. Priority has been given to group projects but has been continuously supplemented with smaller, individual design projects, and study tours.

Students in the specialised programme of Urban Design have worked with town planning and architecture at a large scale. They have achieved competence in architectonic concept development, aesthetic and functional processing of urban building, creation of streets and public squares, infrastructure and street furniture. The specialisation, which has a large IT content, is in part directed towards employment in large drawing offices, and in part toward project development and town planning in larger municipalities, firms of consultants and development companies.

In the specialisation of architecture, the students have worked within the classical areas of the building architect and engineer. This includes among other things, architectural conceptualisation, development of designs, detailing and production and project leadership. As examples of projects, 'An ecological residence in the city', 'a larger institution or commercial building', 'Leadership of complex building projects' can be named.

Industrial design includes an integrated process of conceptual design, construction and product development. Graduates have received professional working methods for a career in industrial design. Aesthetical competence is combined with broad knowledge of construction and product development, ergonomics, materials, environment, leadership and economy. All projects have been solved in close cooperation with outside practices within product design and development.

## 1.3. The pedagogical foundation

A number of educational goals for the programme are described in the 18 study guides produced each year.

Behind this development work, a number of pedagogical tools and goals have been implemented:

- To work in problem-oriented and project-organised ways using themes in the areas of study
- To develop AAU's general pedagogical model, specifically in relation to the design professions, so that the individual abilities of the student are optimally developed. This includes among others, the development of workshops and 'mini-projects' that supplement AAU's project pedagogy on a number of points.
- To develop the students' use of IT. This includes the use of web-based learning material, net-based guidance and communication, IT in the design process and project presentation etc.
- To strengthen the students' ability to organise their own studies and participation in the planning and execution of the semesters. This occurs through student participation in the planning of the semester, group project work, student leadership of management committees, etc.

The study guide is a most important management instrument for the study board tasked with setting the curriculum. The study guide is yet more important for reaching consensus on the pedagogical line and principle concepts of the overall programme. It is a tool for dialogue and communication between students and teachers and it is a tool that ensures the quality of the learning environment.

## 2. THE PBL MODEL AT AAU AND OTHER MODELS

The pedagogical goals are largely achieved as far as we consider the formal organisation of the programme (the study guides), project organisation, IT integration, mini-projects and the students' ability to organise their own studies. However, other models challenge the problem-based pedagogy from architectural academies (master and apprentice), and from traditional universities (lectures).

The problem-based project form of work has been the pedagogical basis for the Aalborg University Centre/Aalborg University since its foundation in

1974. This model has its departure point in a critical evaluation of traditional academic teaching methods and includes the concept of praxis as an essential parameter of its pedagogy. The model enables a double qualification:

* A professional and cross disciplinary qualification
* The development of practical competencies, including competencies of learning, cooperation and attitude.

In the actual implementation of the pedagogical principle at AAU, there has been much focus on group-work, contextual knowledge, cross-disciplinary theory and method, innovation and relevance to practice. In relation to the traditional universities, lectures and a set curriculum with independent examinations etc. are given lesser priority, whereas courses related to project work have high priority. Facilitation and other dialogue characterised teaching methods are the important tools of PBL at AUC.

Project work from the old engineering academies was retained but removed from its 'exercise' form, with emphasis given over to the students' own problem analyses and formulations. Essential elements of the 'master and apprentice' form were thus substituted in project work by the students' own responsibility for learning. A facilitator (a consultant and team member) replaced the »master« and group work was introduced as a general principle. The group constitutes a collective learning environment where students, facilitators and course-givers enter a field of practice of knowledge generation, theory development, analysis and solution. Problem-based project work was extended across research, teaching and praxis and its organisation was based around semester-long project themes, collective responsibility for the projects' progress, and mutual responsibility in relation to examination.

### 2.1. The third way between two international traditions.

In connection with the starting up of A&D, funding in the amount of 2 million DKK was sought from the Ministry of Education for pedagogical development and research. A number of pedagogical models and forms of practice within architecture and design programmes in Denmark were to be analysed and set in relation to the AAU model of problem-based project work. In all, 1 million DKK was granted for the commencement of the programme, although not for pedagogical development work. Nevertheless, a certain amount of comparative mapping and analysis was carried out on Danish and foreign universities and schools.

We were well aware that A&D´s pedagogical line should officially be based on:

- The problem-based project work where one works in groups with projects within a given thematic structure;
- Courses within the thematic structure support project work and building of basic competencies.

However, we were also aware that there are certain issues that this model could not deliver satisfactorily - issues that have been solved well in other pedagogical systems.

In the Danish context, architects and designers have traditionally been educated at art schools. The School of Architecture at the Royal Danish Academy of Arts is more than 300 years old. It arose from the French »le beaux arts« tradition, which included fine art, sculpture and architectural schools. This can be described as the 'master and apprentice' system, where the schools are organised into departments, each with its own professor. The primary pedagogical principle is the project exercise, organised in studios with drawing board teaching, guidance and regular critiques. The exercises are set with increasing complexity, but always with departure in an 'artistic problem' - i.e. the ideal form or spatiality seen in relation to functional and technical concerns. Within this form of pedagogical model, lectures are rare and the methodological apparatus is limited. On the contrary, praxis is as central a parameter as is artistic development.

In contrast to the French schools, we find another international tradition dominated by university pedagogy. This is the lecture-based form of teaching, the set curriculum, and an exercise within the relevant course. Studios are usually not connected to this model, while one finds large libraries for critiques and examinations. This model is often connected with architectural and design education at technical universities worldwide.

Between these two pedagogical models, a number of variations are found but very few educational institutions within the creative programmes have systematically employed problem-based project work.

*Table 1: Pedagogical methods in various educational models*

| Architecture and design | Traditional university | Art/Architecture schools | Project org. universities |
|---|---|---|---|
| Pedagogical concept | Set curriculum, lectures, exercises | Master and apprentice, set exercises and practice | Problem-based project work, courses |
| Professional and personal strengths | Academic competence, Scientific training | Practical competence and artistic training | Problem solving, analytical ability, contextual understanding, cross-disciplinary teamwork and communication |
| Weaknesses and deficiencies | Lacks relation to praxis and collaborative abilities | Lacks academic discipline, theory and collaborative abilities | Lacks academic discipline and individual artistic training |
|  |  |  |  |
|  |  |  |  |

On this background, there are very few role models for architecture and design education based on PBL. One of the more successful is Newcastle University, Australia. Newcastle introduced PBL in the mid 1980s. Problem-based study was started in the first years and it has been successful in overcoming the classic schism between the two traditions.

Project work is organised as individual PBL, but with a greater degree of group work at the commencement of the project. Semesters are organised by year with year-coordinators, lecturers and facilitators/tutors. The students have 15-20 hours lectures and supervision per week and typically work 40 hours a week on their project. The students are placed in a learning environment where a great spread of knowledge and skills occur. For example, older students 'hire' younger students to make models and drawings and younger students have access to critiques by the older students. One has experienced that this 'studio culture' has an important influence on the quality of projects as well as freeing teachers to research.

Newcastle's success with PBL shows itself in the students' individual creative and methodical skills without it having negatively effected the other double qualification of competencies of PBL. The cause is to be found in, among others, the interaction between individual projects, group work, an open learning environment across years, and an organisation of the students in socially binding »tutor groups« of 10-12 students.

## 2.2. Primary projects - mini projects / study circles - workshops/ art and action projects

With a background of experiences and analyses, we chose to supplement AAU's PBL model with a number of »pedagogical interventions«, which are in part derived from the art schools' studio based teaching and in part derived from an analysis of the Newcastle University experience.

From the above table it can be seen that one of PBL's weaknesses and deficiencies is in the training of individual art istic development. Moreover, theoretical schooling is often weak. Other problems the AAU model struggles with include a lack of exchange of experience between 'strong' and 'weak' groups and a lack in the systematic handing down of experience from older students to younger.

Project pedagogy is therefore supplemented with other devices, from the start:

- Project work is organised in open, transparent learning environments with 6-10 groups.
- Mini projects, which essentially reinforce the students' individual, intuitive/artistic works processes, and give training in rapid concept development.
- Workshops and study circles for training of the students' self-organisation of larger theoretical material or cross-disciplinary development.
- Study tours to train the students' personal development, gathering of international inspiration sources and training in design and context analysis.
- Shared critique days on many occasions during semester projects to strengthen the groups' abilities in giving and receiving criticism.

Of these, I would especially emphasise the mini projects and workshops that essentially strengthen the students' ability in working conceptually and place focus on intuitive work methods and artistic development.

In addition, we have introduced critics as an essential supplement to project facilitation. Their strength lies in the diversity of the projects. In the early phases of the project, they are a source of inspiration across groups and years.

## 2.3. Problem and play Based Learning (PpBL) - a work in progress.

In a modernistic way of thinking the development of process competencies in PBL has, in the field of technical science, often been connected with considerations of critical reflection and rational methodology, We know today that these cannot stand isolated. PBL requires intuition, play and action in a continual dialogue with reflection and rational problem solving. This requirement is strong in all educational programmes, but perhaps more particularly those programmes that focus strongly on innovation and artistic development, coupled with technical competences. In this connection, I will refer the interested reader to theories of Kolb (1984) and Schön (1983; 1987), which each in their own way includes the experimental and the intuitive as a working principle - in both practice and learning.

In this connection, I have developed a model for problem-based project work that emphasises both goal-oriented methodical aspects as well as the intuitive and innovative aspects (see fig. 1.). The model's right half has often been the most emphasised in PBL within university education. It is my contention that the more phenomenological left half should receive more focus in the coming years' development of PBL, not only in education that is traditionally considered 'creative', but generally in education that concerns itself with innovation, renewal and with cross-disciplinary competence. I have therefore allowed myself to rename PBL to PpBL, which places focus on the interplay between the intuitive and the goal-oriented aspects of university pedagogy. PpBL stands for »Problem and play Based Learning«. Future development work at A&D and related education must strengthen the initiatives already started in this area, including the development of mini projects and semester projects with the inclusion of both intuitive and reflective tools, artistic progression and critical interpretation etc. It is my hope that it can be expanded theoretically and discipline-specifically across a broad spectrum of educational institutions.

This work will have certain branches particularly related to artistic endeavours in a critical public forum, where dialogue with others on the presented design can give positive experiences with the creative process and the creative product. Another branch will be related to the tools used and IT, which will in future become the media that binds and integrates the different competencies in the future.

*Fig1: PpBL(r), Problem-play Based Learning*

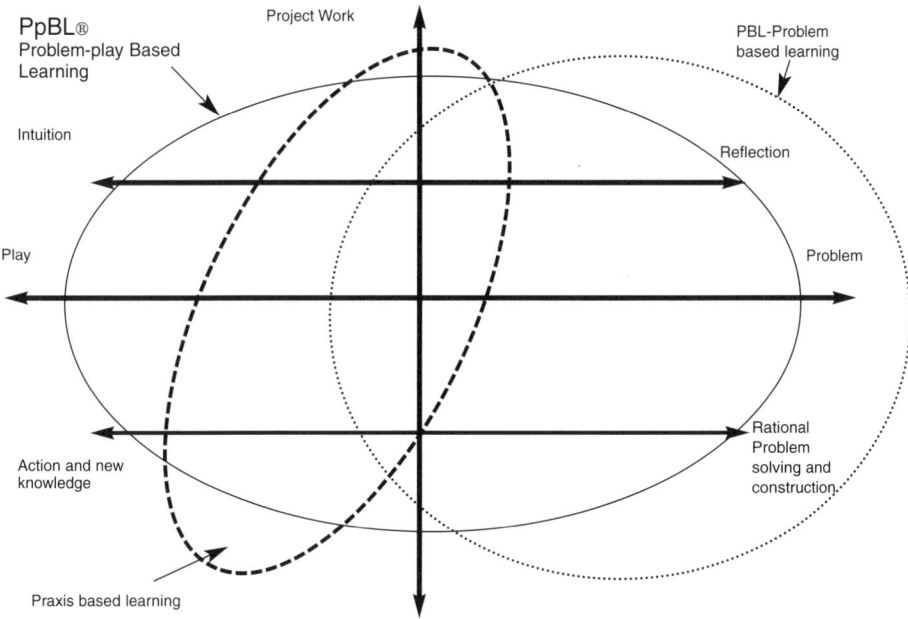

## 3. »SPACE« - THE 4TH PEDAGOGICAL DIMENSION

The experiment with PpBL places focus on the meaning of »space«. In this connection, we perceive »space« as the fourth pedagogical dimension, beyond those of the didactics of professional discipline, the project-based and the problem-play based.

The »space« includes the physical learning environment, as well as the virtual learning environment that particularly includes electronic »space« as the learning environment. In this regard, I will leave the latter but briefly deal with how PpBL and the physical learning environment can supplement each other in the educational model.

### 3.1. Different pedagogical traditions

The different pedagogical traditions have had focus placed on various spatial qualities in the organisation of the educational environment (see table 2). At traditional universities, the auditorium and library are the primary learning »spaces«. The art school uses the studio and workshops as primary learning »spaces« with the cafe and critique room as supplements. In the traditional PBL teaching environment at AAU, the group room and seminar room are the primary educational »spaces«, supplemented by the laboratory and canteen.

It is striking how open the study environment is at Newcastle University, and how much emphasis is placed on students learning from each other. 300 students at the architectural school sit in large open complexes without division between the years. The experience is that the students in this way look after each other socially and with project work, and that the transparent environment strongly encourages learning across year of study. Review sessions take place in the centre of the studio, allowing overlooking from many parts of the building. Thus, 2nd year students can see and hear 3rd year reviews or critiques. Lectures take place in auditoria furnished with writing desks for all students, and with whiteboards and all necessary AV equipment. Laboratory facilities are typically very sparsely furnished, but with good facilities for model making. It is striking that money has not been used on large-scale machine workshops but have instead priority to computer models and cardboard/plastic models, which are worked on in connection with workplaces.

### 3.2. Learning environment for PpBL

At A&D, we have attempted to take the best elements from the various traditions and have experimentally established new PpBL learning environments. We have substituted group rooms with studio-like environments for the project groups, supplemented by the art school's critique room, mini-library and web-library; and we plan to establish café-like kitchen »spaces« for informal meeting. The studios' organisation at art schools is based on individual working situations. At A&D, it is transformed into a collective learning environment where the individual student must constantly be prepared to exhibit his/her work and work organisation. The student sits in a drawing office-like environment with centrally grouped PCs. Work is carried out in groups but there is a large transfer of experience and knowledge between groups and between individual students across year of study. Likewise, supervisors will often be consulted by students others than those he or she is formally responsible for.

*Table 2: Learning environments of various pedagogical traditions.*

| Learning environments of pedagogical traditions. | Traditional university | Art schools Architect schools | Project org. universities |
|---|---|---|---|
| **Pedagogical concept** | Set curriculum, lectures | Master-apprentice, set exercises and practicals | Problem-based project work, courses |
| **Primary learning space** | Auditorium Library | Studio Critique room Workshop | Group room Seminar room and Laboratory |
| **Secondary learning space** | Canteen Cafe | Auditoria Cafe | Auditoria PC room |
| **Contact between teacher and student** | Auditorium Exam halls | Studio Critique room | Group room Seminar room |
| **Evaluation** | Examination | Teacher critique and ped. facilitation | Group facilitation and exams |

There is no doubt that PpBL places other demands on the spatial organisation of the learning environment. In three years time, A&D will move to new accommodation in connection with the building of the House of Music in Aalborg. It is a very important development project for A&D to participate in establishing the foundation for an educational programme integrated in the city itself, and which offers strategic perspectives for the city and cultural activities. Moreover, in a wider perspective it also opens an entirely new education directed toward the area of culture and media. It is anticipated that the gathering of creative educational programmes and musical activities can create the basis for new approaches to educational politics.

A&D is thereby placed in an extraordinary situation in which recent experiences of the relationship between pedagogy and spatial organisation can be expressed in a new building, tailor-made for experimental pedagogy in creative education.

In the coming period, these ideas will materialise into concrete buildings and new projects will follow - partly with respect to the new education and partly to the development of combined learning and production environments within design in its broadest meaning. We hope this building will embrace the pedagogical experiences and goals for a PpBL learning environments. These are desired to be organised around a large, well-lit central »space« (a multi-level internal street) with galleries and balconies. In connection with this central »space«, informal meeting areas, Internet cafes, and information points will be distributed. At ground level, there is the possibility for internal exhibitions, project pin-ups, installations together with music and media art performance from educational programmes in the House of Music.

In general, rooms will be large and flexible, which can be used for many different purposes. In addition, requirements can be tabulated as follows:

- All students shall have a personal »workspace«, grouped in large studio environments with good lighting (through-lighting or light from two sides) and good acoustics. The studios shall be possible to sub divide into smaller units.
- Large and medium sized rooms to be established as double-volume »spaces«, with very good lighting (through-lighting or light from two sides) and good acoustics.
- Corridors to be minimized or avoided and as far as possible integrated into room areas.
- Specialised rooms shall be avoided as much as possible. Instead, we strive for the integration of many functions into flexible »spaces« with great spatial quality.
- Areas shall be disposed such that sectioning is made possible, together with the furnishing of technical 'islands' and smaller seating areas so that students can use the study environment at all hours of the day.
- There shall be easy access to the library and virtual learning fora.
- Close contact and interaction between students across year of study and specialisations.
- Close informal contacts between students, teachers and researchers.
- Close informal contacts between students and staff at A&D, users of the other educational programmes and outside guests.

## 4. CONCLUSION

In connection with the further work of developing and implementing the above pedagogical ideas and visions to a creative learning environment, it will be necessary to experiment. You cannot develop PpBL adequately without experimentation and scientific assessment. This will include both controlled attempts on the small scale as well as development in the broad didactics of the discipline. International experience in the field must be brought to bear and adapted to our own situation. In this endeavour, we must remain open to the good experiences from other pedagogical traditions and from other university levels. Finally, experience in the virtual learning environments must be included. Overall, this must occur with considered respect for the positive results that the PBL model has achieved in the last 25 years at Aalborg University.

# REFERENCES

Kolb, D.A., (1984). *Experimental Learning: Experience as a source of learning and development*, Prentice-Hall Inc, New Jersey.

Schön, D., (1983). *The Reflective Practitioner - How professionals think in action*, Basic Books, USA.

Schön, D., (1987). *Educating the Reflective Practitioner - Towards a Design for Teaching and Learning in the Professions*, Jossey-Bass Publishers, San Francisco.

# EVALUATION OF LEARNING IN ARCHITECTURAL EDUCATION:

## Process and product

**Michael Mullins**

**Abstract**: The integration of the historically separated disciplines of civil engineering and architecture within the Institute for Architecture and Design embraces paradoxes and contradictions. There is a difference between engineering and architecture in their evolutionary backgrounds and their varying degree of emphasis on natural science. In addition, the pervasive influence of assessment on the learning process must be recognized. 'Successful' learning is essentially defined by the criteria on which it is assessed. Information and computer tools now pervade most expressions of modern society and not least, the way in which the built environment is designed and built. These tools have direct influence on education by impelling change in prevalent pedagogical models. A case is made here for the review of assessment criteria in architectural learning and to attempt to develop them within a rapidly changing context of information and communication tools.

## 1. INTRODUCTION: LEARNING AREAS

The Institut for Arkitektur og Design at Aalborg Universitet falls under the faculty of Technical and Natural Science. The Institute was founded in 1998, with the explicit aim to educate for disciplines emerging in the professions of civil engineering and architecture. Teaching and learning are conducted within the wider context of the Aalborg pedagogical model; in consequence design facilitation is carried out in groups of between five to seven students working on project briefs together, with knowledge relevant to the project being disseminated in concurrent courses. Problem-based learning principles of self responsibility for learning are encouraged.

While offering many interesting possibilities, the integration of the historically separated disciplines of civil engineering and architecture also embraces paradoxes and contradictions. Most of the school's graduates will probably practise as professionals in some form or another after graduation, as opposed to entering pure research or teaching, and will deal with problem solving tasks essentially concerned with improving the built environment in one form or another. In this sense, for education to be relevant to professional practice, we must consider educating in ways suitable for the professions, such as it is to be found in 'project-based learning'. On the other hand, the creative design and form-making training, essential for these professions, place other demands on the teaching conditions. It would seem that this is reflected as a distinguishing feature in the difference between 'problem-' and 'project-' based learning forms. In the latter, the project based curriculum is mostly concerned with learning particular proficiencies, and not with the process of learning as experienced by the learner per se; the problem can be external to the learner. Equally, in project-based models, learning assessments spend less time on the evaluation of learning as realized by a learner, but take the form of an assessment of a pre-specified outcome within professional knowledge. Evaluation of 'design talent' or competency is far more prone to aesthetic judgment by examiners; being subjective, it is in the last instance of analysis a matter for self-evaluation by the student him- or herself. In this respect, the Aalborg University model of project-oriented education, allied with problem-based models of learning, does provide a suitable environment for this domain. It can be expected to adapt more easily than traditional Beaux Arts design academies, through legitimising personal discovery and exploration by learners as new tools, for both learning and expression, shape new disciplines emerging in the professions of civil engineering and architecture.

## 2. PROBLEM-BASED PROCESSES, PROJECT-BASED OUTCOMES

Architectural education is centrally concerned with individual design creativity among its students. Creativity is an area of human articulation not easily taught in the lecture theatre, rather requiring a practical component of 'learning by doing' in a studio environment, supplemented, in the Aalborg model, by design work carried out in project groups. Design creativity almost invariably includes some degree of risk taking among students, and particularly in the problem-based process, which is by nature exploratory and often confusing in its apparent lack of clear instruction from facilitators. Dewey's thoughts, though written on reflection and perplexity, may well be applied to this aspect of the creative process: ».... reflective thinking, in distinction from other operations to which we apply the name of thought, involves (1) a state of doubt, hesitation, perplexity, mental difficulty, in which thinking originates, and (2) an act of searching, hunting, inquiring, to find materials that will resolve the doubt, settle and dispose of the perplexity« (Dewey, 1933). This assertion of perplexity as a condition of the creative state is supported by a number of researchers in computer-assisted design (CAD) education, who have pointed out the advantages to legitimising chance, intuition, instability, and ambiguity, and in particular in generating design in the conditions presented by new design methods (Asanowicz, 1999; Yakeley, 1999; Strojan and Mullins, 2002). In problem-based learning, the problems are there to point out the predicament of learning and to provoke creativity as a response in the learner. As such, they support the pedagogical intentions of encouraging individual development of design flair and skill and assessments made accordingly.

However, the pervasive influence of assessment on the learning process must be recognized. The risk-taking factors described above are difficult to place in older didactic models of evaluation and clearly require rethinking if learners are to feel supported in their explorations of territory unknown not only to themselves, but in many cases to their teachers as well. Ramsden has defined three general learning approaches: 'A deep approach involves the intention to understand, and attempt to relate incoming information to previous knowledge and experience in order to extract personal meaning. In a surface approach, the intention is to fulfil the task requirements, which leads to memorisation of only what is thought to be required by the teacher. A strategic approach also focuses on the assessment requirements, but with the intention to obtain the highest possible marks by a systematic allocation of time and effort« (Ramsden, 1988). Deep learning is the ideal form for the engaged learner, but is challenged at the instant that grading of student work is introduced. The astute learner will require knowing the assessment criteria in advance of examination in order to adjust learning efforts accordingly. In the present university context of A&D, this is an inescapable fact of life. Thus, assessment criteria should be explicit and transparent, and it should be anticipated that many, if not most, students will adjust their endeavours accordingly.

These assessment criteria may indeed already be found in the curriculum descriptions and study programs for the relevant semesters of study. However, it will be found that no mention is made of for example 'level of creativity', 'depth of learning', degree of risk in self-selected areas of study, or group engagement for example. This type of criteria is extremely difficult to assess objectively or even in relation between students. As it is, it can be argued that a meeting of the requirements and 'outcomes' described in the curriculum will qualify the learner for a middle grade (an '8' in the Danish '13' system) only, should other more intangible factors such as those mentioned above be wanting. A suggested learner strategy is therefore to use the program goals as a base from which to work, a safety net as it were, but in the knowledge that any self initiated learning goals without an assured measure of success (and thus risky) are legitimate and will be rewarded regardless of product outcome. This must be taken into any account of evaluation or assessment of architectural learning.

There is also a distinct difference between engineering and architecture in their evolutionary backgrounds and their varying degree of emphasis on natural science. Typically, engineering follows the path of correctness in scientific propositions through analysis, while architecture pursues the goal of symbiosis in the environment to satisfy real-world needs. As Ramsden writes »..we would expect that systematic differences in styles of learning should be apparent in professional, science, and humanities students« (Ramsden, 1988), we could similarly anticipate differences between traditional engineering and architectural students. Both present different forms of problem solving that appeal to different learning styles, which raises the question of how to assess the individual student's learning where widely different strategies with widely differing results are employed.

'Successful' learning is essentially defined by the criteria on which it is assessed. Evaluation criteria arise in the context of the university, the academy, the place and the time of their occurrence. However, as far as contextual variables are within the control of instructors, it is possible to structure the environment of learning in such a way that adaptive responses are congruent with the instructor's aims (Ramsden, 1988). The primary present means of assessment in architectural education, including A&D, is the juried review, or critique (widely referred to in architectural schools as the 'crit' or 'review') - the presentation of work to a panel of jurors made up of more experienced academic and practising professionals. While the jury method is internationally applied, it carries certain unsatisfactory elements in relation to problem-based learning. The present measures with which student work is assessed in crits may vary widely, and will to some extent rest on the institution's curriculum, but can rarely be termed 'scientific'. Judgements ultimately are subjective, albeit based on empirical experience, and very often give rise to differences in opinion between the jurors themselves, reflecting their own sense of value in the work before them. This is exacerbated by the professional nature of architectural education, in which evaluation focus is frequently laid on the *object* designed -the building or product for example - and in which it is compared intentionally or unintentionally to a 'real-world' equivalent and assessed accordingly. This is particularly true of external examiners who assess in terms of their own knowledge and experience of the profession, and function as legitimate gatekeepers at the entrance doors to the halls of the profession.

Referring to the limitations of language, Ludwig Wittgenstein wrote »Whereof we cannot speak, thereof we must remain silent« (Wittgenstein, 1922). Much the same could be written on the creative aspects of designing. The subjectivity of, and influence of cultural contextual on aesthetic judgements forces one to reflect on the extent of ones knowledge of what 'good' designing is. There is thus an area of conflict in criteria which simultaneously attempt to assess 'learning-designing' with those which assess professional and technical proficiency[1]. There is a clear case for differentiation. In this respect, the 'crit' serves admirably when viewed as a performance-based method of evaluation - a performance or demonstration, for a real audience and useful purpose; the crit holds the potential to be knowledge-generative - by involving assessments having meaning for the learner, they may produce information or learning in themselves.

## 3. NEW TOOLS, NEW STRATEGIES

Architectural education is again in a period of looking for ways to incorporate new production methods. Information and computer tools now pervade most expressions of modern society and not least, the way in which the built environment is designed and built. These tools have direct influence on education by impelling change in prevalent pedagogical models. In so far as Bloom's seminal taxonomy of educational objectives is close to half a century old, and prepared in an entirely different technological context, it is arguable that its shelf life, so to speak, must soon expire. As a tool for evaluation, its relating of competence and demonstrated skills to the level of abstraction of questions that commonly occur in educational settings (Bloom, 1956) may yet prove extraordinarily resilient to new contexts; this is particularly so in relation to the technical and scientific threads of education at AOD. However, its use as a sole tool for architectural evaluations is limited by its epistemological derivation. This argument will not be pursued further here; it is merely to be acknowledged that many subsequent, and more recent models derive from Blooms taxonomy, and that its application in architectural learning is at present largely untested at AOD.

What is apparent from worldwide trends in education is that the integration of information and communication technologies (ICTs) into curriculum design and teaching practices is effective only if there is a move from older

---

[1] This attempt may easily arise in the integration of engineering and architecture at AOD for example, and may be exacerbated by the integration of project-work with coursework inherent in the Aalborg model.

[2] Distributed, collaborative design-environments have been the topic of discussion and experimentation in universities since at least 1992. Jerzy Wojtowicz reports the term »virtual design studio« as having been used for the first time by William Mitchell in 1993 (Wojtowicz 1994). Virtual design studios, by extending the environments of traditional design studios to include the tools of the information age (ftp, email, web-publishing, tele- and video-conferencing etc.) purports to represent an existing place or building with which students may interact at great distance. Interested readers are referred to an article in the Journal of Architectural Education by the author for further information (Strojan and Mullins 2002).

'didactic' teaching models to more modern 'constructivist' styles of engaged learning (Jones, Valdez et al., 1995). Effectiveness is not merely a function of the new technology, but rather is achieved through adaptation of the learning environment to a changing context. For example, Virtual Design Studios (VDS)[2] offer a complete but limited subsets of architectural education in which one can learn a new, highly context-reliant domain of knowledge. VDS occur in a space particular to themselves and present new opportunities for an investigation and formation of 'place', as that difficult concept is understood in schools of architecture (Strojan and Mullins, 2002).

## 4. PERFORMANCE INDICATORS

To link educational theory and computer technology, a framework developed by Means was expanded and reorganised by Jones, Valdez, Nowakowski and Rasmussen of NCREL in 1995[3]. Their variables and indicators are reproduced in Table 1 as it presents a comprehensive model of objectives upon which assessment criteria can be drawn.

| Variable | Indicator of Engaged Learning | Definition |
| --- | --- | --- |
| Vision of Learning | Responsibility of learning | Learner involved in setting goals, choosing tasks, developing assessments |
| | Strategic | Learner actively develops repertoire of thinking or learning strategies |
| | Energised by learning | Learner is not dependent on reward from others; has a passion for learning |
| | Collaboration | Learner develops new ideas and understanding in conversations. Work with others |
| Tasks | Authentic | Pertains to real world, may be addressed to personal interest |
| | Challenging | Difficult enough to be interesting, but not totally frustrating, usually sustained |
| | Multidisciplinary | Involves integrating disciplines to solve problems and address issues |
| Assessment | Performance-based | Involving a performance or demonstration, usually for a real audience and useful purpose |
| | Generative | Assessments having meaning for the learner; may produce information, product, service |

---

[3] North Central Regional Educational Laboratory, Council for Educational Development and Research, Oak Brook, USA, see: http://www.ncrel.org/sdrs/edtalk/toc.htm

| | | |
|---|---|---|
| | Seamless and ongoing | Assessment is part of instruction and *vice versa*; students learn during assessment |
| | Equitable | Assessment is culture-fair |
| Instructional Model | Interactive | Teacher or technology program responsive to student needs, requests |
| | Generative | Instruction orientated to constructing meaning; providing meaningful activities/experiences |
| | Collaborative | Instruction conceptualises students as part of learning community; activities are collaborative |
| Learning context | Knowledge-building | Learning experiences set up to bring multiple perspectives to solve problems such that each perspective contributes to shared understanding for all; goes beyond brainstorming |
| | Emphatic | Learning environment and experiences set up for evaluating diversity, multiple perspectives, strengths |
| | Heterogeneous | Small groups with persons from different ability levels and backgrounds |
| Grouping | Equitable | Small groups organised so that over time all students have challenging learning tasks or experiences |
| | Flexible | Different groups organised for different instructional purposes so each person is a member of a different group; works with different people |
| | Facilitator | Engages in negotiation, stimulates and monitors discussion and project work but does not control |
| Teacher role | Guide | Helps students to construct their own meaning by modelling, mediating, explaining when needed, redirecting focus, providing options |
| | Co-learner; co-investigator | Teacher considers self as learner; willing to take risks to explore areas outside their expertise; collaborates with other teachers and practising professionals |
| | Explorer | Students have the opportunity to explore new ideas or tools; push the envelope in ideas and research |
| Student roles | Cognitive Apprentice | Learning is situated in relationship with mentor who coaches students to develop ideas and skills that simulate the role of practising professionals |
| | Teacher | Students encouraged to teach others in formal and informal contexts |
| | Producer | Students develop products of real use to themselves and others |

Table 1: Indicators of engaged learning from Jones *et al.*

The table of variables and indicators describes very broadly the components of 'engaged' learning. This provides an intriguing model on which to assess architectural learning. However, while this model acknowledges the necessity of exploring new methods for new conditions, it does lack attention to the particular aspect of the spatial environment which, as architectural educators, we are concerned. Additional factors with relevance to 'place' and 'space' will include such variables as memory in as much as the activity of spatial reconstruction is an act of recollection that gives form to memories of place; way-finding as a means of acquiring knowledge[4]; perception and sensory sensitivity to space, light, color, geometry, detail and material as an experienced continuum; risk taking - design is not a static phenomenon to be recreated, it is continually changing in both individual and collective consciousness, just as it is in the context of the city itself; and a sense of ownership and responsibility, encouraged when the learner sets goals, chooses tasks, develops assessments and evaluates his/her own performance. These factors need to be woven into the fabric of architectural assessments.

Based on work by Trudi Cooper[5], a six-step process for assessment by examiners in project reviews will assist in this endeavour (Cooper, 2000):

### 4.1. Identify learning areas.
These could include: the framework of design conceptualisation; the development of design in terms of 'fitness for purpose'; the integration of technical knowledge; and visual, written and oral communication.

### 4.2. Identify learning outcomes.
Outcomes should be directly related to individual/group goals and curriculum requirements.

### 4.3. Identify the learning strategies employed.
In Ramsden's definitions, the student is engaged in 'deep' or 'strategic' or 'surface' learning.

### 4.4. Identify performance indicators that the student has achieved the learning outcomes.
These may include levels of: responsibility for learning; collaboration; authenticity; innovation; interaction with society and profession; flexibility; exploration; and production.

### 4.5. Collect evidence that the performance indicators have been reached.
This process requires that, in the review, the project portfolio communicates the material in visual, oral and textual ways that are clearly legible for examiners to assess and moderate.

---

[4] As Yi-Fu Tuan has shown in his maze experiments, 'space' becomes 'place' in unfamiliar environments only when space becomes a series of familiar landmarks and paths (Tuan 1977). Way-finding is the means of acquiring knowledge and establishing a foothold in unbounded space, and is equally essential in teaching and learning design.

[5] This material has been based on email correspondence with Dr. Terence Love, Research Fellow at Curtin University, Perth Australia, in PHD-DESIGN List, 03 March 2003.

## 5. CONCLUSION

A case has been made here for the review of assessment criteria in architectural learning. A practical strategy for the development of these criteria is to use the problem-based and project-based pedagogical structures that are, as it were, genetically inherited by AOD from both the Aalborg University model and traditional architectural schools, and to attempt to develop them to their best potential within a rapidly changing context of information and communication technologies. In this respect, the critical review may admirably serve the profession, the students and the teachers when viewed as a performance-based method of evaluation. This performance or demonstration is for a real audience and useful purpose, and a demonstration of both design acumen and technical proficiency as befits student members of the professional fraternity. The jury review holds the potential to be knowledge-generative - by involving assessments having meaning for the learner, they may produce information or learning in themselves. Finally, a review of this nature may provide the space for an assessment of both creative process and product outcomes inherent in problem-based and project-based learning models respectively, and which otherwise contain contradictory and irreconcilable thrusts.

However, the assessment process, rather than being based on subjective preferences of the examiners, should be structured against specific criteria relevant to the encouragement of engaged learning. These criteria could include the identification of learning areas; the identification of learning outcomes; the identification of the learning strategies employed by individual students; and the identification of performance indicators. The review procedure is thus in effect the collection of evidence that the performance indicators have been reached.

## REFERENCES

Asanowicz, A. (1999). *Evolution of Computer Aided Design: Three Generations of Cad.* In: eCAADe 17: Architectural Computing from Turing to 2000, The University of Liverpool, Liverpool.

Bloom, B. S., (Ed.) (1956). *Taxonomy of Educational Objectives: The Classification of Educational Goals.* Handbook I, Cognitive Domain. Longmans, Green., New York ,Toronto.

Cooper, T. (2000). *Portfolio Assessment: A Guide for Lecturers, Teachers and Course Designers.* Praxis Education, Perth, Australia.

Dewey, J. (1933). *How We Think: A Restatement of the Relation of Reflective Thinking to the Educative Process.* D. C. Heath & Company, Boston.

Jones, B. F., G. Valdez, et al.: (1995). *Plugging in, Choosing and Using Educational Technology.* In: EdTalk (online journal). Council for Educational Development and Research. Available from http://www.ncrel.org/sdrs/edtalk/toc.htm [cited 13 June 2001].

Ramsden, P. (1988). *Context and Strategy.* In: Learning Strategies and Learning Styles. R. R. Schmeck. Plenum Press, New York.

Strojan, T. Z. and M. Mullins (2002). »*The Identity of Place in Virtual Design Studios.*« In: Journal of Architectural Education 56(1): 15-21.

Tuan, Y.-F. (1977). *Space and Place*: The Perspective of Experience. Minnesota Press, Minneapolis.

Wittgenstein, L. (1922). *Tractatus Logico-Philosophicus.* Routledge, London.

Wojtowicz, J., (Ed.) (1994). *Virtual Design Studios.* Hong Kong University Press, Hong Kong.

Yakeley, M. (1999). *Simultaneous Translation in Design: The Role of Computer Programming in Architectural Education.* In: eCAADe 17: Architectural Computing from Turing to 2000. The University of Liverpool, Liverpool.

# INTEGRATED DESIGN PROCESS IN PROBLEM-BASED LEARNING

## Integrated Design Process in PBL

Mary-Ann Knudstrup

**Abstract**: This article reports and reflects on the learning achievements and the educational experiences in connection with the first years of the curriculum in Architecture at Aalborg University's Civil Engineer Education in Architecture & Design. In the article I will focus on the learning activity and the method that are developed during the semester when working with an Integrated Design Process combining architecture, design, functional aspects, energy consumption, indoor environment, technology, and construction. I will emphasize the importance of working with different tools in the design process, e.g. the computer as a tool for designing and optimising the building. I will also consider the dilemma of the Integrated Design Process in Problem-Based Learning that emerges when the number of courses in the learning model, as is often the case, clashes with the demand for time and scope for reflection which the students need in order to concentrate, mobilize creativity and find the personal design language which is a precondition for making good architecture.

## 1. THE NEW PROFILE IN ARCHITECTURE

Our intention with the curriculum in Architecture was to focus upon the ability to integrate knowledge from engineering and architecture in order to solve the often very complicated problems connected to the design of buildings. According to the provisions for the Architecture curriculum at Architecture & Design at Aalborg University, the main objective is:
»*To educate graduates who are able to work independently and professionally at the highest level with the architectural and technical design of buildings, and who have a thorough knowledge of project planning and project management in connecting with building projects*«. (Kiib, 2001)
As can be seen from this quotation of the objective, the graduates must through the learning process achieve competencies in design, functionality and aesthetics as well as competencies in technical solutions. This implies - besides a critical, analytical, theoretical, functional and technical approach to the subject - that the students must perform a practical synthesis, i.e. a concrete presentation of a real sketch plan for a building e.g. an office building, resi-

dential buildings or institutions. The process is conducted as an integrated process of creation and design, in which a building with a number of qualities find their form. By using the Integrated Design Process the professional knowledge of architecture and engineering is integrated and optimised. The engineering programs at Aalborg University are based on PBL which is the basic educational model of Aalborg University. But in order to create the professional profile/scope which we expect of our graduates, to enable them to cope with technical and aesthetical problems, focus on the creative element, see new opportunities, make innovative solutions - a product or a building - new elements have to be added to the PBL model. Artistic learning, the creation of ideas, and an ability to see new possibilities and be creative become just as important parameters as the ability to identify problems and suggest a rational solution. Therefore, the curriculum has to be deliberately organized in such a way that the pedagogical and learning objectives are achieved within the core subjects of the curriculum.

During one of the semesters at the master level of the Architecture curriculum's the students produce an energy and climate optimised building as their main project. The objective is described in the study guide for the semester (Knudstrup, 2001, 2002).

*»At the end of the semester the student shall be able to:*

- *analyse the aesthetic, technical and functional problems of the building and through various proposals (synthesis) prepare a building plan with high aesthetic, technical and functional qualities.*
- *use general theories and principles concerning the design of the building and integrate these in the proposed solution, including solutions based on technologies concerning ecology, energy and indoor environment in the design and construction of the building.*
- *produce and present the project graphically, in writing and orally - as importance is attached to both the project report and the presentation in drawings and model.*
- *make a presentation of the office building using a CAD tool.«*

In order to achieve the objective, the project programme is arranged so as to give the students an understanding of the problems connected to an integrated development of the design, the aesthetics, the technical and environmental aspects of the building, and to further develop the student's ability to integrate architectural and technical design in the building. It is therefore very important that the two professional subject areas, engineering and architecture, are both introduced at the beginning of the semester, so that the students conceive them as equal parameters in the Integrated Design Process that follows.

## 2. THE CURRICULUM IN ARCHITECTURE

As mentioned above, the project programme focus on the design of a new office building. The geographical site is chosen in an area, which is currently going to be rehabilitated or developed in order to make the project as realistic as possible and to achieve momentum in the work process. The project must be adapted to the architectural context of the area, and relate to the future wishes for development of the area according to the urban development plan. The architecture of the building and its' position on the site may also substantially influence the solutions and choices with regard to resource consumption, outdoor environment, energy consumption and indoor environment. Besides, in this project special attention is attached to the integration of passive energy technology systems.
The internal functionality and the architectural volumes must be consistent, so that all of the future resident's demands for functionality and logistics of the building are considered in the best way possible. The construction of the building must be clarified.

### 2.1. The Integrated Design Process as a method in the PBL process

The project is conducted as group work. The students work their way through the phases of the project, which are at first described in short terms and later in more details. During the various phases of the project the students are taught by architects[1] and by engineers[2], so that the professional approach of both architects and engineers is ensured. An open-minded commitment from both groups is very important in order to achieve a successful integration of the two professions, or else it will give no meaning to bring the two professions together. For this semester I developed the model described below. In this model the traditional architecture and engineering disciplines are split into different components, and some of the components from engineering are combined with the architecture components into a new method. This is what I call the Integrated Design Process. The Integrated Design Process is a synthesis of the pedagogical method (PBL), the students' personal learning efforts, and the professional learning components from architecture and selected components from engineering.

---

[1] Teaching staff from the Department of Architecture & Design,
[2] Teaching staff from the Department of Building Technology and Structural Engineering.

The Integrated Design Process intertwined in the PBL process.

Problem formulation / project idea

Analysis Phase
Analysis of site, urban development plans, company profile, chart of functions, principles of energy consumption, indoor environment and construction.
Aim and programme.

Sketching Phase
Through the sketching process architectural ideas are linked to principles of construction, energy consumption and indoor environment as well as the functional demands to the new building

Synthesis Phase
Architectural and functional qualities, the construction and demands for energy consumption and indoor environment flow together, and more qualities may be added.
A new building has been created

Presentation Phase
The final project is presented in a report, drawings, a cardboard model and IT-visualisation.

## 2.2. Project phases in the Integrated Design Process

In the following the various project phases will be described in details to give you an insight into these phases and into the Integrated Design Process. Fig. 1 shows the design process map. The process is, in fact, a much more complex mental process, so this map is a simplification of the design process. However it illustrates the various phases and the main loops connected to the process.

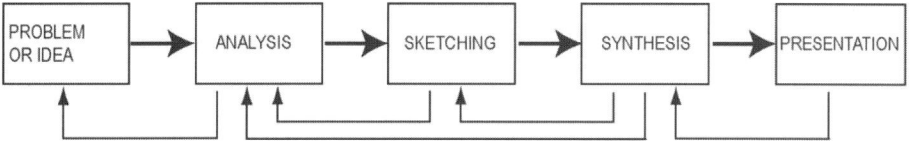

Fig. 1. The design process map.

*Problem formulation or project idea* The first step of the project work is description of the problem or the project idea. The purpose of the project here is to establish energy and climate optimised office building at proximately 3000 m2 with a number of specific properties.

*The Analysis Phase* encompass an analysis of all the information that has to be procured before the group is ready to begin the sketching process, e.g. information about the site, the architecture of the neighbourhood, topography, vegetation, sun, light and shadow, predominant wind direction, access to and size of the area and neighbouring buildings. The group should also consider demands coming from regional plans, municipality plans and local plans which state a number of exact demands and limits for the area such as building restrictions and give information about the site's location in the city and relation to the general urban plan, e.g. connections to the road and path system of the area, and the future development plans for the area. Furthermore, it is important to be aware of special qualities of the area.

In the analysis phase detailed information is procured about the client's demands for space, functionality, logistics etc. It is up to the project group to decide who the building owner is and to make a user profile. It may be a fictive company or a real company to which the group take contact or a company profile described on the Internet. The company can be used for instance as a sparring partner for the elaboration of a room program and logistic needs, a chart of functions and a company concept which can lend inspiration to the design of the building. This is combined with new concept as for instance New Ways of Working. It is also decided if the company may want the building to be an icon for the company in the urban landscape.

The group also works with principles for natural ventilation in a new building, taking the outdoor environment, wishes for the climate shield, the purpose of the building and the demands for functionality into consideration. The group follows lectures, courses and workshops in architecture and engineering, and is conducting parallel studies in literature.
At the end of the analysis phase a statement of aims and a programme for the building is set up.

*The Sketching Phase* is the phase where the professional knowledge of architects and engineers is combined and provide mutual inspiration in the Integrated Design Process, so that the demands and wishes for the building are met. This also applies to the demands for architecture, design, working environment and visual impact, and the demands for functions, construction, energy consumption and indoor environmental conditions. During the sketching phase all demands are considered to find the best solutions as possible, which will meet the demands for the building, the demands for logistics and other demands, which are described in the room programme. New creative ideas and solutions are produced in this phase.

The students have to have capability to visualize their ideas from mind to hand to paper or models. As mentioned above, in this phase the professional knowledge of both architects and engineers are flowing together in the Integrated Design Process. The precondition for designing an energy saving building in an Integrated Design Process is as follows: In the sketching phase the group must repeatedly make an estimate of how their choices regarding the form of the building, the plans, the room programme, the orientation of the building, the construction and the climate shield influence the energy consumption of the building in terms of heating, cooling, ventilation and daylight - and how these choices inspire each other. The mutual influence and inspiration of all the above elements must meet the demands which have been set up for the architectural, functional and technical aspects of the building. The group works with sketches on manifold paper, with physical models, and with computer-designed models.[3] ( Fig. 2.)

Fig. 2. Students' sketches, models and working with computer models.

---

[3] E.g. programmes like „ Auto Cad« or »Autodesk VIZ 4«.

The consequences of the technical choices are calculated by means of rather simple calculation methods/models, which make it possible to compare and select solutions. For example the project group can see which influence a 25% or a 100% glass facade has on the total energy frame of the building. From these calculations the group gains an insight of the parameters that really matters to the energy optimising. In this way the group can sketch various well-founded solutions. At the same time they make an estimate of which of the sketches for the building meet the demands of the architectural expression, and which do not and with that in mind they make their choices.

In this phase the group make a lot of sketches (Fig. 3.) to solve the various problems in order to optimise the final and best solution that hopefully will appear in the next closely connected phase, the synthesis phase. Technical and architectural literature is also studied carefully in this phase.

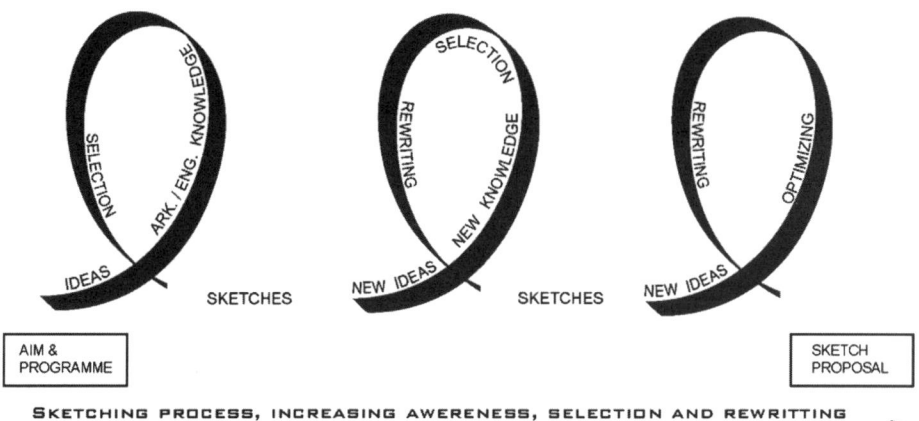

Fig. 3. The sketching process is repeated several times. (Agger, 1983) inspires to this illustration.

*The Synthesis Phase* is the phase where the new building finds its final form, and where the demands stated in aims and programme are met. Here you reach a point in the Integrated Design Process where all elements considered in the sketching phase flows together - and architecture, plans, the visual impact, functionality, company profile, aesthetics, the space design, working environment, room programme, principles of construction, energy consumption and indoor environment technology form a synthesis. In the synthesis phase the various parameters used in the project seen in Fig. 4, should be optimised, and technical calculation models should document the final calculations regarding the climate shield and the energy frame of the building, and the natural ventilation. In this way the project reaches a phase where every item, you may say »falls into place«, and other possible qualities may even be added.

The project finds its final form and expression, and a new building with - hopefully good - architecture, architectural volumes, aesthetic, and visual impacts, functional and technical solutions and qualities have been created.

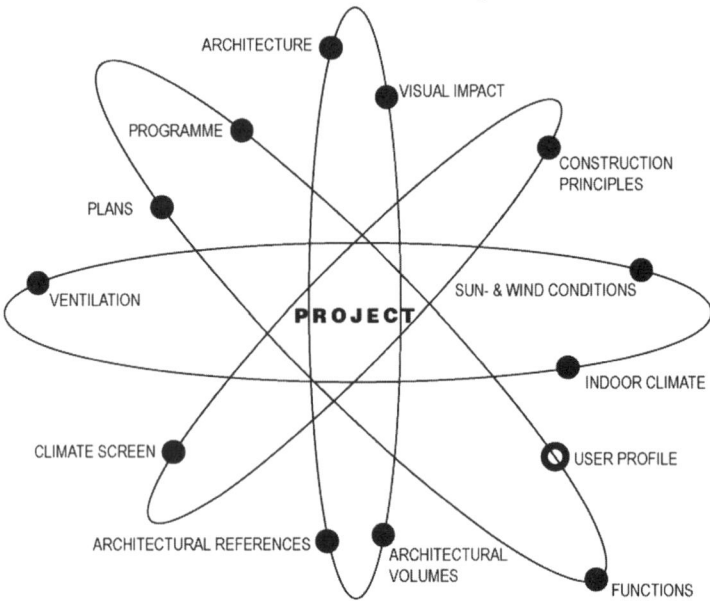

Fig. 4. Illustrate the various parameters that are integrated in the Integrated Design Process

*The Presentation Phase* is the final presentation of the project. The project is presented in such a way that all qualities are shown to advantage, the outcome of the Integrated Design Process is specified, and it is clearly pointed out how the aims of the project have been fulfilled. The presentation includes a project report with documentation of all aspects of the previous phases, and a presentation and description of the finished project in text, diagram's, facades, plans, and architectural volumes, details and calculations, which prove the measurable qualities. The project report also includes a process evaluation, which relates to the plan for the organization and accomplishment of the work which makes the groups aware of their working process and of the learning they have accomplished during the semester. Furthermore, a computer presentation and animation is made together with physical models and posters with text and drawings. The project is also accompanied by a CD witch will be part of the student's portfolio.

## 3. THE PROVOCATION IN THE BORDERLAND BETWEEN THE VARIUS TOOLS AND METHODS

The tools of the sketching process are pencil drawings on manifold paper, building of models in cardboard, plastic or other materials, or 3D models on the computer.

Many different tools are used during the sketching process, at the same time as the students are making calculations on indoor environment optimising and the energy frame in order to solve the often very complex problems attached to office buildings. A tool like the pencil is the traditional tool for architects. It is used in combination with models. These tools all contribute to circumscribe and develop the final form, function and technical structure of the building. The sketches help to maintain the thoughts and ideas, which arise during the process. In this way the sketches become the tool of the student's internal creative dialogue during the sketching process - a dialogue where many ideas on architecture, space design, functionality, room programme and plans are compared to concepts for New Ways of Working and technical demands for indoor environment technology and the cooling and heating.

There are, as it was, various degrees of »resistance« in the sketching tools when the creative thought, the associations and the ideas are tested and formed by means of the pencil, the model and the computer. The resistance provokes the person in charge to consider and test new possibilities, new combinations and solutions to the problems. The synthesis arises in the borderland between the provocations given by the various media, and a synergy effect arises between the various professional worlds when the process is successful.

It is my experience that when the computer is used, other forms are some times generated than the classic geometric forms, and the computer gives another kind of »provocation« to the students than does the physical model and the calculations. In this way the students manage to build a new imagery and think in new ways. In my opinion the computer will be a very important tool for sketching in the future - not only in the presentation phase, but also - and maybe more important - during the Integrated Design Process. As I se it, it offers new professional opportunities and contributes to finding new solutions to the projects. Also, the computer will become a very important tool for handling the increasingly complex problems attached to optimising many different elements at the same time, as suitable programmes are developed for this purpose.

## 4. THE SEMESTER AND ITS ORGANISATION

The semester is planned and organized by an associated professor - called the semester coordinator - who is responsible for the study guide, the timetable and the course of the whole semester. When planning the semester the coordinator meets with a group of students from the previous and the coming semester functioning as a sparring partner. The semester contains a main project and a mini project, and the semester will typically comprise the below elements.

The students do the mini project, which takes about 2-3 weeks, individually. The purpose of the mini projects is to strengthen the students' individual originality and design language, their ability to set forward proposals and their awareness of methods. These are all basic elements, which are important to their professional competencies.

4-5 students groups do the main project, which occupies the rest of the semester. To each group a main supervisor with architect qualifications and a subsidiary supervisor with engineering qualifications are attached. Very targeted project related courses support the project, which is very important for the professional level of the projects. About 50% of the time is used for courses (courses related to the project and courses related to the curriculum), and 50% of the time is used for project work and preparation for examinations. We also have conducted some courses with architects or engineers from the professional practice, which ends up in workshops - successful, but also very time-consuming. But we find that the workshops are important to strengthen the student's theoretical and professional level.
Halfway through the semester we have a seminar with an external guest reviewer, the supervisors and all the students of the semester. The project groups get their work and project sketches evaluated. The evaluation is pointing forward, and all students have the possibility to learn from each others reviews.

The students work in transparent learning environments in a drawing hall with students from different semesters. In this way the students get an opportunity to be inspired by the other semesters and an idea of how it will be to work in a drawing hall in their future professional life. The drawing halls also improve the development of social contacts between the semesters and the synergy effect that will arise from this both professionally and socially. The supervision takes place here at the group's working place and is based on sketches, models, CAD models or text. Both supervisors and students communicate orally, through sketches, models or drawings and calculations. References may be made to existing projects, theory or literature.

The evaluation of the projects is based on the material handed in, the oral presentation on the day of the examination and the following evaluation. We give individual marks after the 13-scale. And the evaluation of the students is based on the aims to be achieved at the end of the semester, which can be seen in the study guide, and the group's aims and programme for its project.

In the end of the semester we also arrange national as well as international study tours to give the students inspiration.

## 5. IS THE INTEGRATED DESIGN PROCES A SUCCESS?

Based on my three years' experience and the evaluations of the semesters it is my assessment that the semester has been successful, and I find that we have managed to fulfil most of the initial aims. The method, the Integrated Design Process in PBL, is so far a success. The students' project shows that it is possible to integrate the engineer skills with the architect skills in the projects, and that the students are learning a method, which enable them to combine other components than the traditional architect components in the process.
The students are, in fact, creating very interesting office buildings with high qualities, where the architecture language is integrated with and inspired by engineering parameters, so that the architectural and technical solutions are optimised. The point is that the students have to integrate the engineer parameters from the very beginning, already in the analysis phase, and further in the process when the sketching of the building is taking place, so that they can make a synthesis of the architectural and engineering parameters.

Seen in relation to the objectives[4] of the semester we have managed to:

- Exploit the professional knowledge of engineers already in the sketching process by developing methods/models that in an easy and transparent way presents the indoor environment and the energy frame of the building. This knowledge can be used for the choices made in the sketching process. Normally these calculations have been conducted ex post.
- Conduct group works in a drawing hall instead of in the ordinary group rooms. In the drawing hall students from different semesters are working in the same creative working space ( Fig. 5. ).
- To include the computer as a learning tool in the sketching or modelling process - and not only as a tool for presentations.

---

[4] cf. page 2 of this article

Fig. 5. Student group working in the drawing hall.

## 6. WHAT HAS TO BE FURTHER DEVELOPED?

As mentioned above the semester has, so far, been fairly successful, but there are still improvements to be done in the following areas:
- The time pressure should be reduced as the courses compete with the time the students have to spend to achieve the necessary sketching competencies and find their personal architectural expression.
- The students' ability to catch ideas and associations, to visualize and to let ideas flow easy from mind to hand to paper.
- The digital tools need to be elaborated to match the professional architectural and engineering demands.
- The technical tools, especially within construction, need further development.
- The interdisciplinary supervisor teams - which have worked well so far - must develop their teamwork and find a more precise definition of what can be learned from each other.
- Interdisciplinary research between architecture and engineering should be encouraged.

Especially the time pressure and the fact that all courses are placed in the first two of the three periods of the semester create problems. It is difficult to

begin the sketching process in due time since only a few days are left for project work during the first two periods. The problem is whether the students in the time available are able to achieve sufficient sketching qualifications.
The students are stuffed with courses and lectures, and may loose the initiative to search for knowledge by themselves. The teachers know how to do problem-based work, but my concern is, are the students learning it, when so much time is devoted for instruction ex catedra?

## 7. THE INTEGRATED DESIGN PROCESS AND THE FUTURE CHALLANGES

It has been exciting and challenging to work with the Integrated Design Process in the Architecture programme with it's' combination of elements from architecture and engineering. It is obvious that it leads to other solutions - other types of buildings and new designs - when the technical disciplines are included in the design process. On the sketching level the projects become better defined than they use to be in the more »artistic« architectural setting. The indoor environmental conditions and the energy frame of the building become clarified. In this way you avoid frustrating problems when e.g. ventilation does not fit into the design of the building.
This is also important for the comfort, and for a good working environment for the coming users. From an economic point of view, the operating costs can be kept at a low level when the climate shield of the building is optimised saving energy for cooling and heating, and the passive ventilation principles are employed, which also reduces energy expenses.

Further development of the computer as a sketching tool is also an exciting challenge. When better sketching programmes are created this tool will be even more useful. Students who use the computer as a modelling tool have a good chance to obtain a good spaceial understanding. Working with the computer also animates you to produce new architectural designs. By using computer simulations of warm and cold airflows you can map in advance the position of cold and warm zones in a building.

It is a huge challenge for the future to develop programmes which can be used for co-optimising a wide number of parameters at the sketching level - both architectural parameters (design, climate shield, facades, plans arrangements, functions, logistics, materials) and engineering parameters (natural ventilation, climate shield, needs for heating and cooling, and construction). One could wish to be 3 - 6 years ahead in time when the immense calculation power of the computer, and its unlimited ability to store large amounts of information such as large collections of indoor environment principles and solutions, principles of construction, and available materials, have been submerged in a combined, computerised design process for the buildings of the future[5].

## REFERENCES

Steen Agger (1983). *Kompendium til kursus i programmerings- og skitseringsmetodik.* [Compendium for course in programming and sketching methods], School of Architecture in Aarhus.

Hans Kiib (2001). *Studieordning for Civilingeniøruddannelsen i Arkitektur & Design. 6. - 10 semester september 2001.* [Curriculum for MSc Engineering with special curriculum in Architecture & Design, 6th to 10th semester], Aalborg University.

Mary-Ann Knudstrup (January 2000). *Studievejledning for 6. semester, Arkitektur og Økologi - Energi og klimatilpasset byggeri. Arkitektur,* [Study guide for 6th semester, Architecture. Architecture and Ecology - Energy and environment in Architecture]. Architecture & Design, Aalborg University.

Mary-Ann Knudstrup (January 2002). *Studievejledning for 6. semester, Arkitektur og Økologi - Energi og klimatilpasset byggeri.* [Study guide for 6th semester, Architecture. Architecture and Ecology - Energy and environment in Architecture]. Architecture & Design, Aalborg University.

Bryan Lawson (2000). *How Designers Think. The design process demystified,* Architectural Press 2000.

---

[5] These tendencies can be seen e.g. in the exhibition »Futures2come« in Dansk Arkitektur Center, Gl. Dok, in Copenhagen 12. March - 9. June 2003.

# THE CONCEPTS OF LEARNING BASED ON THE AAU TEACHING MODEL IN CHEMICAL ENGINEERING EDUCATION

**Erik G. Søgaard**

**Abstract**: During the last thirty years the AAU teaching model has developed into different versions depending on the objectives of the teaching at different faculties and departments. This paper describes a version of the AAU-model used to educate chemical engineers in a number of projects performed in co-operation with the industry, companies and other university departments of natural science.

I present the necessary ingredients in a project and I describe a model of learning that creates the basis of organising the project. This model of learning has a model of memorising integrated. The storytelling concept is integrated in the model of learning as well as in the model of memorising. I describe the problem- and event-based learning by their definitions and normally used problem types and their interface to events are identified. It turns out that by using the narrative concept on projects they will improve in both content and integration.

## 1. INTRODUCTION

The following text is a presentation of how parts of the problem-and mission-based project oriented teaching is arranged and performed by groups on 3. -10. Semester in the Diploma or M.Sc. degree programmes in chemical engineering at the University of Aalborg, Department of Applied Engineering Science in Esbjerg, Denmark.

For all semesters the study board has elaborated study regulations in which the curriculum for the semester is presented. About one quarter of the teaching is based on study unit courses where new and special difficult elements of the curriculum are presented in a way that shows both the classical build-up of a scientific area and presents detailed methods to the understanding of especially difficult abstract ideas and coherence. The result of this classical teaching method gives at its best some skills to the students based on factual knowledge of the presented area of the curriculum. If some parts of the curriculum are already known to some students from an earlier education or other courses maybe the detailed teaching could result in assimilation in which the students will be able to observe their own process of learning. However, we often experience that the students try to identify types of problems from earlier assessments in order to pass examinations and that the students do not ask very many questions which could show a deeper understanding of the abstract ideas and coherence. It is not easy for a teacher to know if the students in connection with that kind of teaching understand the ideas or coherence of ideas.

Therefore, we apply the special AAU teaching model for the main parts of the curriculum. The teaching model has been developed through the whole period of the existence of Aalborg University, now about 30 years. Different departments have tailored their own version of the model so it meets the requirements of that particular department to the education. Besides some general parts the following text mainly describes the engineering education and especially the Diploma and M.Sc. education for a chemical engineer.

## 2. CONTENTS AND THE CONSTITUTIONS OF PROJECTS

The tutors have presented some basic ideas for the project in a written proposal for the specific semester project. All important ingredients of the project shall be presented in the proposals and the tutor shall be able to present the principal ingredients in a couple of versions of the story if he/she wants to be selected as tutor for the semester by a group of students. Some of the more important aspects of the project for a chemical engineer are laboratory work and co-operation with companies. On some semesters also co-operation with other university laboratories is important, especially, when a special chemical or physical method of analysis plays an important role in order to give important solutions to the problem-or event-based project

Obviously, all projects are to be considered as a part of a wider perspective e.g. much greater connection in major areas of chemical technology. About half of the project time is used to obtain new information and knowledge of this new area. In this way the areas of technology of different study groups on even the same semester can be very different. Only the general new basic curriculum from the study plans needs to be involved as a principal part. But of cause this basic curriculum can be used in many very different technologies. One example of the basic curriculum, on one of the first semesters in the education on chemical engineering, is the description of the chemical reaction by help of all normal chemical tools from general chemistry based on curriculum from inorganic, organic or biological chemistry. Depending on the type of technology, this principal part of the chemical reaction on the semester, can give rise to new knowledge in which general chemistry is applied together with one or more of the three mentioned chemistry areas. On the next semester the principles of analytical chemistry play the principal part. Series of methods that together are called chemical unit operations play the next principal part and so on the following semesters. A very important part of the project is to place it in the right connection with the society. How can the results of the project be used? How could a possible new piece of knowledge influence the behaviour of the society that the project group is an integrated part of? The answers to these questions are of substantial importance to the project work. The students may never feel their work as an isolated part in respect to society - that they are performing only to pass examinations before their participation in »real life« in positions outside university.

In order to acquaint oneself with new areas of technology the students of course, obtain new knowledge by reading books and papers and by searching information on the Internet. Also the companies and some foreign laboratories contribute to the enlargement of the students' knowledge. A part of this knowledge can be considered as knowledge accumulated in the minds of the students. Some of it is even assimilated if the student from earlier learning already possesses some accumulated knowledge of a similar kind. However, at the same time as the students accumulate new knowledge from the new area of technology, they also accumulate something that we can consider as non-knowledge. Non-knowledge is the knowledge about some part of the new area of technology that the student now has realised the existence of. Maybe some parts of this non-knowledge will be turned into real knowledge at a later stage of the education. The first time the students become aware of this vast knowledge they do not work with all this information in order to assimilate it by a learning process. On the contrary, by means of both the new knowledge and the knowledge about their non-knowledge they create the limits of the project, taking into account the curriculum as well as the factor of time and equipment and materials that relates to the amount of money that can be spent on the project. The project limits are found when formulating the problem or possibly an event to be dealt with. Both the students and their tutors give ideas to the problem formulation or basis of events. This way the work with the project is considered as governed by all participants in common and not only by either the students or the tutors.

We talk about problem-based learning PBL or event based learning EBL. But what is a problem? Palle Quist has given a very precise definition where he divides problems into three types (Quist, 2003). In the following I will comment on these definitions set into a framework of engineering or natural science. A problem can be an anomaly that is something very different from the expected, different from rules or laws, or just different from the usual

behaviour of either materials or events. Some very fixed laws govern Engineering and Natural Science. Also in our world of description we often find an anomaly especially when we have to do with microorganism that can often be the case in engineering science. Another possibility is antimony, which can be a paradox that often is the result of difficulties in language. By help of a meta language that is the same language but it acts on sentences of the language in question. These paradoxes are often solved. We also find them in very basic science. One of these paradoxes is the story about Achilles and the turtle (Hartnack, 1995). To my knowledge that kind of problems is never dealt with in engineering science. The last type of problem can be a contradiction that is a relation of opposition between obviously same types of materials or events. These kinds of problems are often solved in engineering science. It could be an industrial production suddenly changing its output due to some unforeseen events or it might be an ingredient either in some part of the industrial process or in the raw materials. An event can be a precision of some relations in engineering science. Maybe the performance of a production process or a chemical analytical process works very well, but we do not know enough about it. An event can be the description of that process. Sometimes a precise scientific description will discover new knowledge or at least new models of understanding. We do not solve problems in EBL on the contrary, we maybe create them in order to go on solving.
We even talk about problem fields that are more or less connected in the project.

Maybe the first problem identified will be changed during the work with the project because the focus has turned a little away from this initial area due to the fact that new knowledge of more importance is discovered and that the first main problem identified has proven to play a less significant part than originally expected. The limited economic resources for the purchase of chemicals or laboratory equipment can also change the focus of a project. However, these limitations of resources are normally found already at the very beginning of a project.

## 3. LABORATORY WORK

We have important reasons to involve laboratory work in the projects. One of them being that direct laboratory activities are much less abstract than the imagination of ideas and coherence and therefore they give the students the opportunity to watch chemistry and chemical engineering processes with the naked eye without too much imagination in the first place. When the results of their investigations begin to show up and these results may not always fulfil their expectations then even an laboratory experiment can result in the need of very abstract thinking and require a good instinct of the students and their tutor. Besides some work in setting up and carrying out the experiments, both of which of course can be of doubtful quality depending on the experience of the students, might cause the group and their tutor strong explanation problems. This might also be the case of a very well performed experiment. However, this work is a fine cognitive activity and maybe it can even lead to new knowledge on a high level. Normally, we never permit students to perform experiments that have been done before by other students. Each year all projects are new or at least they are arranged as a continuation of former projects and maybe in some ways based on earlier results. Sometimes a student project can be the start of a new research activity in the research group that acts as tutors of the project and sometimes the student project is based on research that have been going on for some time, but in which a new idea or further examination are the main object of the project. However, in these cases the project also has to fulfil the curriculum of the semester in question and may never be quite similar to a project performed earlier.

If the results of a student project are of such a quality that they can be published, the experiments will be repeated or maybe even expanded by the research group and a paper will be elaborated. The students will act as co-authors on the paper. Normally, this event may happen in connection with some final thesis work, but sometimes it happens already on the third semester, especially with respect to publishing new methods of chemical education activities.

## 4. CO-OPERATION WITH COMPANIES

During the education process of candidates of chemical engineering the co-operation with companies plays an important role. Similar to the laboratory work the co-operation with companies gives the impression of how things work, in the »real world« as opposed to the imagination in connection with abstract thinking in the group room, based on literature and discussions in the group and with its tutor. Normally, the company forms a new picture of the project and some of a problems. Mostly the company is involved from the beginning of the project description. Either the company has contacted the tutor about the project or the tutor has contacted the company. In the first case the company has a specific problem they want to put into a new perspective. It might be a process that sometimes gives some unwanted or not understandable results or it might be that they have a well-know problem, but it requires special attention in order to be elucidated. In these cases the tutor finds a semester that matches the problem to the curriculum, but it is also important that the problem has the tutors interest.. If the tutor contacts the company it is to let the company act as a macro laboratory for the student project . Together with the tutor they will go to the company and incorporate some production or method of the company in their project and try to elucidate some parts of it. Normally, such a project will result in new information for the company useful or not. Sometimes the project report has been copied and distributed to several persons in the company. It is not at all sure that a problem find its solution by the first attempt but the work with the problem normally will give some hints about where to start up a possible new project in the company.

Sometimes co-operation with companies results in research and development contracts between the university department and the company. In some special cases co-operation can result in a Ph.D.-study for a candidate.

## 5. THE IMPORTANCE OF FUNDAMENTAL SUBJECTS.

Without the fundamental subjects, physics and physical chemistry it is not possible to progress the education of the students in chemical engineering. Physics and physical chemistry are the tools to the description and understanding of all natural and engineering science. Sometimes students forget this point and think that these subjects were taught in the first 2-4 semesters and that they on later semesters are of less importance. Indeed that is not the case. If nothing else is learned these two subjects need to be studied. Fundamental chemistry is also important to a chemical engineer. The knowledge and understanding of these subjects are the basis of all jobs at a certain level for a chemical engineer. All other subjects in the education can be re-studied when either forgotten or having become obsolete due to the progression of technology. This will never in a time corresponding to the lifetime of a human being happen to physics, physical chemistry or fundamental chemistry.

In all assessments the students arguments are based on these fundamental subjects that some students are not always aware of. Only some statistical or other mathematical tools together with programming are in themselves independent of the three fundamental subjects in question but these mathematical analytical tools also need to use physics and physical chemistry as their basis to be of any use. Due to this connection the fundamental subjects are ingredients in all projects in chemical engineering.

## 6. STORYTELLING

One of the modern buzzwords in management today is storytelling. The companies use stories to define their own identity. Now, for many years one of these stories was the story of the company itself. The birth of the company. Who started it? When was it done? And why was it done? The story about the company gives rise to new stories today especially involving the new areas of general importance, ethics and also human resources which maybe again gives rise to the brand of the company. The brand is a creation of the present story about the company. How the company wants the story to be told today in relation to customers and partners is an essential part of its marketing affairs. One of the used models in Knowledge-Era Organisations of today involves »springboard stories« that again are based on mutual connections and sympathy to the principal part of the story, strangeness that opposes to the expectations of the listeners and comprehensibility that brings the listeners to a new stage of understanding (Denning, 2000). A result of this storytelling management profile is that new employees are asked to tell parts of the same story and if they fail they maybe do not fit into the company. It works like a kind of marriage.

In the same way the students want to tell their own stories and to identify themselves by it, also involving parts of their closest connections in the future and the past. Among the very basic needs of a human being are of cause the protection from hunger and a shelter for an unpleasant or maybe even a life-threatening climate. Also the protection from wild animals and some threatening human beings belongs to those very basic needs of everybody. As it is very well known also the desire for the posses of useful and sometimes even aesthetic materials is one of the basic needs of a human being. But not at least is the desire for acknowledgement by other people a very important and necessary ingredient for everybody in order to find themselves living a meaning full life. So social acknowledgement indeed also belongs to the basic needs of human beings (Fukuyama, 1993). The story of the student concerns many events, materials and personal relations in their lives but their education is one of most important. It will be told many times and different aspects of it will be told again and again in different connections during the rest of their lives. Social acknowledgement can very easily be obtained and is partly in focus in educational institutions due to assessments, but indeed also in performing the AAU teaching model.

The way we teach and the way students learn at Aalborg University fits perfectly into that storytelling model. Every semester the students and their tutors create a new story. The results and discussions are written down by the students in a report that fulfils the basis of the assessment for the semester in question. In order to be in accordance with the study plans and to make the progress of the education some new basic ideas and their coherence to the former curriculum play the principal part and therefore also constitute one of the main contents of the project.

## 7. LEARNING AND TEACHING

What is the difference between learning and teaching? In his book »Det lærende Samfund« Lars Qvortrup distinguishes clearly between the two phenomena (Qvortrup, 2001). Teaching is an activity that the teacher performs when he tries to give the students a shortcut to the understanding of difficult ideas and coherence, especially, when he acts as a tutor in a project, but also when he is giving lectures in courses on a specific subject. He gives basic definitions and examples and he puts the ideas and coherence in relation to already well-known knowledge. Maybe he also tells about further applications of the new knowledge. By help of different methods and similarities maybe he tries to give the students a sufficient understanding of their new knowledge. Next the students are expected to apply the knowledge in their project in different manners. They can analyse some already agreed part of the story of the project that maybe already is written down in a file on a computer. By analysing the part of the project in question in connection with the new set of ideas and mutual coherence, they maybe want to synthesise that part in another way in order to improve the depth or to expand the solution of one of the problems in the project. An important activity is that they are able to assess if they have improved the project by means of the new part of the project. These activities are called the process of learning. That means learning is an activity performed by the students but the teacher brings some shortcuts and ideas to the learning process of the group by means of his teaching. If the students are expected to obtain progression in their study then both activities are important. Without any kind of teaching the students can never be sure of any progression in their study. Especially, they may face problems when considering the profundity of their learning in the initial semesters of their study.

Another important activity of the students when working on the solution of the problem-and event-based project is the activity of reflection. Did they really learn something that will change their identity and therefore change the story about them? While working in groups the student sometimes needs to reflect about the learning process by watching the activity from a distance. They can watch the other members of the group and maybe try to help these members to understand a particularly complicated problem especially, if they believe having acquired new knowledge in a better and deeper way than the other students. This way a student behaves like a teacher. The student reflects about his/her own learning by comparing him-/herself to a former stage of knowledge and to the apparent knowledge of some other members of the group and he/she will possibly be able to give or receive some shortcuts leading to a deeper understanding. This way the students both teach and learn, because in order to explain something to somebody they need to describe the subject in a clear and logical way and this process is an important part of learning. This is also the reason why we normally say that the teacher is the one who learns the most through his/her performance of lectures in ordinary course teaching activities. Thus reflection and the mutual discussions in the group performing their projects are important factors in the learning process.

## 8. MEMORY

When the students have acquired knowledge they need to be able to keep it also after some assessment. If not, after all they will not have changed their skills or competences and therefore neither the story about themselves or some part of their identity. But how do people memorise? A model of memory is based on a definition of Donald Hebb from 1949 (Siegel, 1999). At the moment this model is progressing very fast giving rise to among many other understandings also a new understanding of memory and learning. The brain consists of a huge neural network that is able to »fire« its neurones in innumerable patterns of neural profiles. Learning is a process in which more of these patterns become connected and will lead to parallel distributed processing. This possibility, the connection of patterns of neural profiles that can be fired parallel, is the basis of learning. The connections between the neural patterns increases as a function of the learning process leading to a very large area of knowledge that can be activated at the same time and used to solve problems. The repeated stimulation of a given pattern increases its probability to be stimulated again. A repeated stimulation can either be brought by an activity of the surroundings, teacher, other students or events in laboratory or in a company etc. But also when you decide to think about a subject or phenomenon yourself. The increased probability of stimulation is caused by changes in the synaptic connection in the network of neurones. Changes on the level of cell membranes results in the probability of »firing« a specific combination of neural pattern. Experience forms the structure of the brain.

Many models of the memory have been given trying to identify the most effective methods of teaching and learning. If you decide to think about an object or a person that you have never thought about for a very long time (it can be difficult not to disturb your own choice) then close your eyes and try to focus on the object or person. What you will find is a set of stories connected to your object or person. In dreams they can behave in a very unlogical way as seen from the point of view of the awakened person remembering the dream. In an awakened position you possibly will find logical connections trying to shape one or more stories that the object or person is a part of. You do not need to think of a person for very long without this person doing something that you remember. In other words it seems as if we remember in small stories the smallest of which can be considered as some basic general primeval stories that we try to connect with names and objects when we need to remember larger areas of knowledge of all kinds. This short story model fits to the model of »firing« neurones in patterns. Integration of short stories and bundles of neural »firing« patterns is the result of learning. If that is true maybe we also understand some of the success of the AAU-model of teaching and learning.

## 9. SKILLS AND COMPETENCES

What is the difference between skills and competences? Skills are to be considered as the result of a learning process in which you have got a distinct factual knowledge about a given subject that was not brought into any kind of use, but that was only brought in connection with an existing framework of possible already existing knowledge (Qvortrup, 2001). In this way this new knowledge is ready to be used in some way in the future if not forgotten. Competences are based on skills and have to do with the awareness of how to find knowledge or maybe even to learn in order to solve problems. This last activity is exactly what we do in the teaching and learning model of AAU. We give our students competences based on their skills obtained by their study unit courses. Sometimes we even give them possibilities to let them redo their learning process if new teaching or other stimulation brings new and deeper understanding to the student of some already, but partly wrongly learned subject.

By the involvement of companies and research-like activities in almost all projects the students are ready to start in a company or as Ph.D.-students right after their completion of their education. An integrated trainee period in a company of the duration of one semester also supports these competencies. In the trainee period the student also write a project report together with a diary about the daily work and finally they present the report and their work in the company as a kind of examination in which also people from the company normally participate in. At the examination a poster with the headlines of the work is presented.

# 10. CASES

## 10.1. Fourth semester project spring 2003:

A solid precipitate that has been investigated by X-ray diffraction spectroscopy, XRD, at Institute of Chemistry, Inorganic Chemical Department, University of Aarhus was found in the wastewater treatment system of Skærbækværket in Aabenraa. The precipitate was found to be a sulphur-nitrogen species salted out as a sodium calcium precipitate that partly clogged the water pipe system from the plant.

A study group working with analytical chemistry as the principal part of their curriculum of the semester found that this species by help of complexing maybe also were involved with a nickel problem at Esbjergværket in Esbjerg. Different kinds of analytical chemical apparatus were involved together with a description of the inorganic synthesis of the possibilities to produce that sulphur-nitrogen species from the flue gas desulpheration plant. A lot of new knowledge together with perspectives of further investigations was produced.

## 10.2. Fifth semester project autumn 2002:

The principal part from the study guides curriculum is the chemical unit operation. In this project active sand filtration plays that role. On the fresh water treatment plant of Fanø, an island next to Esbjerg, the community has troubles with humic substances in groundwater that are used for the production of drinkable water. Normally, help of a coagulation agent of aluminium precipitates these humic substances. However, its sometimes gives a too high rest concentration of aluminium in the fresh water tank, according to new rules from Danish environmental protection agency. Another method using potassium permanganate as an oxidation medium for the humic substances as a substitute for the method of precipitation is proposed by a consultant company.

The students built their own laboratory water treatment system and tried the new method. After a visit at another fresh water treatment plant with similar problems the problem was partially solved but gave rise to other problems. The method will be tried in full scale on Fanø. This project probably will be continued with other ideas for the method of application of the process at the fresh water treatment plant of Fanø and others.

## 10.3. Seven semester final project for diploma engineer autumn 2002:

A lake in Tzerbinia in Poland is polluted with huge amounts of aluminium and some heavy metals in minor concentrations. A former company produced concrete and used the lake as depot for waste materials. The pH of the lake is 12. Water from the lake streams through a tunnel into another lake and a river. The other lake is a tourist and local swimming area. A study group working together with Carl Bro A/S collected samples from the sea and sediment from its boundaries by help of local polish people and brought them to university laboratory in Esbjerg. The group decided together with their tutor to investigate methods of precipitation of aluminium and heavy metals by help of coagulant agents. Also the sediment was investigated for successively extraction of aluminium by water in order to find out if the lake containing 400.000 m3 of water could be emptied and refilled with fresh water. It was shown not to be the case. The results of report were used by the company for further discussion about how to solve the problem in Tzerbinia.

## 10.4. Eight semester project spring 2003:

Modelling of a chemical reaction plays the principal part of eight semester. Our research group work with photochemical degradation of organic pollutants in water by help of photo catalysis.
An investigation together with the group was done by a couple of students. No companies were directly involved but the results of the investigations had an important interest for a company that sponsors one of our Ph.D.students. The results will be presented at an international conference with the students as co-authors on the conference proceeding. After having passed their examination the students performed further investigations in laboratory and a paper was prepared during summer time as a common work between the students and their tutor and it will be submitted to an international journal. Before having started their final projects the students already have contributed to international scientific work.

## 11. CONCLUSIONS

The AAU teaching model supports assimilation instead of merely factual accumulation of knowledge by the student.

Teaching is an activity of the teacher whereas learning is an activity of the student

The storytelling concept of learning fits perfectly into the AAU-model of teaching.

The problems in problem-based learning are most often to be considered as anomalies or contradictions in the projects in chemical engineering education. An event often leads to new knowledge of problems.

The memory model of the activity of neural networks expanding its connections by repeated stimulation fits perfectly into the storytelling concept of learning.

The AAU-model of teaching results in skills of the student but not least in competence based on skills.

The fundamental subjects physics and physical chemistry need together with different parts of fundamental chemistry to be considered as the description and understanding tools of all projects in chemical engineering.

Laboratory work and co-operation with companies during the performance of projects are important ingredients in an integrated education for students in chemical engineering. These activities bring the students important competences for further studies or jobs in companies. Also integrated trainee periods support these competences.

Students are often involved in research during their performance of projects. It makes them eligible for a Ph.D.-study.

## REFERENCES

Denning, Stephen (2000). *The Springboard: How Storytelling Ignites Action in Knowledge-Era Organizations*, Butterworth Heinemann.

Fukuyama Francis (1992). *The End of History and the Last Man*. Free Press, New York. In Danish 1993.

Hartnack, Justus (1995). *Filosofiens filosofi*, CA Reitzel.

Qvist, Palle (2003). *Problemet og PBL. In: Abstracts of Conference of Development. The AAU-model Variation and Development*, Aalborg University.

Qvortrup, Lars (2001). *Det lærende samfund. Hyperkompleksitet og viden*,

Gyldendal, Copenhagen.

Siegel, Daniel J. (1999). *The Developing Mind. Toward a Neurobiology of Interpersonal Experience*, Guilford Press, New York. In Danish 2002.

# SEMESTER PLANNING IN A PROBLEM-BASED LEARNING ENVIRONMENT

## - COHERENCE BETWEEN SEMESTER COMPONENTS AND UNDERGRADUATE PROGRAMME

**Bent Rønsholdt**

**Abstract**: The theme 'Reality of the Models' of the second semester's project unit formed the frame within which the sub-theme 'Equilibriums' was established, and, subsequently, project proposals for student projects were generated. These projects were supported by a project course 'Chemical Equilibrium And Reaction Kinetics'. The objective of this course was to provide a broad theoretical basis for the projects as well as being the first common basic chemistry course in the associated undergraduate programme in biotechnology, chemistry, and environmental engineering. Both sub-theme and course content were subject to constraints. The former should i) originate from the theme, ii) embrace and underline the communality of the specialisations (biotechnology, chemistry, environmental engineering), and iii) provide a basis for creating projects within all three disciplines. The latter should i) stem from the sub-theme, ii) provide a common theoretical basis of the undergraduate programme, iii) be highly applicable in the technical part of the project, and iv) facilitate explanation of experimental observations based on scientific theory. The impact these constraints pose on the problem-based learning approach is discussed.

## 1. INTRODUCTION

The curriculum for the freshman year at the Faculty of Engineering and Science offers a flexible frame within which a number of syllabuses are in place, each aiming at a specific engineering or scientific degree (Studieordning, 2002). Nevertheless, the learning objectives are common to all subjects differing only in the technical and contextual topics covered. The pedagogical model, problem-based learning (PBL), implemented at Aalborg University since its commencement, is specifically outlined as one of the learning objectives and constitutes the methodology by which student projects should develop (Studieordning, 2002, p. 9ff).

A particular feature of this model is that the formulation of problems are ever-changing, partly due to the fact that such problems should stem from practical or theoretical problems encountered in the real world (Algreen-Ussing et al., 1986, p. 4), and ideally these problems can never be planned in advance. Another feature, practised at the University, is that a number of the courses delivered are supposed to be related to the projects and, hence, basically course contents cannot be planned before the actual project areas are identified. Consequently, further planning of undergraduate curricula becomes difficult and demands frequent evaluation and maintenance, as the knowledge base that students are equipped with at the end of the freshman year might well be unpredictable. This appears to be in sheer contrast to planning a whole Bachelor or Masters programme, which must cover those disciplines that characterise candidates acquiring a particular degree.

The recent change in the curriculum of the freshman year reflects the adjustments following a seminar (Laumann, 2002) and an external evaluation (EVA, 2001, p. 83ff) defining the need to incorporate, in particular, the second semester as an integral component of various undergraduate curricula. The second semester, therefore, is no longer identical to all students but specific towards the programme in which the student wishes to enrol. The identity, by which students view themselves, derives from this choice. Accordingly, there is an added demand for coherence not only within the semester but also between the freshman year and the undergraduate programme. This demand is not only experienced by teachers involved in curriculum development, but also experienced by students who in about 95 % of the cases adhere to their first choice of undergraduate programme (Det teknisk-naturvidenskabelige Basisår, 2002).

The objective of this paper is to present the constraints enforced by the recent change of curriculum upon semester planning in the freshman year using, as a case-study, the authors' experience from planning and conducting a second semester aiming at the Biotechnology, Chemistry and Environmental Engineering programme. Subsequently, I discuss what inflictions such constraints might pose on practising problem-based learning.

## 2. SEMESTER STRUCTURE AND PLANNING

The general structure of a semester at Aalborg University is the division between general topics (Kjærsdam and Enemark, 1994, p. 19ff), which are general courses common to the entire programme and individually assessed, and the project unit consisting of the project and the project courses. The project unit, i.e., both project and courses are assessed simultaneously at an oral group examination. The second semester of the freshman year is no exemption from this. Of a total of 30 ECTS (European credit transfer system) the project unit take in 22 ECTS. The planning of these 22 ECTS is targeted towards a specific undergraduate programme and is the responsibility of a teacher affiliated with that particular programme. Especially, the project unit differs in content depending on which undergraduate programme it serves, although this diversion currently is also implemented in the delivery of some general courses (Studieordning, 2002).

The elements of the second semester comprise (Studievejledning, 2002 p.10)

- The theme
- The sub-theme
- The project courses
- The project (which in the planning phase consists of several project proposals)

## 2.1. Identifying the task

The principal aim (goal) in planning a semester is to ensure that topics presented enable that the designated objectives of the curriculum are met. Hence, the semester theme provides the frame within which the particulars of semester should be planned. Secondly, and just as important, is that the content of a semester provides knowledge in core subjects common to disciplines in the undergraduate programme by contributing to the progression in that specific education. In the present case this implies planning a content that equally serves Biotechnology, Chemistry and Environmental Engineering (BCE). Lastly, coherence among study elements (i.e., theme, projects, project and general courses) within the semester, an issue also raised by students, as well as between the freshman year and the undergraduate programme (i.e., the study elements at the freshman year are highly integrated components in the educational profile of the undergraduate programme) is certainly a matter to be strived for. These three major issues determine the common denominator (Figure 1) for the planning of the semester, which according to the curriculum must enable problem-based learning (Studieordning, 2002 p.15).

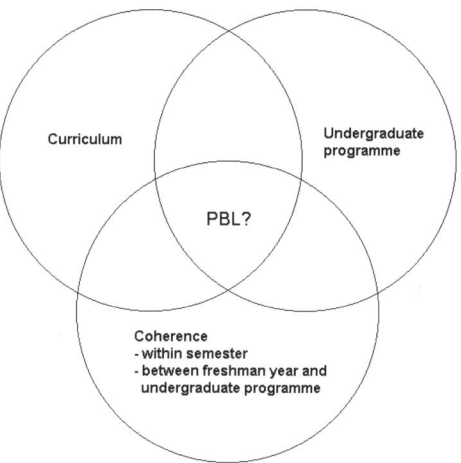

Figure 1. Issues determining the common denominator for semester planning

## 2.2. Case: Biotechnology, Chemistry and Environmental Engineering (BCE)

The general theme of the second semester is 'Reality of the Models'. The concept is that a model, being a simplified description of a particular part of reality, in itself has its own reality. Hence, the reality of the model is that it describes a principle about reality, which may or may not exist. Nevertheless, the application of the model is convenient in understanding the reality.

Applying this concept to the sub-theme specific for students following the BCE programme involves identifying a model that is common to each line of specialisation. The sub-theme chosen was 'Equilibriums'. Equilibrium is a principle (model) in the above-mentioned sense. It is something that in real life rarely and then only in very local areas exists. However, as a model it explains why real, physical, chemical and biological, processes proceed the way they do. Moreover, the principle is very basic and, thus, very suitable at an introductory semester. From a BCE viewpoint it is possible to identify problems based upon this model as all areas basically are working with systems to ensure that an equilibrium situation does not occur and, therefore, necessitates an understanding of the conditions leading to equilibrium.

The project unit, however, does not only consist of the project derived from the sub-theme, but also of project courses. These courses must be evaluated together with the project (Studieordning, 1998, Chapt. 9) and, because the examination evolves from the project, the project must allow incorporation of the outline of these courses. The outline of some of these courses, *i.e.*, 'Scientific Methods' and 'Technology, Man and Society', is given prior to sub-theme development whereas another 'Chemical Equilibrium and Reaction Kinetics' is a consequence of defining a core subject as introductory to the BCE programme[1] - in fact this course served as precursor to the sub-theme. The way in which these constraints influence project proposals is depicted in figure 2.

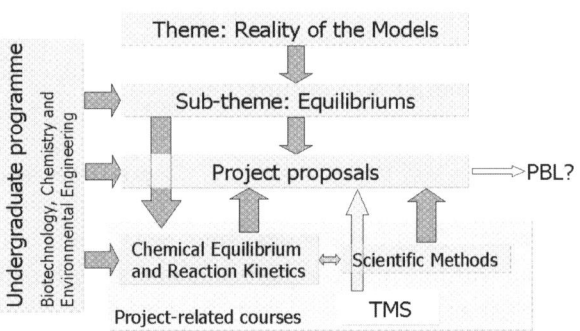

Figure 2. Factors constraining the formulation of project proposals. TMS: Technology, Man and Society.

---

[1] Concurrently, the students are also introduced to 'Collaboration, Learning and Project Management' through course activity, which should be explicitly applied in their project work. This particular objective will not be further addressed here.

All three lines of specialisation in the BCE programme are highly experimental. Although they may be treated solely theoretically, project proposals that incorporate the possibility of practical lab- or fieldwork highly stimulates students' motivation as well as reinforces theoretical training. While it is not problematic to design proposals with such technical content that will suit the interest of students in terms of their specific educational choice, the difficulty encountered with the above constrictions lies in formulating suitable project proposals that are *both* problem-based, have an integrated contextual content, *and* incorporate to a large extent knowledge provided through project courses. The following two examples illustrate project proposals elaborated under the above-mentioned constraints, the first being a successful and the second a less successful project proposal.

*Example 1*
A project proposal incorporating the above-mentioned issues was entitled 'Everyday Chemistry'. This proposal was based on the observation that consumers, including children, has free access to purchasing a number of hazardous household chemicals in ordinary supermarkets, and that their use, both individually and in combination, might constitute severe health risks. It allowed the students to formulate a problem as a paradox (Qvist, 2003), being the contrast between 'protection against health risks' and 'free access to hazardous substances'. It also provided an opportunity to a contextual approach, e.g., consumer behaviour and legislation, in conjunction with a technical approach. Specifically, the technical approach offered the possibility to investigate the chemicals involved and the potential reactions taking place between selected substances upon mixing. The latter, in particular, involving theoretical considerations concerning chemical equilibriums and reaction kinetics, as well as experimental work in the lab to confirm hypotheses based upon such considerations, both integrating knowledge acquired through supporting courses to great extent. Thus, in terms of observing coherence (figure 1) and integration (figure 2) this proposal was appropriate.

*Example 2*
The project proposal was entitled 'Fermentation Processes' and was initiated by student request, as they were interested in a biotechnology-oriented project on fermentation. Focusing on energy budgets of two basic biochemical pathways comprising of series of equilibriums, it was ensured that the project was well within the sub-theme and relevant to the undergraduate programme, would incorporate theoretical knowledge provided through courses, would lead to simple laboratory experiments, and would have a suitable level for students at a second semester. Although students would acquire new relevant technical and scientific knowledge and skills through such a project, the project itself would not fulfil the objectives of the curriculum in terms of

being problem-based and, consequently, the contextual component was obstructed. This led to a fairly backward process of viewing the fermentation process in a suitable context (beer brewing) and inventing a problem (optimisation of the fermentation process - formulated either as a 'why/why not' or 'how' question) that ultimately enabled the students to carry out project meeting curriculum objectives.

## 3. DISCUSSION AND CONCLUSION

When planning a semester in the current situation, one must observe that the freshman year curriculum may have objectives quite separate from those of an undergraduate programme as indicated in figure 1. Since the undergraduate programmes, and also students, have justified reasons to expect that the freshman year will provide them with students with core knowledge in areas specific to their field, changes in already established project courses are likely to be less frequent. Moreover, student expectations of coherence (Laumann, 2002) might secure maximum convergence in the aims of both the freshman year and the undergraduate programme, a matter further accentuated by the recent change towards a 3+2+3 structure of the academic educations (Folketinget, 2003). Semester planning, therefore, has become a complicated task as a number of potential diverging interests must be brought together constraining the process as summarised in figure 2. Moreover, the fact that the educational focus is on technology and science, it is clear that problems relevant to project proposals are confined, which may cause a problem in connection with PBL (cf. Example 2 above) and the expectations to this learning approach, e.g., employing real (Algreen-Ussing et al., 1986) and contemporary problems (Kjærsdam and Enemark, 1994). As PBL is characterised by a problem to which more than one solution is possible (Keiding, 1999), and based upon an analysis of the context in which the problem is seen, the most obvious attempts to solve the problem might be far from technical. For instance, in the 'Everyday Chemistry' project (cf. Example 1 above), solutions might be sought in areas of social science (e.g., legislation) or humanities (e.g., consumer information/education) rather than within technology and science (e.g., replacement with less harmful chemicals). In case such a situation occurred, the project would be beyond the scope of the semester, unless students were restricted to only consider technical solutions, since there is no guarantee in the PBL concept that a student group would automatically choose or even derive to a technical solution. To circumvent that problem, supervisors must, more or less, predict the outcome of a project proposal in advance with the risk of designing solutions that should derive from the students' problem solving process.

So far no attempts have been made to define problem-based learning. It seems unfair to give such a definition here, as the theme of the conference was to establish the various ways in which PBL has developed and is practised at Aalborg University today. Even to the extent that it is argued (Christensen, 2003) that the PBL approach in certain cases deliberately is not practiced. Hence, it appears that every School at Aalborg University practices its own definition of PBL or, perhaps, rather project-oriented group-based teaching, which may explain why the method of instruction is so apparently diverse. As project supervision at the freshman year is catered for by several groups of teachers, each with their own understanding of PBL, this diversity might actually turn out to be the key issue.

Such a conflict was experienced in formulating the project proposal in example 2 and seemed to be a matter of differences in background, tradition, expectations among supervisors, and how this mixed group interprets the curriculum content and PBL. Especially, the definition of a problem differs (see e.g., Keiding, 1999; Qvist, 2003). The lack of a common appreciation of the practiced pedagogical model not only concerns supervisors but has also given cause to much confusion among students and an impression of absence of coherence. Yet, once each group of supervisors, say, in BCE, has come to a mutual understanding on learning aims and objectives as well as constraints, project proposals, which ensure that core subjects focusing at the specific undergraduate programme are covered, might be relatively straightforward (e.g., Example 1 above). Still, such projects will lack the freedom of approach traditionally practiced at the freshman year, in particular when the necessary integration and progression has to be observed (EVA, 2001).

In their book entitled 'The Aalborg Experiment' from 1994, Kjærsdam (Dean of the Faculty of Engineering and Science) and Enemark describes the ideas behind the educational model in Aalborg and how it is implemented at the Faculty of Engineering and Science. It is interesting to note that in particular the project courses should be delivered in support of the projects and are subject to frequent changes depending on the type of projects (Kjærsdam and Enemark, 1994 p.8), ideally deriving from real problems encountered in society at large. While this may be applicable and highly relevant to final semesters this seems pretentious at an earlier stage such as the freshman year. If indeed practised this would lead to frequent changes in undergraduate programmes, as these would have to adjust their curricula accordingly. Everybody involved in course development and planning knows the workload entailed (op. cit.), and it is understandable that teachers would like such courses to run at least more than once. Consequently, according to (idem, p. 22ff) problem-based learning (know-why) is envisaged implemented at graduate level, whereas design-based learning (know-how) should be the means of instruction at undergraduate level leaving the freshman year for teaching how to work in project groups. Nevertheless, the curriculum of the freshman year (Studieordning, 2002, p. 15) explicitly emphasises the PBL approach as the method of learning. In conclusion, if, indeed, this approach is maintained, more explicit definitions of problem-based learning are necessary, and proper training of the supervisors on how to implement PBL is required.

## 4. ACKNOWLEDGEMENT

The author wishes to thank H.H.W. Johannsen for his astute comments to this manuscript.

## REFERENCES

Algreen-Ussing, H.; Fruensgaard, N.O. and Skov-Petersen, B. (1986). *Projekt og Rapport - Rapportskrivning i projektorganiseret undervisning.* 4th ed. Aalborg Universitetsforlag. Aalborg. 54pp.

Kjærsdam, F. and Enemark, S. (1994). *The Aalborg Experiment - Project Innovation in University Education.* Aalborg University Press, Aalborg. 52pp.

Christensen, J. (2003). *Idealet om problembaseret læring på spørgsmål. AAU-modellen Variation og udvikling.* Development Conference held at Aalborg University March 4, 2003. Abstract.

Det teknisk-naturvidenskabelige Basisår (2002). *Tilmelding til overbygningen - Maj 2002. Det teknisk-naturvidenskabelige Basisår*, Aalborg Universitet. http://www.but.auc.dk/stud_info/ob_tilm_f02.html. Last updated: 28-10-02. Visited: 29-04-2003.

EVA (2001). *Basisuddannelserne - ved Aalborg Universitet og Roskilde Universitetscenter.* Danmarks Evalueringsinstitut, København. 189pp.

Folketinget (2003). *Forslag til Lov om universiteter (universitetsloven) - 2002/1 LF2 125 af 29. april 2003.* Retsinformation. http:/www.retsinfo.dk/. Visited: 05-05-03.

Keiding, T.B. (1999). *Kompendium til kurset i samarbejde, læring og projektstyring. Aalborg Universitet.*
http://www.but.auc.dk/~slp0133/SLPkompendie.pdf. Visited: 01-05-03.

Laumann, M. (2002). *Studentersamfundets bud på en løsning for Basisuddannelsen ved Det teknisk-naturvidenskabelige Fakultet. Studentersamfundet.* Aalborg Universitet.
http://www.studentersamfundet.auc.dk/documents/showhtml?fileid=332&.
Last updated: 06-10-02. Visited: 29-04-03.

Qvist, P. (2003). *Problemorienteret erkendelse.* ABZ-net. Aalborg Universitet.
http://www.but.auc.dk/~pal/abz/index.htm. Visited: 01-05-03.

Studieordning (1998). *Fællesbestemmelser for ingeniøruddannelserne - Studieordning.* Det teknisk-naturvidenskabelige Fakultet. Aalborg Universitet.

Studieordning (2002). *Basisuddannelsen - Studieordning.* Det teknisk-naturvidenskabelige Fakultet, Aalborg Universitet.

Studievejledning (2002). *Basisuddannelsen - Studievejledning 2002/2003.* Det teknisk-naturvidenskabelige Fakultet, Aalborg Universitet.

# PBL IN DISTANCE EDUCATION AND WORK-BASED LEARNING

Knowledge at a high theoretical level can only be provided by a very limited number of institutions, universities being among these. Research-based university programmes for adult lifelong learners are still not a major focus at Danish universities. However, since the Ministry of Education in 2001 funded some seed money for stimulating university activity in lifelong learning programmes for academics, many programmes have been developed and offered - mainly on a postgraduate level.

Normally, continuing education programmes mirror ordinary university programmes. Adult learners, however, often request part-time programmes, ICT-supported distance education and other types of flexibility. Therefore, we often see continuing education programmes developed with a content designed by university professors more or less based on the same concept as daytime programmes, but turned into modules for part-timers and using ICT-tools for virtual class-rooms, etc. From a university point of view even adult part-time learners are expected to study with the purpose of obtaining a degree. However, that might not necessarily be the case.

There are various reasons for adult part-time learners to study:
- Some never acquired a university degree and now they find it important to do so
- Some graduated with a bachelor's degree and now want to have a masters
- Some have changed job/professional profile and now need a new theoretical background
- Some want to prepare for a shift in their career
- Some need brush-up courses

- Some need continuing education to learn about new theories and methods within their field
- Some are unemployed and need to improve their skills
- Some just want to improve their work competence
- Etc.

Therefore, continuing education is much more difficult to plan and to market than normal fulltime university programmes with a more homogeneous target group - young full time students.

Annette Lorentsen analyses in her article, »*Quality in Master Programmes in Continuing Education through Problem-Based Project Work*«, the necessary changes in content, methods and culture in continuing education at universities on a general level, and in a concrete case study on a specific distance learning programme at master level for language teachers. If using project work in distance learning programmes, it is necessary to rethink the way project work is organized, e.g. concerning the traditional focus on analytical methods and traditional project work.

One of the main ideas in Problem-Based Learning is to learn by applying theoretical knowledge from courses in solving real life problems. The students in full-time university programmes are »importing« real life problems and using them as tools for learning. However, those students are not involved in the real practice of these problems. In part-time programmes for adult learners we have the opportunity to plan the curriculum in such a way that these learners can have the challenge of working problem-oriented in their own practice.. In the article, »*Back to the Future - Theory and Practice in Adult Practioners' Problem-Oriented Project Work*«, Annie A. Jensen and Helle B. Jensen discuss a series of challenges related to working problem-oriented with one's own practice. They discover that subjects/problems originating from the learner's own work practice give rise to an integration of practice with theory. The part-time adult learners are often more interested in developing the work practice in question than in applying the results from the project work in a subsequent discussion of the theoretical framework.

In the article, »*Project-based Collaborative Learning in Distance Education*«, M. Knudsen et al describe experiences from transferring positive experience with full-time on-campus PBL to ICT-supported distance education on part-time basis. They conclude that the learning model for on-campus engineering programmes cannot be transferred to distance education without significant adjustment. As the project is a joint project for a group, the group members feel a stronger responsibility for the project, than for the courses and their own learning in general. The article describes the didactic changes made according to their findings.

A major task in the transformation of PBL into continuing education is to succeed with problems from the learner's own practice for the project work. This can be very difficult if we organize teams with learners from different organizations. In both articles the programmes described are designed to lead to the learners' attainment of the master's degree. Those university-oriented programmes are for individual enrolment as part of a personal carrier planning.

Learners going through a part-time programme will have a hard time if they cannot see the natural link between their study and their practice. In the article, *»Employability and Work Based Learning«*, the context of continuing engineering education is modelled and discussed. Continuing education is described as university-oriented or company-oriented. This article describes a new concept for company-oriented education, which meets the engineer in his/her daily tasks and integrates the learning process in the job functions. This concept aims at mapping the experiences from problem-based learning in an industrial context in the way of research-facilitated work based learning. Some of the major challenges with this method are the cooperation between organization and university, the teacher's and learner's understanding of the process and the task of identifying the learning objectives to be met.

In spite of the numerous obstacles that arise with the implementation of a continuing education programme, the intensive technological innovations occurring today create a significant need of methods of providing on-going and continuous professional development. To a large number of academics - and especially those who are responsible for the application of new technology within their organization, it is becoming increasingly difficult to obtain and maintain the high level of professional knowledge and skills demanded by the industry. By taking advantage of the research activities and educational experience existing in the university system, private organizations may well be able to satisfy their needs for continuous professional development of their engineers. This is a challenge to be taken in cooperation between companies and universities.

# QUALITY IN MASTER PROGRAMMES IN CONTINUING EDUCATION THROUGH PROBLEM-BASED PROJECT WORK

**Annette Lorentsen**

**Abstract**: Universities have to offer more continuing education and they have to change in many respects to do this successfully. In this article necessary changes in contents, methods and culture in continuing education in universities are analysed both on a more general level and as a concrete case study, presenting a specific master programme for language teachers and producers of language teaching material. Focus on both levels is on how traditional problem-based project work has to change to produce quality in continuing education. Main answers are here: each student's occupation must be given high status and be in focus in all study activities; the traditional focus on analytical methods in project work must be replaced by equal focus on analytical and more creative methods (doing, producing, changing something, making experiments); instead of focussing on traditional group work, future project work should build on combinations of individual work, work in pairs, in networks, in traditional groups etc. dependent on what is needed by the learning objectives defined; if collaborative methods are chosen in virtual settings, highly qualified tools and support are needed to make project work successful.

## 1. UNIVERSITIES AND LIFELONG LEARNING

There is a growing recognition in universities that catering for lifelong learning should be one of the top priorities for universities besides more traditional academic duties such as educating young people and carrying through research activities. This will inevitably lead to new challenges for universities besides already existing ones, calling for responses on many levels, be it on a pedagogical, organizational, managerial level.

Universities are already today faced with many challenges in what may be called their more traditional endeavours: educating young students and carrying out research activities. In teaching young students the main challenge is maintaining quality, going from universities for the elite to mass universities that educate a big proportion of each generation of young people to an academic level. Whereas both student numbers and student characteristics have changed, finances often have not, so universities are faced with a combination of financial, pedagogical and staff related challenges. Also the expectations from future employers and society in a broader sense as to what qualifications and competencies young students should acquire at university have changed. Therefore also contents - and with this also methods - of study programmes have to be reorganised, integrating and focusing on development of more personal and social skills and more meta level skills.

As to research more cooperation with business and industry and more transparency are expected from universities so that the world outside universities will prosper more easily from university research activities and results.

When engaging in lifelong learning universities are faced with even more profound challenges than the ones mentioned in traditional teaching and in research (Knapper & Cropley, 2000), since we are talking about a fundamentally new target group visiting lifelong learning in universities today and even more in the future compared to both existing target groups in problem-based project work activities in universities today and the target groups in earlier university experiences with open and distance learning. Adult students in open and distance learning activities in universities have always been different from traditional young university students since their life experiences and study conditions have differed from those of young students. However, the teaching and learning activities of both young and adult students have often not differed accordingly. Usually, both groups have been introduced to the same study programmes - although one group in an on campus version, the other in some ODL form - heading for the same qualifications, competencies and degrees. This will not work to the same extent in the future, however, because the adult student group in universities will change from second chance students into people already having bachelor degrees - and many also master degrees - seeking continuing education in highly qualified and relevant lifelong learning activities. Therefore, universities are challenged both to develop new programmes for lifelong learning - with new appropriate content using new appropriate methods - and to market these programmes extensively and in new ways to reach people employed in business, industry and public organisations who are often not used to thinking of universities as their main supplier of continuing education.

Profound challenges call for qualified answers. Therefore, universities have to start up both development and research activities in the field of continuing education contents, methods etc. Locally, newly formulated e-learning strategies and strategic ICT initiatives in universities often form the start of a more profound change from traditional universities to universities also offering lifelong learning with renewed contents and methods. On a regional, national and international level strategic collaboration between several educational institutions is often used as the starting point for richer and better continuing education programmes, also from universities. In a Danish context the creation of the initiatives The Digital Northjutland, the IT University in Western Denmark, and the newly established portal Unev.dk ('University continuing education - a virtual approach') for all continuing education programmes in Danish universities (a kind of Danish virtual university) may be seen as such examples of collaborative institutional efforts to promote continuing education in universities. Finally, in an international context many strategic alliances between universities have been formed to cater for the future, also in the field of continuing education. European Association of Distance Teaching Universities (EADTU), European Consortium of Innovative Universities (ECIU), European University Network for IT in Education (Eunite) and EuroPace are just some of the important players in the field in Europe.

Existing initiatives on local, regional, national and international level to promote continuing education in universities often focus mainly on the establishment of appropriate frameworks for continuing education activities in universities and networks of universities. More profound changes in contents and methods of study programmes are often not dealt with in these initiatives. For universities to succeed in future continuing education this is, however, a key problem.

Summing up one must conclude that an increased engagement from universities in the field of continuing education forces universities to face a set of new challenges some of which to some extent have already been taken up in local, regional, national and international initiatives. In this article some of the challenges not yet solved will be analysed and discussed in detail. Focus will be on the need for new contents, new methods and changed staff qualifications which can be derived from universities engaging more profoundly in the field of continuing education. Problem-based learning (PBL) methods as one very important appropriate way of meeting these challenges in the field of continuing education in universities will be analysed and subsequently illustrated through a discussion of concrete use of problem-based project work methods in a specific continuing education master programme for adults.

## 2. CHALLENGING CURRICULA, PEDAGOGY AND CULTURE IN UNIVERSITIES

Continuing education in universities challenges existing university curricula and pedagogy and even university culture as such in a broader sense. To really understand why this is so and to come up with appropriate solutions universities have to take two important steps: they need to abolish the traditional assumption in universities that the same study programmes will work for all groups of students including students in continuing education and they need to get to know the new adult target group in continuing education better in order to be able to base new activities on the way of thinking represented by this new target group.

## 2.1. Towards customisation of study programmes in universities

As mentioned universities already offer a variety of study programmes, mainly to young students, but some also to second chance adult students in open and distance learning. Will it be possible to copy these programmes in a continuing education context in the future? If so this would of course be both more convenient and less expensive for universities than having to create new programmes.

Compared to young students all adult students whether in second chance activities or in continuing education have life and job experiences radically different from young students. Also their study conditions are profoundly different from those of young students. Firstly, time as a scarce factor is essential to all adult students. Also a lacking ability to come to university physically on a regular basis - for residential, job or family reasons - characterizes most adult students. Finally, the priority given to study activities by adult students is different from that of young students. So all in all adult students in general must be characterized as quite different from young students and therefore they need other offers be it content or method wise.

Today and even more in the future university engagement in lifelong learning is and will be changing from second chance offers to continuing education, where adult students to a much higher extent than earlier expect to acquire qualifications and competencies readily transferable to their present occupation. Therefore, much stronger links between general theory and the individual adult student's present occupation must be an integral part of any study programme for adult students offered by universities in the future.

One must therefore conclude that although offering identical study programmes to all target groups would be a convenient model for universities engaging in continuing education - both from a financial and an organisational point of view - this model will not work. Adult students as such are very different from young students, and the group of adult learners visiting university lifelong education today and even more in the future, mainly using it as continuing education, strongly relate studying to their present occupation.

Therefore, all universities - also those with many years of experience in the field of open and distance learning for adults - are faced with the challenge of redefining and developing new study programmes for continuing education.

Consequently, in the future customisation becomes a key word to be successful in continuing education, also for universities. Successful customisation, however, presupposes a deep knowledge of the customer and his way of thinking and defining quality - a knowledge that for the time being is not present in most universities.

As part of an EU project in 2003 Aalborg University carried through a survey with all its existing continuing education programmes about how to define, implement and assure quality and a quality culture in continuing education. This survey (Lorentsen, 2003.a) together with earlier research in the field may help us understand what challenges universities are faced with when they start redefining and developing new study programmes for continuing education, which as described they are forced to in order to be successful, and what possible responses to these challenges they may come up with.

Lorentsen (2003.a) shows that quality in all study programmes at university level is related to two aspects: the contents of the programme and the methods used (for teaching, organising etc.). Superficially, one might think that programmes for different target groups need not be that different to be good, as in all cases what counts is good content and the methods applied. However, this is a wrong conclusion, because common headings - used to summarise the fundamental parameters defining quality in all university education - do not signify the same in different contexts. Although both young and adult students agree that contents and methods define quality, good or appropriate contents and good and appropriate methods are defined very differently in the context of young students and students within continuing education.

As for quality of contents both young and adult students have some common demands stating that contents of good quality must draw upon research in the subject field and make them acquire an overall understanding of the subject field. However, what is essential for universities to realise entering continuing education, is that adults in continuing education besides these very *common* and fundamental demands - due to their often rich subject related ballast gathered through many years of work in the subject field - add very important *specific* demands to contents in order to qualify as good in a continuing education programme. Three of these specific content related quality parameters for continuing education - taken from Lorentsen (2003.a) and Støkken et al. (2002) - should be mentioned here.

Firstly, adults in continuing education strongly prioritise the contents being updated, so that they can be sure to get the newest research based information in the field through the programme. Secondly, they want a continuing education programme to give them the chance of studying some aspects in the subject field more thoroughly than what everyday working life allows them to do. Adults often bring with them from their working experience some sort of overview of the subject field in question, so what they lack - and therefore favour as an important quality parameter - is a deeper understanding of *both* how aspects of the subject field connect and make out a coherent subject field *and* specific details in the subject field. Finally, adults being questioned about quality of contents in continuing education very strongly stress, that contents of the study programme should be relevant to each individual student's present occupation.

As for methods used - for teaching, organising study programmes, information handling etc. - the picture you get from confronting both young and adults students with questions of quality seems to be that adult students generally are much more demanding because of their very different life and study situation compared to that of young students. Methods must be proven successful to be accepted by adults in continuing education. Modern adults have no time for experimentation. Their time budget is scarce, and they must be sure to get value for money. Therefore, professionalism, efficiency, but also flexibility is mentioned as key words when adults define quality related to methods and organisation of continuing education. Finally, service and a proper infrastructure are valued as important quality parameters by adults, too.

Adult definition of quality of contents and methods that differs from traditional study programmes in universities challenges both existing university curricula and traditional university pedagogy and didactics. Also university culture in a broader sense is challenged, because adults' definitions of quality of contents and methods cannot be met by applying traditional university organisational thinking and procedures. On the contrary they call for changes in several respects - for instance in the way we organise ourselves in universities, in the portfolio of qualifications demanded from university teaching staff etc.

## 2.2. Content related challenges in continuing education

Drawing upon adults' definition of content related quality parameters - described above - by far the most important challenge for universities in the field of contents in continuing education is - while still maintaining just as high an academic quality in a narrower sense as earlier - to establish a much closer relation between general theory (in the study programme) and each student's occupation.

This challenge comprises at least two dimensions. Firstly, the *status* of occupational issues must be redefined in continuing education programmes in universities. Secondly, the *focus* of occupational issues in continuing education programmes in universities must shift from being a more abstract one (issues of general interest) to becoming concrete, focusing on each student's actual present occupation.

Adult students' job situation has always influenced on their study activities, and universities have been aware of this fact. Mostly, universities have only recognised and tried to solve the negative part of this influence. However, the negative part being that jobs leave too little time for adults' study activities, if these are not highly structured and described well in study guides etc., for which reason universities for many years have been working hard to improve information, materials etc. in adult education. On the other hand the positive influence between contents of study programmes and adults' job situation - and the other way round - mostly has not been added the agenda explicitly by universities. It has been up to the adult students themselves to interconnect content wise between job and study programme.

However, for students in continuing education, their occupation both forms a crucial part of their lives as such and also serves as a clear denominator for both choice and completion of continuing education study programmes. Consequently, students' occupation has to shift from being defined by universities as a problem in continuing education (*a time robber*) to becoming an *asset* - an integral part - from which study programmes in continuing education in universities may thrive systematically. Such a shift in the status of students' occupation in continuing education study programmes calls for a thorough rethinking and redefinition of the methods in adult education in universities,

Redefining and developing a new status for students' occupation in modern adult education is but half of the solution to the challenge of creating much closer links between theory and occupation. A second dimension of the challenge that must be solved, too, is as mentioned that much more focus must be put on the *individual* student and his *concrete* occupation. So we are not just talking about establishing closer links between theoretical and occupational aspects as such but also about making concrete links for each adult student between theory and his or her own job situation.

The appropriate response from universities to the challenge of establishing much closer links between theory and students' occupation in adult education must be to develop new methods that handle this challenge appropriately. In a later paragraph we shall see that problem-based project work in new shapes may indeed be an important answer to this methodological challenge.

Developing such new appropriate methods calls for a radical shift in cultural attitudes in universities to be successful. Educating young students, which is still looked upon as the main educational effort by most university people, is by traditional university culture viewed as a process of gradual cultural integration of students in a predefined set academic world. With the growing importance of students' occupation in modern continuing education in universities such a - one might say *monocultural* - model which looks upon the academic world as superior to the outside working worlds of students will not work. Instead a model built upon cultures of equal worth has to be established. Cultural theory may here serve as inspiration (Hannerz ,1992). Already it is clear that universities need to improve both the awareness of their own culture and their knowledge of the adult students' world outside the university, and that universities - on the basis of such improved cultural awareness and knowledge - must choose a *multicultural* approach to guide them to a successful synthesis of internal culture and students' external cultures.

## 2.3. Pedagogical, methodological and organisational challenges in continuing education

Modern adults find themselves caught in a world of many - often incompatible - demands. Working life in modern society occupies a growing part of the adult life, because the boundaries between work and non-work continuously are being blurred due to both redefined contents in working life and use of new tools, and at the top of that adults are expected by both society as such and their employers to take actively part in lifelong learning on a continuous basis to keep up and renew their qualifications and competencies. Modern adults therefore experience time as a limited resource, which influences their definition of quality parameters in continuing education extensively.

When it comes to defining what characterises good methods - used for teaching, organisation, information etc. - in continuing education adults therefore stress efficiency, professionalism and proper service. For universities these concepts represent several challenges.

Firstly, a demand for efficiency calls for much more structured - in the sense: well defined, described, planned, delivered - study programmes than university teaching staff are used to in on campus programmes. At the same time efficiency in an adult world presupposes flexibility. To create a successful *synthesis of structure and flexibility* will be a very important methodological challenge for universities in modern continuing education.

Secondly, adults' demand for professionalism and service challenges universities, because what is needed to deliver professionalism and proper service in continuing education are *qualifications, competencies and organisational structures* different from those in traditional problem-based project work in universities.

Defining good methods in continuing education cannot of course rely solely on what adults feel they need, prosper from etc. Also experts in teaching and learning theories must be consulted to give input when universities define their methods in continuing education. In modern theories of teaching and learning collaboration among learners and between learner and teacher (supervisor) is termed very important to have learners acquire the necessary qualifications and competencies needed in modern working life. Collaborative methods must therefore also be a quality parameter in modern continuing education.

However, as described above, modern adults need and value flexibility, which also includes the possibility of studying on their own from home or from the working place - instead of coming to the university on a regular basis as young students normally do. And, as we have also seen above, adults demand contents to be directly relevant to each of them.

Both flexibility and individual focus are not easily combined with a collaborative approach. There-fore, succeeding in creating *true collaboration in a learning environment where students study as individuals from a distance* - from home or from their working place - is a third main challenge to universities when developing future high quality continuing education.

Proper responses to the above three main challenges related to good methods in continuing education:
* synthesising structure and flexibility in continuing education
* creating new qualifications, competencies and organisational structures in universities to serve continuing education
* combining collaboration, individual focus and distance in continuing education call for profound developments in universities.

Developing new versions of problem-based project work in virtual learning environments will - as we shall study in detail below - be one very important response at the methodological level. Other important methodological responses might be to reinforce modular structures of study programmes in continuing education, to handle time in a much more professional way than in traditional university endeavours (to secure no waste of time, better planning, just-in-time learning, transferability of efforts in working life to count also as study time, see Lorentsen 2000), and to give a much higher priority to explicit descriptions and explanations in any aspects of study programmes than what we see in a traditional university.

At organisational level appropriate responses to the above three challenges must incorporate at least the three following aspects: firstly, giving higher priority to teaching in universities - so that teaching and research are equally valued for university professors. Secondly, introducing team working methods and habits in universities - so that former individual working habits are replaced by local, national and international collaboration. Finally, upgrading staff development activities in universities - so that common ideas of university staff being naturally gifted for teaching, promoting courses etc. are abandoned in favour of a much more professional attitude, including formulation of competence development strategies, units and concrete activities.

Below we shall analyse and illustrate how PBL in new shapes can contribute to solving several of the both content related and methodological main challenges mentioned above.

## 3. PROBLEM-BASED PROJECT WORK AS A RESPONSE TO CHALLENGES IN CONTINUING EDUCATION

Project work has often been introduced in universities as a study form that per se secures a close relation between theory and practice and secures collaboration. Several surveys within continuing education show, however, that this is not the case. To meet the challenges in university continuing education that have been discussed above, a profound rethinking is needed.

In this paragraph we shall analyse what *general changes* must be introduced to have project work adjust to new conditions within educational offers for adults in universities. Part of this analysis will be a discussion of what will make out good problems in future problem-based project work in continuing education and what will characterise appropriate ways for students to work with these problems (problem solving approach, organisation of project work etc.).

In the following paragraph 4 a concrete example will follow. A specific continuing education programme will be described to illustrate how problem-based project work may be changed in real programmes to meet the challenges in modern continuing education in universities. The programme in question is a virtual continuing education master programme with the title 'Information Technology, Language and Learning' offered in collaboration between two Danish universities: Aarhus School of Business and Aalborg University.

### 3.1. Project work methods in continuing education

As we have seen above important quality parameters in modern continuing education as such are first and foremost that better relations are established between theory and practice and that methods used should cater for both collaboration and individual work and produce both structure and flexibility.

To produce such quality universities are faced with new conditions and expectations. Firstly, the target group in modern university continuing education more than ever characterise themselves as 'working individuals', each with a specific 'individual occupation'. And each of them defines 'individual occupational benefits' as the key to continuing education.

This makes it a must for successful modern university continuing education that it recognises the importance and legitimacy of this triangle of individual, occupation and continuing education, and that it succeeds in adjusting its contents and methods accordingly. In other words it will not be enough to recognise, tolerate and live with such a learner defined close link between study programme and occupation. On the contrary any successful university continuing education programme must explicitly turn this close link into an asset for the programme and deliver both contents and methods to be applied when each student tries to create his synthesis of theory and everyday practice. As universities are expected to deliver education - and in this case continuing education - at the highest academic level they need to improve their capacities in building bridges between on the one hand the academic abstract analytical way of thinking and on the other hand the everyday concrete action oriented approach to life.

While each adult student - when asked - seems to prefer individual ways of studying (because of higher flexibility and easier applicability on one's own problems in everyday life), experience shows that working on your own often ends up being both too lonely and diffuse and not challenging enough from an academic viewpoint. Traditional project work with its collaborative aspects offers a higher degree of academic challenges for each student and it also offers structure for both social and content related interaction. However, many adult students find traditional project work inflexible.

In short university continuing education is left with serious demands for changes. The following questions sum up the most important areas where changes are needed: How do we make room for concrete everyday issues in continuing education programmes while still maintaining sound academic principles and ways of studying? How can traditional methods be renewed and improved - including a modification of the traditional analytical focus in academic programmes, a higher integration of successful aspects of individual ways of studying (flexibility, a high personal engagement), an abolishment of the weak aspects of traditional project work (collaboration as a 'straitjacket' or negative dependence on others), and an upgrading of the strong aspects of traditional project work (collaboration leading to improved depth and breadth content wise, inspiration and lower drop out rates)?

Working with *appropriate* problems in *renewed* problem-based project working contexts may be the answer to our problems. So success depends on our ability to define and describe what will make out good problems in future problem-based continuing education and how students should study and work with these problems as part of their programme.

In traditional PBL the ideal has been to go for problems that may help us - through exemplification - to reveal bigger issues in society (Jæger, 2002). This is not, however, in accordance with what adults in continuing education today define as their needs, wishes and expectations. Modern continuing education students first and foremost define themselves as practitioners with practical everyday working problems, and taking part in continuing education should according to their expectations help them work on and solve these practical problems. Therefore, University programmes need to rethink what problems will qualify for successful PBL in continuing education. An important part of a renewed PBL in university continuing education must be - in accordance with what we have seen above - that problems should open up to *both* academic theoretical reflection and application of the newest theories *and* actual problem solving in each student's present occupation. Literature on the reflective practitioner and action research (Burnaford et al., 2001; and Jarvis, 1999) can serve as inspiration for a renewal of PBL in this respect.

In traditional problem-based project work in universities students focus on analytical methods and they study in groups. This must be changed, however, to create successful university continuing education in the future.

Students in continuing education in universities often work at managerial level or part of their job is to handle managerial tasks. Therefore, success in their working life is very much measured by how they solve problems and by their actions - to a much lesser degree by how they analyse and understand problems and by their thoughts. Therefore, a need exists for modern PBL in university continuing education to give higher priority to other problem solving methods than analytical methods. A solution would be to give *equal priority* to on the one hand traditional analytical methods, be it quantitative or qualitative approaches, (to secure academic quality) and on the other hand new more creative methods such as experimentation, action, production, change etc. (to secure each student's personal engagement in the learning task and an immediate occupational related concrete output).

PBL has often been carried through in groups. Most adults in continuing education find such total focus on collaborative methods inflexible, but at the same time many adults praise collaboration in groups when it actually works (Lorentsen, 2000). To be successful in the future continuing education in universities therefore needs to rethink the relation between problem-based project work and collaborative methods. In doing so inspiration may be found in the newest research on learning processes. Here individual learning and collaborative learning are both seen as very important aspects of modern learning theories - aspects which must be combined and integrated instead of looked upon as alternatives. Therefore, it seems to be a way forward for problem-based project work to take *learning* - instead of collaboration - as its theoretical starting point. If so a study programmes using problem-based project work will have to decide from learning task to learning task which method is the most appropriate given a specific learning task - resulting in choice of sometimes individual methods, sometimes collaborative methods, sometimes structured methods, sometimes flexible methods etc.

Collaborative methods will of course also in the future be important parts of PBL. In this respect it is very important to recognise that collaboration and communication in virtual learning contexts, which often characterise modern continuing education, call for much attention to be successful. Experience shows that communication tends to weaken in virtual surroundings and that collaboration in virtual contexts is perceived to be more difficult than in traditional physical contexts, although synchronous virtual communication may to some extent help us in the future. Renewed project work methods in virtual contexts - as we are talking about them in continuing education - therefore need to focus strongly on high quality support and guidance to students, on staff development (to be able to deliver such support and guidance) and on developing and applying appropriate tools for both students and staff (Lorentsen, 2002).

To sum up we have seen that problem-based project work is faced with some very important demands for renewal to stay a success also in modern university continuing education. First and foremost the former very strict interpretation of problem-based project work as working with theoretical problems on an analytical level in groups must be abandoned.

## 4. A CASE STUDY: FACING THE CHALLENGE OF NEW PROJECT WORK METHODS IN A SPECIFIC PROGRAMME IN CONTINUING EDUCATION

Aalborg University and Aarhus School of Business - both Danish universities - together offer a continuing education master degree in Information Technology, Language and Learning which may serve as a case study at to what contents and methods may be offered when trying to respond to some of the most important challenges in university continuing education described above.

### 4.1. Contents, structure and study form of the programme

The specific master programme 'Information Technology, Language and Learning' is a two year half time study programme aimed at language teachers, language trainers and producers of language learning materials in all contexts. The programme is in its 4th year.

Content wise the programme is an integration of ICT-theory and learning theory applied on language learning and teaching as empirical field.

The objectives set up by the programme combine and integrate knowledge and skills, theory and practical work. The programme focuses on each student's competence development defined as a progressive continuous process that relates to both each student's occupation and to fundamental requirements of academia.

The programme is structured in three modules, each containing a major task (a project) and related teaching and study activities. Module 1 lasts one year. The theme of the project work in module 1 is 'ICT and (language) learning'. The two other modules last half a year each. The theme of the project work in module 2 is 'Production of ICT resources for (language) learning'. The content of module 3 is left to each student to decide. Module 3 consists of writing a thesis within the thematic field of the total programme.

The programme is offered in a virtual learning environment (as distance education using computers and the internet). Every three months a weekend seminar is offered on campus (in Aarhus).

## 4.2. Methodological developments in the programme

Methodologically the program has tried to achieve three things:
- to develop new project work methods more suited for the target group and the learning objectives in question
- to develop and apply tools in different shapes to support varying project work methods
- to design and try out new dimensions in the assessment processes applied

Each module's project work consists of four elements, which we shall study in more detail below:

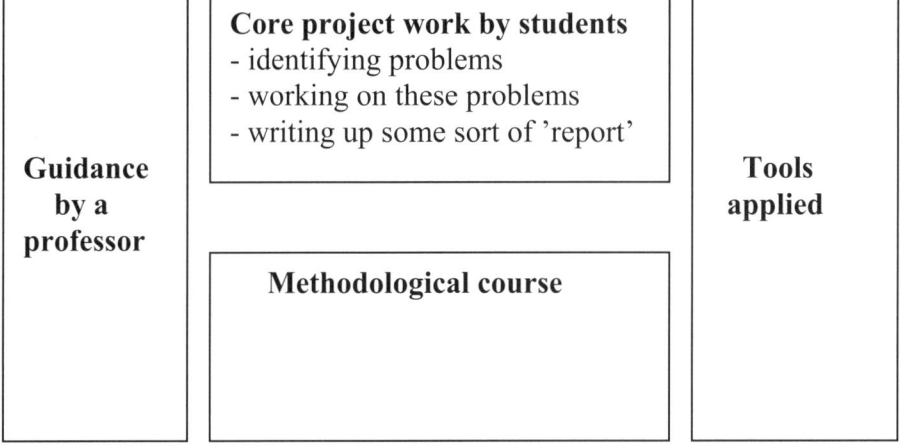

Figure 1: Elements of project work

As input to or as a supplement to this project work a set of courses is offered in each module - except from module 3 (the writing of a thesis), where no such courses are offered:
As input to the project work by the students on 'ICT and (language) learning', module 1, courses in 'ICT and learning' and in 'ICT and language learning' are offered supplemented by a course in 'ICT resources and ICT theory', giving the new students the required background knowledge in the field of ICT.
In module 2, 'Production of ICT resources for (language) learning' also two courses are offered as direct input to the student's project work: a course on

'IT-resources' and a course on 'System development'. A supplementary course on varying aspects of language learning or the implementation of ICT in language learning is also offered.

Returning to Figure 1 we shall now elaborate on each of the four elements to describe how different aspects of each element may be seen as answers to the above mentioned challenges to problem-based project work in continuing education in universities. We here leave out discussions of module 3, as this module is atypical, consisting of each student's writing of his or her thesis.

### 1ˢᵗ element: Core project work by students

Crucial to studying here is: What problems do the students study, how do they work with their problems, and what is the basis for assessing this part of their study programme?

In module 1 the relation between each student's occupation and the theoretical curriculum offered in the course package makes out the problem to be studied in the problem-based project work.
In module 2 designing and creating an ICT system for one's own (or somebody else's) language teaching and learning context is the problem.

The selection of such problems for the problem-based project work, the programme has succeeded in transforming each student's occupation into something valuable for the academic study process, something which the programme could not do without, something which at the same time enriches and is enriched itself by the study process. So theory and occupational considerations are integrated and a synthesis created.

In module 1 reflection is the main activity on which project work is based. As reflection focuses on the individual reflecting, main working method in this module is individual work - supplemented by discussions in pairs to create an appropriate context for raising personal reflections to a more general and abstract level where also others may benefit from one's reflections.
In module 2 emphasis moves from reflecting on status quo to changing status quo by means of an actual ICT product, defining design and production of an ICT product as the main aim of the project work in module 2. This project work is mainly carried out in groups - not because group work as such furthers design and production, but because design and production processes are so complex that normally the capacities of more than one student is needed in order to finish in due time.

In this way the importance of analysis in academic work is stressed, since analysis is part of both reflection and system development, but also other intellectual and creative processes are being recognised and trained deliberately as valuable for creation of knowledge. In all processes working methods are chosen in accordance with the learning task which means that sometimes individual work is preferred, sometimes collaborative work in either loose constellations (discussion pairs, networks etc.) or in (traditional) group work where members of a team share learning objectives, resources etc.

Having introduced new ways of working - as described above - the programme also introduces new ways of assessing the learning processes that have taken place and what has been learned and produced during theses processes. Traditionally, project work in Denmark is assessed by means of oral exams on the basis of analytically oriented project reports. This has undergone changes in this programme. Exam is still oral, but in both modules the analytically oriented report has been replaced by something that corresponds to what has been going on during the learning processes. So, the module 1 exam is based on a portfolio containing selected reflections by the student, the module 2 on the actual IT system (and a relating report) having been produced by the students.

### 2$^{nd}$ element: Tools applied

As seen in much research on project work in ODL success is very much dependant on students having access to appropriate tools. In most cases focus has been on tools for communication and collaboration, since - as mentioned above - project work is traditionally seen as a group activity based on communicative and collaborative processes.

Although this programme has a much broader definition and implementation of project work - ranging from individual work to informal collaboration in different constellations and finally to 'real' team work in groups - it recognises of course the generally acknowledged need for tools for communication and collaboration in ODL. The basic platform in the programme is an intranet combined with an LMS, supporting information, communication and collaboration on a general level.

In both modules this basic platform is supplemented by other tools to cater for specific needs in the learning and teaching processes in each module. In module 1 where students reflect individually and in pairs on the relation between theory given in courses and their own occupation - guided by a professor - experience has shown that quality in both reflection and guidance is very much dependant on being able to structure the processes properly. Therefore, two different kinds of tools have been introduced: reflection templates and a virtual portfolio tool.

In module 2 tools have been introduced to reinforce the objective of the module, which is to simulate a real system development process based on principles from action research. This implies that tools are needed for data collection and analysis, for structuring tasks, resources, collaboration and time during system development processes and for producing the actual systems (tools for home page production, databases etc.). Such tools have therefore been introduced.

Evaluations of the programme show that tools helping to create structure and professional working processes are just as important as tools for communication and collaboration.

Whereas the problem-based project work in the programme is more structured than most traditional PBL for the mentioned reasons, flexibility is still present in the programme (Collis & Moonen, 2001). All course work in the programme is presented as modules, which can be followed or skipped by each individual student according to his or her needs and prior knowledge in the field. This way modern adults' need for flexibility is also met - and from a learning point of view a proper solution to modern adults' very differentiated backgrounds.

### 3rd element: Methodological course

Experience in university ODL shows that students working on projects for several reasons are very much in need of methodological guidance to be successful. Firstly, most adults are not used to project work as a way of studying. Secondly, adults are very much defining themselves as practitioners and are consequently in a high degree focussing on defining success as having solved practical problems - with much lesser focus on problem analysis and the processes before and leading to problem solving.

The most important objective for methodological input linked to project work in continuing education will therefore be to assure that working with one's own occupational problems in projects is combined with proper academic virtues related to knowledge creation and documentation.

In this programme a methodological course and methodological guidance is offered in each module built on the concept of the reflective practitioner with the purpose of producing a synthesis between the practical orientation of the students, ideas from action research and more general academic requirements related to proper knowledge creation and documentation.

### 4th element: Guidance by a professor

Guidance has long been recognised as very important in all project work. Therefore, the key issue is not to question this, but to discuss whether guidance has to be changed in some respects when project work changes and what consequences must be drawn from this.

As we have seen above project work in this study programme may take place individually, in pairs, in networks or in teams, but always stressing the individual student's agenda - very much derived from his occupation - as an important part of the process. Moving towards emphasising the individual is part of a general trend in modern learning processes. Therefore, also a need for more individual guidance is present in renewed project work and in modern learning processes as such. However, most professors are not used to this kind of communication where personal aspects play an important role. Communicating on a personal level, without getting private, is not that easy. Therefore, a need for staff development exists in the communicative field.

## 4.3. Meeting the challenges in the programme

Creating new project work methods, activities and tools must happen within a common framework to be successful. In this case the reflective practitioner in an action research context has served as inspiration, defining the practitioner, who reflects and acts to understand and change his own world and does that on a thoughtful and methodologically sound basis, as the pivotal point of the study programme.

Bringing everyday occupational concerns of working adults into academic study programmes calls for new ways of handling theory and structure - traditional academic virtues. This programme meets this challenge by introducing new processes and new tools.

Firstly, the dominating focus on abstract analysis in traditional project work is replaced by a combination of many methods which taken together secure integration of theory and practice - such as reflecting, experimenting, producing etc. Secondly, a set of new tools - besides the common tools for communication and collaboration - are introduced to produce more structure and a more real life working experience than what is normally seen in traditional academic project work (for instance templates, portfolio tool, tools for professional team work such as electronic calendars, planning tools etc.).

Finally, balancing individually defined objectives and more general academic objectives becomes crucial in study programmes that - like the one here - try to establish a synthesis of theory and practice. The study programme discussed above has chosen to help meet this challenge by giving up the traditional interpretation of project work as equal to group work and by stressing appropriate methodological input to all project work. Project work is here defined as problem-based learning in whatever working constellation is called for by the learning objectives in question (be it individual work, work in pairs, in groups etc.). In this way individual agendas are given much more room in the programme than in traditional project work. This is, however, balanced by continuous methodological input that helps students go all the way from practical experience to proper academic knowledge creation and documentation.

## 5. SOME PERSPECTIVES

We have seen that developing new methods, contents and tools in continuing education is a challenge to all universities today - a challenge which some master programmes have accepted and have met with success.

Problem-based project work seems to be a very powerful way of going forward in university continuing education, as it allows us to relate to problems in real life and to combine such real life problems with appropriate theory to a much wider extent than traditional teaching methods in continuing education. More individually oriented, structured and creative methods must be defined and implemented in project work contexts, however, in order to cope with studying purposes and conditions of modern adults in university continuing education.

In the future a lot of continuing education at university level will be offered by networks of universities - on a national or an international level. This will mean even more challenges, as renewal of methods, contents and tools no longer can build on the experience of individual institutions or cultures. Therefore, resources have to be spent on how to run such networks of universities with success and how the necessary continuous renewal of continuing education programmes can take place also in very complex situations (Lorentsen, 2003.b). The Danish experience on problem-based project work methods in different contexts may be one very important input to a prosperous international collaboration in continuing education in the future.

## REFERENCES

Burnaford, G. et al. (eds.) (2001). *Teachers Doing Research: The Power of*

*Action Through Inquiry.* London.

Collis, B. & Moonen, J. (2001). *Flexible Learning in a Digital World. Experiences and Expectations.* London.

Hannerz, U. (1992). *Cultural Complexity. Studies in the Social Organization of Meaning.* New York.

Jarvis, P. (1999). *The Practitioner-Researcher. Developing Theory from Practice.* Jossey-Bass, Inc.

Jæger, K. (2002). Projektarbejdets principper - et bud på fornyelse. In: Jæger, K. (ed.). Projektarbejde og aktionsforskning. Nye læring- og udviklingsformer i uddannelse og organisation. Publication in Danish from Department of Languages and Intercultural Studies at Aalborg University. Vol.33.

Knapper, C.K. & Cropley, A.J. (2000). *Lifelong Learning in Higher Education.* London.

Lorentsen, A. (2000). *Aspekter af teknologistøttet fjernundervisning på universitetsniveau.* Aalborg: Pædagogisk Udviklingscenter og Videncenter for Læreprocesser. VCL-serien nr.5.

Lorentsen, A. (2002). Om forandringen af læreprocesser og læremiljøer, når læringen er IT-støttet. I: Hertel, F. & Madsen, S. (eds): *Læreprocesser med IT. Virtuel portfolio i undervisning og læring.* Skive.

Lorentsen, A. (2003.a). *Quality and Quality Culture in ODL. Defining, Assuring and Maintaining Quality in Web Based Master Programs in Continuing Education.* In Proceedings from EDEN's conference *The Quality Dialogue.* Rhodes.

Lorentsen A (2003.b). *Potentials of ICT, ODL and Networking when Reengineering Teaching and Learning in Universities. Survey based on interviews in four European universities from the NetCampus project. EuroPace, Belgium.*

Støkken, A.M. et al. (2002). *Mange bekker små... Evaluering av arbeidet med SOFF-støttede fjernundervisningsprosjekter.* SOFF Rapport 3, Tromsø.

# BACK TO THE FUTURE

## theory and practice in adult practitioners' problem oriented project work

**Annie Aarup Jensen and Helle Bækkelund Jensen**

**Abstract**: The relation between theory and practice is a central element in problem oriented project work in master education programmes. This article aims at illuminating a series of challenges related to working problem oriented with one's own practice. With the Master of Learning Processes (MLP) as a case it is examined whether it is a correct assumption that master students take their own practice as a starting point for problem oriented projects. The article's ultimate aim is to draw up a tentative typology of the importance and role of practice in the students' projects. The article takes its starting point in the original theoretical framework of problem oriented project work as it was introduced in Denmark in the 1970'ies, arguing that this framework can be revisited and seen as an important contribution to planning and carrying out master education programmes of today and tomorrow.

## 1. INTRODUCTION

The learners' practice is a decisive aspect in a master education programme for at least two reasons. Firstly, it is a key element in the admission criteria (»*relevant work experience*«). Secondly, the overall targeted learning outcome for students in a master education programme aims at an increased work competence. (Ministry of Education, 2000)

On this background the problem oriented project work would seem an appropriate pedagogical model to apply to master education programmes. The central element in problem orientation is the relation between theory and practice, where project work dealing with a formulated problem enables the learners to gain deeper insight into theory as well as practice (Illeris, 1974). When looking at the on-campus education programmes for younger students and how problem orientation has been implemented as an institutionalised pedagogical model, it can be observed that the theoretical problems have taken precedence over the practice-related problems and the students' personal experience of a phenomenon as a problem (Laursen in: Kolmos & Krogh, 2002, p. 134). This has happened for natural reasons, since young students with no relevant job experience prior to entering the university logically will have no personal practical experience within the specific field of study as a starting point for formulating problems.

With the new and quite large group of students entering the university in master education programmes, which are part-time programmes closely related to the students' work and job practice, it will only seem natural to return to the original theories of problem oriented project work. This student body displays characteristics, which would enable them to work problem oriented, since they have a closer relation to practice and genuine experience with work related problems.

Based on the theory of problem oriented project work combined with the demands specified for Danish master programmes (i.e. as a means of continuing and further education of adult practitioners in order to increase their job competence) this paper reports the first findings from a study of master students' project work. The aim of the study is to determine the importance of students' relations to a work practice that is relevant to the subject of their study, and to examine the role which their experiences from work practice might have in their project work. The first questions to be answered in this respect are:

• Are the students' project work related to practice?
• In the affirmative, do the students draw upon their own practice?
• What is the purpose and function of the work practice in the project work - in relation to the formulated problem?
• In what way do theory and practice combine in these project reports?

For this purpose a number of project reports from the 1st year of a specific masters' programme were examined. As the work is still in progress the findings presented in the following are merely to be considered as tendencies based on the project reports reviewed so far, and consequently further elaboration and additional categories may emerge at a later stage.

## 2. PROBLEM ORIENTED PROJECT WORK - A FRAMEWORK FOR REFERENCE

In order to specify how we define the central terms 'problem orientation' and 'project work' we turn to the original literature from the 1970'ies, when problem oriented project work was first introduced in Denmark as a pedagogical model to be applied at universities and in higher education.

When defining problem oriented project work the literature states that the pedagogical concept consists of two parts: Problem orientation and project work. This is important in so far as it will be possible to work problem oriented, but not organised as project work, and vice versa. For this reason we shall here present and analyse the two components of the pedagogical concept separately.

## 2.1. Problem orientation

The main characteristic of the definition of the term 'problem' has its foundation in a psychological explanation. In order for something to be a real problem it is imperative that it has its starting point in the students' own experience of something as a problem, and that the problem is of a kind which enables a deeper insight into the basic structures underlying the problemi (Illeris, 1974, p.185). Within this conceptualisation of problem orientation this means that the recognition of something as a problem must be internally grounded with the students and originate from them and their frame of reference, as opposed to being externally defined like for instance a problem, which is handed to the students by the teachers. This definition clearly emphasises the students' own process of identifying and formulating a problem. However, this does not mean that anything would be considered a problem as long as the students experience it as such and are motivated to work with it (Illeris, 1974, p. 85; Hultengren, 1981, p. 11-12). Since problem orientation is a pedagogical model institutionalised in university education, external criteria such as relevance for the education programme in question and explicitly defined learning outcomes must be taken into account. That the problem enables deeper insight within the external criteria for the education programme in question is referred to as 'the exemplary principle'.

The term 'problem' is widely used in opposition to the term 'subject'. This emphasises that problem orientation has its starting point in a phenomenon, which is regarded as a problem independently of the scholarly subjects. This is due to the fact that problem orientation was introduced as a pedagogical concept enabling a general and holistic qualification and learning process, whereas the division of education programmes into isolated subject matters was considered to result in a fragmented learning process (Illeris, 1974, p. 78). On this basis problem orientation is often viewed as an interdisciplinary activity. However, this must not necessarily be the case, as it was emphasised as early as 1981 (Hultengren, 1981, p. 19) and has been maintained in more recent introductions to problem orientation (Illeris in: Bisgaard, 1998).

The term 'problem orientation' indicates that we have a pedagogical concept at hand, which emphasises that the students identify and formulate problems within an often very broad framework of reference in the study programme. The term has several characteristics in common with the term 'problem-based learning' (PBL), and it is at times quite difficult to identify the difference between the two concepts. This difficulty may also have its explanation in the fact that the concepts are implemented in the higher education institutions in ways, which appear to be very similar. However, we should like to emphasise that we see two distinct differences between the two. The commonalities can mainly be identified in the underlying understanding of learning processes and learning psychology, since they both rest upon a foundation of constructivist learning theories. The main differences stem from the relation to the curriculum and the degree of independent problem identification and formulation (Dirckinck-Holmfeld in: Heilesen, 2000, p. 222). Where »*Problem-based learning (PBL) provides such 'reasons for learning' by presenting students with practice related problem-tasks*« (de Graff in: de Graff & Bouhuijs (eds), 1993, p. 9), problem oriented project work is not characterised by presenting students with tasks aside from the obvious one that they have to produce a project de Graff continues: »*The theme is introduced to the students by means of study tasks (problems, descriptions of patient cases or other phenomena related to the current theme*« (de Graff in: de Graff and Bouhuijs (eds), 1993, p. 11), and it is clear that the problem at hand is not formulated by the students, but is defined as a task. Problem orientation on the other hand has in its core definition its starting point in the students' experience, not in a subject matter or in the curriculum (Illeris, 1974, p. 80). Since the problems and problem formulations examined in this paper have been identified and formulated by the students and have no direct connection to a curriculum in the traditional sense of the term, and since this is the case for the overall pedagogical concept of the study programme in question, the term 'problem orientation' reflects the study programme's practice in a precise manner.

It does, however, become increasingly complicated to distinguish the two concepts from one another due to the development and interpretation of the term 'subject'. Where the term in the 1970'ies described the traditional scholarly subjects from before the educational reforms of the 1970'ies and 1980'ies, 'subjects' of today have undergone great changes. These changes have resulted in a higher degree of interdisciplinarity, completely new subjects, and a wider use of teaching interrelated subjects in the same course complex, to mention the main characteristics of this development. But the distinction between PBL and problem oriented project work can still be drawn upon the very beginning of the learning process: Is it the problem, which determines the choice of methods and the relevant theoretical knowledge to be applied, and is the problem recognised and formulated by the learners themselves?

In order to work truly problem oriented the students' experience of problems in practice becomes crucial. This is exactly where it can reasonably be assumed that adult practitioners who are studying in a master programme have a well qualified point of departure for seeing and defining problems. Their experience in a certain job, holding a certain position within an institution or company, can be considered their »pool« of actual, self-experienced, and relevant problems.

## 2.2. Project work

Where problem orientation is defined on the basis of the psychology of learning and originally with a clearly specified political agenda aimed at exposing the structures of the society, project work is defined as a teaching method. It can be said that problem orientation is focussed on the ways in which the students' think about the content, whereas project work is the pedagogical form applied to working problem oriented. Only when the criteria concerning both components are met can we talk about problem oriented project work.

*»We here define project work as a teaching method, where students - in cooperation with teachers and possibly others - explore and deal with a problem closely related to the societal reality, in which it appears. This implies that the work must result in a continuing increase in perspective and a deeper degree of knowledge, that the problem is challenged from a number of different perspectives across traditional disciplinary boundaries, and that the choice of theories, methods and tools is determined by the chosen problem.«*
(Berthelsen, Illeris & Poulsen, 1977, p. 14-15)[ii]


The meaning of the term 'project work' or 'project organised' varies depending upon the educational institution, in which it is applied, and it causes in general some difficulty when seeking to point out the determining criteria. This indicates that the understanding of the term 'project work' is widely dependent upon the traditions and culture of the educational institution. But still certain basic criteria can be extracted, of which the following three are ascribed to the term 'project work':

• work/job oriented
• integrating theory and practice
• oriented towards society
(Illeris, 1974, p. 169)[iii]

Two other basic criteria are also specified, which are already built into the understanding of problem orientation, namely interdisciplinarity and research character.iv The concept of interdisciplinarity has apparently lost some of its original importance over the years, and other researchers into project work and problem orientation emphasise only 'research character' and 'integrating theory and practice' as the determining criteria (Hultengren, 1981, p. 19). This leaves us with a wide agreement on project work as an activity, which combines practice and theory in a research process.

The projects dealt with in this paper are characterised by the following criteria: The project work must result in a product (the actual written project report) consisting of 15-25 pages pr. student. It takes its starting point in an overall frame of reference of learning theory and research methods, and courses are offered in both subjects in the first semester of the programme. In the first semester the students have the possibility to work on a pilot project simultaneously with engaging in course activity, and in the second semester the students are engaged in project work. The project period for the reports examined in this paper is limited to one semester part time.

## 2.3. Practice and work orientation

The term practice is widely used in the literature and is ascribed several different meanings. The ideal for a problem oriented study programme is that practice - here defined as practical activities and practical experience - is integrated in the project work without any artificial separation from the theoretical activities (Illeris, 1974, p. 203). This, however, does not clear up the meaning of the term.

Based on reports from Roskilde University, three different understandings of the term in relation to project work can be extrapolated:
* students <u>observe</u> a certain practice
* students <u>participate</u> in a certain practice
* students <u>gather information</u> about practice from informants, who are directly engaged in the practice in question (through interviews and/or questionnaires)

In all three cases practice is something outside the educational institution, where people work in organisations and companies (the cited examples are from factories, courts of law, schools and hospitals), but at the same time these relations between students and practice can be seen as the practice of being a student working problem oriented.

In Danish terminology the word 'practice' has a number of meanings. It may for instance mean 'the real world' as opposed to theories and abstractions, or it may mean a work practice as opposed to the institutions of learning and education. Furthermore, the concept may be used to describe the tacit knowledge inherent in daily life as it emerges through actions, it may be used to describe social and professional relations in communities of practice, or it may describe the norms and standards of a profession per se. For the purpose of this article we have chosen to use the concept of practice in the sense of 'work practice', which combines many of the above qualities, but focusing mainly on the fact that it is a work related context in relation to which the student has gained considerable experience. In opposition to the role of practice originally exemplified above, we use the term 'practice' to identify a natural and daily context for the students in the master programme, since they naturally belong to this work context and do not have to leave the university in order to engage in it. As Jæger (2002) puts it, the master student ideally integrates three roles: that of being a student, a practitioner, and a researcher in relation to a specific work practice.

### 2.4. The relation between theory and practice

The central criteria regarding practice related to problem orientation are that the project work and the problem orientation take their starting point in practice, and that practice (»*the reality, in which the problem is found*« as it is generally referred to) is the basis for defining the problem and determining which theories to turn to in order to gain insight into the problem as opposed to a study programme defining the problem or defining a theoretical problem.

The combination of theory and practice is described as a dialectic interaction between the two: »*The practical problem is understood in the light of a theoretical frame of reference, and the theoretical frame of reference comes to life through its application on the practical problem.*« (Berthelsen, Illeris & Clod Poulsen, 1977, p. 256)v The aim of combining theory and practice is to gain deeper knowledge of both. This indicates that theory should be assessed and evaluated through its application on the practical problem. This can also be viewed as a clarification of the research character associated with project work in regard to dealing with theory and practice.

The term research character is not clearly defined in the literature. Aside from the dialectic relation between theory and practice Hultengren (1981, p. 11) sets up the criterion that a problem formulation (and thus the problem itself) should lead to an investigation, which can be characterised as hypothesis testing as opposed to description.

## 3. PROJECT REPORTS IN A MASTER'S PROGRAMME

We shall now turn to the project reports from the Master of Learning Processes programme in order to examine whether it is possible to extract tendencies concerning the role and function of practice in the project reports and in order to evaluate to what extent it can be argued that the project reports are problem oriented and display characteristics of a research process.

20 project reports were examined. The examined projects stem from the second semester and are in that respect the students' first project reports in the master education programme. All the examined project reports are publicly accessible in the sense that they are not labelled confidential by their authors.

The method used for examining the projects is that the project title, the problem formulation, the problem analysis and the conclusion of each project are analysed in regard to the central themes of this paper, namely the role and function of practice, the students' position in relation to practice and the role and function of theory.

The tentative typology is developed as a framework for further analysis. The contents of the typology should not be viewed as representative, nor is it the aim of the analysis to categorise typologies in a quantitative approach. It is rather the aim to draw up a typology consisting of qualitatively different ways in which practice and theory appear in the projects, and in this respect the method of analysis resembles that of phenomenographic research (Marton, 1988).

### 3.1. Is project work related to practice?

In most cases the reviewed project reports were related to work practice. Brødslev Olsen has previously (1993) examined project reports and problem formulations from ordinary study programmes (full-time day studies) and from open university programmes. He has analysed them in order to determine among other things the degree of problem orientation and to evaluate the project reports as documentation of learning and cognition. Based on a comparison of the project reports Brødslev Olsen concludes that *'many of the subjects for the project reports in Open University are far more specific than in the day studies*[vi]. Being specific means in this respect that there is a considerable delimitation of the subjects of the reports showing already in the title of the reports. The delimitation appears for instance as a concretisation of the context in which the problem in question is set, an aspect which appears to be absent in the examples from the day studies. The concretisation may in some cases take the form of a specific connection to a work practice, which is presented in the students' initial formulation of the problem treated in the project reports. Examples of this are for instance *'with particular focus on the manager as a staff developer', 'in secondary school', 'diagnosing dementia'* (ibid, p. 101)[vii].

This level of concretisation and specific relation to a work practice is precisely what we find in the titles of the examined project reports from the masters' programme. To mention a few,

*'Life-long learning - does that apply to teachers too?'*
*'Training of trainers (ToT)'*
*'Medical students' learning in the community of practice of a hospital ward'*
*'Learning in practice. A study of practice learning among newly appointed nurses'*

Furthermore, it is predominantly the students' own work practice which is made the object of study in the project work. The students often describe their own relation to and role in the work practice which they chose to focus on in the project reports, as is seen in the following.

*'My own interest in the teaching of students at the gynaecological / obstetric ward, Hospital of XXX, springs from my job as manager of the development department of the hospital and being responsible for the implementation of the Ethics Accounts...'*[viii]

In other cases students working in a project group decide on an area of common interest, which is at the same time perceived as relevant for each participant's individual work practice. On that basis the group chooses to examine the work practice of one of the group members, as is seen in the following description.

*'In this project work we have chosen to work with practice learning, as we all work in areas with elements of practice learning. Our experiences cover a wide range, from work with young pupils at production schools, and students in the social and health education, to student nurses and nurses.'... 'Initially, our wish to expand our knowledge of practice learning caused us to consider a number of suitable areas to gather empirical data. Our choice of the neo-*

natal ward at YYY Hospital is due to the fact that through NN's position there we had access to the ward.'[ix]

## 3.2. The purpose and function of work practice in projects

Besides the fact that work practices appear as the object of empirical study in a number of the project reports, a number of other functions are seen, which will be illustrated in the following through quotations from project reports.

A. Work practice <u>as a point of departure for a discussion of theoretically formulated problems:</u> *'Taking my point of departure in primary school and using the teacher role as an example, and referring to the law of 1993 which requires teacher cooperation, I will examine and discuss the problems described by Sennet.*[x]

B. Identification of a problem based on <u>experiences</u> from work practice and <u>combined with the theoretical framework</u> of the master programme: *'I have identified the problems of the assignment partly based on my experiences with the courses through the last 4 years, partly based on the learning theories which I am currently studying at the Center for the Interdisciplinary Study of Learning.'*[xi]

In this case it is worth noticing that the student in question specifies that he/she is actually drawing on the learning theories, which have been part of the course curriculum. In some cases the students seem to draw on knowledge of learning theories acquired prior to their master study.

C. <u>Observation</u> of work practice contributes to the identification of a problem:

*'The point of departure of this project work is a mixture of specific observations, methodological considerations and theories which may illustrate the problem in question and substantiate the preparation of a guide for observation and an interview guide.'*[xii]

D. Work practice as a specific <u>point of departure for formulating the question to be studied</u> in the project report:

*'I personally wonder whether the course description drawn up by ZZ University and the gynaecological/obstetric ward is in fact covering the needs of the interested parties: What are the values of the interested parties in relation to practising the medical profession? Are they considered in the best possible way during the course? And how do the interested parties evaluate the results of the course?'*[xiii]

And, finally, a somewhat different function is seen, namely,

E. Work practice as <u>a practice area for development of a study related competence</u>. Work practice is here used a place where the students may gain methodological experience, in this case experience with carrying out qualitative interviews:
*'Our choice of theory for the chapter on method is based on our desire to work with qualitative interviews, as this is to be considered craftsmanship developed through experience (Kvale, 1997, p.112) we have chosen to use this project work to gain such an experience.'*[xiv]

### 3.3. Combining theory and practice in the project reports

The examined reports comprise relatively few examples of reports, which contain chapters solely reproducing theory. Instead there is a tendency towards integrating theory and practice when presenting the issues in the reports. It is consequently often seen that theories or aspects of theories are presented in a combination with relevant aspects of work practice, for instance in the sense that the concepts or principles of a given theory are interpreted and exemplified in relation to the specific area of research pinpointed in the formulation of the problem of the project report. Often the examples refer to a specific work practice. This way of presenting the theoretical framework of the project work is thus influenced and formed by the students' purpose and research interest in relation to the project work, and the presentation is therefore not only a question of documenting insight into a certain theory in a reproductive form. The students focus their theoretical approach and are guided in this by their particular interest in and knowledge of the work practice, and in doing so they display elements of knowledge transformation (Rienecker & Stray Jørgensen, 1999).

In his study Brødslev Olsen (Brødslev Olsen, 1993, p. 101-108) concluded that as regards project work in Open University there seemed to be 3 ways to do it,

1. To examine an issue by means of two or more theories (comparison of theories)
2. To examine an issue
3. To examine a phenomenon

In our study the reports examined so far tend to use theory in a slightly different way. Often it is the case that a problem or a part of a work practice is examined by means of theory/theories, cf. the above no 1. But when more theories are applied they are often used to examine or highlight different aspects of the work practice or the problem based on each theory's respective premises, i.e. an eclectic approach. Only rarely are there signs that a comparison of theories have taken place, nor are the theories necessarily discussed, neither before nor after application on the problem / work practice.

Theory seems to be applied in order to:

1. Examine a work practice, i.e. deliver the conceptual framework for understanding and/or explaining.
2. Point to solutions of problems, potential development, specific initiatives for development

In some cases the words of the theories are applied normatively with respect to development of work practice.

### 3.4. Development of work practice versus development of theory

Even though the master students' direct involvement in work practices means that they have a strong motivation for thinking in terms of change and development of the work practice they examine and work in, we have not yet come across research designs in the project reports resembling action research. Often, however, the students hold important positions in their work context, as for instance being responsible for staff development and education, consultant etc., which makes it realistic to assume that the student will be able to implement some of the results and thus initiate change. The interest and commitment of the students in this respect may be seen expressed in various ways in the project reports, like for example the following,

*'My interest does not stop with the examination of this project work, but the project report is at the same time a memorandum for a continuing development and evaluation of the courses for medical students at the hospital.'*[xv]

*'This project work gives you a unique opportunity to examine and reflect on your own work practice and to subsequently improve it.'*[xvi]

This illustrates that the natural line of thought and ambition of the students regarding their project work in most cases relate to the development of work practice. This is, of course, not surprising as it is in accordance with the overall purpose of Danish master programmes, as mentioned earlier. It means, however, that it is often at that point that the project work / project report is concluded, i.e. with suggestions of a (number of) solution(s) to the specific problem, trajectories for development etc. Only rarely do the students revisit their theoretical framework for a discussion or critical assessment of its relevance to the problem in question, or its applicability in general, or for reflections on how the specific work practice and the research results could perhaps enrich the theory. This could be viewed as problematic when applying the criteria for project work regarding theory and practice, since critical assessment of theory and the dialectical relationship between theory and practice resulting in a deeper insight into both seem to be absent in this type of project work.

In a few project reports, however, the students do evaluate the applicability of the theory in relation to both the problem formulated and the part of the work practice researched. In those cases there is a tendency that an important factor in such an evaluation is the students' own experience as regards the work practice in question, rather than stringent academic criteria.

If these preliminary findings are considered in relation to Bloom's taxonomy (Brødslev Olsen, 1993, p. 39-57), it seems that the problems regarding the ability to distance oneself from one's own work practice, appear in the project reports in relation to the top levels, such as for instance the ability to synthesise and evaluate. At these levels interpretations and evaluations may take place, which are highly influenced by the practitioner's insight into the domain together with his/her experiences and subjective norms and attitudes. The practitioner's insight gives on the one hand a privileged position as regards interpreting and evaluating. On the other hand this may also lead to interpretations guided by a hidden agenda, more or less consciously, depending on the degree of work on and identification of the student's presuppositions, which have been carried out in the preliminary work when clarifying the problem of the project and the student/researcher/practitioner's beliefs and attitudes regarding the problem.

## 4. TENTATIVE TYPOLOGY

Based on our study it is possible to list the following categories of practice related reports,

a. Retrospective understanding of a given work practice
The student examines empirically a selected part of a given work practice. The situational context, the activity and/or the agents of the practice in question may define the delimitation of the field of research. The point of departure of the project work/report is typically the questions and wondering of the student(s) which have arisen as a consequence of the student/practitio-

ner's experiences in and observations of a given work practice. The ideal outcome of the project work is that the author of the project report understands new aspects of an experienced work practice and enriches his/her understanding by means of a theoretical frame of reference.

b. Understanding of potentials of a given work practice
On the basis of the student's empirical studies of a selected part of a given work practice and a theoretical framework for understanding the problem in question the student seeks to uncover some of the organising principles of the practice. The work may lead to a critique of existing conditions as well as an understanding of the potentials inherent in the practice. The ideal outcome of the project work is an understanding of the demands for a proactive model for development of practice.

c. Development of practice as explicit goal
In this type of project the overall goal is to develop a given work practice or part thereof, which in the experience of the student/practitioner presents certain problems or inconveniences. The understanding of the problem will often be highly influenced by the student/practitioner's role in the specific practice context, and the outcome of the project work will point towards concrete initiatives for improvement of the practice. The author either presents a model for practice development based on a theory or a number of selected theories, or ideally develops a practice specific model for development based on a combination of theoretical deliberations and inspiration, practice related knowledge and work experience.

d. Hidden agenda
Finally, we find that there is a type of projects reports which is characterised by a particular relationship with and mission regarding a given work practice. In this kind of reports the author may have a specific desire to apply theory on a given work practice in order to achieve certain, pre-defined, but not overtly admitted goals in relation to practice. It may for instance be a question of criticising a given practice or of justifying a given practice. The goals in questions will determine the project work and the ensuing conclusions, and from a learning point of view the outcome will be limited.

## 5. CONCLUSION

In most cases the master students take their point of departure in practice when they choose the subject of their project work, and more often than not it is the work practices at hand, i.e. the student's own work practice which in one way or another is made the object of study. In this sense it is fair to conclude that the first criterion for problem orientation is met in the projects. Our findings suggest that problems originating from the student's own work practice give rise to an integration of practice with theory when presented in the project report. The presentation of theoretical aspects is guided by and closely related to the problem in question and that to a higher degree than is usually encountered in project reports written by young students in full-time day studies. It is, however, also apparent that the master students' relation to their work practice leads to a particular perspective in their cognitive interest in the project work. The master student is often more interested in developing the work practice in question (finding solutions, drawing up strategies) than in applying the results from the project work in a subsequent discussion of the theoretical framework. The evaluation of the applicability of a given theory is in some cases carried out on the basis of the student's (common sense) experiences from practice rather than based on a stringent set of parameters related to the problem in question. This is hardly compatible with the demands regarding the role of theory related to practice. The choice of certain theories in order to gain an insight into the practical problem is in complete accordance with the demands as they are defined in the literature, but the dialectic of integrating theory and practice in an almost spiral-like accommodative learning process, where the intended learning outcome should result in a critical assessment of the theory in question, is not present in these types of projects.

The students' primary interest regarding work practice consequently seems to revolve around the following two main areas: an *increased understanding* of practice and the *development* of practice. Finally, there are indications in some project reports that an underlying motive for the project work may exist, which then becomes a task with a given result, which is, however, only known by the author of the project from the outset. Only when there is a real interest and curiosity regarding a problem, will it be investigated. In projects of the hidden agenda type there will be a risk that the theoretical framework is used selectively in order to produce the desired results. In such cases the learning related to the project work may have an undesired character in relation to the learning objectives of the study programme in the sense that the student learns to manipulate rather than to investigate according to academic standards. It remains, however, to be investigated what implications the various types of practice related projects may have on the learning processes of the students, and whether it is possible to detect a development in the quality of the project reports in the areas specified as key criteria for problem oriented project work.

In conclusion, the fact that the students in this masters' programme are deeply rooted in practice means that they focus on concrete and relevant problems which are in touch with reality and which the students are highly motivated to study. At the same time the students' position in relation to practice means that they are more interested in developing practice and translating theory into practice than to discuss the results from their empirical studies in relation to theories and thus contribute to the development of theory. At least this seems to be the case for the project work during the first year of the master programme. The target group is to a large extent focused on the practical use of their study - as they rightly should be according to the general objectives of master programmes. On the other hand, the understanding of job competence in relation to holding a master degree should also include competence in developing theory in relation to the master's own work practice. One important question to pursue in our further research will therefore be whether the tendencies described in this paper based on the students' first year reports are in fact indications of the first step of the students' progression towards a master level as described.

This also leaves us with several open-ended questions related to the theoretical framework of problem oriented project work when taking this as the point of reference. Firstly, we can conclude that the problem orientation seems to be relatively unproblematic for the students in the sense that their problem formulations clearly derive from experienced problems in their practice. At the same time we see indications that exactly this dimension of problem orientation seems to cause problems of another kind in the projects. Working with problems close to the students natural work context apparently causes difficulties when synthesising and evaluating the projects' findings. It can be observed in the project reports that the students do not always succeed in distancing themselves from the well-known practice. In the original understanding of the term 'practice' we concluded that practice is 'something out there' as opposed to the academic university context, and university students originally took part in a certain practice in their capacity of being university students, not practitioners. Where this has lead to the predominance of theoretical issues within full-time study programmes, it could in part time programmes aimed at adult students such as a master's programme lead to a predominance of work practice. Neither of the two can be said to fulfil the requirements of integrating theory and practice, thus leaving us with the need to revisit the framework of problem oriented project work and rethink how we best aid our students to handle theory and practice in a manner which can be characterised as a research process.

# REFERENCES

Berthelsen, J., Illeris, K. & Clod Poulsen, S. (1977). *Projektarbejde - erfaringer og praktisk vejledning.* Borgen.

Brødslev Olsen, Jan (1993). *Kreativ voksenindlæring.* Aalborg Universitetsforlag, Aalborg.

de Graff, Erik (1993). Introduction: the principles of problem-based learning. In: *Implementation of Problem-based Learning in Higher Education* (de Graff, Erik & Bouhuijs, Peter A.J. (eds)). Thesis Publishers, Amsterdam.

Dirckinck-Holmfeld, Lone (2000). Virtuelle læringsmiljøer på et projektpædagogisk grundlag. In: At undervise med IKT (Heilesen, Simon (ed).). Samfundslitteratur, Frederiksberg.

Hultengren, Eva W. (1981). *Problemorientering, projektarbejde og rapportskrivning.* Aalborg Universitetsforlag, Aalborg.

Illeris, Knud (1974). *Problemorientering og deltagerstyring.* Oplæg til en alternativ didaktik. Munksgaard, København.

Illeris, Knud (1998). Erfaringspædagogik og projektarbejde., In: *Pædagogiske teorier* (Bisgaard, Niels Jørgen (ed)). Billesø & Baltzer, Værløse.

Jæger, Kirsten (2002). Praksisorienterede projekter. In: Projektarbejde og aktionsforskning. *Nye lærings-og udviklingsformer i uddannelse og organisation.* (Jæger, K. (ed.)), p. 35-45. Institut for Sprog og Internationale Kulturstudier. Aalborg Universitet, Vol. 33. Aalborg.

Laursen, Erik (2002). Projektpædagogik, konstruktivisme og individualisering. In: *Projektpædagogik i udvikling (Kolmos, A. & Krogh, L. (eds.)).* Aalborg Universitetsforlag, Aalborg.

Marton, Ference (1988). Phenomenography: Exploring different conceptions of reality. In: *Qualitative approaches to evaluation in education: The silent revolution.* (Fetterman, David M. (ed.)), p. 176-205. Praeger, London.

Rienecker, Lotte, Stray Jørgensen, Peter (1999). *Opgaveskrivning på videregående uddannelser - en læreRbog.* Samfundslitteratur, Frederiksberg C.

Undervisningsministeriet (2000): Lov om erhvervsrettet grunduddannelse og videreuddannelse.

[i] In the original definition the political agenda for problem orientation is evident.
[ii] This quote has been translated from Danish by the authors of this article.
[iii] As in ii
[iv] As in ii
[v] As in ii
[vi] As in ii
[vii] As in ii
[viii] As in ii
[ix] As in ii
[x] As in ii
[xi] As in ii
[xii] As in ii
[xiii] As in ii
[xiv] As in ii
[xv] As in ii
[xvi] As in ii

# PROJECT-BASED COLLABORATIVE LEARNING IN DISTANCE EDUCATION

Morten Knudsen, Christine Bajard, Jan Helbo,
Lars Peter Jensen and Ole Rokkjær

**Abstract**: This article describes the experiences drawn from an experiment in transferring positive experience with a project-organised on-campus engineering programme to a technology supported distance education programme. Three years of experience with the Master of Industrial Information Technology (MII) programme indicates, however, that adjustments are required in transforming the on-campus model to distance education. The main problem is that while project work is an excellent regulator of the learning process for on-campus students, this does not seem to be the case for off-campus students. Consequently, didactic adjustments have been made based on feedback, in particular from evaluation questionnaires. This process has been very constructive in approaching the goal: a successful model for project organized learning in distance education.

## 1. INTRODUCTION

Project-organised and problem-based collaborative learning has been a successful learning method at Aalborg University (AAU) since its start in 1974 (Fink, 1999; Kjærsdam and Enemark, 1994; Kolmos, 1996). In recent years a number of continuing education programmes based on technology-supported distance education have been developed (Bygholm, Hejlesen and Nøhr, 1998; Jensen et al., 2003; Lorentsen, 2000), and therefore it has been natural to use the 'Aalborg Model' as a basis in the Master of Industrial Information Technology (MII) distance education programme. This article describes how the MII programme (Knudsen et al., 2000; Masteruddannelse, 2002) has attempted to transfer positive experience from the Aalborg Model in engineering programmes.

The MII programme has been monitored during its first three years of existence (1999-2002) primarily through questionnaires after completion of the basis year, but also through student process reports, plenum discussions and observations made by the supervisors. In addition, an interview based process evaluation was carried out in 2001 (Semey, 2001). Secondary sources of experience from literature, in particular (Bygholm, Hejlesen and Nøhr, 1998; Bygholm, Dirckinck-Holmfeld 1997; Christie et al., 2002; Lorentsen,

2000), conferences, workshops and personal contacts have been a valuable input in both shaping as well in adjusting the off-campus programme.

Three years of experience have shown that the Aalborg Model requires significant adjustments in transferring it into a distance education programme. The MII programme uses the latest information technology, in content as well as in form, but has experienced difficulty in achieving as satisfactory study environment as that of the on-campus programmes. Some of the suspected reasons for this include the fact that the target group is different - students are for example typically employed adults - and the fact that the MII learning environment and forms of communication are fundamentally different from those used on-campus.

The primary element in the Aalborg Model is project work, where the students work in groups making a project each semester. The project work takes up half of the study time, and in the rest of the time the students are offered courses. There are two types of courses, general study related courses with exams, and project related courses, examined via the project. Project related courses provide tools (e.g. Java programming), as well as theory and methods (e.g. object oriented analysis and design) required to carry out the main project. Consequently, direct relationship between courses and project work and a balanced emphasis by the students on courses and project work respectively is of utmost importance. Project work is an excellent regulator of this balance between course assignments and projects with on-campus students, as it helps and activates the students in the selection of what is most important to learn. Our experience indicates, however that this is not the case when it comes to the off-campus students. To compensate for that, didactic adjustments were made at the end of each year.

## 2. THE MII PROGRAMME - PEDAGOGICAL AND THEORETICAL BACKGROUND

### 2.1 Content

The Master of Information Technology educations, MII (Masteruddannelse 2002) is a 3-year programme, corresponding to 90 ECTS (European Credit Transfer System units) with an expected study load of 20 hours per week. It consists of a 1-year general basis programme combined with one of five different 2-year specialisations.

The purpose of the basis year is to introduce the most important theories, methods and technologies. The general theme is Distributed Information Systems with focus on system development, data nets and tools.

Courses and project work take place concurrently. A small first project (called a pilot project) focuses mainly on training project work in groups in a learning situation where an important part of the communication is mediated via the Internet. This leads up to the subsequent main project, which can, for example, deal with analysis, design and implementation of a system for processing production data from a database via an Internet browser.

Specialisations have been offered in: IT in Civil Engineering, IT in Industrial Production, IT in Process Control, IT in Distributed Real Time Systems and IT in System Administration. The two-year specialisations consist in selecting special-related courses and project.

## 2.2 Form

The programme is organised as a technology-based distance education framed by seven two-day seminars per year. A special web-based distance education system, Uniflex (Borch et al 2003, a and b), has been developed, to support courses as well as project work. Amongst other things, Uniflex makes the courses available in a standard form comprising introduction, course description, technical content, references, self test, problems with hints, and course evaluation. Each course unit has a built-in newsgroup for discussions, questions and answers.

The seminars take place at Aalborg University from Thursday afternoon to Saturday afternoon. The face-to-face contact with project group members and with supervisors is used intensively for the parts of the project work, which is difficult to handle electronically, general discussion and planning in particular. Also new courses are introduced, typically with a lecture and problem solving assignments to match. Current courses are reviewed with question and discussion sessions and elaborated through further lectures. In addition, there are guest lectures, study course exams, project exams, and evaluations and discussions about the programme.

Project work between seminars is based on weekly synchronous virtual meetings with audio, text and recently video, as students and supervisors have home computers with Internet connection, headsets and web cams. The supervisor follows these meetings, lasting one to two hours. Most groups have chosen to use Yahoo Messenger. In addition to these synchronous meetings, there is asynchronous communication via e-mail and through Uniflex where documents are uploaded and reviewed.

## 2.3 Target group

Students enrolled in the MII programme are typical distance education students and differ in several important respects from ordinary on-campus students. They already have an education, formal or informal, corresponding to a bachelor degree. Typically, students are full-time employed and have a family, and consequently have less time for studying.

They form a very heterogeneous group, with respect to age, education and expertise. However, all students have a professional expertise in IT, usually related to their daily work. This is of consequence in an education programme where IT is central in terms of form as well as content.

## 2.4 Learning theory foundation

The programme is based on social-constructivist learning principles, combined with Cowan's 'reflection loops' (Cowan, 1998), as it is commonly recognised that reflection has a predominant place in problem-oriented group-based learning. Cowan has combined Kolb's 'learning cycles' (Kolb, 1984) and Schön's ideas about reflection in learning processes to a concept based on three planned reflection loops for, in (the middle of), and on (after) the learning process. The so-called modified Cowan diagram is illustrated in Figure 1:

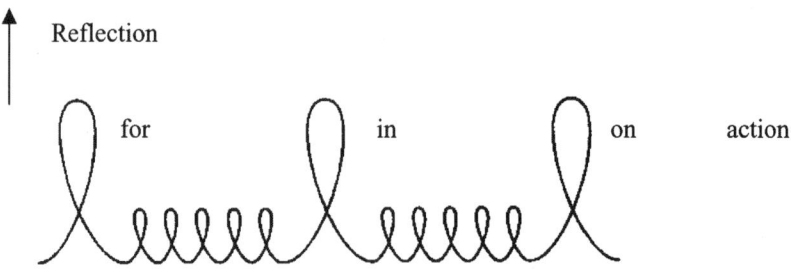

Figure 1. Modified Cowan diagram with three planned reflection loops

In the MII programme, these major reflections are set to take place in three specific seminars. The main purpose is to enhance the quality, depth and relevance of what is learned. In addition, reflection should take place in other seminars and at virtual group meetings. These small, unplanned reflection loops are supposed to level out differences in knowledge between the individual group members, which is indeed needed in distance education.

## 3. GROUP WORK IN THE PHYSICAL AND IN THE VIRTUAL ROOM

To understand the challenges in adapting on-campus collaborative project and group organised programmes (AAU engineering programmes) to distance education (MII), a further analysis of the differences is required. We have chosen to divide these into three partly overlapping categories:

* Work forms and social structures
* Communication forms
* Personal issues

### 3.1 Work forms and social structures

In on-campus educations programmes at AAU, students have their physical group room, which is their base every day from 8 a.m. to 4 p.m. They go to lectures together, do course assignments together in the group room, work on the project - often in sub-groups - and take most breaks together. This causes and allows a great deal of relevant informal communication, easy opportunity for help with various minor problems, and a strong social contact.

Off-campus students are only together, face-to-face, during the seminars, while daily studying is done alone at home. Initiative is required to create contact with another group member, e.g. to ask for help, and students have to overcome the risk of disturbing. Consequently, small problems can take a long time to be solved and cause frustrations.

On-campus students are continually motivated by their fellow students, teachers and supervisors, while off-campus students have to motivate themselves when they start studying, typically around 9 p.m., after a long day's work and time with the family.

### 3.2 Communication forms

Formal communication in MII in relation to project work occurs in synchronous group meetings, with or without participation of the supervisor. With today's technology, synchronous communication over the Internet is an obvious opportunity, and with a little training, efficient virtual group meetings can be conducted. These require more preparation and meeting discipline than face-to-face meetings, though experience shows, that brainstorming, general discussions, solutions to person-related problems, and planning can be difficult to carry out in virtual meetings. The differences between face-to-face and virtual group meetings are otherwise of lesser importance, in particular when the participants already know each other. Experiments in the e-Learning Lab at AAU indicate that better technology with full duplex, whiteboard and better video, can possibly further decrease the difference.

Spontaneous communication, regarding the technical content of the courses, occurs automatically when on-campus students go to courses together and do their assignments together in their group room with the teacher dropping in. The off-campus students, on the other hand, follow courses alone, at different times, so there is no natural communication with fellow students or the teacher about course content. The course newsgroups especially created to cover this communication need are not used sufficiently in spite of motivation efforts from the teachers and a few of the students.

### 3.3 Personal issues

Distance students identify themselves as mature professionals more than as regular students (Lorentsen 2000). Their job and their family life is their base and have first priority. When lacking time for their studies, the time available is prioritised where the obligations are the strongest, that is on the project. This is because the students' sense of responsibility and solidarity with the group appears to be more important than personal acquisition of course material.

Furthermore, distance students have a lesser need than regular students for both social and professional/technical network within their study groups, as they already to a large extent have a network privately and at work. Contact to the university and in particular to fellow students is nevertheless important to them. They just do not have much time for it.

Many distance students have adapted a more results oriented attitude from their work, and do not identify themselves with the university study environment and form

## 4. RESULTS OF QUESTIONNAIRES AND PLENUM MEETING

Each year (2000, 2001 and 2002), within a week after completion of the exam, MII students have been asked to complete an evaluation questionnaire containing approximately 60 questions in 7 categories:

- Pilot project
- Main project

- Group work
- Courses
- General about curriculum
- Technology and software tools
- Organisation and private/family life

Any modification and/or addition of questions from year to year have been made with the attention of keeping a valid basis for comparison between the three years. The response rate in 2000 was 10 out of 14 students, in 2001, 9 out of 13 students, and in 2002, 8 out of 8 students.

The questions most relevant to the relationship between project work and courses are listed below in Table I. The answers for each question are given either as typical answers in condensed form, direct quotes in » », or e.g. 'yes/no = 3/6' meaning 3 answered yes and 6 answered no.

| | Question | Response 2000 | Response 2001 | Response 2002 |
|---|---|---|---|---|
| | **Pilot project** | | | |
| Q1 | Do you feel that the pilot project was beneficial to the main project? | Yes | Yes | Yes/no: 4/2. |
| Q2 | Do you have recommendations for alteration in the pilot project? | No | More control | Yes/no: 3/2 More technical. Include Java and OO* |
| Q3 | Mention some positive experiences you had during the pilot project. | Group collaboration | Virtual collaboration | Group collaboration |
| Q4 | Mention some negative experiences you had during the pilot project. | Technology (Luvit (www.luvit.com) and www-based learning environment). | Uncertainty | None in particular. "The project appeared irrelevant" |
| | **Main project** | | | |
| Q5 | Was the project suitable for distance education? | Yes | Yes | Yes/too complex: 2/4 |
| Q6 | Do you prefer that the supervisor propose the projects or, as it was done, that everybody does? | Everybody | Everybody | Everybody/supervisor: 3/4 |
| Q7 | 2000 & 2001: Did the project work take up too much room compared to the courses?<br><br>2002: How much of your study time was spent on project work during the course intensive period December-March? | Yes/no: 4/4 "The main project took too much of our time – it had to be done, it is easier to dismiss the courses." "The project took 80% of the time" | Yes/no: 5/4 "We were not able to limit our project. We were warned not to be too ambitious, but…"/ "The students should have been asked to work on the courses before the project." | Too much: 5 |
| Q8 | 2000 & 2001: Do you have suggestions how a better, more equal distribution of time on projects and courses can be obtained?<br><br>2002: Do you feel that you divided your time optimally between courses and project work? | Better courses "The courses should be introduced earlier, so we can see the relations between project and courses." | Tighter control, hand in solutions "Tighter follow-up on courses"/"Each group hands in a solution of problem for each course"/"Deadlines for handing in problem solutions"/"More communication and discussion in relation to courses"/"Cut down on the projects" | No: 6 "In retrospect I can see: there was too little course studying and too much project." "Tighter control of projects" |
| Q9 | 2001: Was there sufficient time for both courses and project work? 2002: Is it too difficult to work on several courses and the project simultaneously? | | Yes/no: 3/6 | Yes: 6 |
| Q10 | 2001 & 2002: Could you use the courses for solving problems of the project? | | Yes | Yes/no: 2/2, some: 3 |
| Q11 | Would it be all right if the supervisors make one project proposal, giving a tighter coupling between project and courses? | No | Yes | Yes/no: 5/2 |

| Q# | Question | 2000 | 2001 | 2002 |
|---|---|---|---|---|
| Q12 | What is your opinion of the Aalborg model applied for distance education? | Good but difficult | Good but difficult "The danger is that the courses are given a lower priority at home [...], because in the project you have some deadlines as agreed with your fellow group members." | Good/Adjustments required: 2/3 "Too much energy is spent on less relevant activities, a tighter control is necessary." |
| Q13 | What is the hardest part of distant project work? Name examples. | Slow communication | Discipline, motivation | Communication Java |
| **Group work** | | | | |
| Q14 | What was your experience of the group work? | Difficult, slow communication | Surprisingly good | Fine, difficult, positive, fiasco |
| Q15 | Do you feel that your contribution live up to the expectations of the others? | Yes/no: 4/4 | Yes/no: 6/2 | Yes |
| Q16 | Do you consider your own contribution satisfactory? | Yes/no: 6/4 | Yes | Yes |
| Q17 | Do you consider the others contribution satisfactory? | Yes/no: 6/3 | Yes | Yes/no: 4/2 |
| Q18 | Were all agreements kept? | Yes | Yes, mostly | Mostly |
| Q19 | Did you make sufficiently clear and specific agreements during seminars? | Yes | Yes | Yes |
| Q20 | Was the supervisor kept abreast of events? | Yes | Yes | Yes/no: 5/1 |
| Q21 | Do you have recommendations for improvements of the communication? | Sound is missing | Better technology | Full duplex |
| G9 | How were the interaction and the collaboration with the other members of the group? | Good | Mostly good | OK |
| Q22 | Did you have to modify your prior impression of group work routines? | Yes/no: 4/5 | Yes/no: 5/2 | Yes/no: 2/3 |
| **Courses** | | | | |
| Q23 | Have you used knowledge from all courses in the project? | Yes | Yes | Yes/no: 3/1 |
| Q24 | Did you work on courses primarily during the recommended period? – If not: why? | | | Yes/no: ¼ "Strong focus on the project" |
| Q25 | Your opinion on compulsory handing in of project relevant assignments by groups? | | | Good idea "This type of education requires a little coercion." |
| Q26 | Your opinion on a project free period, where you can concentrate on courses? | | | Good idea "… if there are tests." |

Table I: Questions and responses from 2000, 2001 and 2002.

Selected responses about project/courses at plenum meeting:
The unofficial project course exam seminar in Feb. 2002 became an impromptu evaluation meeting, as students were not adequately prepared for the exam situation. A constructive discussion arose. Many constructive and useful points were noted.

The students stated that:
- as the project was a collaborative assignment, the group members felt a heavier responsibility towards the project than towards the courses and their own learning in general
- they spent more time on the project than the courses (up to 80%)
- they were behind with the project courses, so the technical level in the group varied a great deal and was generally too low
- due to lack of technical insight required for the project, the project work took too long, which in turn decreased the time available for course studying - a vicious circle!

The students also gave recommendations for adjustments to acquire a better balance between course and project work:

- Give project work a lower priority in certain periods
- Work on course content in groups (transfer some of the group-responsibility sense from project to courses)
- Compulsory course assignments by each group
- More course evaluation exams

## 5. CHARACTERISTICS AND DIDACTIC ADJUSTMENTS

The first three basis-year programmes (ending in 2000, 2001, 2002) all had some different technical, didactic or pedagogical characteristics, and based on experiences, adjustments were made for the following year.

### 5.1 First year (2000)

Characteristics: LUVIT (Manufactured by Luvit AB, Lund, Sweden, www.luvit.com), a www-based learning environment was used for overall organisation. Unfortunately, this system performed rather poorly, in part because it was not intended for project work, but mostly because of numerous technical problems. Synchronous communication was text based chat on Netmeeting.

Adjustments: A new WWW-based system, Uniflex, was developed by the MII-staff to replace LUVIT. Better chat tool with sound was introduced. Control of project work was tightened. Changes of form and content of certain courses were performed.

### 5.2 Second year (2001)

Characteristics: All main projects had to comply with a client-server structure to strengthen the relationship between courses and projects.
The groups learned to conduct efficient virtual meetings with text-based chat, and some had success with sound-based chat as well.

Adjustments: An even stronger integration of courses and projects was required, and a tighter control was asked for.

## 5.3 Third year (2002)

Characteristics: A stronger integration of courses and projects was implemented by:
* introducing phases for concurrent courses and project work with specific technical subjects
* giving small problems and assignments in the course units that were relevant to the projects
* conducting unofficial project course exams, in the form of discussions of these assignments and their relations to the project at a seminar at the end of each course unit.

As the feedback from the questionnaire and the plenum in section 4 indicates, this did not succeed.

All groups successfully used voice-based chat for project meetings.

Adjustments: see section 7.

## 6. ANALYSIS

From the contact with the third year's students during seminars and virtual group meetings, the supervisors got the definite impression that most students had trouble prioritising their time optimally between several courses and project work. This leads to frustrations and inefficiency. The information from the students at the plenum meeting also clearly confirmed this impression of how they felt, when they were in the middle of the process.

The evaluation questionnaire, on the other hand, presented the students' opinion after they had finished the semester when the students had a better overview of the semester. They also had satisfactory project reports and a successful examination behind them and the frustrations at a distance. This might have lead to an exaggerated satisfaction with things as they were.

The answers to the questionnaire, Table I, are, true enough, more ambiguous, but there were also fairly distinct trends, supporting the impression above:

There was a clear positive opinion about project-oriented study, which was characterized as 'good but difficult' (Q12). Many mentioned group collaboration as a positive experience (Q3). All the respondents wanted the freedom to choose their own project, but the students in 2001 would also have allowed the supervisors to make the choice if that had lead to better coupling between project and courses (Q6, Q11). An increasing number of respondents indicated, that the main project was too complex and supervisor planned projects might be preferable (Q5, Q6, Q11). About half of the respondents in 2000 and 2001 thought that the project work took too much time compared to courses (Q7, Q8), but in 2002, almost everybody thought they spent too much time on the project and too little on courses and found several simultaneous courses with the project too difficult (Q7, Q8, Q9). Many, in particular in 2001 and 2002 mention a general need for tighter control (Q2, Q8) of the project work as well as the project related courses. In 2002, less satisfaction with the Aalborg model in the implemented form was expressed, as half of the respondents wanted adjustments (Q12). There was, for example, strong support of a project-free period combined with compulsory assignments and examination of assignment problems (Q25, Q26). In the response selection (Table I) and in particular the direct quotations, it is impossible to be completely neutral, but we believe that our premises are fairly correct, and the conclusion is well founded.

Our conclusion is that our efforts in tightening control after the first and second year (see section 4) did not have the desired effect and that a more efficient adjustment should be implemented.

Although we hesitate to deviate too much from the problem-oriented project-based model (Aalborg Model), we believe this is a natural and necessary adjustment for distance education - and in any case, that this experiment gives us a valuable experience.

## 7. DIDACTIC ADJUSTMENT PLAN

To obtain a better learning process for the students, the following plan has been agreed upon for the 2002/2003 academic year.

The semester is divided into three distinct phases; see Figure 2 and the description below.

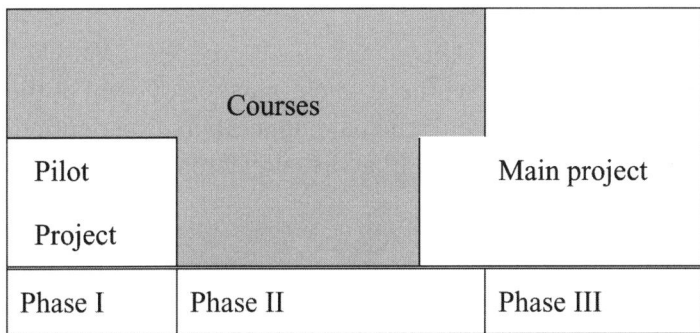

Figure 2. Distribution of project and course time in the basis year.

Phase 1- The Pilot Project

*Duration*: 2 months

*Aims*: The primary aim is to learn group-organised project work in web-based distance education, including a familiarisation with relevant collaborative and communicative tools. The secondary aim is to become familiar with the technical content of the project, in this case construction of databases.

*Content*: Introduction to the education and solution of practical problems. Project work, two project related courses and one study related course unit.

*Comment*: The pilot project period has been reduced from 3 to 2 month, and the content changed to involve design of a database, which can be useful to the main project.

Phase 2 - Courses

*Duration*: 4 months

*Aim*: To acquire knowledge and comprehension of course subjects, (c.f. Blooms taxonomy (Bloom)).

*Content*: Remaining five courses. For the four project-related courses: compulsory course assignments by groups with strict deadlines, and oral examination of these assignments at seminars. An objective is to transfer some of the group-responsibility sense from project to course work.

*Comment*: The project-free period is a drastic change. Control of course work is strengthened.

Phase 3 - Main Project

*Duration*: 3 months

*Aims*: Application, analysis, synthesis, and evaluation (Bloom) of the technical subjects, in particular interdisciplinary application. Experience from project work in a learning situation in a virtual environment, including documentation in a report.

*Content*: Project work.

*Comment*: The duration of the main project is reduced considerably and the students can choose between 'problem' and 'assignment' type projects (Kolmos 1996).

Requirements from the course teachers:
* They must be very active in answering questions promptly and set an alarm if the deadlines are not met.
* They must be active in keeping the dialogue between the students running so that the groups collaborate virtually on the assignments, asynchronously in newsgroups and synchronously at chat meetings.
* They must supply assignment problems relevant to the project, preferably subsets of the project, and of a complexity that makes it possible for most students to cope with. It is essential that the students frequently experience success.

## 8. CONCLUSION

Three years of experience with the MII basis year indicates that a successful project-based and group-organised learning model for on-campus engineering programmes cannot be transferred to distance education without significant adjustments. While project work is an excellent regulator of the learning process for on-campus students, this does not seem to be the case for off-campus students.

As the project is common for a group, the group members feel a heavier responsibility for the project, than for the courses and their own learning in general. A vicious circle sets in as the majority of the time available is spent on the project, leaving too little time for the project related courses, which leads to weaker technical and theoretical insight to solve the project problems. Time is spent inefficiently on the project, which in turn decreases the time left to work on courses.

Didactic adjustments were made after the first two years, but these adjustments have not had sufficient effect. Therefore, new and more drastic adjustments are planned based on the first three years of experience with the off-campus programme. The main feature of these adjustments is a project-free period where the students concentrate on course work. This is supplemented with a stronger control of the course work, including compulsory course assignments by groups. The objective is to transfer some of the group-responsibility sense from the project alone to both the course units and the project. A stronger correlation between courses and projects is also planned, by relating the course assignment problems to the projects.

These adjustments are based on student feedback, in particular from evaluation questionnaires, formal and informal discussions, and they are in agreement with the general experience that distance education programmes require a more strict planning and control than on-campus programmes.

Although the didactic adjustments implemented so far have not lead to an indisputable success, the students have presented satisfactory projects and improved in both the process of making the project and in documenting during the specialisation semesters. It is therefore our contention that the adjustments that have been implemented in the first three years of the experiment of adapting the Aalborg model to distance engineering education have been on the right track towards the ultimate goal: a successful model for project-based, group-organized learning in distance education.

## REFERENCES

Borch O, Helbo J, Knudsen M. and Rokkjær O. (2003.a). UniFlex: A WWW-environment for project-based collaborative learning. In: Proc. *4th International Conference on Information Technology Based Higher Education and Training ITHET*, 03 July 7-9, 2003, Marrakech, MOROCCO.

Borch O, Knudsen M. and Rokkjær O. (2003.b). *Pedagogical and technological challenges in on/off campus education* (This Anthology).

Bygholm A, Hejlesen O. and Nøhr C. (1998). Problem oriented Project work in a distance education program in health informatics, In: *MIDINFO 98, 1M1A* (B. Cesnik et. al. (Eds)), pp. 740-744, IOS Press, Amsterdam.

Bygholm A, Dirckinck-Holmfeld L. (1997). Pedagogic in the virtual learning environment. In: *Læring og Multimedier* (O. Danielsen et al (Eds)), pp. 63-68, Aalborg Universitetsforlag, Aalborg.

Christie M.F., Jaun A., Johnson L.E (2002). Evaluating the use of ITC in engineering education, In: *European Journal of Engineering Education, V27, no. 1.* Taylor and Francis, London.

Cowan J. (1998). On becoming an innovative university teacher - reflection in action. In: *SRHE and Open University Press*, London.

Fink F.K., (1999). Integration of Engineering Practice into Curriculum. In: *Proc. 29$^{th}$ ASEE/IEEE Frontiers in Education Conference*, Session 11a2. San Juan, Puerto Rico

Jensen L.P., Helbo J., Knudsen M. and Rokkjær O. (2003), Project organised Problem-based Learning in Distance Education. In: *International Journal of Engineering Education* (to be published). Taylor and Francis, London.

Kjærsdam F. and Enemark S. (1994). *The Aalborg Experiment* - Project innovation in university education, Aalborg University Press http://www.teknat.auc.dk/teknat_home/experiment/

Knudsen M., Helbo J., Borch O., Jensen L. P., Rokkjær O., Østergaard J.(2000). Project Work in Networked Distance Education. In: *Proc. 2nd International Conference on Networked Learning, at Lancaster University*, Lancaster.

Kolb, D. A. (1984). *Experimental Learning. Experience as the Source of Learning and Development.* USA: Prentice-Hall, Inc. Wilton (1998). http://proquest.umi.com/pqdweb

Kolmos, A. (1996), Reflections on Project Work and Problem-based Learning. In: *European Journal of Engineering Education, Vol. 21, No.2,* pp. 141-148. Taylor and Francis, London.

Lorentsen A. (2000). *Aspekter af teknologistøttet fjernundervisning på universitetsniveau,* Pædagogisk Udviklingscenter, Aalborg Universitet.

Masteruddannelse i Industriel IT, http://www.mii.auc.dk/

Semey, M. (2001), *Evaluering af samarbejdet i projektgrupper med fokus på samspillet mellem teknologi og kommunikation,* AAU (internal report in Danish)

# EMPLOYABILITY AND WORK BASED LEARNING

**Flemming K. Fink**

**Abstract**: The main natural resource in Denmark is human capital. Therefore, well-trained workers and well-educated engineers are a basic asset in Danish industry and Continuing Professional Development is consequently a prerequisite for the survival. In Denmark universities have no tradition of being active in continuing education, and in 2001 the Ministry of Education funded the establishment of competence development centres at six universities. One of these is the ELITE centre at Aalborg University. ELITE is based on research on continuing professional development. Some results from modelling the context of Continuing Engineering Education are presented in this article. A new mode of continuing education called Facilitated Work Based Learning is presented. This new learning process is based on a transformation of the basic Problem-Based Learning concept into an industrial context.

## 1. INTRODUCTION

In order to maintain a competitive advantage engineers always have to be »one step ahead« of their competitors in their efforts to integrate new knowledge into their products. For this reason Continuing Professional Development (CPD) of engineers has become increasingly vital. CPD includes the development of professional theoretical skills in addition to the practical work functions i.e. a combination of Continuing Engineering Education (CEE) along with productive engineering. In the knowledge society we have to stress the importance of learning as the mean of attaining competitive advantages, which knowledge by itself does not possess. Knowledge, once obtained becomes stale or out of date, but learning and application of knowledge continue to create, adapt and build on existing knowledge and this is what might create a competitive advantage. There is a new focus on the importance of human resources as a significant resource for the industrial development.

The awareness of the importance of professional development of engineering staff differs from company to company. As more and more consumer products, industrial equipment, etc. include an increasing amount of advanced functionalities and features the demands for skilled engineering staff increase as well. Most innovative companies are aware of the importance of improving the professional competence. From description of the context of CPD (Fink and Kolmos, 2000) it is known that even though professional development is identified as vital for the future of the company, the individual engineering staff member often tells that he has to find the time for such courses himself - they are not integrated in the time-plan for the project. Money for financing the course is normally no problem - but time is.

## 2. COMPETENCE AND HUMAN CAPITAL

The main natural resource in Denmark is human capital. Therefore well-trained workers and well-educated engineers are a basic asset in Danish industry. Continuing Professional Development is consequently a prerequisite for the survival of Danish industry.

The industrial context is following fast innovative changes, and the planning of professional development activities must therefore be highly dynamic in order to accommodate these processes and cannot be rigidly scheduled. Further, the framework of the professional development courses must include fast, continuous follow-ups on the needs identified by the organisation, in order to ensure that the engineers continuously are improving their never-static knowledge and skills necessary to attain their goals.

Modern companies, including Small and Medium Size Enterprises (SME's), basically compete on the best employees with the highest levels of education and competence who can keep abreast of new developments. To maintain the competitive level of the production apparatus and sufficient flexibility enabling companies to adapt quickly to heavy knowledge demands, the company has to have a frequent turnover of staff or a continuous investment in the maintenance and expansion of the organisation's total competence. This competence have to be maintained and developed continuously both by the company and by the individual employees. New research results must be integrated into product development as quickly as possible. Therefore, companies need a model for quick transfer to industry of the knowledge, which evolves from research results. The technical staff members have to develop professionally on an ongoing basis, e.g. by taking part in appropriate learning processes such as lifelong learning.

Small and Medium size Enterprises (SME's) have the same needs as larger companies. However, because of their size it is even more important that employees are on-the-job. Spending days following a professional development programme is neither feasible nor necessarily advisable. SME's are especially vulnerable regarding their ability to maintain and to attract well skilled employees. Employees must be able to see possibilities for their personal professional development and carrier. Therefore SME's need to find other ways to receive and develop new competences, ways of integrating new knowledge into their activities without too much interruption.

## 3. UNDERSTANDING THE CONTEXT OF CONTINUING ENGINEERING EDUCATION

Exchange of information between the university and the company is crucial in the establishment of an effective framework for professional development. The first schedule for a model for organising professional development between the company and the university is explained in details in (Fink and Kolmos, 2000; Fink, 2001.a). The constructed model is composed by eight elements based on the background of research and development within didactics and organisational learning. All of the elements and their unique characters play a role in a flexible continuing education process.

The organisational correlation between companies and universities, the different strategies of the companies and the universities for continuing education, and especially the objectives and contents of professional development, are of a more cultural and society-like character than the other elements. However, it is the relation between all elements that is of decisive importance to the concrete arrangements. The primary element concerns the professional development process and its objectives and content. Questions related to the specific types and levels of technical and knowledge-based needs must be answered in cooperation between the university and the company. Particular attention should also be given to the technological capacity of the society in which the company is based, as these needs may vary greatly across countries and in the individual companies. The findings related to this element in the model will significantly influence the selection of strategy for carrying out the analysis of needs. Based on experience of understanding and using the rather complex model given in (Fink and Kolmos, 2000) a revised model has been developed as shown in the figure and described in more detail in (Fink, 2001.a).

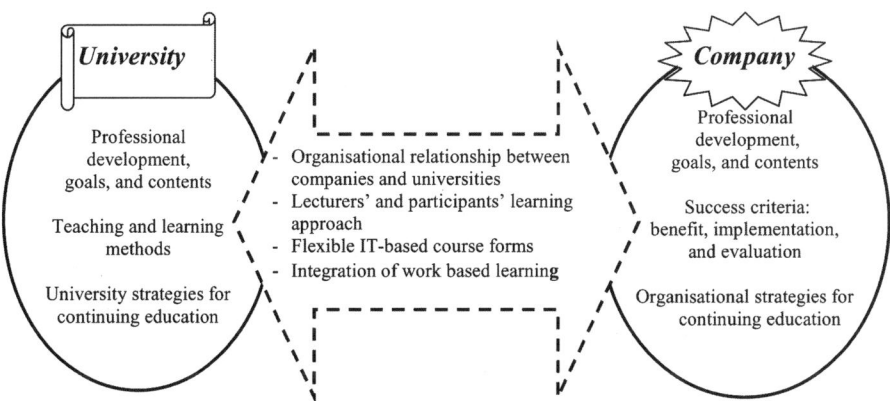

## 4. CONTINUING PROFESSIONAL DEVELOPMENT AS A UNIVERSITY ACTIVITY

The field of continuing engineering education is still relatively new to universities, and programmes may not yet be integrated into the university's educational and administrative practices. It is important to consider **why** the university teachers should be involved in this activity, **what** will be the objectives to achieve and **how** should it be implemented.

The university set-up as organisation and particularly the procedures of the administration have to be prepared for new procedures and routines before implementing a continuing education programme. It is quite possible that those universities wishing to integrate continuing education programmes into their system will encounter perceptual barriers among academic staff. State-universities like the Danish are economically controlled by very strict rules, which rarely are intended to work together with activities of more commercial character. Selling and delivering courses-on-demand is different from giving classes to university students.

Industrial engineering is application oriented and we might find it difficult to interface professors from fundamental research with industrial needs. Universities with more application-oriented research, including cooperative research with industrial partners, will be much more prepared for educational activities applied to the needs in industry. However, it can still be at difficult task to obtain a common frame of references for discussion of professional content and academic level of a specific course, in order to distinguish between academic learning and tool development.

The dynamic nature of the continuing education may also present a barrier in adopting these programmes because the university-culture usually is based on rigid planning and clear administrative practices that are not applicable in this case. The university must be prepared to offer courses on demand, rather than according to a rigid and pre-determined schedule. Further, flexibility in terms of class size, content, and scheduling will make it necessary to allocate additional personnel resources in order to prevent overburdening of existing lecturers. This is a real challenge to the traditional university system for allocation of scientific resources.

## 5. TEACHING AND LEARNING METHODS

Basically, there are two broad types of teaching and learning methods from which the company and/or the engineer may select: *company-oriented* methods or *university-oriented* methods.

Company-oriented methods may then vary according to structure and strategic decisions, such as:
- Just-in-time courses or courses-on-demand, in which the company defines its actual needs for knowledge development and the university quickly plans special courses to satisfy these needs.
- The project forms that may be characterised as a co-operative agreement between the university and the company (development departments) to have university researchers participate in development teams and to incorporate work-based learning.
- Part-time programmes implemented as IT-based distance education (flexible in time and place) - courses or projects
- Work based learning with professors facilitating the learning process integrated in normal productive engineering (Fink, 2001.b)

To a great extent, the **university-oriented** methods can be thought of in terms of ready-made courses within given subjects, offered to both the individual company as in-plant courses or to groups of companies or engineers with individual enrolment.

Traditionally, university-oriented educational programmes or courses are taught to equip the students with credits in formal terms - such as a full degree programme. It is also discussed whether single continuing education courses should be valued with credits according to the European Credit Transfer System (ECTS). This could form the basis for the employee to document his activity in maintaining his academic skills. It can however still be questioned to what extend the employer will acknowledge a list of academic courses showing the employees level of knowledge, or he will focus on documented engineering competences in terms of prior job tasks.

At a more specific level the choice of the specific teaching methods to be used is also important. Again the relationship between the company and the aims of competence improvements play an important role, as more participation-oriented and interactive methods can be linked to the internal company work. The integration of formal engineering education and productive engineering is a new challenge to meet on the basis of many years of experience from Problem-Based Learning (Fink, 2001.b; Fink, 1999).

Organisational strategies may vary greatly from *total strategic planning* for the company, where a basic education course plan is established for a number of employees to *individual employee strategies*, where employees select their own continuing education courses, which may or may not be the same as the choices of their colleagues. Often, a company's strategy for the professional development will fall somewhere between these two extremes and it is also quite possible that the company adopts a »laissez-faire« attitude by never fully formulating a strategy. In any case, the strategy that the company selects will greatly influence on the formulation of the professional objectives, success criteria, and the nature of co-operation and interaction between the university and the company during developing processes. Most important in terms of selecting a particular strategy (or combination of strategies) is that the professional needs and goals of the organisation can be met and that the strategy in the best way possible reflects the dynamic industrial environment in which the engineers function.

Based on several years of dialogue with industry concerning engineering staff development these strategies can be divided into different idealised categories as described in (Fink, 2001.b). Another parameter that has to be considered is the recognition of the course as being part of the personal curriculum - does it improve the engineer's employability? Is it important for the future carrier planning? This means that CPD-programmes must be developed to meet the expectations of both the managers as well as the engineers, programmes that integrate new academic knowledge into the productive daily process of the engineer or vice versa.

## 6. FACILITATED WORK BASED LEARNING

Continuing Education by following face-to-face courses is only possible if a course is accessible - either for individual enrolment or as in plant courses. These courses must be taken at a given speed at a given time without any possible consideration of individual needs. Streamed or videotaped courses are flexible, but normally there will be no dialogue between participants or between participants and a teacher.

We have at AAU implemented some specific »Master programmes« as research based PBL (Fink, 2001.b). In these master programmes IT-based distance education is very important (Borch et al., 2000; Knudsen et al., 2000) - se also M Knudsen et.al. in this book. The mentioned concept for CPD-programmes has been implemented at AAU for several years. These »Master programmes« are 1-11/2 year programmes on half-time basis, which means that it takes 2-3 years to complete. The programme consists of courses and project work. As in the ordinary daytime studies the project must involve at least 50% of the time and some of the courses must be applied in the project. The programme is also organised in themes and for the engineers attending the programme it should be possible via the project to integrate his job tasks into his study - or to integrate the application of the courses into his job tasks. In this way the workload from following the study will be reduced nominally. We have however realised that this is not always easy. New ways of more direct cooperation between university and company on management level to define the framework of the educational process are being developed right now. One of these new methods is Facilitated Work Based Learning (FWBL).

## 6.1 Definition of Facilitated Work Based Learning

Work-Based Learning has been described as a type of university programme or course, which unites the university and the organisation to create a »new learning opportunity in work places« (Boud and Solomon, 2001). The idea of FWBL as a tool for Continuing Professional Development is to develop a learning process that

- is integrated in the job task
- does not require absence from work or family
- has take-off in needs, not in academic programmes
- ensures professional relevance
- is integrated in the organisation
- adapted to the individual regarding level and learning speed

With take-off in our experience since 1974 in Problem-Based Learning (PBL) and the experience from Caledonian University in Glasgow in work based degree programmes (Burns, 2000), WBL is recognised as a vocationally oriented further development. Facilitated Work Based Learning is Problem-Based Learning in an industrial context. FWBL is learning on the job with a learning process facilitated by research-based knowledge transfer from the university. Following individual learning objectives by work based learning the learning process will be integrated into the daily engineering productive work. The learning speed as well as the professional content and objectives are defined individually.

The transformation of identified competence deficiencies into learning objectives will be a new task to take part in for competence providers such as university professors or centres for continuing education. This transformation must be carried out in cooperation between the competence provider, the competence receiver and the company represented by the human resource manager or the team leader. The deficiencies will normally be identified or defined in terms of competences. Building up new competences is composed of knowledge transferred from the university and mentoring the learner in applying this knowledge in new job tasks. When some competence deficiencies are identified among individuals or a group of engineering staff, a plan of knowledge transfer is negotiated between the engineers, their manager and the university. This negotiation ends up with a contract between the three partners defining

- Learning objectives
- Learning/pedagogical means
- Milestones/tasks for the learner
- Success criteria
- Involvement of the company
- Involvement of the university

## 6.2 Implementation of Facilitated Work Based Learning

The idea of developing a method for continuing professional development as Facilitated Work Based Learning is based on our 30 years of experience with Problem-Based Learning. In the PBL curriculum we try to adapt real life problems into the students learning projects. The students are not part of the practical situation from where the problem is imported, and normally they do not have experience from practice. The problem is for the students only a tool - learning is the objective. The students are learning by applying theories from the courses in the problem analysis, problem solving and documentation. Whether they reach a final solution is not decisive for the learning process.

FWBL is PBL organised as company based teamwork. The teams will be mixed teams. The team members will differ in educational background and in their involvement and job task in the FWBL programme. FWBL team members will be actively involved with the problem in practice, and their main focus is to acquire the skills needed for them to perform satisfactory in their job task. FWBL may of course be planned to meet the academic requirements described in a formal university programme to qualify the learner for a degree. This will normally involve more time from the learner than needed for his job task, extra time that he normally has to take from his private time, as degree programmes will be considered a personal investment in your carrier.

A university professor will act as mentor for the industrial learning team - the FWBL team. The learning process may according to the contract involve lecturing, discussion of work outcome and review from mentor, ICT-based/interactive learning tools, reading, discussion, etc. A senior staff member may also be involved.

The learning process must regularly be reviewed and the contract revised according to the situation. As such FWBL programmes will normally be in progress for a year or more, the conditions are expected to change: The strategic plan may change, the final objective of the work tasks may change, unforeseen technical or political situations may occur, the number of people involved may change etc. However, as the FWBL programme is based on cooperation between two fundamentally very different organisations, the importance of the contract reference frame for the work must not be understated, and therefore regular review of the contract is needed.

The individual learner and his daily activities are influenced by many factors beyond his control. Depending on the size and the organisation of the company his superior, other teams he is cooperating with and dependent on, technical possibilities beyond his control, administration etc. The mentor from university is also involved in many different activities meaning that his daily schedule is very vulnerable to ad hoc changes. To have success with the programme implementation it is important from the very beginning to agree on the management of the contract, including definition of priority of the FWBL programme tasks compared to other tasks for the learner and for the mentor. The FWBL learning process will end with an assessment of the process to evaluate the result. In situations where we organise this assessment as a workshop where all FWBL participants are presenting their experiences for as many relevant colleagues as possible, this will be part of the organisational learning process.

## 6.3 Organisational Learning

Individual oriented competence development like courses with individual enrolment includes the risk of being a waste of money and time for the organisation. The course might not be 100% relevant to the participant and the timing of the relevant issues to his/her needs might not be optimal. Bad timing means knowledge input too late or too early, i.e. the engineer is not going to use the new knowledge with the risk of not consolidating his/her competence. In order to benefit optimally from the investment in the development of new competences the single element of competence development has to be pre-defined in the CPD plan for the individual and for the team or the company. Each learning element has to include a definition of the purpose of this activity, identification of correlation between the content of the learning element and the overall learning strategy and evaluation of the outcome of carrying out the task. Too many participants in CPD-courses are never faced with the demand of justifying the relevance of the course afterwards - only beforehand. It is perhaps even more relevant to go through the course in a very condensed form for a group of colleagues and highlight the most important issues of the course. In this way the learning process of the course participant will be improved and the organisation as such will also benefit.

In work based learning the benefit of the organisation is more obvious. The learning process, objectives, content, form, and timing is planned to optimise the situation for the participant and for his team. The content, form or timing can be revised based on the context and transformation of knowledge into the organisation can be an integral part of the strategy.

## 7. DISCUSSION

Depending on the organisational culture, history, and management insight in the mentioned problem presentation, the nature of the organisation's strategies for continuing education will vary considerably. Most companies are aware of the necessity to allocate additional resources to continuing education and these expenses become a part of the operating budget, but in many companies the management trusts the ability of the individual engineer to access his own needs pertaining to professional development and it is thus the engineer who determines whether he will participate in a continuing education programme.

Other companies are organised into teams of engineers and the team managers are responsible for currently accessing the professional skills of the group as well as the planning of continuing professional development. This means that implementation of CPD will mainly be a function of this team manager's ability to cover all his responsibilities - if he is rather busy having his team meeting the deadline; CPD is not on his mind.

The innovative company has an active management practice in which the product strategy is continuously revised requiring continuous evaluation and re-evaluation of the engineer's technical and professional skills. Whenever lack of necessary skills is encountered, the engineers are either replaced or professional development programmes are implemented.

Only a few managers still believe that graduate engineers, who have a research-based education by definition, do not need continuing education, as they should know how to acquire new knowledge. In such companies time and financial resources will not be allocated for continuing education.

The University organisation and strategy is similarly influenced by cultural, historical, political and economical factors, in addition to the prevailing research traditions. Especially, in older traditional universities there are very »proud academic traditions«, which often mean that little to no basic educational and pedagogical changes have occurred. Research in these institutions is often »basic« or aimed solely at reaching higher levels of theoretical knowledge in narrow fields.

Other more innovative, universities have directed research towards a combination of application-controlled and discipline-oriented research. Universities in which there are sustained interest in applied theoretical education may be much more open to the demands and changes which occur outside the university environment and may thus be more open to undertake new tasks.

In spite of the numerous obstacles that arise with the implementation of a continuing education programme the intensive technological innovations occurring today create a significant need of methods of providing on-going and continuous professional development to industrial engineers. To a large number of these engineers-and especially those who are responsible for the application of new technology within their organisation, it is becoming increasingly difficult to obtain and maintain the high level of professional knowledge and skills demanded by the industry. By taking advantage of the research activities and educational experience existing in the university system, private organisations may well be able to satisfy their needs for continuous professional development of their engineers. It will be a challenging development for both companies and universities.

## REFERENCES

Borch, O., Knudsen, M., Helbo, J. (2000). *From Classroom Teaching to Remote Teaching*, EURO Education Conference 2000, February 2000, Aalborg, Denmark.

Boud, D. and Solomon N. (2001). *WORK-BASED LEARNING an New Higher Education?* Open University Press, 2001.

Burns, G.R., Chrisholm, C.U. and McKee, W.A., (2000). *Work Based Learning - an economic and strategic issue*, 2.nd Global Congress on Engineering Education, July 2000, Wismar, Germany.

Fink, F. K. and Kolmos, A. (2000). *Model for Continuing Professional*

*Development In an Innovative Context*, ICEECEE, Davos, Switzerland, September 2000.

Fink, F. K. (2001.a). *Modelling Continuing Professional Development in an Innovative Context*, Journal of Computing and Information Technology, Vol. 9, No 3, Zagreb.

Fink, F. K. (2001.b). *Integration of Work Based Learning in Engineering Education*, Frontiers in Education Conference (FIE'01), Reno, Nevada, October 2001.

Fink, F. K. (1999). *Integration of Engineering Practice into Curriculum - 25 Years of Experience with Problem-Based Learning*, Proceedings of Frontiers in Education Conference (FIE'99), Puerto Rico, November 1999.

Knudsen, M. et al. (2000). *Project Work in Networked Distance Education*, International Conference on Networked Learning, April 2000, Lancaster, UK.

# SKILLS DEVELOPMENT AND SUPERVISION

One argument in favour of introducing project-based study programmes at many universities has been the development of the students' competencies in co-operation and project management. These competencies are on one hand a precondition for making the PBL models work - on the other hand, the competencies are developed through practice. However, they are not merely developed on the basis of practice. Research in the development of process competencies has shown that if the process competencies are not developed at a deliberate process level, which means that the students reflect and experiment with e.g. various ways of co-operation, the students' ability to co-operate will remain tacit knowledge, which will be difficult to transfer to new contexts.

This is exactly the problem which Lise Kofoed, Søren Hansen and Anette Kolmos deal with in the Article, *»Teaching Process Competencies in a PBL Curriculum«*. Aalborg University has more than 20 years' experience in teaching students process competencies in a project-organized and problembased (PBL) educational system, although the teaching has undergone radical changes during the years. In this article, the background, the didactic model and the contents of the course, »Co-operation, Learning, and Project Management« (CLP), for first year students in the Faculty of Engineering and Science at Aalborg University, Denmark are presented. The objective of this course is to facilitate the students learning of process com competencies in connection with a PBL approach. The students have to document their abilities in writing a process analysis.

Staff development is a necessary part of the development and improvement of PBL models and the development of the students' process competencies and the pedagogic competencies of the supervisors is closely connected. Søren Hansen and Lars Peter Jensen deal with this theme in the article, »*Supervision is also about Addressing the Group Dynamics*«. As the title indicates, an important aspect of supervision concerns the students' collaboration; however, a lot of teachers do not know how to handle this aspect. The problem is not only found at Aalborg University, but also at the engineering colleges in Denmark. To address these issues, a special course was developed and offered with success several times to supervisors at the engineering colleges as well as at Aalborg University. This article points out aspects of supervising collaboration, and points out strategies for staff development.

# TEACHING PROCESS COMPETENCIES IN A PBL CURRICULUM

Lise Busk Kofoed, Søren Hansen and Anette Kolmos

**Abstract**: Aalborg University has more than 20 years' experience in teaching students process competencies in a project-organized and problem-based (PBL) educational system. The way the students have been introduced to this pedagogical concept has changed and developed during the years.
In this article, the background, the didactic model and the contents of the course, »Co-operation, Learning, and Project Management« (CLP), for first year students, Faculty of Engineering and Science at Aalborg University, Denmark, will be presented.
The objective of this course is to facilitate the students' learning of process competencies in connection with a PBL approach. The course includes theories and methods within the areas of co-operation, learning and project planning and supports the students' work with a process analysis prepared in connection with their project report. The objective of the process analysis is for the students to develop awareness of the work-and-learning processes, in order to become better project workers. Completion of the process analysis, which involves the student to document his/her reflections of the project process, has been a requirement in the Basic Study Program since 1982.
Both the course and the process analysis have undergone major changes throughout time and this development has occurred in three phases: instruction; theory and on-reflection; experiments and portfolio. The quality of the students' process analysis has improved increasingly with the development of the course.
We have reached four conclusive conditions for this development: 1) students already have experiences with project work and group processes; 2) the project supervisors' support is necessary to create a reflective learning culture; 3) teachers involved in these courses have to be qualified in both the subject area and in the learning process competencies and 4) it is important that there is a team researching and developing this area.

## 1. INTRODUCTION

Process competencies are an important part of the problem-based and project-organized engineering curriculum at Aalborg University. However, teaching and learning processing skills are not easy tasks. The learning of process competencies cannot be acquired purely through mental activities, such as a number of subject area competencies can. They are not analytical, technical, or scientific abilities but rather expressions of the individual's personal approach to learning and managing of the subject competencies along with a variety of other abilities, such as working co-operatively, communicating effectively, working independently, behavioural changes, planning and directing, and self-evaluation. They represent a metacognitive level of both action and knowledge. They represent a form of knowledge in action, which may be tacit, as it may be difficult to put into words.

Such skills can be very difficult to value, especially in an engineering culture characterized by technical and rational knowledge. They can be hard to value, because it may be difficult for the learner to experience his or her own progression in the management of these skills. On the other hand, engineers at the university now are much more aware of the necessity to achieve these skills, because e.g. co-operation, project management, communication etc. are recognised as core skills within engineering work. Compared to other subject areas at Aalborg University, engineering has progressed much more in the development of a curriculum within this area.

Teaching and supporting the learning of these skills are important. They cannot just be achieved by organizing the students' learning environment. The PBL and the project work provide the basis for students »automatically« to acquire a number of process competencies at least through experience, and the course has to support these experiences. Research with master's students reveals that this is actually the case, with students taught in project-organized and problem-based programmes being evaluated by their employers as having an easier transition from the academic world to the business world than those with traditional educational backgrounds (Jensen & Wagner, 1990; Nielsen et al., 2003). Other studies indicate, however that assimilation of these personal competencies is restricted to a tacit level-in other words, the students do not appear capable of verbally articulating their own experiences in developing these skills (Kolmos, 1999).

In this article we focus on the development of process competencies for students at the Faculty of Engineering and Science at Aalborg University. An essential part of the working life of an engineer takes place in project-organized environments. Therefore, by applying the problem-based and project organised learning processes at Aalborg University, we want to educate students who will become qualified project workers, and who are able to enter directly into a project organized working environment after their studies. The students must be able to plan, manage and be in charge of projects. They must be able to organize internally in the project group and acquire competencies within co-operation and communication. In short, they have to develop the necessary project competencies to be able to work as partners in a project organized working environment (Hansen, 2000).

Since Aalborg University was established, a part of the education for students of engineering has been organized with a view to achieving these ambitions. The teaching of process competencies is implemented by the project supervisors and through a course in Co-operation, Learning and Project Management (CLP) in the first year programme at the Faculty of Engineering and Science, Aalborg University. The course is taught by a group of teachers, who have their background in both engineering and educational research. The following gives a definition of process competences and describes the development of the course, the didactic principles on which the teaching is based, and the content of the CLP course. Finally we present conclusion and perspectives.

## 2. HISTORY OF THE CLP-COURSE

Since the establishment of Aalborg University in 1974, there has always been a course dealing with the practice of project work in the curriculum. We have studied the development of this course by use of students' evaluation of the courses during the time (Algreen-Ussing and Kolmos, 1996) analysis of students' process analysis, studies of course material, interviewing the lectures and using our own experiences as we have been actively involved in the course development. This course has undergone major changes throughout time and this development has occurred in three phases: instruction; theory and reflection-on-action; experiments, reflection-in-action and portfolio.

### 2.1 Instruction

Throughout the 1970's and 80's, the scope of the process analysis (which was part of the semester project) was limited to a few pages, mostly written in the course of a half-days time after delivery of the project. The particular subjects, which were selected by the students were essentially random within the areas of project planning, project direction, cooperation, utilization of supervisors, the relationship between project and project unit courses - and the process analyses were at that point quite meagre. The process analyses were generally not explicitly included in the project supervisors' agenda-leaving a great deal to the students' own initiative —and they were seldom given much attention in the final project exam.

Introductory courses for project work were also held during this period. In the 1980's, the project form was new for many students starting at Aalborg University, which necessitated an introduction to the special work form involved in both the model-and just as importantly, the work and-learning processes in the project. The courses were called, »Methods in Project Work (PA courses), and the basic literature was written with special emphasis on providing an introduction to the problem-oriented project work in the first year of the Basic Study Program in the Department of Engineering and Science (Algreen-Ussing & Fruensgaard, 1990). The primary focus of the course was to provide an introduction to make a project and to handle the project process. Therefore, it consisted of typical introductory lectures with presentation of the principles of the problem-based project work and examples of, how the project work should be carried out; subsequently, accompanying assignments provided students with the opportunity to implement a number of the presented tools and methods. The teaching of the course was often quite difficult, in that the students perceived the material as either too abstract - or too banal. The course was sporadically supported by the project supervisor.

## 2.2 Theory and reflection-on-action

During the 1990's these courses underwent considerable development. Professor John Cowan served as a consultant for the basic educational programme and contributed to the further development of the course and the process analysis. On the basis of theories on reflection loops (Cowan, 1998), a plan was implemented for conducting a more fundamental assimilation of experiences shortly after the project delivery. In other words, once the project was delivered, a day was scheduled for the students to discuss their experiences with other project groups, in order to make the students more aware of their own experiences with the group process. Thereafter, the students were expected to conduct an analysis of their own experiences, which would in turn be incorporated into the final process analysis. In this model, it was still the supervisor's function to support the preparation of the project analysis, but it was further supported by the organised days for experience assimilation.

Further development of the course occurred at that point - not directly for the preparation of the project analysis, but to support the project process. At this point, the courses, referred to as the »PG-Courses« (project-and-group work), were on a far more theoretical level. The students' reaction to the content of the teaching was still that it was too basic or too abstract -basic because the specific advice seemed so self-evident (even though it perhaps was/is not self-evident at all) - and abstract because it was difficult for the students to relate the abstract learning theories to their own practices. Also far more students entering the university during the 1990's were experienced with the project model.

The developmental work which occurred at this point provided support in the area of the study plan development, within which three overriding, intermediate objectives for the basic educational programmes were formulated: technical subject matter, contextual subject matter and developing the project qualifications. In terms of the technical and contextual subject matter, it was determined that further congruence to Bloom's Taxonomy (Bloom, 1956), which was selected as a shared reference framework for the description of the subject-depth should be sought. As an example of the emphasis on theory students should use Bloom's taxonomy to state their own learning aims related to their different specific learning goals. The quality of the process analysis decreased, as neither the students nor the project supervisors were able to combine theory and practice. So the students did not really use the course content for their process analysis.

## 2.3 Experiments and portfolio

The third phase in the developmental work took place in 1999. At this time, the portfolio model was established as a fundamental new model. The novel aspect of the portfolio model was that the students were to gather documentation regarding their own project and learning process along the way. They could choose themselves, how they would organise the work with the process analysis - a great deal of good advice is given in the courses - but the most critical feature is that they experiment and gather documentation of their experiences. These experiments and the accompanying documentation constitute the foundation of a final reflection on the process, at which point the students would write their process analyses - which could also be referred to as their »public portfolio« (Kjær Andreasen & Kolmos, 1999).

The portfolio method is quite applicable for achieving the objectives of the on-going experimentation, documentation and reflection (Black et. al, 1994). In the »Co-operation, Learning and Project Management« course (CLP), the overall objectives for the portfolio work are provided; in addition, there are a number of predetermined themes, to which the students are expected to relate. Specifically, students will be considering issues, such as project-management, organising of the work and learning processes, co-operation within the group and collaboration with the supervisors. From within these themes, students are expected to establish more specific goals for both the group as a whole and for the individual group members. The defining of objects for the process portfolio is followed by arranging experiments and consequently documenting and reflecting experiences with these experiments.

Through these means, the courses were also more closely related to the process analysis during the course of the project process. The main reason for this being possible was that the students had more extensive experience with the project work form - in fact, only the minority of students experienced this teaching form to be completely new. The specific project model, which is practised at Aalborg University, is new to the students - but they do have experiences from similar processes - therefore they can quickly adapt to this practice. Only the very first course is dedicated to the introductory aspects of the project model; otherwise, the courses contain a theoretical element including examples of the various practices and examples which document different aspects of their processes in various ways.

Similarly, much more focus is attributed to the individual in these phases, whereas previously, the courses were directed towards »the group«. This is where the students show an interest in the subject, and their motivation to internalise the concepts has become quite evident methods with respect to their position in the group. The co-operative group work is regarded as important in itself and the students recognize the importance of understanding their own individual perspectives, in order to fully understand the group. This is a way, in which to create much more reciprocal understanding in the group's dialogue.

The responsibility for the supervision related to the portfolio and the final preparation of the project analysis remains with the supervisor, but it is supported by those conducting the course. They will write a response to the completed project analysis, which is sent to all involved supervisors, external examiners, and peer groups associated with the project exam. This procedure gives the process analysis seriousness and a focus - thus, it becomes an explicit item on the exam agenda. The process analyses have clearly not only developed quantitatively - but also qualitatively, to the overall highest degree and with such an effect that it is given much more respect than previously (Kofoed and Kolmos, 2001). In order to gain respect in a cultural context we have increased the subject level of the process analyses.

## 3. REFLECTION AND EXPERIMENTATION - DEVELOPING A DIDACTIC MODEL

During the third phase of the course development, we developed our understanding of reflection because a part of this establishment of experiments became a more and more important element to facilitate the learning of process competencies, especially the awareness of practice and the creation of innovative experiences (Kofoed et al, 2001).

Throughout the course, the student is provided with small experiments embedded as exercises and over time, they are challenged to conduct tests in their groups and to reflect over the results in their portfolio. An example of these experiments can be a communication diagram, in which a group member or supervisor spends time (e.g. 15 minutes to an hour) drawing a diagram which depicts, how communication occurs in the group. Visualising communication provides a specific basis for discussion of the group's mode of communication which is generally not difficult for the students to reflect over on all three of the abstract levels, (see figure 1) which in turn leads to potential solutions for extraneous communication. A possible solution for the group can be to elect a chairperson-others could be to switch places or impose time allotments. The selected solution is then to set up a new experiment to be described and evaluated.

As can be seen from the following our basic approach to facilitation of experimentation and reflection is based on Schön (1983, 1987), Kolb (1984) and Cowan (1998). The three authors have different understandings of how experiments and reflections can be used as learning strategies. Schön's basic concepts are »reflection-in-action« and »reflection-on-action«. »Reflection-in-action« is a process where reflection and experimentation take place at the same time - in any case it is difficult to separate the two processes. »Reflection-on-action« is reflection at a distance, and it contains an element of evaluation of former actions. Cowan (1998) adds reflection before action as an important part of the learning process. Kolb (1984) does not deal with reflection as a method - but with an element in a learning process consisting of experience, reflection, conceptualization and experimentation.

In our analytical work, we found that the students were using different types of reflection when they worked with their portfolio and the final process analysis. These different types of reflection did not correspond to the types of reflection defined by Schön, Cowan and Kolb. Our research data lead us to define three different types of reflection: *Common Sense Reflection* means to be conscious of the experience. The knowledge, which is gained from the experience, is not questioned. The *Comparative Reflection* is learning through comparing different experiences. Finally, *Vertical Reflection* is based on induction and deduction - to be able to pass from single experiences to more abstract categories and vice versa (Kofoed and Kolmos, 2001).

In our model we also work with the three types of experiments developed by Schön (1983): *The Explorative Experiment, the Move-testing Experiment* and *the Hypothesis Testing Experiment.* All three types of experiments can be contained in reflective practice, so the practitioner jumps from one type to the other. In the model (figure 1) the experimental processes necessarily imply corresponding reflective processes. The explorative experiment implies a type of common sense reflection, where the primary aim is to test for establishing awareness. Move-testing contains the intended action and thus imply the comparative reflection. The hypothesis testing experiment also implies generalization of experiences and conceptualization, because experiences have to be analysed before new actions are taken. Therefore, this type of experiment is connected to the vertical reflection.

Basically, we do not understand Kolb's learning circle as a circle, where learning only takes place if the learner reflects forms his/her own conceptual understanding, tests hypothesis, acquires new experiences as the basis of reflection etc. (see figure 1). Analysing our own students' learning, they do not always go the whole way round the learning circle - on the contrary, at the beginning of the CLP-course they tend to go directly from the reflective observation to new experiments without any conceptualization. Therefore, we found it is important to define different types of reflection and experimentation. If the students are going to conceptualise and make more profound hypothesis testing, they must be facilitated into doing so through questions and through learning concepts, theories, models and methods connected to the field in question.

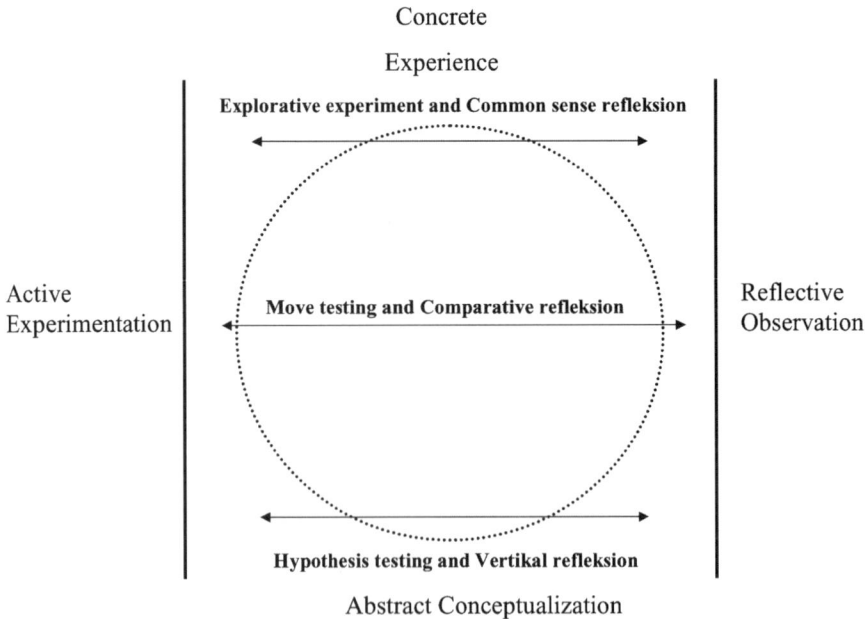

Figure 1. A didactic model developed to understand the theoretical approach to the CLP course.

## 3.1 The explorative experiment and common sense reflection

Below we present the concept of experimentations related to different levels of reflections. Common sense reflection is a preserving reflection, meaning that it is based on everyday awareness, but it is also an expression of gathering energy for processes to which you will pay special attention (Kolmos and Kofoed, 2002). In connection with the education of reflective practitioners Schön's reflection-in-action concept is central. Common sense reflection is one of the elements included. A reflective practitioner does not use a general theory and method uncritically - but through explorative experiments he/she curiously tests to see how it works, what will happen - and reflects on a common sense level during the process. (Schön, 1987), (Hansen, 2000).

## 3.2 Move-testing and comparative reflection

Move-testing and comparative reflection are also elements in Schön's reflection-in-action concept. Move-testing and the comparative reflection are fundamental elements in the practice of the reflective practitioner. Among others, it is through reflection on similarities and differences in his/her experiences that ideas for further development are born - and development can take place through testing these experiences. For example, if the learner is going to establish a better social environment in the group, he/she uses her experiences and tries e.g.to bring a cake for next group meeting to support the social atmosphere. But if this does not work - he/she has to try something else.

The comparative reflection is an element in the vertical reflection (Kolmos and Kofoed, 2002). But it can also take place without leading to the abstract conceptualization. In connection with a reflective and experimental practice the conceptualization is not essential to development.

Schön's move-testing experiment is an example of this (Schön, 1987). The purpose of this type of experiments is that they should lead the student to a better understanding of a given problem. The student tries to understand a problem or a situation by changing it. He/she continues until he likes the entirety of what he/she experiences. Then the experiment is a success. He/she does not necessarily expect a certain outcome, but observes closely the changes caused by the intended experiments. This is quite another objective than by the hypothesis testing experiment (as described later). The reflective student does not try to control his/her »test set-up«. He/she becomes a part of it and evaluates entirety, which is the outcome of his/her experimental »reframing« of the problem. The understanding obtained by the student in this way contains both tacit and explicit knowledge. The explicit or conscious part of this knowledge can be the object of a subsequent vertical reflection, which may lead to conceptualization. However, the tacit part of the understanding will not lead to any conceptualization - but still, it is an important part of the competency which the student has obtained from his/her experiment.

## 3.3 Hypothesis testing and vertical reflection

Hypothesis testing is the type of experiment, which is most like the traditional controlled experiment. It is a test of relations, which implies a conceptualization of cause and effect. The conceptualization is among others the outcome of a vertical reflection, where the learner climbs the ladder of abstraction. These experiments are planned and the reflections are rational - they may be difficult, but in some cases they are necessary parts in changing practice.

Vertical reflection is especially suitable for connecting theory and practice. The teacher use vertical reflection in connection with theoretical reflections on the examples used during the course. The students use vertical reflection when they try to become conscious of their experiences through reflection on e.g. a theory about co-operation. This is a reflection based on the comparative reflection, where the students relate various experiences and make their own understanding of e.g. the concept »good co-operation« - or »organization of co-operation processes«. This is when the experiences are made explicit or oral.

The vertical reflection will contain a reflection-on-action. Contrary to reflection-in-action this is a »Stop and Think« reflection, which follows a finished act (Hansen, 2000). This kind of reflection is supported in the CLP course by presenting a number of facilitating questions to the students in order to make them reflect on their process experiences in relation to the theory they have learned during the course. The results are shown in the student's process analysis.

This didactic model is the basis for continuous development of the CLP course and vice versa - the course is questioning the model for development of theories and methods.

## 4. THE CONTENT OF THE CLP COURSE

The course in Co-operation, Learning and Project Management consists of 10 lectures of 4 hours each. 7 lectures are taught at the 1st semester, and 3 at the 2nd semester. The following is a short description of how the above didactic method has been translated into the CLP course. The structure of the course is based on four subjects: Learning and problem-based project work, project management and project control, organization and co-operation, and the portfolio model.

### 4.1 Learning and problem-based project work

The concept of Problem-based project work refers to a method, where the students are working with problems in their projects. At Aalborg University the students have to find, formulate and solve / discuss a problem, which can be guiding for their project. We want graduates that are able to find and solve problems through critical analyses - and an understanding that the process of solving problems consists of an interaction between formulating the problem and focusing on the solution. Therefore, we have chosen to call the total process »problem managing«.

The applicability of a certain solution to a problem is absolutely dependent on where the analysis had its focus, during the problem analysis. During the first two terms of the education, focus is on the students' ability to make a broad analysis of a real problem connected to a specific technical problem area, which they find themselves in the context where the problem has arisen. It may be a ward at a hospital where the management or the staff is discussing the introduction of new technology. The students are asked to analyse social structures and actors involved, and other conditions that are important to understand the problem and to find a solution to it. Furthermore, we want the students to learn to be responsible for the content of their projects. Therefore, they currently have to formulate learning objectives in the actual project. The written outcome of these reflections is called a statement of learning objectives. It is a kind of mutual contract between the students, and between the students and their supervisor stating what the students are expected to learn from their project and its actual problem (Hansen, 2002), but taking the study regulation in consideration.

## 4.2 Project management

It is important that the students obtain competencies in project management. Project management is defined as answering the question: What do we want and how do we carry out our plans? It is a question of pinpointing the aim of the project and the means to achieve the aim. We do not use much literature, which advises finished solutions to how projects are planned and managed. The argument in favour of this is that a specific project-planning tool can be seen as an integrated part of the project group's way of co-operation, principles of organization, and communication. Teaching is based on the principle that project plans are seen as a visualization of the project group's common understanding of the aims and means of the project. Therefore, they have to be adapted to the organizational structure, which is used by the project group, and which fits into the actual composition of personalities and experiences.

In the CLP-course the principle of our understanding of project management is therefore that it is first of all about structuralization and visualization of the project process. That is why the students are presented to a number of fundamental methods for structuralization and visualization of a project process. First of all in the form of examples of project plans from former students' process analyses. Much importance is attached to demonstrate multitude and creativity instead of finished models, which all students must try to use. It is a basic principle in our teaching that through reflective experiments the students learn to develop their own approach to accomplishing a project. An approach, which has its starting point in the students' own personality and the unique composition of the project group.

An example of a creative and dynamic method of structuralization and visualization is »Post It Structuralization«. This method is very simple, and the system is that the members of the group write central words or concepts of e.g. the problem content on Post It slips, which are placed on a piece of cardboard, e.g. a door. To make the system as dynamic as possible only one word is written on each slip. During the initial brainstorm each student writes the words he/she finds relevant to the subject, which has to be structured. Afterwards the students gather around the table and they place the slips in order to organise the brainstorm input. There are special rules to follow, which are taught at the course. The result is a visualization of content of the problem indicating what to be dealt with in the project.

## 4.3 Organization and co-operation

A prior condition to carry out an innovative and creative project process like the Post It Brainstorm is that the project group's communication is open, mutual, reflective and uncritical when creating ideas. Therefore training in this kind of communication is part of the course. The project group has to solve a purely hypothetical situation e.g. they have lost their way in a dessert and must try to survive together. During the case they train communicative behavior, which is, categorized in the following way:

- Task-helping contributions that are helping the group getting on in the discussion. E.g. by proposing a new concept, summarizing the discussion, or testing, whether there is a common understanding in the group.
- Contributions that promote the communicative environment. E.g. by encouraging others to participate, to follow others ideas and to be open-minded.
- Contributions that are categorized as non-functional behavior. E.g. defending their own position, attacking another person's position, over-talking or chattering.

The aim of this exercise is to develop the students' awareness of their own contribution to the communication in the project group.

One way to explain the inspiration from Schön's reflective practitioner is to compare the working project group with a blues band doing a jam session. Each participant continues to compose on the contributions of the other participants, and invites them to continue the development of the communication, which can be described as open, uncritical, reflective in relation to the theme, and creative. Creativity arise when the participants illustrate their descriptions and analyses by examples, at the same time as they use the others' examples to mirror their own understanding of what has been communicated. In relation to the didactic model this approach can imply the use of experimentation based on the explorative and move-testing experiment and the comparative reflection (Kolmos and Kofoed, 2003).

During the course the project groups are inspired to experiment with their internal organization and forms of co-operation. Teaching mainly consists in challenging the group's initial organization through a number of facilitating questions. For example we ask them about their form of management, how they share the work, roles and functions as chairman, secretary etc. Furthermore, the students are presented to a number of inspiring examples of how former project groups organized themselves.

## 4.4 Process analysis/portfolio model

The experiences obtained by the students from the training during the course and their own experiments are presented in an additional report called a process analysis. The process analysis, which is an external group portfolio, works as a tool for development of competencies, documentation of competencies, and as the basis of evaluation of the students' process competencies. The process analysis must contain a description and analysis of the process experiences obtained by the group during the project period. Furthermore, it should contain proposals for improvement of future processes. These proposals must be described on an operational level, which more or less can be used as the basis of the following project period. This means that the process analysis contains both comparative and vertical reflections. The comparative reflections reflect the qualitative development obtained by the group through explorative and move-testing experiments. The vertical reflections reflect this development in relation to the theories and methods of the course. On this background the process analysis is also expected to contain hypotheses of how the group is going to develop in the future.

Before examination the students receive a written response to the process analysis from the course teacher. It consists of a number of facilitating questions, and the aim is to initiate further reflections by the students. The response is sent to the students, their supervisors and the external examiner, and it can be used as a discussion paper at the examination if anybody wants to do so.

## 5. CONCLUSION AND PERSPECTIVES

In our analysis of the course development, we found four main issues that have been central. The experience from the course shows that the four elements are very important for achieving the learning goal. In our further development of the course these four premises will be taken much more into account.

The first one is the student's knowledge and expectations. During the first phase in the late 80'ties, project work as a learning method was not known to students - so they needed much more specific guidelines for »how to do things..«. Students' evaluation of the courses at that time indicated that they were satisfied with the practical approach, but theories on project work they regarded as banal or too abstract because they did not have any experiences to relate to. Today, the majority of our students have tried out project work during their primary and secondary school, and they enter into the university with some experiences. However, their experiences vary a lot, so in order to co-operate, they have to be much more aware of their former experiences compared to the new demands. The first parts of the CLP-course challenges exactly this and is supported by the documentation and the reflections in the process analysis - and because the students become aware of the differences in practice, they recognise to conceptualise their practice.

Furthermore, it is also important that the project supervisors support and value the development of these competencies, in order to create a much more reflective culture, but not all of them do. In all the phases of the course development, the commitment of the project supervisors has been a problem, only solution to that problem has been to select teaching methods where we were more independent of the supervisor's commitment. In our analysis of the third phase process analysis we find that students still complain about the lack of support from the supervisors and the tendency seems to be that there is a correlation between the supervisor's commitment and the level of content. The role of the supervisors and influence on the students project work has to be studied much more to give a scientific documented statement.

Teaching the course requires that teachers involved have knowledge about the project theme and qualification in both the subject area (technical knowledge) as well as in learning process competencies (project management, learning and group processes). It is important that the teachers are able to give specific examples in very specific technical matters, otherwise the students are not always able to identify themselves or to relate the course content to their own situation. Therefore, all lectures within the CLP course have to be double qualified knowing the content and theories on learning and process competencies.

The teachers can only become double qualified if they are closely connected to a team researching and developing this specific pedagogical area. Development of process competencies must be research-based as well as other university subjects are research-based. There is a need for continuing development of concepts, theories, and methods in order to avoid a common sense level. Therefore, we have created a close interaction between the Research Group on Higher Engineering Education and the CLP group. The relation between the two groups has always existed, but during the second and the third phase of development, more and more research has been addressed to issues in the CLP-courses.

**NOTE**

Parts of this paper has former been published in Kolmos and Kofoed (2002).

**REFERENCES**

Algreen-Ussing, H., & Fruensgaard, N. O. (1990). *Metode i projektarbejde (Methods in project work: Problem orientation and group work)*. Aalborg University Press, Aalborg, Denmark.

Algreen-Ussing, H and Kolmos, A. (1996). *Progression i uddannelsen fra basisuddannelse 1992-93 til 5. semester 1994*, The Teknatbas Evaluation. Department for Development and
Planning, Skriftserie no. 99, Aalborg University.

Black, L., Daiker, D. A. Sommers, J., & Stygall, G. (Eds.). (1994). *New directions in portfolio assessment, reflective practice, critical theory and large-scale scoring*. Boynton/Cook Publishers, Portsmouth, N.H.

Bloom, B. S. (1956). Taxonomy of Educational Objectives, Handbook 1: Cognitive Domain, David Moaky Company, New York.

Cowan, J. (1998). *On Becoming an Innovative University Teacher: Reflection in action*. The Society for Research into Higher Education and Open University Press, Buckingham.

Hansen, S. (2000). Vejledning og evaluering af den refleksive praktiker i det problemorienterede projektarbejde på ingeniørstudiet ved Aalborg Universitet, Aalborg University.

Hansen, S. (2002). Vejledning som faglig forståelsesdialog set i lyset af den operative konstruktivisme, in Kolmos, A. and Krogh, L.: Projektpædagogik i udvikling, Aalborg University Press, Denmark.

Jensen, S. A. & Wagner, M. F. (1990). *Ingeniørers arbejde og kvalifikationer (Engineers work and qualifications: A continuous Study of work- and qualification conditions among AUC engineers)*. Aalborg: Institute of Systems Engineering, Aalborg University, Denmark.

Kofoed, L. and Kolmos, A. (2001). *Empowering Transferable Skills in Problem Based Learning*, in Penny Little and Peter Kandlbinder: The Power of Problem Based Learning, Australia.

Kofoed, L. Rosenoern, T. & Jensen, L.P. (2001). Experimentarium as Arena for Common Learning Processes. In Dawson, P. and Langaa Jensen, (Eds), Human Factors and Ergonomics in Manufacturing (Vol. 11, No. 2).

Kjær Andreasen, B. & Kolmos, A. (1999). *Undervisningsportfolios på højere uddannelsesinstitutioner (Teaching portfolios in higher education).* (VCL Series, nr. 2). Centre for University Teaching and Learning: Aalborg University, Denmark. [Online]: http://www.puc.auc.dk/publika/portfolios,ak-ba.htm

Kolb, D.A. (1984). *Experiential Learning: experience as the source of learning and development.* Prestice-Hall, New Jersey.

Kolmos, A. (1999). Progression of Collaborative Skills. In J. Conway and A. Williams (Eds.), *Themes and variations in PBL* (Vol. 1, p.129-138). Australian Problem Based Learning Network, Callaghan, NSW.

Kolmos, A. and Kofoed, L. (2002). *Developing process competencies in co-operation, learning and project management,* paper for the 4th World Conference of ICED, 3-6 July, 2002. http://www.csd.uwa.edu.au/iced2002/publication/toc.html.

Kolmos, A. and Kofoed, L. (2003). *Development of Process Competencies by Reflection, Experiment and Creativity,* submitted at the conference: Teaching and Learning in Higher Education, University of Aveiro, 13-17 April, 2003, Portugal.

Nielsen, C., Bøgh Jensen, F., Nielsen, O., Amskov, D. (2003). Kandidat og aftagerundersøgelsen 2002, Aalborg Universitet, www.can.auc.dk

Schön, D.A. (1983). *The Reflective Practitioner - How professionals Think in Action.* Basic Books, USA.

Schön, D. A. (1987). *Educating the reflective practitioner: Towards a new design for teaching and learning in the professions.* Jossey-Bass Publishers, San Francisco.

# SUPERVISION AND GROUP DYNAMICS

Søren Hansen and Lars Peter Jensen

**Abstract**: An important aspect of the problem-based and project-organised study at Aalborg University is the supervision of the project groups. At the basic education (first year), it is stated in the curriculum that part of the supervisors' job is to deal with group dynamics. This is due to the experience that many students are having difficulties with practical issues such as collaboration, communication, and project management. Most supervisors ignore this demand, because either they do not find it important or they find it frustrating, because they do not know, how to supervise group dynamics. This problem is not only found at Aalborg University but also at the engineering colleges in Denmark. For that reason a course was developed with the aim of addressing the problem and showing, how it can be dealt with. So far, the course has been offered several times to supervisors at the engineering colleges as well as at Aalborg University. The first visible result has been participating supervisors telling us that the course has inspired them to try supervising group dynamics in the future. This paper will explore some aspects of supervising group dynamics as well as, how to develop the Aalborg model in terms of staff development.

## 1. INTRODUCTION

The authors have been part of the Aalborg experiment for many years starting as students more than twenty years ago and later on working as teachers and supervisors but also doing research in the area of, how the students learn to be competent team workers. The research was mainly carried out as action research, as we at the same time were engaged in developing the problem-based and project-organised study by experimenting with our own practice. Over the last six years, we have also been part of a group of teachers, who has agreed to do experiments together and afterwards share experiences. One experiment was to focus more on group dynamics, when supervising. We believe that a study model such as the Aalborg experiment is dynamic, always changing through a process of continuous experimentations and reflections. Through our own experiments, we have developed what can be regarded as a toolbox containing different practical ways of supervising group dynamics.

## 1.1. Students need more from their supervisor than a technical consultant

From our own practice, we know that students working in groups often find it difficult to collaborate and to benefit from being a team. Typical problems, which they are facing, are:

- They have different ambitions and different ideas about, where to focus in the project that they do together.
- They have none or very little experience in project management.
- They do not know how to handle a conflict between group members.
- They are not used to motivate themselves to learn.
- Often they do not know how to handle a meeting in an efficient way.

It seems obvious that they need teambuilding. This is documented by (Algreen et. al., 1995) and (Kolmos, 1999). It has also been documented that, the group will develop as more reflective and concerned with that aspect when the supervisor address group dynamics (Hansen, 2000) and (Langeland, 2000).

At the first year of the engineering education in Aalborg, the groups have two supervisors. The main supervisor is typical an engineer with a background within the engineering area, in which the students are studying. According to the curriculum, the main supervisor is responsible for supervision in technical part as well as, what we here call group dynamics. The second supervisor is more likely to have a background within social science. The second supervisor is responsible for helping the students to focus on; how society can make the best of the technology that they are working with. It is our experience that very often the second supervisor will also help the students with problems concerning group dynamics, whereas the main supervisor will only be concerned with the technical part. It is our belief that the main reason for this is that the second supervisor often has an educational background that makes it more obvious to focus on group dynamics.

Supervisors from other engineering colleges state that they do not regard group dynamics as something, which they should address. They do not know how to address it or they are simply afraid of, what will happen, if they try.

Although it is known that if the supervisor addresses group dynamics, the group's teambuilding will be improved, it is seldom done. Pedagogical Network for Engineering Education in Denmark (IPN) is helping teachers at the engineering colleges to improve their pedagogical skills giving courses and establishing networks for sharing experiences. IPN has identified the above problem and asked the authors to develop a course for supervisors about the addressing of group dynamics. In this paper, we will present ideas and methods of how to address group dynamics during a supervision session. We will also present and discuss how we have organised a course for supervisors and how it can contribute to the further development of the Aalborg model.

## 2. A MODEL FOR TEACHING AND LEARNING GROUP DYNAMICS

To a supervisor who is not familiar with supervising in group dynamics it can seem quite overwhelming to start doing so. To make it easy understandable what to do, and how to do it, we will introduce a special version of Kolb's learning circle, (Kolb, 1984) with extra words (in italics) paraphrased by the authors (figure 1). Kolb's learning circle describes how people learn either from their own experience or from abstract theories. Kolb calls this the prehension dimension of learning. The knowledge can then be transformed trough a reflective process or through carrying out experiments. This is the transformation dimension of learning.

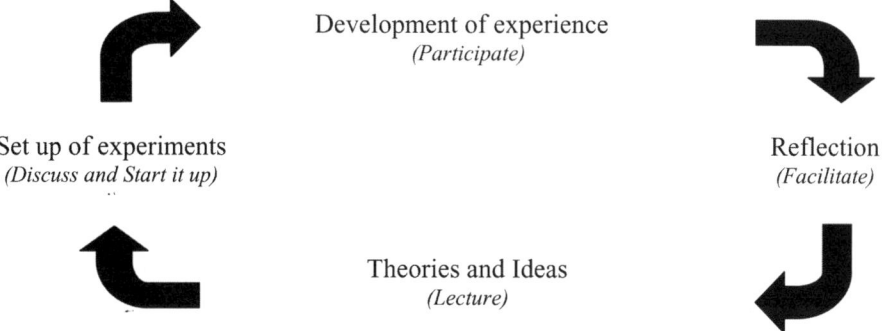

Figure 1. Kolb's learning circle, (Kolb, 1984). The authors paraphrase the words in italics. The supervisor can participate in action, facilitate reflection, lecture on new theories and ideas or set up experiments for the students to try out.

Our contribution to the model is to suggest how a supervisor can help the students through respectively the prehension and transformation dimensions when learning group dynamics. According to the model, the supervisor can take initiative to create a learning environment based on reflections and experimentations. The supervisor may give a small lecture with inputs and ideas on, how to improve practice within the group work. To follow up, he/she can help the students prepare experiments for them to try out during the supervision session that follows. During the session, the supervisor may participate directly in the students' development of new experiences. After the session, he can facilitate reflection by asking reflective questions about the procedural topics in the preceding session. By acting reflective and experimenting, the supervisor demonstrates to the students that this is the way to do project work and to develop group dynamics. By inviting the students to join and by presenting options to choose from, the supervisor can initiate change processes, from which students will develop. It is important that the supervisor deals with all aspects of the model. If the students are to develop affective competences such as group dynamics, they must try out ideas in practice and afterwards reflect on them to develop further.

## 2.1. How to use the model in daily supervision

A way to implement this model in the supervision is proposed in figure 2. The »ordinary« professional supervision session can be expanded with a pre-session and a post-session as illustrated in figure 2. In the pre-session, group members decide which part of the process to focus on (communication, collaboration etc) and what to do. This is something that the supervisor can prepare in advance using his knowledge about the group's lack of competences. Here we are referring to group dynamics, but it could also be the professional aspects of the students project. In the post-session, the supervisor can facilitate, which might lead to further development. Facilitating should be asking questions that initiate a reflective dialogue in which the participants alter between looking back at what they have been doing to looking forward and planning what to do as the next step. John Cowan has named these specific reflections respectively reflection - on - action and reflection - for - action (Cowan, 1998). The idea of expanding the supervision session with app. a 5 minutes pre- and post-session is to make it easier to include the aspects of group dynamics in the supervision without making many changes in the supervision methods in general.

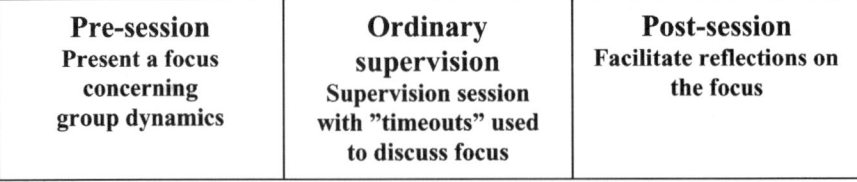

| Pre-session<br>Present a focus concerning group dynamics | Ordinary supervision<br>Supervision session with "timeouts" used to discuss focus | Post-session<br>Facilitate reflections on the focus |
|---|---|---|

Figure 2. The »ordinary« professional supervision session is expanded with a pre session and a post session where a focus concerning group dynamics is discussed with the students.

## 3. EXAMPLES OF TOOLS AND IDEAS PRESENTED TO SUPERVISORS AT A COURSE

In this section, we present examples of the tools and ideas presented to the supervisors during a course. The form of the course is a two-days workshop, where dialogue and exchange of experiences between the participants is emphasized. From the response we get from the participants, we are aware that the content presented must be very specific, motivating and inspiring. There is no need for introducing pedagogic or didactic theories of learning. The content must be related directly to the supervisors' own experience. Therefore, we find it important that the participants get the opportunity to reflect and discuss their own practice against our ideas. One way of doing that is to ask facilitating questions that initiate reflection of practice. Just like, we want the supervisors to facilitate their students' reflection. Another important aspect is to make it as much a hands on experience as possible, so about half of the time is used on exercises and role-plays and the other half on a continues mix between the teachers presenting tools and ideas for supervision and discussions among the participants.

### 3.1. Focusing on improving the students´ communication

A supervision session with a group of six students, where theoretical aspects of a problem were discussed, is tape recorded, in order to be able to have a succeeding discussion of the communication in the project group. First, there is a pre session with a short presentation of both positive and negative types of contributions to the following discussion (bottom of figure 1). The used model for communicative behaviour categorises contributions in tree categories:

- Task-helping contributions that are helping the group getting on in the discussion. E.g. by proposing a new concept, summarising the discussion, or testing, whether there is a common understanding in the group.
- Contributions that promote the communicative environment. E.g. by encouraging others to participate, to follow others ideas and to be open-minded.
- Contributions that are categorised as non-functional behaviour. E.g. defending his or her own position, attacking another person's position, over talking or chatting.

Throughout the following session (top of figure 1), the supervisor should be communicating in the same way, as he wants the students to communicate (task helping and promoting contributions). He or she could also use small timeouts to remind the students on the focus.

In the post session, a part of the tape was played for the students. While listening to the tape, the students categorize their own contributions in accordance with the communication model presented ahead of the session (right part of figure 1). Afterwards the supervisor and the students discuss, how to improve the communication in the future (left part of fig 1).

While reflecting on the communication, examples of functional and non-functional contributions will be recognized, and each student should write down, in which way he or she wants to improve in the following discussions. Throughout the rest of the semester, the supervisor may, from time to time, make a short timeout during a supervision session and ask the students about the communication. Has it improved? In what way has it improved? How can it improve further? In this example, consciousness about communication is developed and compared with a theory of good communication.

## 3.2. Addressing project management using facilitative questions to start reflection

Very often, a group of students who are novices in project management will set out to agree to have a collective management, where everybody makes decisions in common. They do not want a chairman during the meetings and they have no rules for good behaviour, or how to work as a team. It is possible as a supervisor to facilitate the groups' development of skills in project management by asking questions such as:

- Why do you not have a project manager in the group?
- How are the group organising project management?
- Which tasks are the management system facing?
- How are you going to organise to deal with those tasks?

Such questions can initiate a reflection of the group's experiences with project management. During the discussion, the supervisor may present concepts of good management rules and reflect together with the students about similarities and differences compared to their own experiences. A result from such a discussion should be the students´ own list of operational learning objectives.

## 3.3. Introducing the communication diagram

Having groups of five to seven students, we often see that discussions within the group are unbalanced in the sense that not all the students participate or some of the students almost do all of the talking. A simple way of revealing this is to draw a diagram of who is talking to whom during the discussion. It is called a communication diagram (see figure 3) and can be used in several ways.

The supervisor might use it to show that the discussion is unbalanced, simply by drawing the diagram, when he participates in a meeting/discussion and then the supervisor may show it to the group afterwards, in order either to discuss the pattern with them or leave it up to the group to discuss what to do. This is a special way of facilitating a reflection (right part of figure 1) about communication.

A common example is that two group members sit next to each other and discuss other matters than the rest of the group (e.g. football). In other words, if the two people in the right down corner of figure 3 had several arrows between them. A simple solution of this could be to move one of the two people to the upper left corner and draw a new diagram during the next discussion to see, whether the communication pattern has improved.

The supervisor might also suggest an experiment (left part of figure 1) of replacing the students around the table using the communication diagram (Jaques, 2000) to see whether it changes the communication pattern. The students often use this solution, when they have seen the communication diagram in use.

Draw how the members of
the group are placed around the table

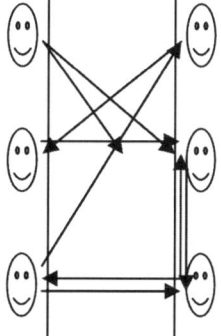
Draw arrows for each contribution to the
discussion for about 5 min.

Figure 3. The communication diagram (Jaques 2000), showing all contributions made by the group members in a discussion.

## 3.4. Participating in structuring a project

A supervisor may experience that discussions with the students are insufficient to make them understand ideas about proposed changes to the project. Sometime the supervisor's participation (top of figure 1) in doing the project is needed. One example of this could be the task of structuring the project after having formulated the problem.

As a tool for structuring the project, the supervisor can introduce the »Post-It brainstorm« method. The idea is to write down everything that comes to mind concerning the project on Post-It notes. Then the group should structure the notes. The good thing about Post-It notes is that they can easily be restructured, when there is a good argument for doing so.

The supervisor may then tell the students that for the next hour or so, he is member of the group taking part in the Post-it brainstorm. In that period, he is no longer a supervisor but an experienced member of the group who has an idea about, how to proceed. During the session, it is important that the supervisor acts as a group member and not as an authority. He or she most NOT do all work, but instead bring forward suggestions and insist that they are followed up by action. After the session, it should be clear to the students, how they can complete the structuring task.

At the end of the session, the supervisor can facilitate a reflection (right side of figure 1) about the methodology, which they have just used. This might make it easier for the students to complete a similar task in the future.

## 4. EXAMPLE OF HANDS-ON EXERCISE - ROLE-PLAYS

Role-plays are very useful to obtain hands-on experience, when a real world situation is not present. The entire morning of day two is used for approx. six role-plays, where the participants switch between playing the role of different groups with some kind of difficulties, and the role of the supervisor trying to supervise these groups.

The role-plays illustrate supervisor meetings. The group will have already given an agenda to the supervisor (the topic that the group wants to have discussed at the supervisor meeting). The group members assign roles between themselves, so that the outlined situation in the role-play occurs. The participants who are not playing are observing the plays. Each role-play lasts approximately 15 minutes. Afterwards there is a discussion on, how the supervisor dealt with the situation, based on the observations and the participant's experiences, and a more general discussion about, how this kind of conflicts can be handled. The use of role-plays has proven to be a good way of initiating reflections about supervision. The participants very often get ideas about their future experimental supervision

### 4.1. Example of a role-play:

The group is a very nice and extremely bright group. They work hard and read everything that they are told to. However, none of them does anything, which are not supported 100% by their supervisor. In other words, this group is very orthodox. Meaning that the group has a hard time carrying out a real discussion on their own. This is expressed at the supervisor meetings. Everyone is very quiet and cautious and finds it hard to take a critical position to each other's work. At the supervision session, everyone in the group delivers nice work papers. However, none of the work papers has been discussed beforehand within the group. Everyone wants the supervisor's evaluation first.

Besides illustrating a situation, where the supervisor have to address group dynamics, if he wants to assist the group to improve their work by themselves, it is also an argument for doing it, because otherwise the supervisor will have to do all editing work for the group. On the other hand, if the supervisor can convince the group of the necessity of reading and discussing their work papers themselves, the group's work and ability to take critical positions will improve dramatically and the supervisor will be presented with work papers already well edited.

## 5. HOW CAN THE COURSE INFLUENCE STAFF DEVELOPMENT AND CONTRIBUTE TO THE DEVELOPMENT OF THE AALBORG MODEL

We believe that the development of a learning culture mainly is taking place in a process of continuous reflections and experiments. This is exactly what this course represents. The course content is developed through years of experiments. The course is structured to initiate reflections among the participants and to inspire them to make their own experiments. As teachers we also gets inspiration from the dialogue with the participants. In a way, the course can be considered as a workshop where changes in learning cultures are initiated. The question is of course whether anything will change when the participants get back at their home institution. We do not know that, but from Delphi evaluations, where each participant write down tree good experiences from the course and tree things that did not work so well, we know that most of the them felt inspired to address group dynamics in their future supervision. They liked the hands-on parts like role-plays very much, because, besides the actual experience it was an excellent opportunity to exchange many experiences and ideas from the participants' own practice. They also favoured the presentation of specific ideas and tools that they can use more or less directly in their future supervision. This result is very satisfactory, because in the beginning of the course many of the participants expressed concern about, how to discuss group dynamics with their students.

### 5.1. Further development of the Aalborg model

Giving courses like the one described in this paper is a contribution to spread elements of the Aalborg model to other institutions. This process has been going on for many years. The Aalborg model has inspired most engineering colleagues in Denmark together with many institutions in other countries, but they do not necessarily implement it the same way as we have done in Aalborg. Learning about how the Aalborg model has been implemented in other institutions is a vast source of inspiration that we can use in our own development. This is exactly what we experience through the discussions with the course participants. This way we consider a course, as the one described in this paper, a way of developing the Aalborg model. Here are some examples of that we have learned:

- A much more focused view of our own model and method for supervision due to reflections, when developing a course for experienced teachers and the actual discussions with the participants
- A deep knowledge of a lot of different practices for both project work (length and type of projects), supervision and examination
- A lot of good ideas for handling group dynamics (different kind of conflicts)
- Specific ideas of other usable exercises and different ways to use our exercises
- Specific ideas for new teaching experiments

### 5.2. Lessons learnt from similar courses

Due to the great interest in the Aalborg experiment and its special way of handling PBL, the authors have also been involved in other courses, where we have used the hands-on exercises from this paper to give people from other countries and learning cultures an idea of both, how we do in Aalborg and the potential of this. In these cases, the role-plays once again proved extremely good for both hand-on experience and exchange of practice and ideas on an equal level, in order for the teacher also to benefit. One lesson learnt was that the participants in one course might have another professional background than in the last course, hence, they will benefit more from an exercise, if it is slightly altered. To find out, whether this is the case, it is a very good idea to present not only the idea of a specific exercise for the participants but also the »hidden« why's and what's that we as teachers considered (reflected), when planning the course. In that way, the participants are able to reflect upon, how they can benefit the most from the exercise, and it will help them and the teachers to focus on the learning outcome of the actual exercise.

### 5.3. An example of didactic development at Aalborg University

The learning model presented in figure 1 can be regarded as a general model for teaching and supervising in the problem-based and project-organised study at Aalborg University. Teachers and researchers responsible for giving the course »Collaboration, Learning and Project Management« (CLP) which is offered to students at the basic year have developed this model. The CLP-group is an example of, how a didactic approach in higher education is developed, when teachers and researchers combine their efforts to do so. The actual development was made by using figure 1 as a development approach combining learning theory and our own experiments. The reason for pointing that out, is to suggest that didactic development in higher education often depends on having a group of staff members who feels committed to develop their teaching and who wants to exchange ideas and experiences.

## 6. CONCLUSION

The Aalborg experiment were launched almost thirty years ago, but it is still alive and maybe more popular than ever. Although we often talk about the Aalborg model, this model is not the same at all faculties and it is not a static model, because the implementation of it is ever changing, according to both study guidelines and teaching. From the start, it has been a part of the culture at the University to do excellent teaching and throughout the years, the teachers have struggled to get the most out of the Aalborg model. Looking at the engineering educations, a lot have been gained in teaching courses and supervising technical issues, so one of the potential of greater improvements now is in addressing the group dynamics, which can improve group performance and learning capacity significantly.

This paper has argued that although it is stated in the curriculum for the first year studies that the supervisors must address group dynamics, they have difficulties in doing so because they do not know (have not learnt) how to do so. Experiments with short courses for supervisors from engineering colleges have shown that it is possible both to inspire them to address group dynamics and to give them tools and ideas of how to do so. The main reason for accomplishing this in a short time is that teachers have many experiences that is shared and discussed during the course. This great potential of knowledge about what to do as a supervisor in different situations is seldom shared at the home institution, due to lack of time and low status in discussion of pedagogical issues.

It is the belief of the authors that a simple and low cost way to staff development and improving the practice of the Aalborg model is to create legal forums, e.g. at the first year of the engineering studies, where teachers can discuss supervision in group dynamics, exchange experiences and knowledge about theories and new ideas. Then the supervisors should plan small experiments with this kind of supervision and later on report the results to the forum, in order to reflect upon their experiences.

There is probably still a need of actual courses, such as the one described in this paper, e.g. for newly employed teachers or teachers at other engineering educations. So another possibility to develop yourself is to take the challenge of giving such a course and sharing your experiences with others, and that way gain very much by getting access to the participants experiences.

## REFERENCES

Algreen-Ussing Helle & Dahms Mona (1995). TEKNATBAS-PROJEKTET, *Sammenfatning, diskussion og konklusion, Kvalitet i uddannelse og undervisning, en undersøgelse af den teknisk-naturvidenskabelige basisuddannelse 1992-93*, Centertrykkeriet, Aalborg University.

Cowan John (1998). *On becoming an innovative University Teacher. Reflection in action*, The society for research into higher education & Open university press.

Hansen Søren (2000). *Vejledning og evaluering af den refleksive praktiker i det problemorienterede projektarbejde på ingeniørstudiet ved Aalborg Universitet*. Department for Development and Planning, Aalborg University.

Jaques David (2000). *Learning in Groups - a handbook for improving group work*, Kogan Page, London.

Kolb David A. (1984). *Experimental Learning. Experience as the source of learning and development*, Prentice Hall.

Kolmos Anette (1999). *Progression of collaborative skills in Themes and variations in PBL*, volume 1, ISBN 0 7259 1068 2.

Langeland Christensen, Jonna (2000). *Evaluering af forsøg med undervisningen i projekt og gruppearbejde på den Teknisk Naturvidenskabelige Basisuddannelse*, VCL-series no. 12, Centertrykkeriet, Aalborg University.

# INTERCULTURAL PERSPECTIVES

Are PBL models a Western phenomenon - or is the project work model at Aalborg University a typical Danish phenomenon, which cannot be transferred to other cultures? That is a question which has been brought up several times, especially through the last 10 years, where we have had many visitors at the university, and the number of international students has increased. Experience and knowledge from the area shows that of course there will always be a strain of culture - but it is possible to transfer PBL models to other cultures - and international students and staff can learn in the Danish version of the PBL model. Still, it is not always easy - which can be seen from the last two articles.

In the article, »Problem-Based Learning and the Agency of Mapping the Contemporary City«, Gitte Marling points out that problem-based learning was a very helpful approach to mapping and analysing unknown and very complex urban contexts. The article is based on a problem-based workshop held at Chulalongkorn University (Chula) in Bangkok in February 2003. The goal was to show how problem-based learning could be used in an intercultural learning process - both for a group of Thai students and groups of Danish students. The conclusion is that problem-based learning is a very strong tool for intercultural problem analyses and problem-solving.

The last article is based on the personal experiences of a German professor at a Danish PBL university. Being a professor in Germany is a very powerful position, and the professor plays an important part in the organizational structure; however, in Denmark the organizational structure is determined by numerous committees and boards, so the Danish professor is regarded more or less as equal to all the other colleagues. This situation is described by Joachim Höhle in the article, »The AAU Model seen from a Foreign Professor's Point of View«. The author, who has a German educational background, an international career in industry, and 17 years as professor at Aalborg University, uses his experiences in an analysis of the advantages and the disadvantages of PBL models. Specifically, »The Chartered Surveyor Education in the 7th to 10th semester« is used as case and basis for the discussion of two questions: »Can foreign teachers adapt to the AAU model?« and »Can the AAU model be exported to foreign countries?«

# PROBLEM-BASED LEARNING AND THE AGENCY OF MAPPING THE CONTEMPORARY CITY

Gitte Marling

**Abstract**: The article will present a problem-based workshop held at Chulalongkorn University (Chula) in Bangkok in February 2003. The goal is to show how problem-based learning can be used in an intercultural learning process.
In the workshop new mapping methods in urban design were tested and developed in a 3-level learning-lab.
The background and the context of the workshop will briefly be presented as well as the organization, the process and the results of the workshop. The Danish participants have evaluated the workshop, and the article ends with statements and reflections from this evaluation. The main experience is that problem-based learning was a very helpful approach to mapping and analysing very complex urban contexts. The conclusion is also that once again problem-based learning showed its strength as a unique pedagogical approach.

## 1. DUCED-WORKSHOP AT CHULALONGKORN UNIVERSITY IN BAGKOK

The drive from the airport to The University was an amazing experience for the Danish urban design students. They were stretching their necks, turning their heads and pointing out of the windows, as they met the city outside the windows of the bus. Huge billboards with advertisements as big 10-storey houses were the first impression of the city; then followed the steady stream of cars floating through the city on highways on several levels. The highways and the sky-train system take up a lot of space, and influence the image of the city.

Bangkok has grown dramatically over the past few decades. Not only has its size increased - it cannot be measured in dimensions - its structures have changed, too. It is difficult to map the identity of this huge and fractal city with its endless repetition of the same simple structural module and with industrially produced high-rise buildings in »international style«. They have been built at an incredible speed, by architectural offices nobody has ever heard of.

17 Danish urban design students from the Department of Architecture & Design (A&D) at Aalborg University were very excited. They were going to

spend a couple of weeks in Bangkok, exploring the city and participating in a workshop about how to map the city. This was our second workshop in Bangkok supported by DUCED, a Danish University Consortium for Environment and Development - Industry & Urban Areas (DUCED-I&UA). DUCED was established in 1998 in order to strengthen the human resource base of environmental expertise, especially in industry and urban areas.

The consortium consists of five Danish universities that offer a variety of environmental courses and degrees. Through DUCED-I&UA, the universities cooperate in strengthening environmental education and research in Denmark as well as in countries receiving Danish environmental assistance. (DUCED)

In 2002 we held a DUCED-workshop in Bangkok and one in Aalborg with another group of students. Most of the planning was then done by Aalborg University but this time we had worked together with staff members of the faculty in Bangkok. The program, the field, the approach and the process had been discussed before we started the workshop. In order to overcome the intercultural gap between the Thai students and the Danish students, we had agreed to work with problem-based learning.

The title of the workshop was »*Water Based Cities - Urban Development and Transformation in Bangkok. Local Traditions versus Global Perspectives*«.

As mentioned before, the participants were 17 students from A&D Aalborg University and 14 students from Chula, Bangkok. Leaders of the workshop were Dr. Angsana Boonyobhas, Chula, and associate professor Dr. Gitte Marling, A&D.

The aim of the workshop was to learn about planning and urban design in large cities in an unknown cultural context. Furthermore, the aim was to learn about methods or the agency of mapping the city. Four new methods were to be used and tested during the workshop.

As the workshop was placed at the beginning of the semester, the idea was to use the workshop as a kind of kick-start for the main project of the semester, at least for the Danish students, and it was our plan that the Danish students would bring a lot of information about Bangkok home in order to continue the work in Aalborg.

Figure 1-2:   Bangkok between tradition and global development

## 2. WORKING IN BANGKOK CREATED A LOT OF OPPORTUNITIES AND A LOT OF PROBLEMS

It was a great challenge to work in Bangkok. First of all we were to work in a foreign architectural and cultural context. We had to learn about Thai culture, the religion, the traditional ways of living and the traditional settlements. We had to learn about the history and the development of the city and the modern way of living in Bangkok. We had to make a registration of the urban architecture and the physical conditions; within a very short time we had to learn much of very complicated social, economic and political systems and structures. This challenge forced us to be very open-minded and to see, hear, smell and feel the city. It was also very important to collaborate with the Thai students and others with knowledge about the local conditions. For the Thai students, it was a challenge to understand our approach to understanding and mapping their city. Besides, problem-based learning was new for them.

Another challenge was that the participants hardly knew each other. The professors did not know the students, as none of us had worked together before, so they did not know whom of the students to rely on in a pressed situation. The Danish students did not know the Thai students. Both parties were a little nervous as they considered the other part to be very skilful and clever.

At the beginning of the workshop, we had to overcome this social barrier and we had to overcome it very quickly as the workshop only lasted 21/2 weeks. This time limit was one of the most difficult challenges to overcome, together with practical problems like the computer systems, the network and the capacity of the system at Chula. Even though we were offered the use of the best and most modern computers at the faculty, we ran into many problems because we worked with maps and pictures in very heavy IT-documents. Nevertheless, most of the students managed to finish their work before the workshop ended, although a few had to do the rest afterwards.

## 3. THE AGENCY OF MAPPING THE CONTEMPORARY CITY

The main question for the workshop was how to understand Bangkok - and which methods could be used as mapping tools?
There is currently an ongoing development in urban theories and the debate on planning methods among urban planners, architects, sociologists and others with an interest in larger cities. The debate is influenced by the fact that new types of huge cities are developing in these years, for instance in East and South East Asia. In Japan, Hong Kong, Singapore, South Korea,

Thailand and Taiwan, economic, cultural and political life is shifting rapidly. The most visible sign of this rapid development is the pace of construction in cities and, connected to this, the pervasive expansion and explosion of urban space and metropolisation.

A considerable number of new cities have emerged all over the Asian Pacific Region. In these cities, hundreds of thousands of high-rise buildings have been erected from land which was agricultural fields or abandoned until very recently. Similar situations can be seen across the whole continent. The cities are studied and described as generic cities, flow cities, networks cities and cities on the move etc.

Figure 3: Working on investigation results

The Dutch architect Rem Koolhaas is one of the main theorists. He has studied large cities like Bangkok around the world, and he calls these very fast developing cities for »generic cities«.
He starts his article about the generic city with a question and a provocation:

»Is the contemporary city like the contemporary airport - »all the same«? Is it possible to theorize this convergence? And if so, to what ultimate configura-

*tion is it aspiring? Convergence is possible only at the price of shedding identity. That is usually seen as a loss. But at the scale it occurs, it must mean something...What if we are witnessing a global liberation movement: »down with character!« What is left after identity is stripped? The Generic?«* (Koolhaas, 1999 p. 1248).

Koolhaas has the idea that the potential of these generic cities like Bangkok is that they are liberated from the captivity of the old city centre, with all its straitjacketed identity. It seems as if these cities have no histories, developed as they are during a few decades. They grow and grow, developing new centres, new networks of infrastructure and communications etc. The generic city is big enough for everybody, he says.

*»It is easy. It does not need maintenance. If it gets too small it just expands. If it gets old it just self-destructs and renews. It is equally exciting - or unexciting - everywhere. It is »superficial« - like a Hollywood studio lot, it can produce a new identity every Monday morning.«* (Koolhaas,1999 p.1250).

Koolhaas argues that the generic city represent the final death of planning. Not because the city is unplanned - but because planning makes no difference whatsoever.
*»What is becoming of much greater significance for inventions in the urban landscape is the interrelationship among things in space, as well as the effects that are produced through such dynamic interactions.«* (Koolhaas, 1999 p. 1250)

The dynamic and the relationships are very central in this understanding. The American landscape architect, James Corner, agrees with Koolhaas. In his article »the Agency of Mapping« he also brings in David Harvey's arguments:

*»That the struggle for designers and planners lies, not with spatial form and aesthetic appearances alone, but with the advancement of more liberating processes and interactions in time«*


Corner summarizes:

*»Harvey's point is that projecting new urban of regional future must derive less from utopia of form than from utopia of process - how things work, inter act or inter-relate in space and time. Thus, the emphasis shifts from static object-space to space-time of relations systems«.* (Corner, 1999)

Corner is concerned about mapping as a cultural project, creating and building the city; not just measuring and describing it. Mapping is according to Corner a very complex and dynamic agency, and the mapping act may emancipate potentials of a given site and enrich experiences. The mapping process is more important than the map itself, because in the process of mapping lies the uncovering of realities, which have previously been unseen or unimagined. Maps have to give more than what is already known, he says. (Corner, 1996)

In his own work, Corner combines all the information of what already exits, for instance, physical conditions (topography, rivers, roads, buildings, places, parks etc.), or hidden forces as natural processes (wind, sun, rain), historical events, legislative conditions, programmatic structures or economy. Corner visualizes these interrelationships and interactions. Doing that, mapping itself becomes a design process.

»*It allows designers (and planners) not only to see certain possibilities in the complexity that already exists, but also to actualize potentials*«. (Corner, 1999)

## 4. USING AND TESTING MAPPING TECHNIQUES

Inspired by Koolhaas' and Corner's assertions about the contemporary city, we realized that mapping is, in Corner's words, more than mapping geometrically defining parcels of land. It is mapping an active milieu, which has no beginnings or endings, but is surrounded by other milieus or middles, in a field of connections, relationships, extensions and potentials. The job student's task was to test methods to map »sites« or milieus as boundless fields of phenomena - some physical, some imaginary.

Before the workshop started we had decided to test 4 thematic ways or techniques, in which new practices of mapping are used:

DRIFTING is a cognitive mapping method developed by the Situations theorist, Guy Debord.
The aim is to create series of »psycho geographic maps« the method is to walk aimless around the streets of the city turning here and there wherever fancy takes you. It is a kind of dream-like drift through the city, mapping alternative impressions.(Corner, 1996). A similar method is used by earth-artist Richard Long. He walks in geometrical figures. They may have a particular measuring unit: a mile, sixty minutes or seven days. His maps are open, cognitive, mental maps, rendering new images of space and relationships (Corner, 1999).

LAYERING is a technique of producing independent and non-hierarchic layers - one upon the other - to make a heterogeneous surface. Each layer has it own database and its individual logical structure.

The layers are a way of separating enormous amounts of data and information. You can study the layers separately like the differently coloured painted lines on a gymnasium floor. One layer is legible for each play. Looking through all the layers, the structure of the whole will give form to a sort of pattern to the »site« or milieu. Like children who develop new games from the mixture of lines on the gymnasium floor.

RHIZOME is a technique connecting any point to any other point. Like a network with no beginning and no end, but always with a middle from which it grows.

A Rhizome is non-hierarchical and continuously expanding like a mushroom mycelium. Rhizome maps are a kind of collages, but unlike the collages the rhizome map is systematizing its material into more analytical and denotative schemas. It is a kind of systematic montage, where multiple and independent layers are incorporated as a synthetic composite. Rhizomatic mapping affords many diverse entries, exits and »lines of flight« each of which allows many ways of reading and using the maps (Corner, 1999).

GAME BOARD is a game or play technique developed by Raoul Bunchoten and his London firm named Chora.

Bunschoten sees the city as dynamic and multiple with a range of players or actors, who are the forces behind the development. Selected sites are pointed out (by throwing some beans on a map). The bean site is investigated and so are the possible actors. It is the point of view that urban design practice is less like spatial composition and more like orchestrating the conditions and by doing this, a process of urban renewal and development will start. Bunschoten calls this »stirring the city«. The goal is to develop new kinds of projects in the city, new »urban prototypes« (Bunchoten, 1999).

He sets up some rules for the game developing and testing new urban prototypes. The maps consist of symbols referring to a kind of database and cards presenting different prototypes (Bunschoten, 2000).

Figure 4: Presentation and discussion in forum

## 5. THE PROBLEM-BASED LEARNING-LAB.

As mentioned before it is impossible for the students - and for anybody else - to analyse Bangkok from one end to another and it is insufficient to use rational mapping techniques. The complexity is too huge for an approach like that. That is the reason we have chosen more intuitive methods. The questions to be answered thorough the workshop were: What are these techniques all about? How can they be used in the design process? How can they be presented? What are the potentials in the techniques - and the limits?

We organized the workshop as a learning-lab in 3 levels:

### 1st Level was the forum or Chora:
The whole group participated in a forum comprising of all the students, the advisers (the leaders of the workshop) and invited guests (the dean, the vice dean, 2 associate professors at Chula and a visiting professor from Colombia University, USA)

The questions discussed in the forum were, among others: what are the potentials and limitations of each method used? Has the method been used in the right way? Has the result - the maps - been created and communicated in a proper way. Is there a connection between the design proposals and the agency of mapping? How can the methods be developed?

The leaders of the workshop were responsible for the forum, which met at the beginning of the workshop in order to present the idea of the workshop, the program and the methods to be used.

During the process, there was one pin up-session in forum in order to discuss the ongoing work.

At the end of the workshop, there was a final presentation by the students in forum.

During the workshop, much data and information were collected and many pictures were taken. Some students got hold of geo-maps; other students found articles, internet links, and data or air photos of the area we worked in. The forum organized a folder on the net, where the collected information was stored for collective use.

In forum, we organized a study-tour to the selected area of Bangkok and 4-5 lectures about the mapping methods, urban design and planning in Bangkok, landscape planning etc.

### 2nd Level was the project groups:

The students were divided into 6 mixed groups (Thai and Danish students). Each group selected a mapping method to be used and tested. The project groups worked as home base for each student. The students worked together in the project group and met every day during the workshop, arranged tours to the area and helped each other collecting data, discussed the impressions and the work of the individual group members.

The group planned the work to be made, that is the problems to be mapped, the field, the subject, the approach, the labour division and the time schedule. Questions to de discussed in the project groups were: How to understand the method? Which information to collect? How to organize the mapping? Etc.

### 3rd Level was the individual student:

Each student had to create a map, presenting registrations and analyses of a milieu in Bangkok.

The challenge for each student was to give his or her personal presentation of how the registrations and the analyses could be communicated to the forum - and to give a proposal for an urban design strategy or urban design proposal for the investigated milieu.

Urban design education is not only about learning to analyse, it is also about learning to communicate and give design proposals. To train this latter skill, we decided to have a 3rd level in the workshop.

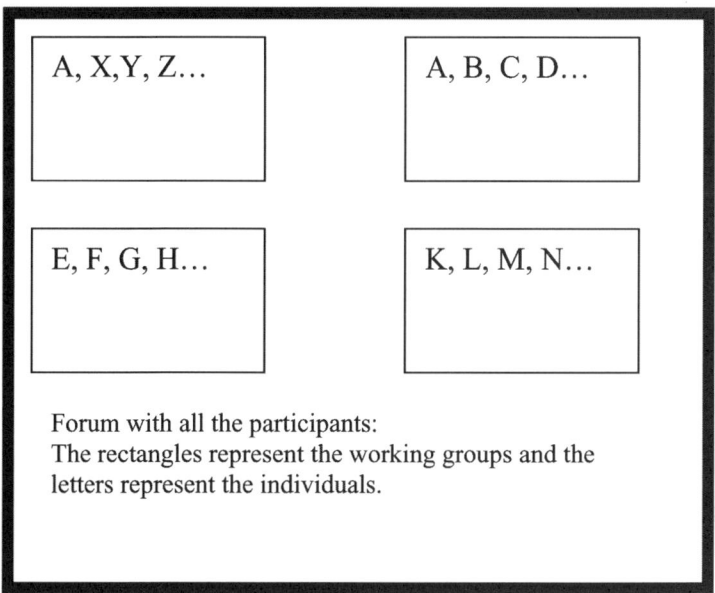

Figure 5: The organisation of the problem-based learning-lab.

## 6. PROCESS ADVISER

As leader of the workshop, you have to plan the process very carefully. You have to prepare which information you are going to give the participants about the idea of the workshop, the aim, the process and the expected results. When the participants are an international group of students you have to write everything down to be sure that everybody has received your messages.
Another thing, which we learned, as teachers and advisers, was that you have to give the most important lectures and presentations yourself, and you have to follow up with advice at all 3 levels.

You have to give advice in forum about the process, you have to inform about plans, and especially about the plans that have been changed (in Thailand you plan by means of the mobile telephone. The mobile telephone gives you the freedom to chat about the plans, to change a little here and a little there, and that's the way it is!).

The whole situation with Danish students in a foreign cultural context, at a foreign university and collaborating with Thai-students whom they have not seen before, creates many questions, which need creative answers. So even if you are well prepared, you cannot plan everything before you start. The easiest way to handle this is to function as a kind of »chaos-pilot«, who guides the group through the unexpected.

At the group and individual levels, you have to guide the students through the working process from mapping to design of strategies or urban design projects. As in all problem-based learning processes, it is important not to give the students all the answers. Here the complexity of the city helps you, because you are not able to give the answers yourself. You have to support the students in planning an investigation strategy and to focus on the project in order to help them to help themselves. You have to discuss with the students, ask questions about their work, and guide them to answer the questions - doing this you cannot avoid being much involved in the whole process yourself.

One of the building blocks of problem-based learning is reflection. In this workshop, we worked with reflection on several levels and subjects: What have we learned about a city like Bangkok? What have we learned about mapping and designing urban projects in Bangkok? What have we learned about mapping techniques? And what have we learned about communication and presenting maps?
It is important to make these reflections both during the process and at the end in order to have a full outcome for the work; and it is important to give the students a chance to formulate their own statement of »what did we learn in school today...«

## 7. EVALUATION OF THE WORKSHOP

The Danish participants evaluated the workshop twice: the day we finished the work and again two months later. The evaluation took place in forum (with all Danish participants), where everybody had the chance to speak up and give his or her opinion. The evaluation took place as an open talk about the workshop, only guided by at few questions about the problem-based approach to mapping, the organisation of the workshop, the theme and the field.

Forum agreed in the following statement about the workshop:

- The programme was too pressed. The students were in lack of time to do all the investigations.
  Evening and nights were used to produce the maps, especially

because there were some problems with the computers.
It might be a good idea with two or three more days - with a break in between.

- The theme and subject of the workshop were fine. It was a good idea to test not only one but several methods; and it functioned very well to give the same methods to 2 different groups in order to bring about some discussions of the methods.

- The organization and structure of the learning-lab was prized. The three levels (forum/ group/ individual) functioned very well. The students found that the shifts between individual work and collective group work was invigorating.. They supported each other in the groups and challenged their own creativity in individual work. The common opinion was that the forum was a must - as a social and organizing frame.

- The students were very happy with the whole process. »It is incredible what we have been through«... »We have learned a lot in a very short time«.
»It has been hard, but also fun, interesting and unforgettable!«

- At the beginning the Danish students were sceptical about our plans for bringing Danish and Thai students together in the same project groups. They imagined it would be very difficult and take a long time to bridge the cultural gaps.
After the workshop ended, the Danish students had changed their minds.
»We could not have done it without the Thai students!« was one of the statements. Another statement was: »The Thai students were very good partners. They were skilful and they helped us to understand the culture and the context«.

- Before the workshop started, I had imagined that problem-based learning would be a challenge for the Thai students and the professors at Chula. I knew that the Danish students were used to problem-based learning. They did not even think about it as something special. But I had imagined that Thai students would find it difficult.
After a short introduction to the workshop, the groups started to plan their work. The Thai students were a little shy and did not say much in the beginning. After a while they participated eagerly, and I realized that urban planners - at least at master level - always

have a problem-based approach to their work. They are used to solving problems in the complex urban fabric. So as we have seen many times before, problem-based learning was not at problem at all - it was a help not only as a method of learning but also in order to bridge the intercultural gaps.

## 8. FINAL COMMENTS

The mapping workshop was a very fine experience and a pedagogical challenge for me. When I came home, there were many things to do (more teaching programs, research and so on), but I am happy I took the time to write this article, because it gave me the chance to talk to the participating students again. Reflecting on the whole process again also gave me new ideas for future workshops.
The staff members from Chula were very fond of the workshop and the problem-based learning approach. Even though they were not used to problem-based learning, they soon used the pedagogical principles. After participating in another workshop at Department of architecture and design, Aalborg University in May 2003, they had decided to continue our collaboration. Next year, they will arrange another intercultural workshop at Chula. The workshop will be based on problem-based learning principles.

During the workshop both the Danish and the Thai students produced many creative maps in presenting their work. We have decided to publish a book with these ideas and results. The book will be finished during August 2003.

## REFERENCES

Bunchoten, Raoul (1999). *Stirring the City*, the Aarhus School of Architecture, Aarhus.

Bunchoten, Raoul(2000). *Flotsam City*, 2000.London.

Corner, James & MacLean, Alex S (1996). *Taking Measures across the American Landscape*, London.

Corner, James (1999). *Recovering Landscape*, (p. 1-26), New York.

Corner, James (1999). *The Agency of Mapping*, in: Cosgrove, Dennis (ed) (1999): Mappings. London.

DUCED: website. See *under www.udenrigsminiteriet.dk*

Stephen Graham (2001). *Flow City. In: DISP 144 no. 4.*

Stephen Graham & Marvin (2001). *Splintering Urbanism*, Cambridge.

Koolhaas, Rem (1999). *S, M, L, XL*, (p. 1248-1264), New York.

# THE AAU MODEL SEEN FROM
# A FOREIGN PROFESSOR'S POINT OF VIEW

**Joachim Höhle**

Abstract: By means of the case »The Chartered Surveyor education in the 7th to 10th semester« the AAU model is discussed. Based on a German educational background, an international career in industry and 17 years as professor at AAU the author analyses the advantages and the disadvantages of this educational approach. Considering this analysis and the many changes in the world since the foundation of AAU in 1974 two questions are answered: »Can foreign teachers adapt to the AAU model?« and »Can you export the AAU model to foreign countries?« In an outlook, possible changes in the AAU model as well as in the organizational structure of AAU are also dealt with.

## 1. INTRODUCTION

Aalborg University (AAU) was founded in 1974, shortly after the students' revolt in Denmark and in some other European countries. Professors should no longer be at the top of the power pyramid. The result of the reformatory efforts was that power and responsibility were distributed among many persons, and the students got influence and co-responsibility. The academic staff at AAU today consists of professors, associated professors and assistant professors; PhD students and technical assistants also participate in the education. Normally, AAU recruits its teachers from its own rows. Interested and qualified candidates are put through scientific and pedagogical training programmes. Staff positions are offered to such persons, but they must compete with other applicants. Some of the appointed professors got their education and experiences from abroad.

How can such persons adapt to the AAU model? The AAU-model will also be exported to foreign countries. Will it function there? These are the two main questions, which I will try to answer in this paper. Before that, I will try to characterize the project-organised studies from my point of view, and analyse the advantages and disadvantages of the AAU model. I will use the education of the Danish Chartered Surveyors in the last semesters as a case, because my experience mainly comes from there. It is not necessarily valid for all of the educations at AAU.

I myself come from another culture, the German one. My education and teaching practice I received in Germany, experience in practice I obtained also in Switzerland and USA. The Danish language and culture were nearly unknown to me when I came to AAU 17 years ago. Professors at German universities have great power in their work.

Personnel and other resources support them in fulfilling their many-sided obligations. A subject group, called »Lehrstuhl« (chair), is hierarchically organised. A professor in ordinary (today named C4 professor) is the leader of a

Figure 1:
The book »The German professor«

subject group and bears the full responsibility for the education and research in his field. He can decide by himself on the research goals of the »Lehrstuhl« and is the mentor of his PhD students. At the final semester, the student's topics of the diploma thesis are formulated by him and will often support the goals of the selected research line. Furthermore, he holds the major lectures in his field and leads together with his colleagues seminars for the students about new research and achievements. Furthermore, he has the final decision about the investments for research tools and the co-operation with other people and organisations. All of this gives him the possibility for continuity in the research and high achievements. Professors have a long education and there is a great competition for these positions. The German university system is based on Humboldt's principle of »unity of teaching and research«, which means that a university teacher should do research and teaching at the same time. German professors and those aspiring to become one publish a lot, seven to eight scientific publications a year is not a rare sight. The authoritarian professor, as depicted on the cover of the book »Der deutsche Professor« (cf. figure 1), does not exist in the present Germany, but it fits the prejudice of many people.

## 2. THE AAU MODEL

Danish people are, in my experience, especially anti-authoritarian. They do not want to be dictated by anyone from above. In the beginning at AAU, the term »leader« was completely avoided. All types of professors are equal in their rights and the term »unity teacher« was introduced. In the AAU managing bodies (committees), students and technical personal are represented and have influence on decisions. If decisions have to be made, the majority decides. Minority groups can oppose decisions of the majorities, but this is in my own experiences a difficult undertaking. The majority group are the associated professors. All professors do have a lot of freedom regarding their research and external activities. In recent years, the situation changed somewhat, responsibilities were placed and leaders became more powerful. According to the law for the Danish universities of 1993 the Director of Studies, for example, has the direct responsibility for the studies.

The key element of the AAU model is the **project-organised study**, which means that projects are carried out in a team from the first to the last semester. Quite a lot of literature has been written about it, for example (Algreen-Ussing, et al., 1986 and Enemark, 1999). Today, the new teachers and researchers from abroad can receive a short training in this form of study when they start their work at AAU. My experience comes from the counselling at AAU's basic year and later from the education of the Danish chartered surveyors. In this contribution, I like to discuss the study in the 7th to 10th semester of AAU's »School of surveying and planning« only. Figure 2 illustrates who are the actors in this project-organised study.

The project group, consisting of 3-5 students, is placed in the centre of the diagram. Either supervisor comes from a subject group, or a research centre connected to AAU, or from external organizations. The students form the project group after a tough selection process where »chemistry« plays a key role. The teachers propose projects, but the students search for topics as well. Very often, they decide on their own project topic. A semester coordinator prepares the semester together with a planning group. He keeps an account of the resources and arranges for completion of the semester evaluations. Projects are evaluated by an internal examiner ('censor'), or - at final projects - by two external examiners. The chairman of the body of examiners has to approve the external examiners. Furthermore, there is an educational board where representatives from the practice are counselling. There are still more bodies who influence the projects as regards resources and rules: Faculty, department, division, subject group and the research school where official leaders are seated. Other positions, which are important for the project groups are: Administrators of group rooms, administrators of system- and application software and laboratory technicians. As in each organisation informal groups exist and they try to achieve goals that may differ from the goals set by the official leaders.

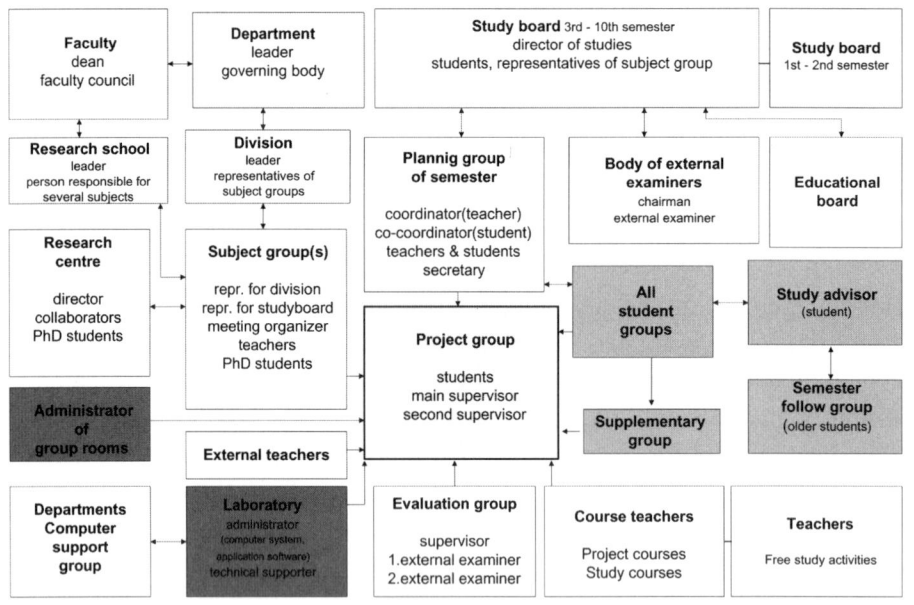

Figure 2: Student projects and its actors at AAU's
»School of surveying and planning«

Supervision of a project takes place through a dialogue between the project group and the supervisor. Every student himself is responsible for his or her own learning. Project supervision aims to support and guide the students in this learning process. This means that the students have great freedom in their projects and do not have to follow a supervisor's advice or ideas. An important element of the AAU-model is the evaluation of courses and of project supervision by the students. Teachers of courses and supervisors of the projects participate in these evaluations. By means of constructive critique, courses and supervision can be improved.

To a newcomer from abroad it will take some time to understand how the system works. It may take many meetings to come to a consensus, when the semester is planned, carried out, and evaluated, or if the curriculum has to be changed. Responsibility is placed on several persons. It is a general rule of thumb that, if responsibility is divided between two persons, each person will feel responsible with 25 % only. If good leadership does not exist, chaotic situations can quickly develop. The course content is not coordinated then, and investments will possibly be distributed to the wrong hands, or distributed in small pieces in many hands. It will only work if all persons involved in the education act responsibly.

The education of the Danish chartered surveyor ('landinspektør') takes five years. After a basic education of one year, a superimposed education of four years follows. In its first part (3rd-6th semester) the students learn the basic qualifications of the profession and in the second part (7th-9th semester) they deal with complex problems including the relevant theories and methodologies. In the last semester of the study (10th semester), a final project has to be done. The last three semesters are specialization semesters, and currently a specialization in mapping, land management, and planning can be chosen. The graduates of this study are named M.Sc. in surveying, planning and land management (AAU 2001).

At the Chartered Surveyor study (7th to 10th semester), the following characteristics are special:

a. There is one project per semester. For students choosing the technical specialisation the topic has to be in subject areas of »Geographic Information Systems« (7th semester), »Technical Surveying« (8th semester), and »Mapping and Geoinformation« (9th semester). A final project is done in the 10th semester where a project group of maximum three students can choose a topic from one of the mentioned three subject areas.

b. According to the study regulations, about 30 % of the scheduled study time is used on courses and 70 % on the project (average for the 7th to 9th semester). Several courses will contain knowledge for the selected project. Non-project related courses (SE courses) and guest lectures are also given.

c. Only one examination is held at the end of the semester, where the project group presents the results of the projects and where some of the knowledge connected to the project is examined. The SE courses are not examined.

d. Each project has two supervisors. In the $7^{th}$, $8^{th}$ and $9^{th}$ semester an internal examiner evaluates the project. This means that the project group has to deal with a group of teachers, who need to have knowledge about the subject of the project and practise constructive cooperation.

e. The group rooms are equipped with appliances which give some comfort to long working hours. Each student owns a computer where field measurements are processed or project reports are produced. The studies are occasionally interrupted by leisure and sport activities. Figure 3 gives some impression of the students' lifestyle at a project-organised study.

## 3. CHANGES IN THE WORLD AND IN THE FIELD OF GEOMATICS

Since the foundation of AAU in 1974, many changes outside of the university have occurred which have influenced the contents and form of education. Only a few keywords are mentioned here: Nowadays education is global, which means that studies are internationalised. For example, students study at a foreign university for a period. English is the major language at conferences and textbooks. Education is a lifelong process. Distance learning and direct learning at the university use the Internet. Private industry and trade unions have influence at the universities. As the knowledge in the technical sciences explodes, many resources are required for a modern education. Many changes occurred also in the knowledge, which Chartered Land Surveyors need to have in their professional careers. Today the study is called »Geomatics« and it embraces new subjects like global positioning systems, geographic information systems, and remote sensing beside the traditional subjects like surveying, photogrammetry, and cartography. Geomatics relies on theories of mathematics, physics, computer science, satellite technology and uses tools such as data base management, computer graphics, and image processing. Its application is in topographic and thematic mapping and spatial data management for a number of fields (e.g. civil engineering, environmental science, agriculture, geography). Special areas of professional and economic interest have traditionally been the cadastre, land use planning, and land management. In these tasks, subjects like law, real estate management and economics have to be known. A comprehensive discussion of the global changes in the Geomatics education has recently been published in (Konecny, 2002).

Figure 3: Project groups and their »homes«

## 4. ADVANTAGES AND DISADVANTAGES OF THE AAU MODEL

The students have a very active role in the education. The model contributes to independent action of the students and strengthens their self-confidence. There is a short distance between teacher and student - both physically and concerning the power. Group rooms are situated near the teachers' rooms, and students can get help at all times of the day. (There can also be a lot of noise, when the students enjoy their »Friday bar« while the teachers have to concentrate on their tasks. Figure 4 gives some impression of the working condition at such a day.) New knowledge and information flow both ways. The teacher is forced to update his knowledge continuously, also in areas which are not his specialty or interest. However, the unity of research and teaching is endangered. Some professors engage themselves in research centres, private firms or administrative posts. This can result in, that some professors are doing research only and some teaching only. The students in the education of chartered surveyors are often very job-oriented; their projects rarely contribute to the subject group's research work. The students concentrate on the projects and reduce participation in those courses that are not evaluated in any way. This results in many as well as big gaps in the students' knowledge. The student is largely self-taught. Semester evaluations, where teachers and supervisors are criticised unconstructively, may restrain a teacher's joy and creativity. The system is very vulnerable when the number of students increases. Group rooms and equipment are then lacking and teachers are overburdened if no extra resources are granted. However, the AAU model has first of all the freedom and the flexibility to adapt quickly to new knowledge areas.

Figure 4: Working conditions for teachers at times of the »Friday bar«

## 5. HOW CAN FOREIGN TEACHERS ADAPT TO THE AAU-MODEL?

If foreign teachers and researchers come from countries where a hierarchical structure is common, it will be quite a task to adapt to the new conditions. It will require help and support from colleagues and the management of the university. In principle, foreign teachers can easily learn counselling in project-organised study and after a while they will like it. I myself consider the counselling in projects as a »raisin« in the teacher's tasks. Therefore, to be a supervisor in interesting projects with good students may give rise to a competition between teachers.

The foreign teacher's problem at the AAU is first of all the Danish language. For new teachers it should be possible to hold lectures in English. To use English in project work should also be a goal in the internationalisation of the studies. Unfortunately, this is not so much the case in the education of Chartered surveyors so far. In my opinion, all AAU students should be able to publish in English about their projects in foreign journals or on the Internet. In order to obtain the mentioned qualifications for the students, technical English should be introduced as a course at the basic studies. With a good proficiency in English, students are also able to study abroad for a semester. After completion of their studies, they can more easily find jobs at international companies, organisations, and educational institutions in their home country or abroad, and thereby successfully compete with the candidates from other universities. The many possibilities to prepare for international careers also require that foreign exchange students will come to AAU for a short stay. The integration of such students into project groups and the conversion of some courses into English spoken courses is a great challenge for students and teachers of AAU. A lot of work has to be done in this respect.

## 6. CAN YOU EXPORT THE AAU MODEL TO FOREIGN COUNTRIES?

When the AAU model is transferred to foreign countries, cultural factors will play a role. A short power distance in the relationship between teacher and student is necessary. Furthermore, some flexibility in evaluation of the student's knowledge has to be applied. This so-called uncertainty avoidance and the power distance are both rated low in Scandinavia, UK and the Netherlands (Stubkjær, 1992). Therefore, the AAU model has good chances to be used in these countries. The project-organised study requires mature students, who can handle the granted freedom and act responsibly. Whether the AAU model works successfully at other places will also depend on the willingness of the professors to give some of their power away. In projects, they have to act as an advisor and facilitator for project groups.

## 7. OUTLOOK

The AAU model has many advantages. However, the model has to be adapted to new developments. For example, courses for the Internet have to be created and this requires new approaches in pedagogy and technology. In addition, organisational changes in the management of the university will take place. According to the new law of 2003 for all Danish universities, leaders at all levels will be appointed and external persons will have the majority in the governing body of the university. Today AAU, therefore, seems to be in a transition stage adapting its organisational structure and its educational model to the new times.

## ACKNOWLEDGEMENTS

The author wants to thank Esben Clemens for his drawings (figures 3 and 4) and Michael Höhle (who was educated at AAU) for discussions about the topic.

# REFERENCES

AAU (2001). *Landinspektøruddannelsen - studieordning* (Education of the Danish Chartered Surveyor - study regulation).

Algreen-Ussing, H. et al. (1986). *Metode i projetktarbejde ved teknisk-naturvidenskabelige uddannelser* (Method in project work in the education of technology and science). Aalborg universitetsforlag, ISBN 87-7307-340-7.

Enemark, S. (1999). En uddannelse i stadig fornyelse (An education in continuous innovation). In: *Landinspektøren*, Vol. 39, pp. 388-397

Konecny, G. (2002). Recent Global Changes in Geomatics Education, In: *IntArchPhRS*, Com.VI, San Jose dos Campos, Vol.XXXIV Part 6, 22p, CD-ROM

Rheder, W. (1985). *Der Deutsche Professor* (The German professor), Rasch und Röhring, Hamburg.

Stubkjær, E. (1992). Quality Management and the Land Surveyor Education - Unification or
Diversity? In: *Proceedings of the 1$^{st}$ Seminar »Education in Land Information Systems«*, Delft.

# NOTES ON CONTRIBUTORS

**Bajard, Christine:** received a B.A. in Literature at the University of Montréal, Québec, Canada in 1983, followed by an extension in Education at the University of British Columbia, B.C, Canada in 1984. She has taught from 1984 to 2001 in schools ranging from French Immersion to International schools in Denmark and in Canada. She has had a leading role in use of IKT in teaching/learning in all her workplaces, culminating with a sabbatical to engage in a Pædagogical Diploma Study in Multimedia in Holbæk, Denmark. Her main interest has been in guiding teachers on their path to becoming users of IKT both in their teaching and in their daily life, focusing on the interactive form of learning between teachers and students. Reflection and study have been aimed at the effect of use of IKT as a form of communication in learning on varying combinations of learning styles.

**Borch, Ole:** Associate Professor, Department of Control Engineering, Aalborg University, Denmark has more than 30 years educational background as supervisor and teacher in an problem based learning (PBL) organization. The main areas in teaching are modern software development and computer networking and programming. The major and recently research focus areas are PBL and project work methods and technology in the framework of engineering distance learning education.

**Borchmann, Thomas:** Mag. art. et Ph.D., Assistant Professor, Department of Communication, Aalborg University. Thomas Borchmann's educational background is in philosophy and business studies. Since 2000, he has been at the Faculty of Humanities where his teaching obligations are within three areas: technology studies, methodology and organization theory. His research is centred on critical and value-oriented analysis of discourses concerning work, organization, management, technology and learning, as these get articulated in local contexts, theory-building, media and curricula. A large part of his research has been done as collaborative action research.

**Bækkelund, Helle:** Ph.D.-student at the Department of Education and Learning at Aalborg University. She has worked in the field of ICT-supported education for adult practitioners since 1996, doing teaching, development and research into problem oriented project work and collaborative learning models in course teaching. She has also carried out several evaluations of ICT-implementation in other areas of education and developed several teacher-training programs for teaching with ICT. Currently she is carrying out research into the use of web technology and conceptions of teaching among university teachers.

**Cancino, Rita:** Associate professor, Ph.D. Associate professor at the International Business Communication Study Programme (Spanish) at Aalborg University, Department of Languages and Intercultural Communication. In 1999 Ph.D. from Aalborg University in translation, legal language and lexicography. In 2002 Vice Dean at the Faculty of Humanities, 1999-2002 Director of the International Business Communication Study Programme. Main field of research is the language for specific purpose and translation, legal language and language policy. Other field of interest is problem-based learning and its implementation in different environments due to my close co-operation with universities in Latin America.

**Caspersen, Sven:** Rector of Aalborg University 1976 - 2004; Member of Confederation of Rectors' Conferences in the EU, Brussels 1986 and Chairman 1992-94. President Federation of European Stock Exchanges, Brussels 1995-96; Member of the Executive Board of FIBV (Fédération Internationale de Bourse des Valeurs) International Federation of Stock Exchanges 1993-95; Chairman European Capital Markets Institute, Copenhagen 1993-94; Chairman Danish Parliament's Advisory Board on European Matters 1993 - 2001; Chairman Danish Rectors' Conference's International Committee 1994-2002; President of International Association of University Presidents 1999 - 2002; Member of the Hochschulrat of Hamburg-Harburg Technical University 2003-; Member of the Kuratorium of Dortmund University 2003-. Doctor Honoris Causa: University of Central Florida , Orlando 1988; Vilnius Technical University, Lithuania 1993; Vilnius University, Lithuania 1999; Universidad Autonoma de Guadalajara, Mexico 1999; Universitatea »Politehnica« din Bucaresti, Romania 2000; Universidad Autónoma de Nuevo León, Mexico 2000.

**Christensen, Jens:** Ph.D., Dr. of Science. Associate Professor at the Department of Development and Planning, Aalborg University. Jens Christensen is educated as a land surveyor. He has been employed at Aalborg University for more than 20 years. His teaching obligations are within two major areas, a) technology, man, and society, b) theory of science and knowledge. Since 1996, he has been a member of the study board for the education in philosophy and theory of knowledge. His research is within the field of theory and philosophy of science and knowledge. A major focus is the view of nature, including knowledge of nature and attitudes towards nature in relation to the technological practise with nature, perceived in historical, subcultural, and intercultural perspectives. He is a member of The Research Group of Theory of Knowledge, Engineering Education and Organisational Learning, and he is attached to The Centre of Philosophy and Theory of Knowledge, Aalborg University.

**Fink, Flemming K.:** Professor, Director of UCPBL, Director of Studies, Head of ELITE, received his M.Sc.E.E. from Aalborg University in 1978. Subsequently he was a researcher at Odense University and established an educational programme in Digital Signal Processing at the Engineering College in Odense. Since 1986 he has been with Aalborg University doing research and teaching within speech recognition and digital signal processing. His major engineering research is in auditory modelling and in co-operation with three colleagues he has patented a new concept for parametric hearing aids. F. K. Fink has been Director of Studies since 1993 and initiated an internationalisation of the curriculum. He is very active in setting up Life Long Learning programmes on postgraduate level and head of the Centre for Continuing Engineering Education in Electronics and IT (ELITE). His major research activity is now on Facilitated Work Based Learning based on PBL. Fink has published several papers on Problem Based Learning, University - Industry co-operation and Continuing Professional Development. F. K. Fink is Senior Member of IEEE and representing Aalborg University in several national and international boards and co-operations.

**Hansen, Søren:** Ph.D., Associate Professor, Aalborg University. Søren Hansen is member of The Research Group of Theory of Knowledge, Engineering Education and Organisational Learning at the department of Development and Planning Research Group Technology and Society at Aalborg University. He holds a master degree in Engineering in the field of medical informatics and electronics. Dr. Hansen has conducted research in the following areas: Supervision of project groups in the project organised PBL study, organisational change processes, assessment in higher education, creativity in the learning process, work based learning. He holds a Ph.D. in »Supervision of project groups« (2000).

**Helbo, Jan:** received the M.Sc. degree in electronic engineering from the Technical University of Denmark in 1972. From 1972 - 1974 he was Assistant Professor at the Engineering Academy of Denmark, Aalborg. From 1974 - 1976 he was Assistant Professor at Aalborg University, Department of Control Engineering and since 1976 - Associate Professor at Aalborg University, Department of Control Engineering. From 1993 - 1999 he was Head of Department of Control Engineering at the Institute for Electronic Systems, Aalborg University. His main interests have been Robotics and Piezo Motors and control, e.g. Construction of flexible robot links and use of Piezo Motor for space use. In recent years his time also is spend on IT-Based Learning, in particular in relation to distance education in control engineering.

**Höhle, Joachim:** Dr.-Ing., professor, Aalborg University, Department of Development and Planning, subject group for GeoInformatics. Joachim

Höhle studied surveying engineering and photogrammetry at German universities (Technical University of Dresden and University of Karlsruhe). After completion of his Doctor of Engineering degree in 1971 he joined the Swiss company Leica (formerly Wild Heerbrugg) and got involved in the design and project management of instrumentation for the mapping industry. Three years of his 13 years with the Leica company he worked in the U.S.A. as a consultant for surveying and photogrammetry. Other experience in project management he collected as chief engineer in a mapping company in Hamburg. In 1985 he became guest professor at the Danish Technical University in Copenhagen and at the University of Trier in Germany. In 1986 he accepted the offer of Aalborg University to become an associated professor for digital mapping and a year later he became professor for photogrammety and digital mapping. His research and teaching activity deals mainly with topographic mapping by means of digital images. He has a special interest in computer-assisted learning and development of Internet-based teaching material. As the Danish representative for the pan-European organisation EuroSDR he got acquainted with many other universities and colleagues of his subject area.

**Jensen, Annie Aarup:** Associate professor at the Department of Education and Learning, Aalborg University, and the head of the department's study board. Annie Aarup Jensen has carried out research into various aspects of adults' learning processes, such as continuing education, learning through ICT, and learning in multicultural practice.

**Jensen, Lars Peter:** received his M.Sc. from Aalborg University in 1980. He has been working there ever since, at the Department of Control Engineering, holding a position as Associate Professor. His first research project was the development of a ground speed controller for a Combine Harvester, and from there he moved on to design of Man-Machine Interfaces within the Process Industry. He has as special interest in the Ergonomics in the control room especially during organisational changes. This has led to a new research focus on learning processes both within companies trying to establish a 'developing workplace', and at the University trying to improve the Team Work skills among first year's students both on-campus and in our distance continued education programme.

**Jørgensen, Frances:** M.A., Ph.D., successfully defended her Ph.D. thesis on group and organizational learning and Continuous Improvement (CI) in August 2003 and is currently employed as amanuensis at the Department of Development and Planning at Aalborg University, where she teaches courses on co-operation, learning, and project management to first year students within the Faculty of Engineering and Science. Her research interests include team and employee development, CI and change management, the facilitation of group learning, and self-assessment and performance measurement as tools to support learning and team development. Dr. Jørgensen obtained a master's in industrial and organisational psychology at Middle Tennessee State University, USA, and was a self-employed organisational consultant specialising in team and management development.

**Kiib, Hans:** Professor, Department of Architecture & Design, Aalborg University. Hans Kiib has more than 30 years of experience in teaching and research within Urban Design. As one of the mainstays in the start-up and structuring of the graduate engineer education in Architecture & Design, he has developed the technical profile of the education and the adaptation of AAU's Problem Based Learning Model to the particular didactic subject matter with a combination of technical and aesthetic areas in an entirely new education.

**Knudsen, Morten:** received the M.Sc. degree in electronic engineering from the Technical University of Denmark in 1963, and the Ph.D. degree from Aalborg University in 1993. From 1965 to 1971 he was with the Servo Laboratory, the Technical University of Denmark, General Dynamics, Rochester, New York, and Measurex Corporation, Santa Clara, California. Since 1971, he has been an Associate Professor, and from 1990 Reading Professor (Docent), in control engineering at the Institute for Electronic Systems, Aalborg University. His main interests have been modelling, system identification, and control, e.g. in relation to cancer hyperthermia systems and loudspeakers. In recent years a considerable part of his time is spend on IT-Based Learning, in particular in relation to distance education, and on The IT-Initiative, a program for adjusting Aalborg University to the IT-age.

**Knudstrup, Mary-Ann:** Associate Professor, Aalborg University. Her educational background is Architecture. Since 1980 she has been holding various positions at the Faculty of Engineering and Science and is now employed at the Department of Architecture and Design. Mary-Ann Knudstrup was from the beginning a member of the Interim Study Board for the Civil Engineer Education in Architecture and Design, which was established in may 1997. Earlier she was a member of the Department of Development and Planning. In 2001 she was elected to the Executive Board of the Department of Architecture and Design. Her primary subject fields are Architecture and Planning. She has published books and articles on these topics. She is currently working with Urban Architecture, Office Buildings, Energy and Indoor Environment in Building Design as well as Methodologies. Her teaching is based on the Problem Based Learning methodology, and she has been actively involved in the development of PBL in relation to the Civil Engineer Education in Architecture and Design.

**Kofoed, Lise Busk:** Ph. D., Associate Professor, Head of Department, Architecture&Design, Faculty of Engineering and Science, Aalborg. Research in technological and organizational changes with special focus on: The learning processes connected to changes, Pedagogical methods within the project organized and problem based curriculum, Changes within learning institutions - from traditional to Problem Based Learning, Methods for staff development, Employee participation, Management of changes, Developing of teaching and training methods e.g. gaming and simulation. Research is based on action science and action research with interdisciplinary perspectives. During the years Lise Kofoed has been project leader of several research projects (e.g. EU projects) and has also been involved in developing Ph.D. courses and supervision.

**Kolmos, Anette:** Ph.D., Professor, Vice Director of UCPBL, Aalborg University. Anette Kolmos was formerly the Director for The Center of University Teaching and Learning. Her educational background is in social science and psychology. Since 1984, she has been employed at the Faculty of Engineering and Science. She is now member of member of The Research Group of Theory of Knowledge, Engineering Education and Organisational Learning, at the Department of Development and Planning. Her primary teaching focuses have been on co-operation, learning and project management for engineering students and since 1995, faculty development and change processes in higher education. Her major research interests are in the areas of PBL and project work within engineering education, change processes in higher education and the development of process skills. Dr. Kolmos has published several articles and books on these topics.

**Krogh, Lone:** Leader of The Centre for University Teaching and Learning at Aalborg University. Lone Krogh's educational background is Master of Public Administration and Politics. She is teaching, researching and consulting within university education and staff development. She is especially engaged in the relationship between Society, labour market and the educational systems in analysing and transferring these general aspects into »best teaching and learning practice« at the universities and other educational systems. Didactic analyses and problem-based teaching and learning have been main principles behind her teaching for more than two decades. Her major research focus is on teaching and learning elements within the University context.

**Laursen, Erik:** Research Professor, Department of Education and Learning, Aalborg University, in 1974 Graduated from Sociology, University of Copenhagen, from 1974 - 2000, Assistant professor, later associated professor in Social Psychology and sociology, Department of Social Studies and

Organisation. Aalborg University, from 2000 - 2003, Research Professor at the Centre for Interdisciplinary Study of Learning, Aalborg University, from 2003, Research Professor in the Department of Education and Learning, Aalborg University. Has taught in many fields of study at Aalborg University, among others the programs in Sociology, Social Studies, Adult Education and Learning processes.

**Linhardt, Søren:** Cand. mag., Assistant Professor, Department of Communication, Aalborg University. Søren Lindhardt's educational background is in humanistic informatics. Since 1995, he has been at the Faculty of Humanities where his teaching obligations are within three areas: technology studies, methodology and organization theory. His research is centred on critical and value-oriented analysis of discourses concerning work, organization, anagement, technology and learning, as these get articulated in local contexts, theory-building, media and curricula.

**Lorentsen, Annette:** Professor, IT Innovation, Aalborg University. Annette Lorentsen's educational background is in humanistic informatics and foreign languages. Since 1998 she has been heading the central unit for IT Innovation at Aalborg University, and since 2002 she has been national project leader on behalf of the Danish Rectors Conference for the development of a Danish portal for virtual university education. Her teaching obligations are within ICT implementation in educational institutions and ICT and teaching/learning. She has developed and delivered substantial distance education activities within languages and within ICT and learning theories. Her major research focus is on implementation and use of ICT in ODL and in educational institutions as such. She has published several articles and books on this subject.

**Marling, Gitte:** Architect Ph.D., Associate Professor in Urban Design is engaged at Department of Architecture and Design, Aalborg University. She is the author of several books and articles on Urban Planning, Urban Architecture and Environment. Resent books are »Urban Environmental Indicators - Assessment of Danish Housing Settlement«, 1999 and »Urban Songlines - Dream Lines of Everyday Life« 2003 and several articles on relates issues.

**Mullins, Michael:** Architect, M.Arch. (Natal), Cand.Arch. (Copenhagen). Michael Mullins was born in South Africa, where he also ran a successful architectural practice for over 15 years. Research and teaching interests in computer applications for 3-D design visualization, led him to take a senior lecturer's post at the University of Natal in 1999, prior to accepting in 2002 a teaching and research position in the Department of Architecture and Design in Aalborg, where he now lives.

**Qvist, Palle:** Mag. art., Amanuensis, Department of Development and Planning, Aalborg University. Palle Qvist is a member of the CLP Group (Co-operation, Learning and Project management). His educational background is in modern history, communication and international relations. He has since 1977 given lectures in PBL at all faculties of the university. He is now teaching engineering students. His main interests in relation to PBL is related to understanding the nature of the problem in PBL, PBL and democratic learning, faculty development and ICT and excellent teaching practice in engineering education. He is co-authors on a much quoted book about PBL, has published articles and numerous web-pages on the topics and is editor of GRUPPExperten (The Group Expert), a on-line help site on world wide web - a »group doctor« - for project groups with co-operations problems or conflicts.

**Rasmussen, Jørgen Gulddahl:** MSc. PhD. Professor in organisation and management at the Department of Business Studies, Aalborg University. He is Head of Study of the Business Administration program at the university. He has been teaching and doing research at Aalborg University for more that two decades and has served as Dean and Vice-dean of the Social Sciences for several periods been doing administrative and managerial work. His research is within management, governance, organisational learning, strategic development, and competence development within different types of firms and institutions. His teaching is within some of the same fields mostly for students in business administration, but also for students in other programs. Outside the university he is engaged in training, supervising and lecturing for different professional groups on organisation development, learning and management.

**Rokkjær, Ole:** is working with Continuing Engineering Education in IT and Electronics, and he is the co-ordinator of the Master in Information Technology education at Aalborg University. He holds a B.Sc. degree in Electronics Engineering from Aalborg University in 1989, and among numerous interests he has studied adult pedagogy. He has been teaching at Aalborg Day College and been employed as a consultant in the Unemployment Fund for Danish engineers (IAK).

**Rønsholdt, Bent:** Associate Professor, Section of Environmental Engineering, Department of Life Sciences, is currently the planning co-ordinator for the biotechnology, chemistry and environmental engineering section at the freshman year. He holds a M.Sc. Eng. degree in chemical engineering from the Technical University of Denmark from 1983. Since 1989 he has been employed at the Faculty of Engineering and Science, and has been involved in planning the curriculum of the biotechnology programme and its later integration with chemistry, partly as head of the study board. Teaching responsibilities currently involve project supervision and lectures in Scientific Methods and Chemistry in the freshman year. His major research interest focuses on growth, chemical composition and product quality of rainbow trout, which has resulted in a number of scientific publications. He is the national co-ordinator of the EU funded AQUATT-network for aquaculture education's.

**Søgaard, Erik G.:** Master of Science, Physical Chemistry, University of Aarhus, Denmark, from 1976 - 1978: Medical Representative, Hoffmann LaRoche, Denmark, 1978 - 1984: Associate Professor, Physics and Chemistry, Teacher Training College, Tønder Statsseminarium, Tønder, Denmark, 1983 - 1990: Lecturer, Physics and Chemistry, Aalborg Katedralskole (High School), Aalborg, Denmark, 1990 - 1995: Associate Professor in Physics, General Chemistry, Inorganic Chemistry, Organic Chemistry, Analytical Chemistry, Physical Chemistry and Technical Chemistry, Engineering College, Esbjerg Teknikum, Esbjerg, Denmark, 1995: Associate Professor in Physical Chemistry, Colloid and Interface Chemistry and Technical Inorganic Chemistry with Special Emphasis on Water Supply and Soil and Groundwater Remediation Technologies, University of Aalborg, Department of Chemistry and Applied Engineering Science, Esbjerg.

**Sørensen, Olav Juul:** Professor of International Business, Department of Business studies, Aalborg University. Olav Jull Sorensen holds an MSc-degree in Marketing from the Aarhus Business School, Denmark and an MBA from University of Wisconsin, USA. He has worked in Aalborg since 1972, at first as lecturer attached to the Aalborg affiliate of the Copenhagen Business School, and later as lecturer an professor at Aalborg University, when the Business Administration programme became part of the new University. He has also hold a position as Senior Lecturer in Ghana, 1976-78, at the School of Administration, University of Ghana. His primary fields of interest in teaching are Internationalisation of Companies, Theory of the Firm, and International Industrial Dynamics. Of late, he has included Entrepreneurship as a teaching field. The major research interests are within International Business, focusing on the internationalisation processes of firms from developed, developing and transition economies. Another major interest is the Government-Business relations, pertaining especially to export promotion. He has been a key person in the establishment of the International Society of Marketing and Development, a global association of researchers with an interest in marketing systems in developing and transition economies. He has also been very active in building an international network of university partners in Lithuania, Russia, China, Vietnam, Ghana, the UK, Germany, and the US. Olav Jull Sorensen has been very active in building relations to the local and international business communities.

Among others, he is a board member of The North Jutland Exporters Association.